D1518411

The Philosophy of the Western

The Philosophy of Popular Culture

The books published in the Philosophy of Popular Culture series will illuminate and explore philosophical themes and ideas that occur in popular culture. The goal of this series is to demonstrate how philosophical inquiry has been reinvigorated by increased scholarly interest in the intersection of popular culture and philosophy, as well as to explore through philosophical analysis beloved modes of entertainment, such as movies, TV shows, and music. Philosophical concepts will be made accessible to the general reader through examples in popular culture. This series seeks to publish both established and emerging scholars who will engage a major area of popular culture for philosophical interpretation and examine the philosophical underpinnings of its themes. Eschewing ephemeral trends of philosophical and cultural theory, authors will establish and elaborate on connections between traditional philosophical ideas from important thinkers and the ever-expanding world of popular culture.

Series Editor
Mark T. Conard, Marymount Manhattan College, NY

Books in the Series
The Philosophy of Stanley Kubrick, edited by Jerold J. Abrams
Football and Philosophy, edited by Michael W. Austin
Tennis and Philosophy, edited by David Baggett
The Philosophy of the Coen Brothers, edited by Mark T. Conard
The Philosophy of Film Noir, edited by Mark T. Conard
The Philosophy of Martin Scorsese, edited by Mark T. Conard
The Philosophy of Neo-Noir, edited by Mark T. Conard
The Philosophy of Horror, edited by Thomas Fahy
The Philosophy of The X-Files, edited by Dean A. Kowalski
Steven Spielberg and Philosophy, edited by Dean A. Kowalski
The Philosophy of Science Fiction Film, edited by Steven M. Sanders
The Philosophy of TV Noir, edited by Steven M. Sanders and Aeon J. Skoble
Basketball and Philosophy, edited by Jerry L. Walls and Gregory Bassham

THE PHILOSOPHY OF
THE WESTERN

Edited by

Jennifer L. McMahon
and B. Steve Csaki

THE UNIVERSITY PRESS OF KENTUCKY

Scholarly publisher for the Commonwealth,
serving Bellarmine University, Berea College, Centre College of Kentucky,
Eastern Kentucky University, The Filson Historical Society, Georgetown College,
Kentucky Historical Society, Kentucky State University, Morehead State
University, Murray State University, Northern Kentucky University, Transylvania
University, University of Kentucky, University of Louisville, and Western
Kentucky University.
All rights reserved.

Editorial and Sales Offices: The University Press of Kentucky
663 South Limestone Street, Lexington, Kentucky 40508-4008
www.kentuckypress.com

14 13 12 11 10   5 4 3 2 1

Library of Congress Cataloging-in-Publication Data

The philosophy of the western / edited by Jennifer L. McMahon and B. Steve
Csaki.
    p. cm. — (The philosophy of popular culture)
  Includes bibliographical references and index.
  ISBN 978-0-8131-2591-6 (hardcover : alk. paper)
    1. Western films—History and criticism. I. McMahon, Jennifer L. II. Csaki, B.
Steve.
  PN1995.9.W4P485 2010
  791.43'6278—dc22   2010007780

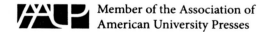

Member of the Association of
American University Presses

Contents

INTRODUCTION

Philosophy and the Western

Jennifer L. McMahon and B. Steve Csaki

What is it that compels people's fascination with the American West? What motivated (and still motivates) individuals to pull up stakes and head west? Why do the travails of the cowboy remain so captivating when cowboy culture is virtually extinct? Arguably, the perennial appeal of the American West is anchored in myth, a myth whose power persists in large part because it finds expression, among other places, in the literary and cinematic genre known as the western.

The myth that westerns convey is both anchored in the history of the West and itself helped shape the historical settlement of the American frontier.[1] It emerged from the stories of westward expansion: stories of those who moved west made their way back east as quickly as their subjects moved in the opposite direction. They came in the written forms of letters, chronicles, newspaper articles, serials, comics, and dime novels, as well as in performances such as Buffalo Bill's Wild West Show.[2] Whatever form they took, stories of life on the American frontier settled in the minds of all who heard, saw, or read them. Thus, as new Americans laid claim to native lands of the West, stories of the western territories staked their own claim on the popular imagination. These stories motivated a cultural fascination with western figures, famous and infamous, and catalyzed interest in the prospect of a western life. Not only were stories of the American West anchored in westward expansion; insofar as they captivated the popular imagination, they encouraged it. However, to the extent that they typically refashioned the reality upon which they were based, these stories blurred the line between fact and fiction. As a consequence, most who migrated to the West had little idea what truly awaited them. They were drawn west by the myth, by the vague yet inexorable allure of a wild, untouched land, of terrain laden with

1

golden opportunities; however, this is rarely what they found. While rooted in history, the myth of the American West quickly took on a life of its own. And while the historical reality to which it refers is all but lost, the myth of the American West is alive and well, and continues to command an abiding interest in the western genre.

There are few genres that capture the hearts of their audience like the western. Though many westerns have simple plots and stock characters, they also have an unwavering appeal. This collection of essays is focused principally on western film, specifically the American western.[3] As those familiar with the western genre are well aware, it is nearly as vast as the West itself. There are thousands of westerns, and an abundance of literature exists on the western genre.[4] Though there is ample historical and literary criticism of the genre, little scholarship exists on the relationship between the western and philosophy. This volume addresses this lack by focusing on the philosophy of the western.

At first glance, westerns and philosophy may seem to have little to do with one another. Whereas philosophers epitomize the contemplative life, western heroes exemplify the active one. Indeed, the characters in westerns typically eschew the intellectualism associated with philosophy. Nonetheless, as the essays in this collection show, the relationship between philosophy and the western is significant because philosophy not only influenced the history of the American West, it also influenced the western genre. Indeed, as several chapters in this volume attest, some of the canonical features of western films trace their history back to the early days of western philosophy, days when individuals like Plato and Aristotle were the new sheriffs in town, and logic and rhetoric were used to cut down the opposition rather than a Winchester or a Colt. Examining the relationship between westerns and philosophy is also important because philosophy can help us understand the western and its appeal. Because philosophers aim to understand human nature, they frequently examine commonplace attitudes and desires, perspectives that often find expression in westerns, and desires that they often fulfill. Furthermore, philosophic analysis of western films is significant because it sheds light on various aspects of American culture and values, helping us come to a clearer understanding of the American mind. Finally, to the extent that westerns illustrate a number of well-known philosophies, examining the link between westerns and philosophy is worthwhile because westerns can help us obtain a firmer grasp on philosophic theories and concepts that might otherwise seem intractably abstract.

One of the obvious interests that philosophy shares with the western has already been mentioned: history. One of the earliest philosophic theories of art issued from the ancient Greeks. It held that art is imitation, or *mimesis*, and this theory retains adherents today.[5] The mimetic theory of art maintains that art is a representation of reality: namely, that it reflects, or mirrors, life. Perhaps more than any other cinematic genre, the western is grounded in, and reflects, the historical phenomenon of western settlement. As various authors in this collection discuss, westerns command philosophic interest not merely because they reflect aspects of a definitive period in American history, but also because they transcend that frontier, representing either the period in which they were produced or more enduring aspects of the human condition.

Philosophers are also interested in the aesthetic qualities of westerns. Aesthetics refers to the branch of philosophy that studies art. Philosophers who specialize in aesthetics consider the formal features of westerns, features such as character and setting, as well as the rhetorical strategies employed in individual works. To be sure, parallels exist between these sorts of critical analyses and those offered by literary theorists. At the same time, the interpretations offered by these philosophers tend to go beyond literary analysis to consider issues of philosophic interest. These issues include the individual, cultural, and moral aspects of western films.

These interests correspond to the major subdivisions of this volume. Part 1 of this collection, "The Cowboy Way: The Essence of the Western Hero," contains essays that consider the relationship that westerns have to identity. Philosophers analyze identity from a variety of different perspectives, including personal identity, gender identity, and cultural identity. The essays in the first section of this volume consider the way in which westerns have established—and continue to establish—powerful ideals with respect to identity. Shai Biderman's essay, " 'Do Not Forsake Me, Oh, My Darling': Loneliness and Solitude in Westerns," explores the essence of the western hero, particularly one of the hero's perennial features: solitude. As fans of the western will attest, western heroes are, with rare exception, lone figures. Though they are figures upon whom others depend, they remain estranged from society. Drawing primarily from the works of Aristotle (384–322 BCE) and Descartes (1596–1650), Biderman examines a range of films including *High Noon* (1952), *Shane* (1953), *The Searchers* (1956), and *Unforgiven* (1992), and makes a case for the epistemic and ethical benefits of solitude.

Douglas J. Den Uyl takes another look at the loneliness of the western hero in his chapter, "Civilization and Its Discontents: The Self-Sufficient Western Hero." Like Biderman, Den Uyl asserts that the western hero is usually a lone figure and that westerns both express and reinforce our cultural preoccupation with individualism. Distinguishing solitude from self-sufficiency, Den Uyl applies Aristotle and Spinoza's (1632–77) notions of self-sufficiency to the films of John Ford and argues that Ford's films both elevate this trait and at the same time suggest that it is on the decline.

B. Steve Csaki's essay, "Mommas, Don't Let Your Babies Grow Up to Be Pragmatists," examines another integral feature of the western hero: his propensity for action. Focusing specifically on the quintessential western hero, John Wayne, Csaki argues that Wayne achieved his iconic status as a western hero in large part because he embodied the ideals of American pragmatism. Drawing primarily from William James (1842–1910) and John Dewey (1859–1952) and focusing principally on *The Cowboys* (1971) and *Rooster Cogburn* (1975), Csaki argues that the defining feature of the pragmatic individual is his or her ability to perceive the salient features of his or her environment, adapt to circumstances, and act to achieve specific ends.

Stephen J. Mexal's "Two Ways to Yuma: Locke, Liberalism, and Western Masculinity in *3:10 to Yuma*," uses the philosophy of John Locke (1632–1704) to explain how the western both sets a standard for individual identity and also serves to reflect the prevailing view of particular historical periods. Comparing the original 1957 version of *3:10 to Yuma* to the 2007 remake, Mexal argues that the differences between the two films reflect the changing ideal of masculinity from one that emphasizes civic-mindedness and filial duty to one that associates masculine identity with property. Moving us toward the issue of community that will become the focus of the next section, Mexal relates this shift to the different contexts in which the two films were produced: namely, the transition from a cold war mentality and a nation preoccupied with defense to post–cold war politics and a nation defined by an unbridled commitment to capitalism.

Like Mexal, Lindsey Collins focuses on *3:10 to Yuma* and argues that it, like most westerns, promotes an ideal of masculinity associated with the appropriation and control of property. In her essay, "Landscapes of Gendered Violence: Male Love and Anxiety on the Railroad," she analyzes the symbolism of the railroad in western films. According to Collins, while the incursion of railroads into the frontier landscape symbolizes the domestication of space by male force, films such as *3:10 to Yuma* and *Tycoon* (1947) that foreground railroads also articulate the anxieties associated with the transformation of landscape and life that such technologies entail.

Part 2 of this volume, "The Code of the West: The Cowboy and Society," extends the analysis of community introduced in the section on identity to consider how western films explore the nature of human relationships and social organization. Of particular interest is how westerns illustrate competing philosophic theories regarding the nature of community, including theories proposed by well-known social and political philosophers such as John Locke, Thomas Hobbes (1588–1679), and Jean-Jacques Rousseau (1712–78). In his essay, "Order Out of the Mud: *Deadwood* and the State of Nature," Paul A. Cantor examines David Milch's popular series *Deadwood*, particularly how the series illustrates the relationship between order and law. In fact, Cantor argues that *Deadwood* can help us arrive at a positive answer to the question: Is there order without law? Cantor examines the philosophies of Hobbes, Locke, and Rousseau, all of which informed popular perceptions of the conquest of the American frontier during the nineteenth century, and argues they also find contemporary expression in *Deadwood*.

Continuing the discussion of the relation between order and law initiated in the previous chapter by Cantor, as well as the discussion of the relationship between power and space introduced in part 1 by Collins, Aeon J. Skoble explores the parallels that exist between *The Magnificent Seven* (1960) and Kurosawa's *Seven Samurai* (1954). In his chapter, titled "Order without Law: *The Magnificent Seven*, East and West," Skoble explores not merely the similarities between the Japanese samurai, particularly the masterless *ronin*, and the western hero, but also the way in which the two films illustrate how grassroots social order can arise spontaneously with the aid of individuals with integrity.

The next two chapters in the volume continue to examine the social and moral impact of individuals with integrity. In his essay, "From Dollars to Iron: The Currency of Clint Eastwood's Westerns," David L. McNaron argues that individuals with uncompromising integrity are necessary conditions for the possibility of community and justice. He focuses specifically on Clint Eastwood's films, arguing that Eastwood repeatedly portrays characters who, though often violent, epitomize strength of character.

Similarly, in his chapter, titled "The Duty of Reason: Kantian Ethics in *High Noon*," Daw-Nay Evans examines the classic *High Noon*, particularly its main character, Marshal Will Kane. According to Evans, Kane embodies the absolute dedication to duty that Kant argued was necessary in order for our actions to have moral worth, while at the same time illustrating how difficult it is to adhere to such a strict moral code.

Part 3 of the volume, "Outlaws: Challenging Conventions of the Western," contains essays that take a critical look at the code of the West that westerns promote by examining westerns that defy that code. In the aptly titled "The Cost of the Code: Ethical Consequences in *High Noon* and *The Ox-Bow Incident*," Ken Hada challenges the moral absolutism that is characteristic of many westerns. Bridging the gap between the last essay in part 2 and the first in part 3, Hada focuses at length on the classic *High Noon*; however, rather than celebrate the moral absolutism of Marshal Will Kane as Evans did in the previous chapter, Hada gives us cause to question his unflinching ethics. Drawing primarily from the work of Martha Nussbaum, Hada argues that while films like *High Noon* and *The Ox-Bow Incident* (1943) present us with characters for whom ethics are absolute, they at the same time undercut the codes their characters embody by illustrating the often fatal consequences that follow from moral inflexibility.

In his essay, "'Back Off to What?' The Search for Meaning in *The Wild Bunch*," Richard Gaughran examines a film that challenges audience expectation by undercutting the assumption of morality altogether. Focusing on Sam Peckinpah's *The Wild Bunch* (1969), Gaughran examines moral relativism as it is illustrated by the film, relating it not only to changing political and economic conditions of the twentieth century, but also to prominent literary and philosophic movements of the period, such as existentialism. Though Gaughran recognizes that audiences might be troubled by the film's questioning of traditional values, he employs the work of Jean-Paul Sartre (1905–80) to argue that *The Wild Bunch* can be interpreted as an empowering film, to the extent that it emphasizes human freedom.

William J. Devlin continues the discussion of westerns that challenge our expectations in his essay, "*No Country for Old Men*: The Decline of Ethics and the West(ern)." In this chapter, Devlin examines an increasingly common characteristic of contemporary westerns: moral cynicism. As Devlin notes, whereas classic westerns tend to have easily recognizable heroes and villains, the moral situation depicted in contemporary westerns is rarely so clear. Influenced by figures like Peckinpah, Devlin argues, contemporary westerns not only incorporate moral ambiguity, they are also considerably more cynical than their classic predecessors. Devlin argues that this is nowhere more evident than in *No Country for Old Men*, a dystopic western that not only offers contemporary audiences a new sort of villain, but utterly confounds audience expectation by failing to have the hero rescue the community from the risk personified by the villain.

In their essay, titled "The Northwestern: *McCabe and Mrs. Miller*," Deborah Knight and George McKnight examine a film that defies not only the moral but also the aesthetic conventions of the genre. Rather than command audience interest with familiar panoramas and an uplifting conclusion, they argue, Robert Altman reverses familiar conventions such as the shoot-out to produce an end-of-genre western sufficient to inspire critique of several of the ideals upon which many early westerns are based.

Finally, part 4 of the volume, "On the Fringe: The Encounter with the Other," contains essays that consider the tendency westerns have to emphasize particular values and exclude, marginalize, or misrepresent figures who are nonetheless integral to the history of the American West, such as Native Americans, African Americans, Chinese, Hispanics, women, children, and animals. Studies in otherness, the essays in this final section look at the code of the western from the perspective of what it distorts or excludes and assess the ethical consequences of those omissions and obfuscations.

Though archetypal figures in the western, Native Americans are certainly one of the most seriously misrepresented groups in the genre. In his chapter, "Savage Nations: Native Americans and the Western," Michael Valdez Moses relies upon the philosophic discussion of indigenous peoples in Jean-Jacques Rousseau, Adam Ferguson, and Tzvetan Todorov to analyze the representation of Native American people and culture from the early films of John Ford, such as *Fort Apache* (1948), and Arthur Penn's *Little Big Man* (1970) to Kevin Costner's *Dances with Wolves* (1990) and Jim Jarmusch's *Dead Man* (1995), among others. While Moses sees a positive trend toward less caricatured and more sympathetic portrayals of Native Americans, he notes that with the exception of films written and produced by indigenous Americans, representations of Native Americans are less concerned with an honest depiction of their subject than with a polemical representation of the changing landscape of American political life.

Richard Gilmore's "Regeneration through Stories and Song: The View from the Other Side of the West in *Smoke Signals*" also analyzes the representation of Native Americans in western films. However, its focus is one of the few films produced by and told from the perspective of Native Americans. Linking back to Csaki's pragmatist interpretation of John Wayne in part 1, Gilmore places a similar emphasis on American pragmatism, even though the characters in Sherman Alexie's *Smoke Signals* (1998) are more suspicious of the Duke. As Gilmore notes, though *Smoke Signals* is about the distress that arises from failed relationships, it is also about resilience, reconciliation, and growth. With its symbolism and humor, Gilmore suggests that *Smoke Signals* illustrates important principles of Native American philosophy, principles it shares with American pragmatism, particularly their mutual emphasis on holism and process.

In their chapter, "Go West, Young Woman! Hegel's Dialectic and Women's Identities in Western Films," Gary Heba and Robin Murphy shift the focus to the representation of women in western films. Using Georg Wilhelm Friedrich Hegel's (1770–1831) dialectic to frame their discussion, Heba and Murphy trace the portrayal of women through three distinct but related phases. Analyzing not only the visual depictions of women but also their linguistic and structural functions, Heba and Murphy assess many of the classic westerns treated previously in the volume, including *The Searchers* and *Shane*. However, rather than focus on how those films promulgate and elevate masculine ideals, they discuss how these films also set definitive and typically restrictive standards for women.

Finally, the last essay in the collection considers another marginalized figure in westerns: the horse. In "Beating a Live Horse: The Elevation and Degradation of Horses in Westerns," Jennifer L. McMahon offers an existential explanation for the polarized treatment of horses in western films: namely, their simultaneous celebration and subjugation. Drawing from philosophers such as Georg Wilhelm Friedrich Hegel, Friedrich Nietzsche (1844–1900), Jean-Paul Sartre, Martin Heidegger (1889–1976), and Michel Foucault (1926–1984), McMahon analyzes the desire to dominate horses that westerns illustrate and promote. She speculates that by overcoming this desire, we can improve our relationships not only with horses and other animals, but also with one another.

Given the scope of the western genre and the vast array of subjects it encompasses that are suitable for philosophic examination, this collection aims to offer an intriguing glimpse into a new area of exploration, rather than an exhaustive mapping of it. Whereas ample scholarship exists on the history of the western, and the domain of western literary and film criticism is likewise heavily populated, the philosophy of the western is an open and promising frontier. Though the territory is not uncharted,[6] there is much yet to be explored. The terrain is promising because it can offer audiences not only a greater understanding of the discipline of philosophy, but also a fuller appreciation of the origins and continuing influence of the ever-popular genre we know as the western.

Notes

1. Here, with the term *settlement,* we are referring to the incursion of nonnative peoples into the western territories of the United States beginning in the early nineteenth century. In truth, these territories were already settled, insofar as they had been occupied for thousands of years by the indigenous peoples of North America. A wealth of scholarship exists on this nonnative settlement of the American West. Historical sources include William C. Davis, *The American Frontier: Pioneers, Settlers, and Cowboys, 1800–1899* (Norman: University of Oklahoma Press, 1999); William Deverell, *A Companion to the American West* (Malden, MA: Blackwell, 2004); and Clyde Milner, *A New Significance: Re-envisioning the History of the American West* (Oxford: Oxford University Press, 1996). Studies that consider the relation between that history and the western genre include Scott Simmon, *The Invention of the Western Film: A Cultural History of the Genre's First Half-Century* (Cambridge: Cambridge University Press, 2003); Janet Walker, ed., *Westerns: Films through History* (New York: Routledge, 2001); Jenni Calder, *There Must Be a Lone Ranger: The American West in Film and Reality* (New York: Taplinger, 1974); and Peter C. Rollins and John E. O'Connor, *Hollywood's West: The American Frontier in Film, Television, and History* (Lexington: University Press of Kentucky, 2005).

2. For further discussion of William F. Cody's famed theatrical portrayal of life on the western frontier, see Joy S. Kasson, *Buffalo Bill's Wild West: Celebrity, Memory, and Popular History* (New York: Macmillan, 2001); Don Russell, *The Lives and Legends of Buffalo Bill* (Norman: University of Oklahoma Press, 1960); Richard Slotkin, *Gunfighter Nation: The Myth of the Frontier in Twentieth-Century America* (New York: Atheneum, 1992); and Henry Nash Smith, *Virgin Land: The American West as Symbol and Myth* (Cambridge, MA: Harvard University Press, 1950).

3. It should be noted that several articles in the volume do reference works outside the scope of American western films insofar as they incorporate discussion of western novels or Sergio Leone's spaghetti westerns. Likewise, one article is focused on the recent HBO television western *Deadwood.*

4. See our selected bibliography, which identifies a variety of secondary source material on the genre, yet still only scratches the surface of this vast body of literature.

5. Most notably, Kendall Walton, who continues to promote the mimetic tradition in his work *Mimesis as Make Believe: On the Foundations of the Representational Arts* (Cambridge, MA: Harvard University Press, 1993).

6. See, for example, Peter A. French, *Cowboy Metaphysics: Ethics and Death in Westerns* (Lanham, MD: Rowman & Littlefield, 1997); and Will Wright, *Sixguns and Society: A Structural Study of the Western* (Berkeley: University of California Press, 1975) and *The Wild West: The Mythical Cowboy and Social Theory* (London: Sage, 2001).

Part 1

THE COWBOY WAY

The Essence of the Western Hero

"Do Not Forsake Me, Oh, My Darling"

Loneliness and Solitude in Westerns

Shai Biderman

> Shouldering your loneliness
> like a gun that you will not learn to aim,
> you stumble into this movie house,
> then you climb, you climb into the frame.
> —Leonard Cohen, "Love Calls You by Your Name"

"Solitary Man"

One of the common attributes of western films is the "lone hero." Whether it's in the final scene, where he takes that inevitable "lone ride" off into the sunset or in his heroic acts throughout the film, where he saves the town folk from danger, the lone hero keeps to himself. He is the quintessential "strong silent type" traditionally prized in the American psyche. He is strong in the sense that he is powerful in his physical, intellectual, and moral capacities. He is silent in the sense that, despite the social benefits earned by his outward actions, he remains secluded and keeps to himself. He appears to outwardly and inwardly manifest the notion of loneliness. Many famous Western protagonists manifest this characteristic. Ethan Edwards (John Wayne) in *The Searchers* (1956) must rescue his niece after he finds that nearly all of his family members have been massacred in a Comanche raid. While he ultimately saves her, he nonetheless must take the lone ride to do so. "The Man with No Name" (Clint Eastwood) in the *Dollars* trilogy (1964, 1965, 1966) is a gunslinger who represents the notion that the lone rider is one without a significant identity, one who acts for money, makes superficial friendships, and then rides off alone. Shane (Alan Ladd) in the movie of the same name (1953) is introduced as a lone rider, a gunslinger who saves the homesteaders of a small town from a cattle baron and then leaves, just as he came, alone in solitude (possibly riding to his death). Finally, Marshal Will Kane (Gary Cooper) in *High Noon* (1952) tries to give up the lone life of the town's marshal in order to marry his Quaker sweetheart, only to find out that loneliness goes with the territory and cannot be overcome. Other instances in many other films support the claim that this characteristic of loneliness is not a random feature of the western hero; rather, it is the hero's trademark.

But why must the hero ride alone? How does he benefit (if at all) from a life of loneliness and solitude? Is it purely accidental or does it imply an intrinsic quality of the western protagonist? In this chapter, I will examine the condition of loneliness and solitude in the western hero, asking such questions as, "What is the condition of loneliness?" and "How is it different from solitude, if at all?" I will analyze the nature of these predicaments, as both a state of mind and a state of affairs, using and echoing related terms and distinctions like isolation, privacy, seclusion, alienation, disengagement, and the difference between being alone and being lonely.

In order to find out why it is crucial for the western hero to be all (or some) of the above, I will pursue the philosophical nature of this condition. I will argue that loneliness and solitude have a philosophical significance, in the sense that those who are subject to the condition of loneliness might have a "philosophical benefit" over others who are not. I will discuss this philosophical benefit by analyzing how the hero's lonely road of solitude is the most conspicuous trademark of his character. This analysis will help to show why this trait has been so influential in other cinematic genres. Characters like the modern cowboy, including Travis Bickel (Robert De Niro) as the angry lone rider in *Taxi Driver* (1976), and Clint Eastwood's urban mutation of his early western roles as Harry Callahan in the *Dirty Harry* film series, pay homage to the western hero by applying the characteristics of loneliness and alienation to the modern area, thereby moving the sense of estrangement from the country to the city.[1]

As I follow the lone hero on his journey, I will examine solitude and isolation from two philosophical perspectives. First, I will examine the hero's loneliness from the point of view of *epistemology*. As the field of philosophy that concerns knowledge (in terms of analysis, application, and limitation), epistemology applies to loneliness as an issue concerning the limits of knowledge. I will examine the hero in terms of both what he knows and what he doesn't know, as well as what he reveals and doesn't reveal to others. Second, I will examine the hero's loneliness from the point of view of *ethics*, or the field of philosophy that concerns what we ought to do. Here, the ethical examination of loneliness focuses on whether or not the hero's tendency toward isolation inhibits or advances his moral character. As we will see, the western hero is a man motivated by his will to "do the right thing": save the western lawless frontiers from stray gunmen, from acts of injustice, and from evildoers. His loneliness has ethical relevance, I will argue, and as such is a philosophically significant aspect of his character.

"Are You Lonesome Tonight?"

In the film *Heat* (1995), the elusive robber Neil McCauley (Robert De Niro) breaks his professional oath—"Don't let yourself get attached to anything you are not willing to walk out on in thirty seconds flat if you feel the heat around the corner"—when he befriends a shy girl, Eady (Amy Brenneman). Eady, noticing Neil's softer side behind his tough guy's mask, admits that life in LA has left her feeling "very lonely" and she wonders if Neil feels the same way. Neil, however, retorts: "I'm alone—I'm not lonely." This distinction, which Neil expresses as he and Eady stand on a balcony observing the night falling on LA, the crown of the West, is a distinction between a subjective, inner, self-proclaimed depiction of one's state of mind, and an objective, outer, public and universal depiction of a state of affairs. In order to begin our journey with the lone hero, it is important to flesh out this distinction carefully so that we can understand the epistemic and ethical issues of loneliness, as well as how these distinctions are portrayed in westerns.

As suggested in the scene from *Heat*, there are two sides to loneliness. On the one hand, there is the subjective, personal, inner feeling of isolation and estrangement from other people, in the sense of feeling lonely. On the other hand, there is the objective, public, outer view of one being physically away from others, in the sense of being alone. Though we can conceptually separate the two sides of loneliness, they can relate to one another in various ways. First, both the internal and external conditions can be absent from a single individual. For instance, when I am at work, I can be neither estranged nor alone, as I have my colleagues around me, and I feel a strong bond with them. Second, both conditions can be presented together. I may end up working late, while my colleagues find it best to have dinner together. Desiring to be part of their companionship, I wind up not only *being* alone but *feeling* alone. That is, upon realizing that I am (objectively) alone in the building, I feel (subjectively) lonely. Here, my feeling of loneliness may take on the face of self-pity and envy. Third, these two conditions can be separated from each other. McCauley represents this separation, as he objectively remains alone, in solitude from others, but this isolation does not make him *feel* as if he is lonely, in the sense that he has a desire or need to be with others. Thus, for McCauley, the objective state of being alone does not entail the subjective feeling of loneliness. These conditions can be separated in another way. For example, in *The Thin Red Line* (1998), First Private Witt (Jim Caviezel) asks Sergeant Welsh (Sean Penn), "Do you ever feel lonely?" Welsh responds, "Only around people." Welsh's response helps to crystallize the categorical differences between being alone and feeling lonely but, at the same time, undermines this difference by blending the two together. One can, accordingly, "feel" alone (despite obvious objective data that proves otherwise), and one can thus "be" lonely (despite being surrounded by loved ones).

As we investigate the western hero with this conceptual distinction of loneliness in mind, we immediately run into a problem. Namely, we have no access to the character's state of mind, unless he tells us how he feels. But it is important to note that, as the "silent type," the hero is not the kind of individual to relate his feelings to other people. Still, we can deduce his state of mind from his actions, and from the way he handles himself in front of the camera. When we follow this procedure, we find that the lone hero often illustrates the two sides of loneliness. In *The Searchers*, when Uncle Ethan first comes back from the war, he is surrounded by his family. Thus, objectively, he is not alone. However, his body language and mannerisms reflect deep uneasiness about being around people. He doesn't feel at home with his family; rather, he acts as if he'd rather be left alone. In other words, like Welsh, Ethan is feeling lonely around other people. Even though these people are his family, Ethan carries himself as if he were a stranger in a strange land, unable to identify and work with others. This image of Ethan as the lone rider who feels lonely only around others is encapsulated in the final scene of the film. There, after spending years (and most of the film) searching for his kidnapped niece, Ethan literally carries her to the doorstep of friends. As the family walks his niece into their home, Ethan hesitates at the doorstep, and the camera views him from the inside of the home. This revealing shot conveys a sudden and unpleasant feeling of loneliness. We feel lonely because we believe Ethan feels lonely. Abandoned by family and victimized by his ragged (and somewhat brutish) nature, Ethan cannot help but feel lonely. And the camera makes a noticed effort to convey this message. He stands there, lonely (and alone in the frame), holding his elbow in a somewhat exhausted way. His life goal is completed; he is depleted and tired. More importantly, nobody needs him anymore. The camera reflects all that by showing him at the doorstep, framed by the door, against the background of the wilderness.[2]

In *Unforgiven* (1992), the question of loneliness (in both its subjective and objective senses) is discussed on several occasions. William Munny (Clint Eastwood) used to be the western hero's archnemesis: a vicious outlaw who "killed women and children," as his reputation goes. Now he is a born-again pig farmer, still devoted to his dead wife, who reformed him from the bad ways of his youth as he cares for his two children. But since the wife is no longer there to keep him straight, Munny conjoins with his old partner in crime, Ned Logan (Morgan Freeman), and with a new admirer, the Schofield Kid (Jaimz Woolvett), to avenge the unjust abuse of a whore by two local cowboys. Now old and pathetic, Munny makes a very poor excuse for a spokesman for justice. While on the road, Munny and his friends discuss the absence of female companionship. Logan has a wife at home whom he misses. Though he is with two companions (and so is not objectively alone), he feels lonely: he misses his bed and his wife, longing to be with her. Later, he tries to fend off his feeling of loneliness by cashing in an advance on the bounty offered by the bordello for the death of the two cowboys. The Schofield Kid, on the contrary, doesn't feel lonely. He is pumped up with stories of wild gunfights and heroism, and cannot wait to add his share to the ongoing myth of the Wild West. However, by the end of the film we see him on the ground, miserable and remorseful, both lonely and alone, as he realizes that his dream to be an outlaw is something that he cannot and does not want to strive for anymore. Munny, much like Neil McCauley, is objectively alone. But though he may not feel lonely when alone, he is concerned about being trapped forever in physical isolation: as he tells the Kid, "I won't kill you; you are the only friend I've got." Ironically, this sentence means that Munny has no friends. He might not feel lonely—but he is alone.

There are two paradigmatic examples of loneliness and solitude in the westerns. First, the hero rides alone. Second, the hero faces his enemy in the final duel alone. And in between these two narrative scenes, he is usually on his own. Take, for example, Shane in *Shane*. The film's opening scene is of Shane riding in the mountainous countryside of Wyoming. Though he befriends homesteader Joe Starrett (Van Heflin) and his family, in several crucial scenes, he acts alone. In his first fight he is alone, and more importantly, he is alone in his final showdown. In that case, Shane wants to enter the final showdown alone so strongly that he beats up Joe (the man whom he is helping through the showdown) so he can do this alone. Shane is thus strongly compelled to fight objectively alone, without companions.

Fighting alone is also exemplified by Marshal Kane in *High Noon*. There, following his duty as marshal (that is, his duty to protect everyone else), Kane fights four gunmen. But ironically, though he accepts his duty to protect others, no one protects him—he must enter the final showdown alone. Similarly, in *Unforgiven*, after learning of Logan's death, Munny seeks revenge all alone. Though, with respect to the final showdown, Shane desires to be alone, Kane is forced to be alone, and Munny is too raveled in his drunken desire for revenge to care one way or the other, all three lone riders are similar in at least one respect: they are subjectively comfortable in their objective solitude.

In conclusion, I have shown the dual nature of loneliness. On the one hand, loneliness is a state of mind, a self-inspection of one's feelings and self-perception. This is the subjective condition of being lonely. On the other hand, there is the objective perception of being alone. We can use this distinction to expound on related terms that designate descriptions of these two conditions. For example, isolation (or seclusion) is the condition of being hidden and shunned from the company of others. Seemingly an objective term ("The patient was isolated for fear of contamination"), it can also reflect a subjective inner state of mind, much like the feeling of loneliness. "Privacy" has a positive connotation to it (in some legal systems it is a sacred right); "alienation" has a negative connotation, and it usually refers to either the condition or the feeling of being cast out from society. "Disengagement" is a neutrally sound term, which has the hint of reciprocity. All these terms have to do with the conditions of loneliness and solitude. And they all play supporting roles in the construction of the western protagonist. Now, having clarified the notion of loneliness, we can turn to discuss its philosophical nature.

"One Is the Loneliest Number"

What are the philosophical applications of loneliness? What might be philosophically gained from a lonely or a solo figure's point of view? The conditions of loneliness and solitude appear in philosophy in many different contexts. One major context concerns the epistemic quest for certainty and true knowledge. The epistemic quest is encapsulated best by Socrates (469–399 BCE), who maintained that "the unexamined life is not worth living." Aristotle (384–322 BCE), meanwhile, added that philosophy begins with a sense of wonder. The wonder is to be pursued by a life of examination and investigation. The desire to know achieves its greatest fulfillment in the philosopher who understands the principles and causes of the world.[3]

Solitude is a primary position for such an epistemic quest, as it is the context that isolates and manifests the wondering voice who seeks for knowledge and truths. Following contemporary philosopher Philip Koch, we can say that "the more given to reflection a person is, the more a philosopher; and when, in addition, the objective of reflection is a connected vision of the whole reality, we have a philosopher in the strongest sense of the term." In order to follow these two declarations about human life and goals, the individual is better off on his or her own, encountering the world and him- or herself in an unmediated and uninterrupted way. The ability to retreat from the immediacy of the world, of other people, and to examine the world "from a distance" (the distance of solitude) is, as Michel de Montaigne (1533–92) notes, a clear philosophical advantage: "We must reserve a little back-shop, all our own, entirely free, wherein to establish our true liberty and principal retreat and solitude."[4]

French philosopher René Descartes (1596–1650) understood that this individualistic state of mind is required for the true soul searching for, and gaining of, true knowledge and an understanding of the world. In his *Meditations on First Philosophy* (1641), he springs from "a little back-shop" of solitude into the most skeptical of epistemic searches. His solitude quickly evolves into the disposition of *solipsism*, the extreme epistemic position that states that, lacking contrary evidence, the only thing that I can be certain of is my own individual, and isolated, existence. He begins his search by isolating himself, in the objective sense, by withdrawing to the seclusion of his room. There, in isolation, he turns his attention to the epistemic quest for knowledge and certainty. He opens the first meditation with a very personal standpoint about himself: "Several years have now elapsed since I first became aware that I had accepted, even from my youth, many false opinions for true, and that consequently what I afterward based on such principles was highly doubtful." In other words, Descartes begins his epistemic quest by employing *methodological doubt,* or the method under which nothing is certain unless proven to be so, and whatever isn't certain is systematically abandoned as a falsehood.[5]

Those dubitable knowledge-claims multiply when he recalls that "I must nevertheless here consider that I am a man, and that, consequently, I am in the habit of sleeping, and representing to myself in dreams those same things, or even sometimes others less probable, which the insane think are presented to them in their waking moments." Here, Descartes asks, "How often have I dreamt that I was in these familiar circumstances, that I was dressed, and occupied this place by the fire, when I was lying undressed in bed?" Descartes is deluded and misguided. He cannot trust his senses, nor can he trust that he's not dreaming. As Descartes points out, nothing is known for certain, and this is a very lonely, subjective disposition: "Just as if I had fallen all of a sudden into very deep water, I am so greatly disconcerted as to be unable either to plant my feet firmly on the bottom or sustain myself by swimming on the surface." In other words, life and the world have subjectively become very lonely places for Descartes.[6]

The only certainty Descartes finds is that he, himself, exists. His reasoning for such a conclusion is as follows. Even if one assumes that there is a deceiver, from the very fact that one is deceived it follows that one exists. In general, it will follow from any state of thinking (for example, imagining, sensing, feeling, or reasoning) that one exists. While one can be deceived about the objective content of any thought, one cannot be deceived about the fact that one exists and that one seems to perceive objects with certain characteristics. Since one can be certain only of the existence of one's self insofar as one is thinking, one has knowledge or certainty of one's existence only as a thinking thing (*res cogitans*). Whereas this certainty rescues Descartes from his "feeling" of loneliness, it leaves him, strictly speaking, alone in the epistemic sense of solipsism. For Descartes, at this point, his own existence, as a thinking thing, is the only verifiable reality. In this sense, then, solitude, in its epistemic form, becomes the methodological preference for developing one's knowledge of the world.[7]

Loneliness thus has an epistemic value. It is both the primary and preferred condition for philosophical investigation and examination and a possible end result of such a quest. This is why many writers and philosophers, such as the poet Octavio Paz Lozano (1914–98), have insisted upon our "essential loneliness." Loneliness, then, is not merely the aberrant state of a person or culture, but rather "the profoundest fact of the human condition."[8]

The loneliness of the western hero reveals itself in two epistemic contexts. First, as already suggested, he is, after all, "the silent type." Language is not his strong side—he doesn't speak much, and he hardly ever asks for advice or shares his thoughts (and hence his contemplation) with others. As opposed to reflecting publicly, at a town meeting, perhaps, or in a group conversation, the hero reflects largely in private. The philosopher Ludwig Wittgenstein (1889–1951), who builds on the linguistic characteristic of Cartesian solipsism, notes, "The limits of my language means the limits of the world." That is, since we cannot say what we cannot think, it follows that one's world is limited by one's language so that "the world is *my* world" (my emphasis).[9] And, since the lone rider is one who, more often than not, remains silent, he embraces this epistemic notion of linguistic solipsism. Second, the western hero keeps to himself. He doesn't seek information from others, and he doesn't share information with anyone, either. We rarely know his thoughts, his feelings, or even his name. He makes decisions and acts on them without sharing with others (and us) his deliberation process. Whenever he contemplates and assesses the knowledge he has, he does so in private. He never asks others what he can find out himself, on his own, by himself. This "alone," or private, aspect of the epistemic loneliness makes the western hero rather mysterious.

We can see this lonesome and mysterious characteristic in Marshal Kane of *High Noon*. Kane decides that his duty as sheriff is above everything else. He gains this knowledge of himself, his duties, and his correlate plans without (and even against) the advice of anyone else. His wife, his former mistress, his deputy, the town's assembly—all tell him, in one way or another, to flee town. But he has already made up his mind. We would say nowadays that he "looked into himself" and found out what he ought to do. In epistemic terms, we can say that he gained certain knowledge about what he should be doing next. And, again, this knowledge was gained without the help of others.

Likewise, Shane in *Shane* is the quiet type. He rarely speaks, he hides his past as a gunslinger, he reveals but very few details about himself, even hiding his full name. The same goes for William Munny in *Unforgiven*—there, even when the Schofield Kid gets his facts wrong about Munny's past, he remains quiet, refusing to reveal the truth. Finally, in *The Good, the Bad, and the Ugly*, Blondie (Clint Eastwood) holds a rare piece of knowledge: the name on the gravestone where the treasure is buried. This knowledge is of no use if it is shared, especially with his shady companions, the vicious Angel Eyes (Lee Van Cleef) and the crooked Tuko (Eli Wallach). When he finally shares the info with Tuko, the knowledge is not relevant anymore, since Angel Eyes is lying dead in an open grave and Tuko is hanging from the rope of his own doing. In short, whether it is Kane, Shane, Munny, Blondie, or many other western heroes, all of them are similar insofar as each lone rider remains, more or less, silent, finding comfort in his subjective epistemic and solipsistic solitude.

"All the Lonely People"

The most important philosophical aspect of the western hero's loneliness focuses more on what he does than on what he knows. The western hero is, after all, a man of action. Whether he is a sheriff or a bandit, a keeper of the law or an outlaw, a member of conventional society or a vigilante, the lone hero is not a man of words. He is a man of deeds. Ethan Edwards in *The Searchers* is a man of few words. So is Marshal Will Kane in *High Noon*. Blondie in *The Good, the Bad and the Ugly* rarely opens his mouth (as opposed to the chatty Tuko).[10] And the shy Shane finds it hard to make verbal connections. But all of them are men of action: they go on an expedition for years to find a lost niece, they save the town from evildoers, and they go on a treasure hunt (and briefly join the Union army in the Civil War). As a man of action, the lone hero must be able to justify his actions as morally sound because of, or in spite of, his solitude. And so we must investigate whether or not the condition of loneliness interferes with the hero's effort to do the right thing.

When considering ethics and loneliness as two character traits that might contradict each other, one may wish to refer to Aristotle. Aristotle's ethics revolves around the state of happiness (*eudaimonia*) as the goal of humankind (and, as such, as the justification of ethics) and around the concept of excellence (*aretē*) as the prerequisite of character needed in order to lead the virtuous life of happiness and flourishing. Being ethical, according to Aristotle, involves leading a harmonious and balanced life of flourishing and excellence. What is excellence and how does one become excellent? Aristotle presents the golden mean, or the mean between two extremes of vices, which crystallizes the excellent, and thus virtuous, behavior (or trait). The most common example, used by Aristotle to expand on the nature of the golden mean, is the condition and character trait of bravery. Bravery is the character disposition that is the mean between cowardice (deficiency) and recklessness (excess). In order to be excellent (virtuous), one has to act in moderation.[11]

Aristotle designates many external goods that can help, to various degrees, in the process of habituating virtuousness. Such goods include proper education, nourishing, and upbringing, having inspiring role models, and the acquisition of habits, practicing those habits, and developing them into skills (what Aristotle calls "practical knowledge"). One external good that is necessary for acquiring excellence is having friends and social relations. As Aristotle points out, "Man by nature is a political [social] animal." Thus, for Aristotle, one cannot be fully virtuous and excellent if one has no friends and is estranged from society. Aristotle compares this lonely, friendless condition to sleeping or being in a coma: one cannot be said to be "virtuous" or "excellent" (or "moral") when one is asleep or in a lifelong coma. Similarly, one cannot be said to be ethical if one keeps to oneself, is alone and alienated from society, has no friends or family, and does not nourish and cultivate one's social skills.[12]

Following Aristotle's ethical standards, the western hero cannot act on his full potential as an ethical figure as long as he is a lone rider. His lack of social skills, while proven to have some possible epistemic benefits, is devastating as an ethical disposition. The lone hero cannot fully acquire the moral and noble roles of pursuing justice, fighting evil, saving towns, and amending wrongs unless he opens up and abandons his loneliness for a life that essentially embodies social interactions.

"I'm Lonesome but Happy"

Aristotle's virtue ethics cherishes the virtue of friendship and social interaction. To that extent, it presents a problem for the lone rider. This approach rests on the Aristotelian presupposition that human nature entails solidarity and camaraderie (as "man is a social animal") and so ethics should reflect this disposition as a necessary condition of the moral being. However, this premise can be debated. British philosopher Thomas Hobbes (1588–1679), author of the political manifesto the *Leviathan*, still scarred by his firsthand experience of the British civil war, believed human life to be "nasty, brutish, and short" and human interaction to be a constant and self-defeating war of all against all. We have thus to acknowledge the possibility of a different premise of the motivating force of human nature, and, accordingly, a different system of ethics, which cherishes other qualities and character traits.[13] Such systems, or, better yet, such premises, are adopted by two philosophical movements, one ancient and one modern: namely, the Greco-Roman system of Stoicism and the nineteenth- to twentieth-century movement of existentialism. The common grounds of both Stoic ethics and existential ethics can be harnessed to our purposes and pinned to the condition of loneliness. According to the Stoic doctrine, loneliness is, in fact, the better way to approach human existence. Life has no meaning. It is short, full of disappointments and mishaps, and then we die. The only thing left to be done is to accept that, and then detach ourselves from the terror and anguish of this realization. That is, we must accept the fact that our existence is characterized by suffering, but ignore the consequences and implications that follow. The Stoic aim is to live a life of "freedom from disturbance" (*ataraxia*) by eliminating the two main sources of human anguish, the fear of god and the fear of death. Stoicism teaches us that cosmic phenomena do not convey divine threats, and that death is merely the disintegration of the soul, with hell an illusion. Being dead will be no worse than not having yet been born.

In short, Stoicism makes basic distinctions between that which is up to us and that which is outside our control, aiming to attain a state of detachment (*apatheia*). Those things that are in our control include our thoughts, impulses, and the will to get and to avoid. Those things outside our control include material things, property, reputation, our station in life, and so on. For Stoicism, the key to happiness, as it were, is to attend only to those things in our control. The Stoic Epictetus (55–135), a freed slave, writes: "Never say about anything 'I have lost it,' but instead, 'I have given it back.' . . . [Treat life] just as travellers treat an inn." Here, Epictetus is endorsing a sense of detachment toward those things beyond our control. This sense of detachment applies to how one should treat not only material items and goals in life, but also other people: "If you kiss your child or your wife, say to yourself that you are kissing a human being, for then if death strikes it you will not be disturbed." In this sense, for Epictetus, human existence is similar to the lives of actors in a play: "Remember that you are an actor in a play, which is as the playwright wants it to be; short if he wants it short, long if he wants it long. If he wants [you] to play a beggar, play even this part skilfully, or a cripple, or a public official, or a private citizen. What is yours is to play the assigned part well. But to choose it belongs to someone else." Finally, he suggests that by embracing our mortality, we shape our morality: "Let death and exile and everything that is terrible appear before your eyes every day, especially death; and you will never have anything contemptible in your thoughts or crave anything excessively."[14]

The Stoical emphasis on detachment toward and around others can thus be seen as a way to endorse the internal sense of solitude. Here, the lone rider embodies the Stoical view that one should focus only on what is in one's control. For instance, in *The Searchers*, once Ethan learns while traveling that his family is in danger of being killed by a Comanche raid, he does not let his emotions get the best of him. Though his companions attempt to race back to the homestead, Ethan calmly decides to give his horse a rest, realizing that his horse will never make it back, otherwise. In this sense, Ethan, like a Stoic, realizes that the prevention of his family's death is beyond his control; what he and his horse need right now is sleep, so that he can do what he can tomorrow. Likewise, in *Shane*, once Shane is victorious in his showdown, he chooses to leave town. As he explains to young Joey (Brandon DeWilde), he cannot stay: "A man has to be what he is, Joey. Can't break the mold. I tried it and it didn't work for me. Right or wrong, it's a brand . . . a brand sticks." In other words, Shane views his life as that of an actor in a play—his role, a role determined by the playwright, is to be the lone rider. Hence, he cannot settle down and embody a complete social identity in the Aristotelian sense. According to Stoicism, because the lone rider accepts this role, he is able to be happy.

A similarly profound approach to life, death, and human nature can be found in the eclectic movement called existentialism. The basic existential belief is similar to the Stoical viewpoint in that human life has no innate purpose or meaning. Rather, as the existentialist Jean-Paul Sartre (1905–80) maintains, our "existence precedes [our] essence." That is, our own nature, and the meaning, or purpose of our lives, is not preconditioned or predetermined. Instead, existentialism emphasizes that each individual has the power and the personal freedom to create his or her own meaning in life. And, since in existentialism there is no necessary set of rational laws to follow, the individual can allow a central role for his or her passions—so that for the existentialist, to live is to live passionately.[15] The call to create one's essence and so one's happiness is thus a call for us to be individuals, or to live *authentically*. Authenticity can be understood as the attitude an individual has toward his or her life insofar as it is acknowledged as his or her own project. That is, to live authentically entails that the individual acknowledge his or her own life not just as any life; rather, one lives in such a way so that one creates or makes one's self as one intends. The existential call for authenticity advises us to not simply fall in with the crowd, as it were. Rather, our individuality and freedom are truly expressed when we can escape from the groupthink and labels of a social identity. In fact, one's social identity can be so detrimental to our freedom that Sartre maintains, "Hell is other people." Similarly, Søren Kierkegaard (1813–55) maintains that the human life is best understood as finding oneself: "The thing is to understand myself . . . the thing is to find a truth which is true *for me*, to find *the idea for which I can live and die.*" In this sense, for Kierkegaard, the human being should live not according to what is objectively true, but rather according to what is personally and individually meaningful, even if this meaning is discovered within, and expressed through, the subjective feeling of loneliness. Likewise, Friedrich Nietzsche (1844–1900) maintains that one of the central tasks in human existence is to determine the meaning of one's life by creating one's own self: "*What does your conscience say?*—You shall become the person you are." For Nietzsche, then, an individual's true existence is understood to include the manifestation of one's passions, talents, and virtues.[16]

Perhaps the clearest example of the lone rider who embodies the existentialist response to the Aristotelian challenge is William Munny from *Unforgiven*. In his youth, Munny was a notorious outlaw, said to have killed women and children. But he changed his life after meeting his wife and raising two children on a very small, impoverished ranch. As such, Munny lives out the Aristotelian ideal as a social animal with his family, and even seemingly buries all acknowledgement of his sordid past, as he often tells people, such as Ned, "I ain't like that no more. I ain't the same." Ultimately, however, his existential calling to "become the person you are" takes hold. By the end of the film, Munny embraces his past, acknowledging who he was, and once again turns to his outlaw-ish (yet still heroic) ways, as he announces to a saloon full of his enemies: "I've killed women and children. I've killed just about everything that walks or crawls at one time or another; and I'm here to kill you." Munny, then, comes to realize who he is—the real life that he has created for himself. He is someone who can neither completely bury his past nor hide what is true for him as his created essence, and therefore cannot live comfortably according to the Aristotelian depiction of the human being as essentially a social animal. Instead, Munny's essence is that of a lone rider.

Thus, overall, the western hero tends to keep to himself, sometimes in both senses—of loneliness and of being alone—and otherwise in one or the other. This predicament, as I have shown, can serve to help him carry out his job and tasks, both as an epistemic stand (I am the only reliable source of knowledge) and as an ethical stand (I am what I do; my deeds and actions define who I am as a moral person). However so, both philosophical advantages are really two-edged swords: epistemic solipsism might end up being a very limited perspective and a very narrow source of knowledge; moreover, the ethics of loneliness consistently ignores the embedment of ethics in the social domain, which, according to Aristotle and many others, is what ethics is primarily all about. One is therefore left to wonder why the western hero is portrayed in this fashion. Is it because he is usually created in the image of real historical figures (who were, supposedly, lonely characters)? Even if this is partially the case, it does not explain such a portrayal of totally fictitious characters. It is my idea, therefore, that the lone hero is indeed "a lone" hero because he must be so. In order to be a "hero"—he must be "lone." The lonesome predicament is integral to the idea of a western hero figure: the pioneer who wanders the wilderness, who has no steady home or domestic affiliations, who does what he does and says what he says only for the sake of his mythological heroism. He is authentic, detached, and in harmony with himself, living his life as he chose freely to live, and positions himself as a hero, a myth, a mystery, and the totem of generations to come.

Notes

The title of this essay is taken from the song "The Ballad of High Noon" (music by Dimitri Tiomkin, lyrics by Ned Washington), sung by Tex Ritter over the opening credits in *High Noon*. The epigraph is taken from Leonard Cohen, "Love Calls You by Your Name," from *Songs of Love and Hate* (1971). The heading titles are likewise drawn from songs: "Solitary Man" by Neil Diamond (lyrics by Neil Diamond, 1966); "Are You Lonesome Tonight?" a popular song written by Lou Handman and Roy Turk in 1926 and recorded by a number of singers, most notably Elvis Presley; "One" by Three Dog Night (lyrics by Harry Nilsson); "Eleanor Rigby" by the Beatles (lyrics by Paul McCartney); and "Cowpoke" (lyrics by Edwin H. Morris).

1. It is interesting to note that Martin Scorsese has acknowledged that his *Taxi Driver* was consciously influenced by John Ford's *The Searchers* (1956). Both Ethan and Travis Bickel are angry war veterans and social outcasts who become obsessed with rescuing a young girl, restoring her virtue, and returning her to society in order to purify their own souls, although they remain outsiders.

2. It might be argued that in this scene Ethan is unable to enter the door—a symbol of reconnecting with community—in large part due to the dehumanizing effects of his experience. It seems that many western heroes share this quality. Their experiences have disclosed the dark side of human sociality. Though they may display a sort of nostalgia for a time when they trusted others and took consolation from their company, their experience makes them incapable of ever "going back." Their loneliness is chosen in part due to their discovery that everyone is out for him- or herself anyway. (I kindly thank Jennifer McMahon for this illuminating note.)

3. Plato, *Apology, Five Dialogues*, trans. G. M. A. Grube (Indianapolis: Hackett, 2002), 38a. For Aristotle's account of the sense of wonder, see Aristotle, *De Poetica: The Basic Works of Aristotle*, ed. Richard McKeon (New York: Random House, 1941), 1455–87.

4. Philip Koch, *Solitude: A Philosophical Encounter* (Chicago: Open Court, 1994), 128; Michel de Montaigne, "Of Solitude," in *The Essays of Montaigne*, trans. E. J. Trechmann (New York: Modern Library, 1946), 205.

5. René Descartes, *Meditations on First Philosophy: The Philosophical Writings of Descartes, volume II*, trans. John Cottingham, Robert Stoothoff, and Dugald Murdoch (Cambridge: Cambridge University Press, 1984), Meditation I, p. 12.

6. Ibid., Meditation II.

7. It is worth noting here that the epistemic disposition of solipsism, while holding a necessary role in the Cartesian skeptical move, can nevertheless be taken as a rather dubious epistemic stand. Solipsism denies the certainty of anything but oneself, thus eliminating the reliance on others. For the solipsist, others might not exist, if only for the fact that their existence cannot be verified in the same way as his own existence is. And so, the lone individual can lose perspective and, without feedback provided by others, would have no means to correct subjective distortion. This is pretty much the end of the road for the solipsist. In its strict form, solipsism is almost an impossible epistemic thesis to live by. However so, since it does have some philosophical distinctive attributes (and advantages), it is worth considering its value as a trademark of the western lone hero.

8. These quotes have been attributed to Paz Lozano in conversation. Philosophers who promote solitude, either in word or action, include Descartes, Isaac Newton, John Locke, Blaise Pascal, Baruch Spinoza, Immanuel Kant, Gottfried Leibniz, Arthur Schopenhauer, Friedrich Nietzsche, Søren Kierkegaard, and Ludwig Wittgenstein. All lived lives of solitude, some of celibacy, and most of them never married.

9. Ludwig Wittgenstein, *Tractatus Logico-Philosophicus*, trans. D. F. Pears and B. F. McGuinness (London: Routledge, 1974), 5.6–5.6.2.

10. And even Tuko cannot resist crystallizing the priority of deeds over words when he famously mocks his former victim and now assailant: "If you have to shoot—shoot, don't talk."

11. See Aristotle, *Nicomachean Ethics: The Basic Works of Aristotle,* ed. Richard McKeon (New York: Random House, 1941), books 2, 6–7.

12. Aristotle, *Politics: The Basic Works of Aristotle,* ed. Richard McKeon (New York: Random House, 1941), book 2; Aristotle, *Nicomachean Ethics,* books 2, 6–7.

13. Thomas Hobbes, *Leviathan* (Mineola, NY: Dover, 2006), 72.

14. Epictetus, *The Enchiridion,* trans. Nicholas P. White (Indianapolis: Hackett, 1983), secs. 3–21.

15. Jean-Paul Sartre, "Existentialism Is a Humanism," in *Existentialism and Human Emotions* (Secaucus, NJ: Citadel, 1957), 15.

16. Jean-Paul Sartre, *No Exit and Three Other Plays,* trans. Lionel Abel (New York: Vintage International, 1989), 46; Søren Kierkegaard, "The Journals," in *A Kierkegaard Anthology,* ed. Robert Bretall (Princeton, NJ: Princeton University Press, 1946), 5; Friedrich Nietzsche, *The Gay Science,* trans. Walter Kaufmann (New York: Vintage, 1974), aphorism 270. See also Albert Camus, *The Rebel* (New York: Vintage, 1992).

CIVILIZATION AND ITS DISCONTENTS

The Self-Sufficient Western Hero

Douglas J. Den Uyl

> Trust thyself: every heart vibrates to that iron string.
> —Ralph Waldo Emerson, "Self-Reliance"

Perhaps no image is more symptomatic of the American western than the lone hero, abandoned by all, skillfully performing some act of courage in the cause of justice.[1] In this respect, a movie like *High Noon* (1952) comes immediately to mind: Marshal Will Kane (Gary Cooper) is forsaken even by his fiancée as he faces a deadly opponent. However allegorical the film may be, it is perhaps paradigmatic of the majority of western films—namely, it showcases a hero possessed of extraordinary self-sufficiency facing problems that ordinary men would be either unable or too fearful to handle.[2] The western hero has been described as "mythic" and compared to the great mythic heroes of Western civilization.[3] Those earlier heroes, whether Homeric warriors or Norse avengers, possess awe-inspiring strength, skills, and courage that stand out so significantly that the contributions of all others recede completely into the background. Heroes of the American western also evoke this sense of standing apart from, and above, ordinary men and women; yet they simultaneously seem more human and closer to us than those other mythic heroes. No doubt the cultural context plays a role as to which heroic traits are emphasized and resonate.[4] American westerns are certainly no different in this respect, for they represent narratives central to the American consciousness, particularly those connected to foundings and democracy. The western hero, for example, compared to heroes of other cultures, seems more "democratic," seldom wanting to stand out in the end, but more comfortable melding back into the community or floating off into the sunset as one equal among others.

But the legacy of Western civilization offers up other "heroes" likewise admired for their self-sufficiency, virtue, and skills. These heroes are ones touted by philosophy. How does the philosophic ideal of self-sufficiency compare with the picture of self-sufficiency found in the American western hero? With thousands of western movies available, there are potentially thousands of possible heroes to consider. Similarly, philosophy is filled with a myriad of thinkers and interpretations. There are simply too many westerns and too many thinkers to give any one of them a full hearing here. Fortunately, our goal is more modest than any pretense at completeness. We shall limit ourselves primarily to a couple of philosophers and a few examples from western films. Our purpose is to evoke, rather than to conclude, a conversation about the dimensions of self-sufficiency and the contribution that can be made to that concept by the American western.

The two philosophers we shall use to guide us are Aristotle (384–322) and Spinoza (1632–77). They both give self-sufficiency central importance in their theories of human action, while at the same time they represent rather different periods and ways of "doing" philosophy. We shall look at both with the idea of arriving at a composite picture of self-sufficiency to use when considering the heroes of western films. For our westerns, we shall draw upon the films of John Ford, in particular *The Man Who Shot Liberty Valance* (1962). There are some important reasons for doing so. First, John Ford is arguably the person who defined the nature of the western film for the modern talking cinema.[5] Second, Ford's heroes are often more complex than the typical "B movie" type of western hero, which thereby has the benefit of encouraging more subtle and probing analysis. Finally, Ford's heroes seem especially human, which should help us in our reflections upon an idea of self-sufficiency that can actually be practiced. Mythic heroes may be awe-inspiring, but the heroes of western films often serve as exemplars of the kind of persons we should ourselves try to become.

Philosophers on Self-Sufficiency

Aristotle is the philosopher most usually connected with the notion of self-sufficiency (*autarkeia*). For this reason we should begin by citing in some detail the most well-known passages from his *Nicomachean Ethics* on this subject:

We call that which is pursued as an end in itself more final than an end which is pursued for the sake of something else; and what is never chosen as a means to something else we call more final than that which is chosen both as an end in itself and as a means to something else. What is always chosen as an end in itself and never as a means to something else is called final in an unqualified sense.[6] This description seems to apply to happiness above all else. Honor, pleasure, intelligence, and all virtue we choose partly for themselves . . . but we also choose them partly for the sake of happiness, because we assume it is through them that we will be happy. . . .

We arrive at the same conclusion if we approach the question from the standpoint of self-sufficiency. For the final and perfect good seems to be self-sufficient. However, we define something as self-sufficient not by relevance to the "self" alone. We do not mean a man who lives his life in isolation, but a man who also lives with parents, children, a wife, and friends and fellow citizens generally, since man is by nature a social and political being. . . . For the present we define as "self-sufficient" that which taken by itself makes life something desirable and deficient in nothing. It is happiness, in our opinion, which fits this description.[7]

Much later in the *Nicomachean Ethics* Aristotle adds the following: "What is usually called 'self-sufficiency' will be found in the highest degree in the activity which is concerned with theoretical knowledge. Like a just man and any other virtuous man, a wise man requires the necessities of life; once these have been adequately provided, a just man still needs people toward whom and in company with whom to act justly. . . . But a wise man is able to study even by himself, and the wiser he is the more is he able to do it."[8] These passages seem simple enough but actually connect a number of different and complicated concepts to the notion of self-sufficiency. First among them is "happiness," which is itself tied to "final ends" or ends pursued for their own sake. We learn from these passages of the connection between happiness and virtue and that self-sufficiency is not to be thought of in the absence of other persons. We learn too in the second passage cited that self-sufficiency is tied to theoretical reasoning and that the philosophical life is the most self-sufficient life of them all. Aristotle supports this last notion by saying that "what is by nature proper to each thing will be at once the best and the most pleasant for it. In other words, a life guided by intelligence is the best and most pleasant for man, inasmuch as intelligence, above all else, is man. Consequently, this kind of life is happiest."[9]

Aristotle is well known, as a result of the points made in passages like these, for holding that the best and happiest life is the philosophical one, with a practical life of virtue being happiest in "the secondary sense."[10] It is clear that if the life of the contemplative philosopher must be our model of self-sufficiency, then our western heroes seem quite distant from that ideal; however, there is a controversy about how intellectualistic one should make Aristotle when reading these passages.[11] If we were to look strictly at the last passage cited, however, we can see that a life guided by intelligence (sometimes translated as "reason") is not exactly the same as the life of the philosopher as we would normally understand it. Since our subject is the western hero and not interpreting Aristotle, we need not finally decide certain matters of interpretation here. What is both clear and of value to us in the present case is that the self-sufficient life, however interpreted, is one that is guided by reason or intelligence. We shall make this a central component of our understanding of self-sufficiency in what follows.

We cannot proceed without some comment on the words *happiness* and *virtue,* because their connotations in English are different from those Aristotle meant to convey. Happiness in English, for example, connotes the idea of a passive mental state of feeling untroubled. For that reason the Greek *eudaimonia* is often translated as "human flourishing" rather than "happiness" to suggest a more active understanding. Indeed, for Aristotle happiness is a form of activity, whether that activity be thinking or performing some virtuous act.[12] When Aristotle considers happiness he thinks of someone *doing* something. The virtues themselves—some of which are mentioned in the passages above—are also forms of activity. Any happiness associated with them comes from their exercise, not from their being possessed by us as dispositions. In addition, the term *virtue* sometimes has a static ring to it in English, not to mention a strictly moral one. Yet "virtue" in Aristotle can refer more broadly to simply excellence. The virtuous man, then, is someone who demonstrates excellence in action. Excellence can be connected to skills, and no doubt a virtuous person possesses skills. But virtue and skill are differentiated because virtues are concerned with doing or acting well, while skills are concerned with making or producing something.[13] Both the western hero and the western villain are highly skilled, and thus both have a kind of excellence. But the sort of excellence in action that Aristotle wants to capture with his notion of virtue requires excellence of action in the service of some worthy end.[14] The villain's deficient moral character prevents us from saying that he exhibits more than just skill, because the central question of what those skills are for, and what good they might produce, is either ignored or perverted. The hero, by contrast, acts well, and his skills are in the service of the excellent doings in which he engages.

For an action to count as virtuous for Aristotle it must meet three criteria: first, the agent must have knowledge, which means minimally knowing what he is doing and why; second, he must choose the actions for their own sakes; and third, he must choose them out of a fixed disposition to do so.[15] We shall be considering aspects of all three of these elements in our discussion to come, but the first and third are especially important. A steady fixed disposition seems to be a trademark of the western hero and the reason for part of our admiration of him.[16] Those heroes often seem, in this respect, oblivious to the normal distractions to which the rest of us might succumb, such as money or sexual pleasure; they do not waver in pursuit of the end they know they must pursue.

Aristotle thinks that although we habituate ourselves to virtue by practice, that habituation process is thoroughly mediated by intelligence.[17] Virtues do become a "second nature" to us, indicating that although virtues must be developed by us, they often seem to exhibit themselves as if they were a "first nature"—that is, like a natural, untrained disposition.[18] Nevertheless, we train and habituate ourselves to virtue in order to encapsulate dispositions that can transcend particular circumstances. The virtue of courage is not just for gunfighting but for any situation for which that virtue would be appropriate. It would be strange to regard as "self-sufficient" someone who was able to function well only in one situation but not others. Moreover, functioning well is not something that can be done *for* somebody but something that must be done for and by oneself.[19]

In the opening passage we cited from Aristotle he mentions that self-sufficiency means "deficient in nothing." But as Julia Annas points out, this cannot require the possession of *every* conceivable good, but rather those goods that are "required by the deliberated projects that life contains."[20] Notice that in this interpretation the virtues assist a life filled with "deliberated" projects, plans, and activities. Through the use of our intelligence we must weave together the particular projects and activities we undertake, using the virtues to help arrive at consistent actions and a unified life plan.

The standards of excellence in Aristotle's theory of happiness, virtue, and self-sufficiency are not, however, subjectively determined. Rather, the standard of excellence for him is "nature," and not whatever desires, feelings, or wishes one may happen to have. "For those things are natural which, by a continuous movement originated from an internal principle, arrive at some completion: the same completion is not reached from every principle; nor any chance completion, but always the tendency in each is towards the same end, if there is no impediment."[21] We complete ourselves when we live according to human nature. This amounts to integrated excellence of activity in the company of others directed by reason or intelligence. A life guided by something other than reason or intelligence (for example, by authority or pleasure) is not a *human* life or an excellent one. The movement toward "happiness" is thus our "internal principle" that draws upon resources both internal and external to ourselves: "We may define happiness as prosperity combined with virtue; or as independence of life. . . . A man cannot fail to be completely independent if he possesses . . . internal and . . . external goods."[22] There has been controversy throughout history as to how many external goods and of what kind a person needs to be happy.[23] Aristotle includes among the external goods such things as wealth, friendship, and children. He mentions the need for bodily goods as well, such as health and strength. For our purposes here, it is enough to say that human beings are material creatures living in and utilizing a material world. We would be living according to our "internal principle" when the use of those goods is intelligently directed in such a way as to produce excellence in action.

It is at this juncture that we can move nearly seamlessly into a consideration of Spinoza, for Spinoza is especially insistent upon the connection between acting from one's own nature and independence or freedom. Freedom is the ultimate good for Spinoza, and when one thinks about it, freedom can certainly be characterized as a form of independence and thus self-sufficiency. Indeed, Spinoza shares a number of concepts with Aristotle when it comes to thinking about the connection between freedom and self-sufficiency. First among them is that the free person acts from his or her own nature or from an "internal principle."[24] Spinoza defines true virtue as living "by the guidance of reason, and so weakness consists solely in this, that a man suffers himself to be led by things external to himself and is determined by them to act in a way required by the general state of external circumstances, not by his own nature considered only in itself.[25] Notice that for Spinoza, freedom, which we are now identifying with self-sufficiency, is a function of the degree to which we act from and within ourselves. The passage may suggest that Spinoza is even less willing than Aristotle to allow external goods to be a part of what it means to be self-sufficient or free. If things are "external" to us, they are for Spinoza impediments to our freedom; but like Aristotle, this does not mean we must live in isolation. Indeed, we must live among other things, and especially other persons, if we are to have any real freedom.[26] If freedom is not a form of separateness from other things and persons, what, then, does Spinoza mean by "external circumstance"? External circumstances are those forces that impede our acting from our "own nature considered only in itself." Other things and persons *can* be impediments for us, but that is not so much a function of them as it is with whether we are guided by reason or knowledge in dealing with them. In other words, the mere "externality" of things or persons is not the issue, but whether our actions with respect to them are guided by knowledge and reason.

Being guided by reason is, again like Aristotle, a form of activity for Spinoza. To be active and not passive is to be free.[27] A life guided by reason is thus the active and therefore the free and self-sufficient life. However, the primary way in which we impede our freedom has little to do with what is actually outside of us, but rather with what is inside—namely, our emotions.[28] As Spinoza puts it, "We shall readily see the difference between the man who is guided only by emotion or belief and the man who is guided by reason. The former, whether he will or not, performs actions of which he is completely ignorant. The latter does no one's will but his own, and does only what he knows to be of greatest importance in life, which he therefore desires above all. So I call the former a slave and the latter a free man."[29] To do "no one's will but [one's] own" is to make reason our internal principle.[30] Why is reason so important? It is because the person guided by reason is one who has what Spinoza calls "adequate ideas." Adequate ideas concern knowledge of the world within which we move, and we move successfully within that world when we understand it and how to deal with it. When we don't have adequate ideas, the world, in a sense, moves us, for we are the passive recipients of the forces "out there" (or in the case of emotions, "in" there) that push us here and there. The more adequate our ideas, the more free, active, and independent we become. Emotions are essentially passive states for Spinoza. They happen to us rather than function as things we do. In this respect they are "external" to us because they seem to move us rather than us moving them.[31] They are also not efficient tools for dealing with the world, but rather more reactions to it. Spinoza, then, like Aristotle, holds that the life ruled by reason is the perfected form of human activity.[32]

With respect to virtue, Aristotle emphasizes excellence in action, as we saw. Spinoza's perspective is consistent with Aristotle's but carries with it a slightly different tone, namely, that virtue is competence in action.[33] Both regard the moral virtues as forms of excellence, and the scope of the term *virtue* in both cases extends beyond what we typically think of as moral. In Spinoza's case, virtue is essentially efficacy. In Aristotle's case, all excellences of action qualify as "virtuous" in some sense. For both thinkers, however, "competence" and "excellence" are circumscribed by the moral virtues.

If what we have said is reasonably accurate, then we have arrived at a composite picture of self-sufficiency as a philosopher might define it: *The self-sufficient individual is the self-motivated person guided by reason whose actions are virtuous in nature.* Given that characterization of what a philosopher might look for in determining self-sufficiency, how do western heroes stack up against it?

White Hats and the Heads They Cover

One of the tropes of western films is that the good guy always wears "a white hat." Sometimes this is literally true, but the expression is in all cases meant to convey that the western hero is in the service of some good. The particular goods may vary from securing justice to protecting the weak, but heroes are the "good" guys because they actually are securing some good.[34] It is true that a number of the "antiheroes" of many more contemporary western films, such as *Unforgiven* (1992), blur the distinction between good and bad. But the ones who command our allegiance, such as William Munny (Clint Eastwood) of that same film, are still generally in the service of some overarching moral good (in this case bringing "justice" to the cowboys who cut up one of the town whores). Generally speaking, it seems safe to assume that western heroes have fulfilled that condition of self-sufficiency that requires some demonstration of, and commitment to, moral excellence. Certainly the virtue of courage is almost always present, and some form of the virtue of justice is typically a part of the hero's character as well.[35]

But do these virtues emerge from a life guided by intelligence? We noted earlier that western heroes seem to be men of action rather than reflection. But does that imply that reason is not at the center of their actions? Reason might be considered along at least two dimensions. In the first, reason would include the idea of wisdom gained through experience. If so, most western heroes would seem to qualify. Such wisdom, for example, is the case with Wyatt Earp as John Ford depicts him in *My Darling Clementine* (1946); Earp, by the time he gets to Tombstone, has been marshal elsewhere long enough to handle virtually any situation.[36] This example is not an isolated one. There are very few "greenhorns" among western heroes. Most heroes, even if they are young in age, have the sort of experience that gives them a kind of practical wisdom. Indeed, hinting at that past experience is often a part of the way in which the hero's character is developed on-screen.

The second way in which reason has a role to play in self-sufficiency is with respect to self-knowledge. The self-sufficient man would know himself, his plans, his purposes, his goals, and why what he's doing needs to be done. Perhaps the term *self-motivated* captures this sense of reason, but a strongly driven person might be self-motivated and yet driven irrationally and obsessively. The foregoing point brings to mind Ethan (John Wayne) of John Ford's *The Searchers* (1956). Though a compelling man, and a man in possession of some of the other characteristics of self-sufficiency we have identified, Ethan is essentially "unfree," as Spinoza defines that term. He is so obsessed by his quest to find Debbie and purge the world of her racial impurity that it is difficult to think of him as a western hero. Indeed, even the good he serves at the beginning of the film in seeking to return Debbie home is corrupted by his obsessive quest. Though redeemed in the end, Ethan's fascination for us comes precisely because he possesses so many of the characteristics we expect from a western hero yet puts us off from quite according him that honor.[37] The ending of the film, however, where Ethan returns Debbie home, does strongly suggest that Ethan has gained something significant in self-knowledge and thus a form of freedom or independence he lacked through most of the film. In general, then, we expect self-sufficiency to include a significant level of self-understanding, and we can safely look for that element when considering western heroes. Our conclusion thus seems to be that western heroes are likely to be men guided by reason and would not be heroes if they were not.

The Call of the Wild

It would seem that the general characteristics of the self-sufficient man as described by our philosophers are arguably present in the typical western hero. Yet such a conclusion is no doubt still being drawn at too generic a level to be of much analytical value. If nothing else, we have yet to say much about the western hero's connection to community. I believe one of the best films for exploring a number of issues connected to self-sufficiency is John Ford's *The Man Who Shot Liberty Valance*. Ostensibly, the film could be said to have two heroes. The first, Tom Doniphon (John Wayne), is the quintessential western hero—strong, fast with a gun, sure of himself, and he even wears a white hat! The other possible hero is Ransom Stoddard (Jimmy Stewart). After being away for some years, Stoddard has traveled back to Shinbone to attend the funeral of Doniphon. By this time Stoddard is a U.S. senator with a long record of accomplishments, all as a result of his instrumental role in leading the territory to statehood, a feat that was itself predicated upon his reputation as the man who shot Liberty Valance (Lee Marvin). The film is organized as a narrative Stoddard tells to some newspapermen about the old days in Shinbone. At the opening of the story Stoddard is a young lawyer traveling west because he took Horace Greeley's advice to go west literally. We do not know if Stoddard was headed for the town of Shinbone; but the stagecoach conveying him was robbed, and Stoddard was whipped by Liberty Valance and left for dead. He was subsequently brought to Shinbone, and from there the rest of the story unfolds. Given Stoddard's attributes—his importance to the town and the territory, his winning away of Doniphon's girlfriend Hallie (Vera Miles), and his reputation for having shot Liberty Valance—he would seem to have all the necessary credentials for being one of the heroes of the film.

Stoddard does indeed possess many of the qualities we have identified with the self-sufficient hero above: he has a tremendous sense of purpose, self-knowledge, and self-directedness. His courage and acceptance of responsibility are unquestionable, and he is, by the standards of the day, a learned man, who even opens a school to teach others to read and to understand their civic history and responsibilities. But Stoddard is not the central hero of this film, nor even perhaps *a* hero. The story he tells reveals that Doniphon, and not he, shot Liberty Valance, though Stoddard did show courage by facing Valance directly at the time of the shooting. Stoddard has secretly lived with the truth that it was not he who shot Liberty Valance, though he is the one who reaped the glory from it. The lie he lived had instrumental value in bringing about the "good" of the taming of the West. But its cost was clearly a loss of self-sufficiency for Stoddard. Stoddard could never "be himself" so long as he lived as someone else, and for that reason alone, his heroism is tarnished.

But that is not the only reason Stoddard is not the hero. Ford indicates throughout the film that something important about what the West represents is lost with the arrival of the world that Stoddard brings with him. Ford films the story in black and white, and there are virtually no landscapes (unlike other Ford westerns), thus draining the West of all its color and strongly reinforcing a sense that something good has been lost. The opening and closing shots of the film, in addition, are of a moving train—Ford's symbol for civilization and the incursion of the East.[38] The sacrifices, compromises—and in this case, lies—that go into taming the West provide a dark contrast to the bright optimism we see with Doniphon until the point in the film where he loses Hallie and the coming of civilization seems inevitable.[39] Ford clearly means for us to see Doniphon as the hero, but he is a tragic hero whose own goodness and sense of justice are his very undoing in the end. Doniphon's skill, courage, and knowledge of how to function well in the precivilized West are used time after time to save Stoddard and to make possible what is to come. Ford's point is clear: the coming of civilization is inevitable and it is brought about on the backs of men like Doniphon. Moreover, Ford is suggesting as well that the qualities of character men like Doniphon possessed are being lost, and the viewer has the sense that it is precisely something connected to the self-sufficiency of such men that is sacrificed.[40]

Yet Stoddard, more than Doniphon, is the man who appears to possess the central good of the philosophers with respect to self-sufficiency: namely, reason. Through his law books he at once represents to us both the order and impartiality of civil society and the education needed to understand such books. Indeed, education is actually depicted as the *central* good of civilization, as witnessed in the schoolroom scene where behind Stoddard on the blackboard is written: "Education is the basis of law and order." If all law and order is grounded in education, then encouraging education is the key to the difference between an order imposed by men like Doniphon (or for that matter Liberty Valance) and the order that comes under the impartial rule of law. Indeed, Stoddard's law books are symbolic of the institutionalization of reason. They are reason socialized. His activities as a teacher are an effort to instill reason among his students. The two are meant to be integrally connected. Typically in Ford films women embody the good of education, but in this film Hallie is uneducated; yet her thirst for education portrays the ineluctable drive toward it that is both a feature of and a precursor to civilization. Hallie is so drawn to the call of education and civilization that she, perhaps to her later regret, leaves Doniphon for Stoddard. In this connection it is interesting to note that Doniphon, unlike

Hallie, can read, though not particularly well. Yet while the scene indicating Doniphon's ability to read also, no doubt, demonstrates his intelligence, Ford shows that Doniphon thinks reading to be of generally little value, and knows only so much of it as might be needed to conduct business or to keep informed.[41] Hallie, by contrast, seems to crave education for its own sake, and she seems to crave it for the sake of the good, since she wants to be able to read "the Good Book" for herself.[42]

As Aristotle noted in the passage we cited earlier, once the "necessities of life" have been provided, the virtues connected to self-sufficiency, including intellectual ones, can be engaged. But this point raises some significant issues for our topic here. Ford films in particular, and perhaps most other westerns as well, take place either prior to or at the transition toward that point in which the "necessities of life" are provided—namely, toward what we are calling "civilization." Arguably the most basic necessity is some sort of law and order, for without that any other necessary good is precarious at best.[43] Now Doniphon protects Stoddard at every turn, including allowing him to gain the reputation as the "man who shot Liberty Valance." In this respect, the film demonstrates that the sorts of skills and virtues Stoddard possesses cannot be exercised in the precivilized world where Doniphon reigns. At least for Aristotle, self-sufficiency, to have a chance of being exercised, presupposes a certain level of material and social well-being. The man, in this case Stoddard, put in precivilized circumstances is actually no longer self-sufficient. Indeed, what this film, along with many other westerns, teaches us is that such a person may be *more* dependent and thus less in a position of self-sufficiency than others who had not devoted themselves so singularly to the pursuit of virtues made possible by civilization.

But Ford's message goes in the other direction as well—namely, that Doniphon cannot make the transition to Stoddard's world. His self-sufficiency is also highly context bound. He could perhaps make the transition to Stoddard's world if he had paid more attention to what philosophers recommend, that is, the development of his reason to the point where he could figure out how to apply the virtues he does possess to the new order. But Doniphon is not really in a position to put his own house in order in that way. His reason for not doing so is not because his habits all go in the other direction, as our first reflections about this matter might suggest. Doniphon cannot devote himself to cultivating virtues suitable to civilization because of his apparent devotion to another good, namely, bringing civilization to the territory. Doniphon protects men like Stoddard, and thus the entrance of civilization, at the cost of his own well-being. This point is most clearly demonstrated at the political convention where Doniphon—having already fallen precipitously from his former glory—shows up to ensure that Stoddard gets elected territorial representative and recounts to him the true story of the shooting of Liberty Valance. By contrast, during the film Stoddard never quite processes the nature of the world in which he finds himself and the degree to which he needs a man like Doniphon in order to succeed. In other words, he, unlike Doniphon, does not see beyond his own narrow framework until the poignant end of the film, when we sense that Stoddard does finally understand what he and others owe to Doniphon. Ironically, for all Stoddard's learning, Doniphon is clearly the wiser man. Doniphon has the sort of reason that sees the good, but tragically cannot prepare for it himself. The nature of his devotion to the good in the precivilized world he inhabits—that is, as the counterweight to the violence and disorder Liberty Valance represents—puts him in the position of being unable to turn to his own self-development without sacrificing the very good he sets out to secure. That, of course, is the tragedy of his situation.

Whether this sort of tragedy is *necessary* is a question we cannot answer here. Instead, we must ask whether self-sufficiency is necessarily inapplicable to those in a precivilized condition, where most westerns take place. Aristotle seems to conveniently answer this question affirmatively, indicating not only that Doniphon cannot be self-sufficient, but that Stoddard cannot, either, despite his learning. Conceptually this solution is clean; no one in a precivilized state can be self-sufficient because the goods needed are simply not available. By the same token, such a solution seems to rub against common sense. Doniphon certainly, and even Stoddard to a large extent, appears to have at least some degree of self-sufficiency, even according to the general criteria laid down by our two philosophers. Perhaps it is at this point that we may wish to separate Spinoza from Aristotle a bit, for his approach to the issue seems more internally focused than Aristotle's. Rather than giving considerable weight to external goods, the Spinozistic approach, following the Stoics to some extent, would center upon the degree of self-directedness within one's circumstances. By this standard, Doniphon is clearly self-sufficient—at least until his circumstances change, and Stoddard is not out of the running for this form of self-sufficiency, either.

Most Ford westerns depict the intersection of the precivil and civil orders. That dividing line of civilization highlights an opportunity for us to recognize a possible difference between the two philosophers not so apparent above in our efforts to unify them. Aristotle has a teleological view of human nature, one that supposes a natural movement toward fulfillment and maturity by each of us. When Aristotle looks at the nature of something, including human nature, he looks at it from the standpoint of the best condition it can realize. For him, therefore, self-sufficiency would be present only in that full state of completion and maturity of which human beings are capable. Teleology need not, however, be linked to Spinoza's conception of activity or freedom. Here activity, as knowledgeable self-direction, seems to be enough.[44] The question of completeness is left alone. This difference allows us to draw a distinction between ontic self-sufficiency on the one hand and procedural self-sufficiency on the other.

Ontic self-sufficiency would be a condition in which all the primary goods needed for human excellence, including the external ones, are present and being exercised.[45] Ontic self-sufficiency would be possible only in civilization, where all the materials for self-realization are available. Neither Doniphon nor Stoddard are self-sufficient in this ontic sense, nor would we typically expect westerns to provide us such examples. But they (and other heroes) may be, to various degrees, *procedurally* self-sufficient, if their actions are fully self-directed and guided by knowledge and intelligence appropriate to their circumstances.[46] Though not all the elements needed for completion are either present or yet acquired, the individual manages to successfully negotiate his environment, pursue real goods, and act from understanding and a sense of self-purpose. Doniphon and Stoddard may both qualify on this basis. The philosophical question here is whether procedural self-sufficiency is (or can be) seamless across contexts. John Ford's answer to this question is negative:[47] the characteristics of self-sufficiency in the precivilized context are different from those in the civilized one to the point where one set must be traded for the other, producing some inevitable loss.[48]

The worlds of Doniphon and Stoddard intersect as civilization is being realized, but they never merge. It is, paradoxically, the ordinary, apparently non-self-sufficient, individual who makes the transition from precivil to civil society seamlessly. The heroes are the bridge upon which the common man walks. That is the democratic "final cause" of the American western that renders its heroes so different from other mythical heroes of Western civilization. No better illustration of both the democratic purpose and the tension between Stoddard's and Doniphon's worlds can be found than the schoolroom scene. Led by Stoddard, the class is a model of democratic diversity, including a Swedish immigrant, a number of Latino (Mexican) children, white males and women (including Hallie herself) and an African American, Pompey (Woody Strode), who also happens to be Doniphon's helper. When asked what she has learned about the United States, the Swedish immigrant says that the United States is a republic and a republic "is a state where the people are the boss!" And Pompey, with a picture of Lincoln off to his side, when asked to speak about the Constitution, confuses it with the Declaration of Independence.[49] These are the people who will benefit once Liberty Valance is cleared away and order and civilization brought in, as Stoddard fully explains to them. But the whole exercise is interrupted suddenly by Doniphon, who bursts in the room telling Pompey he's been wasting his time reading, as he points out to Stoddard that Liberty Valance has hired some guns to prevent the democratic process from taking place. The world belongs again to Doniphon, and Stoddard is forced to admit, after erasing the sentence mentioned earlier from the blackboard, that "when force threatens, talk is no good anymore." Each man is thus a master in his own world, but their worlds do not mesh easily.

"Rugged" Individualism

Perhaps the most poignant symbol of *The Man Who Shot Liberty Valance* is the "cactus rose" that Hallie picks at the beginning of the film near the burned-out house Doniphon had built for the two of them. At the end of the film she places it upon Doniphon's coffin. Years earlier Doniphon had given a cactus rose to Hallie as a kind of courting gesture, and at the end of that scene Hallie shows it to Stoddard and mentions how beautiful it is. Stoddard agrees, but then asks Hallie if she has ever seen a "real" rose. She responds that she has not but that she hopes they will dam the river one day and bring lots of water to the area so there can be all kinds of flowers. The cactus rose could symbolize many things: from the thorny barren beauty of the West to Tom Doniphon himself. But it is the comment that the cactus rose is not a "real" rose that is especially arresting. Real things, including, one must suppose, real human life—importantly, *civilized* life—are to be found in the East. The West is at best a shadow of something more real. But what exactly is so unreal about the West, and would not something be lost if cactus roses were replaced with more conventional flowers? Moreover, based on our argument above, if both procedural and ontic self-sufficiency can be found in civilization, what could possibly be left to lament in the disappearance of Tom Doniphon's West, especially if ontic self-sufficiency is not possible there?

There is, I believe, an important virtue, threatened by civilization, that may be a species of self-sufficiency, but that nevertheless needs a separate mention here. That virtue is self-reliance. To suggest that the cactus rose is somehow less real than the "real" rose is an indication of a failure to understand self-reliance. As Emerson (1803–82) expresses it in his famous essay of that title, self-reliance is truth to oneself as a distinct and unique individual.[50] It is not action in isolation from others, but it is action willing to be separated from others, if there is no other way to remain true to oneself. Its enemy is thus not cooperation but conformity. To suppose that the cactus rose must be evaluated by a standard applicable to some other flower is to enforce a kind of conformity upon the cactus flower. The cactus rose has its own nature, and it must ultimately look there for its standards of excellence. This is Emerson's message for human beings as well. Civilization has a conforming element to it that dulls our sense of what we are as individuals and what we can do on our own. As Emerson puts it, "The civilized man has built a coach, but has lost the use of his feet."[51] He is carried along more luxuriously, perhaps, but at a price of forgetting that he has his own set of legs.

It may be that the concept of self-sufficiency as we have been discussing it would, upon more extended reflection, lead one necessarily to the virtue of self-reliance. Yet logically there is nothing in the accounts of self-sufficiency we have given to this point that speaks of the individual as ruling him- or herself according to his or her own unique and individual nature. The definitions and explanations we have presented are all consistent with *general* ideas of human excellence, activity, or virtue. Even our account of procedural self-sufficiency does not refer directly to standards predicated upon uniqueness of self. Philosophers, of course, tend to be comfortable with universals, but our admiration for the western hero does not stem from recognizing a more perfect rendition of a general model of human excellence, however self-sufficient the model. It is the hero's fidelity to *his own* truth that makes the western a unique genre. The western hero often rides off alone, not because he is antisocial, or because he is able to survive without help from others, but because there are no "companions" for him, given the truth he must follow. If doing so ends tragically, as it does for Doniphon, we are all the more moved and sympathetic, but our opinion of him remains high because, even in the face of personal sacrifice, he carries on according to what he is and not according to something he is not. Doniphon cannot be Stoddard; and if he were in a position to devote himself to ontic self-sufficiency and make the transition to civilization, he would not look like Stoddard when done.

In *The Man Who Shot Liberty Valance,* Ford clearly laments the loss of self-reliance as civilization encroaches, but oddly enough not just with respect to Doniphon, but more so with respect to Stoddard. Stoddard has the same material for true self-reliance that Doniphon does, but we see in the closing scene on the train a glimpse that he may have compromised that self-reliance in the process of bringing on civilization. I am not speaking here just of Stoddard's unwillingness to correct the conductor who repeats the myth about the man who shot Liberty Valance, but rather of the indication that Stoddard's and Hallie's true selves belong more to Shinbone than to Washington (Hallie says, "My heart is here") as well as the game of politics Stoddard plays when he promises the conductor to write the railroad about the good job it is doing. The disingenuous posturing by Stoddard, confirmed by the look on Hallie's face, seems a far cry from the principled man we saw earlier in the film. Hallie and Stoddard have compromised themselves as they have distanced themselves from Shinbone. Doniphon, by contrast, always seems true to what he is, which, as we've seen, is part of the tragedy in the end. Ford may be mistaken in believing that civilization is the inevitable corruptor of self-reliance, if not self-sufficiency. That is an interesting point for reflection. Certainly the philosophers we have mentioned regard self-sufficiency as being fostered by civilization, not diminished by it. But Ford is doing art, not philosophy, and as such can point us to real concerns without necessarily arguing for a necessary connection.

It is not just the individual who is diminished by the loss of self-reliance, but democracy as well. The disappearance of self-reliance in a democratic setting is a license for mob rule. For if sovereignty is democratic in nature, the only possible check upon mass conformity is the willingness of some of society's members to stand up for a truth that others may not share. Democracy can be a great power for wealth and equality, but that same power can be an overwhelming detriment to self-reliance. The leading figures in a Ford western are perhaps not always self-sufficient, as we noted with Ethan in *The Searchers,* but they are all self-reliant. That distinction raises numerous interesting questions about the relationship between self-reliance and self-sufficiency and the role of the former in the development of the latter.[52]

We, unfortunately, have no space to explore such questions here. Suffice it to say that these sorts of questions are naturally evoked by the western film or novel, and thus can serve the cause of philosophical reflection. If self-reliance is a virtue, as I believe it is, it is no accident that one of the great American thinkers, Emerson, devotes an essay to it, or that it is repeatedly championed in the American western film and novel. Self-sufficiency may broadly identify a form of human excellence that has been handed down to us from the reflections of Western philosophers; but self-reliance is America's contribution to the pantheon of particular moral virtues and the American western is its cultural signature.

Notes

I would like to thank Jennifer L. McMahon, Douglas Rasmussen, Jonathan Jacobs, and Margarita Molteni for helpful comments on drafts of this essay. I would especially like to thank Liberty Fund, Inc. whose conferences on western films have reinvigorated my own interest in them.

The epigraph is taken from Ralph Waldo Emerson, "Self-Reliance," in *Emerson: Essays and Poems* (New York: Library of America, 1996), 260.

1. In the pioneering early talking western *The Big Trail*, directed by Raoul Walsh (1930), the mother says to her daughter during the daughter's prayer before bed, "Aren't you going to ask God to help Breck Coleman [the hero]?" And the daughter answers, "They say Breck Coleman can take care of himself."

2. The film, which came out in 1952, is considered to be a symbolic call to face up to the House Un-American Activities Committee during the era of Senator Joseph McCarthy, who was looking for Communists in Hollywood.

3. Robert B. Pippin, "What Is a Western? Politics and Self-Knowledge in John Ford's *The Searchers*" (Castle Lecture, Yale University, February 2008). This lecture will be a chapter in a forthcoming book entitled *Hollywood Westerns and American Myth* (New Haven, CT: Yale University Press). In this connection, Pippin cites André Bazin and Robert Warshow, whose various articles provide a foundation for the way scholars and critics look at westerns. See also Paul Cantor, "The Western and Western Drama: John Ford's *The Searchers* and the *Oresteia*" (paper presented at the annual meeting of the American Political Science Association, Hyatt Regency Chicago and the Sheraton Chicago Hotel and Towers, Chicago, August 30, 2007).

4. An extreme example of this sort of emphasis is the so-called Saxon Gospel, in which Jesus is depicted as a Viking warrior. G. Ronald Murphy, S.J., trans., *The Heliand: The Saxon Gospel* (Oxford: Oxford University Press, 1992).

5. See, for example, Tag Gallacher, *John Ford: The Man and His Films* (Berkeley: University of California Press, 1986); Ronald L. Davis, *John Ford: Hollywood's Old Mas-*

ter (Norman: University of Oklahoma Press, 1995); William K. Everson, *The Hollywood Western* (New York: Citadel, 1992); and Joseph McBride, *Searching for John Ford: A Life* (New York: St. Martin's, 2001).

6. Julia Annas prefers to translate *teleia* as "complete" rather than "final." I have left "final" here because it is the most common of translations, but the difference between "complete" and "final" in English could be significant. Since I mainly follow Annas's interpretation of self-sufficiency in what follows, I felt it important to note that translation difference here. See Julia Annas, *The Morality of Happiness* (Oxford: Oxford University Press, 1993), 39–40.

7. Aristotle, *Nicomachean Ethics,* trans. Martin Ostwald (Upper Saddle River, NJ: Prentice Hall, Library of the Liberal Arts, 1999), 1097a28–1097b17.

8. Ibid., 1177a27–33.

9. Ibid., 1178a5–7.

10. Ibid., 1178a8.

11. See, for example, the discussion in Fred D. Miller Jr., *Nature, Justice, and Rights in Aristotle's Politics* (Oxford: Clarendon, 1995), 347–57.

12. Aristotle, *Nicomachean Ethics,* 1102a5.

13. See Annas, *Morality of Happiness,* 67–69.

14. Aristotle notoriously draws a distinction between wisdom and cleverness as a way of distinguishing a kind of true practical wisdom from a false one (*Nicomachean Ethics,* 1144a26). Cleverness is simply skill at achieving one's ends. It is interesting that western villains are often "clever" in this sense, indicating again that the western hero approaches more closely the philosophers' requirements for self-sufficiency.

15. Ibid., 1105a29–33.

16. I use the masculine pronoun throughout because the heroes of most westerns are male. This may be "sexism," but it may also represent the sort of "masculine" virtues the West requires, which could be found as well among many western women.

17. In this connection see Jonathan Jacobs, *Aristotle's Virtues: Nature, Knowledge, and Human Good* (New York: Peter Lang, 2004), 116–20.

18. Aristotle, *Nicomachean Ethics,* 1152a30.

19. The Aristotelian philosopher Henry Veatch has said that "attaining one's natural end as a human person is nothing if not a 'do-it-yourself' job." Henry B. Veatch, *Human Rights: Fact or Fancy* (Baton Rouge: Louisiana State University Press, 1985), 84.

20. Annas, *Morality of Happiness,* 41.

21. Aristotle, *The Basic Works of Aristotle: Physics,* trans. R. P. Hardie and R. K. Gaye, ed. Richard McKeon (New York: Random House, 1968), 1105a29–33. See also Annas, *Morality of Happiness,* 150.

22. Aristotle, *Rhetoric,* trans. W. Rhys Roberts, in *The Complete Works of Aristotle: The Revised Oxford Translation,* vol. 2, ed. Jonathan Barnes (Princeton, NJ: Princeton University Press, 1984), 1360b14, 25.

23. A good discussion of many of these points is to be found in Annas, *Morality of*

Happiness, chap. 18. See also Martha C. Nussbaum, *The Fragility of Goodness* (Cambridge: Cambridge University Press, 1986), chap. 12.

24. It is interesting to note that Annas (*Morality of Happiness*, 40n46) holds to the idea that "something like self-determination is nearer to the suggestions of the Greek [*autarkeia*] than is self-sufficiency." If true, this would move Aristotle significantly closer to Spinoza.

25. As with Aristotle, referencing here is fairly standard among Spinoza scholars, and the reference here would be E4P37Schol. 1. "E" stands for Spinoza's *Ethics*, with the number referencing the book within the *Ethics* (in this case book 4). Spinoza's *Ethics* is laid out in geometrical fashion such that it has axioms, propositions, proofs, corollaries, scholiums, and the like. In this case, the scholium of proposition 37 is being referred to. Typically I use the following edition for my citations from the text: *Spinoza Complete Works*, trans. Samuel Shirley, ed. Michael L. Morgan (Indianapolis: Hackett, 2002). There are many helpful commentaries on Spinoza's philosophy available, and one would profit from looking at virtually any of them. I am, no doubt, partial to my own little introduction concerning a number of issues relevant here. Douglas J. Den Uyl, *God, Man, and Well-Being: Spinoza's Modern Humanism* (New York: Peter Lang, 2008).

26. Spinoza, E4P35Cor.2Schol., E4P40.

27. Ibid., E4Appendix#4.

28. Spinoza actually allows for both passive and active emotions, with only the former being an impediment to freedom. We cannot discuss all the appropriate distinctions here, so our focus is primarily upon passive emotions. We can think of them as emotions that have not been rationalized—that is, as emotions that are not the result of knowledge and reason in action. E4 and E5 are particularly good at indicating the ways in which reason can or does not attach to emotions.

29. Spinoza, E4P66Schol. The word "emotion" is a translation of the Latin *affectus*. It is generally thought that the term *emotion* is a bit too imprecise to qualify as a useful translation for scholars, and thus it tends not to be used these days. For our purposes, however, the term serves just fine, for part of our admiration for the western hero inheres in his mastery over emotions. For that very reason we wonder, as mentioned below, about the degree to which Ethan in John Ford's *The Searchers* qualifies as a hero.

30. It is important to note that our essence for Spinoza is desire, not reason (E3P9-Schol.). Yet reason can be a form of desiring for Spinoza, what would be for him an "active" form, for emotions themselves can be either active or passive (E3P58). These and many other important distinctions must be glossed over somewhat here for the sake of brevity and the development of some sort of composite picture of the self-sufficient individual. Given the task at hand, I do not believe we are distorting Spinoza too severely here.

31. Western heroes often appear to exhibit a stoical distrust of emotion. In this regard, the western hero is generally in line with the Western intellectual distrust of emotion and emphasis on reason.

32. Spinoza is not averse to talking about perfection (E3P11) despite the fact that his theory is not teleological. The most we can say here is that Spinoza thinks of "reality" and "perfection" as the same (E2Def.6), meaning that the more perfect a thing is, the more it exerts its reality on the things around it. For humans that sort of perfection comes with knowledge.

33. Spinoza says that "by virtue and power I mean the same thing" (E4Def. 8). Power is competence of action within one's environment. His definition of virtue, then, is less teleological than Aristotle's notion of "excellence," which may suggest standards and hierarchies of the good.

34. In *The Big Trail* mentioned in note 1 above, Breck Coleman says: "I'm the law out here; that's all; and the law is justice."

35. There remains, however, the interesting question (which we are unable to answer here) of the so-called unity of the virtues (the doctrine that we cannot really possess any virtue without all the others). The issue is especially interesting if considered in a "precivilized" state, as discussed below.

36. For example, rather than shoot and kill the drunk Indian causing trouble in the saloon during an opening part of the movie, Earp finds a way to disarm him harmlessly and to simply throw him out of the bar. This suggests not only an ability to recognize alternatives, but an understanding of the meaning of proportionality in the use of force, as well as a concern for harm to others.

37. There is much we could talk about here, and Ethan provides a good example of how the model of self-sufficiency we are using might encourage insights into the film. For example, the ending of the film, where only Ethan remains outside the home into which the others have returned, leaves open the question of whether Ethan has resolved his internal difficulties and is thus a candidate for self-sufficiency, or whether this is the end of but one form of searching, to be followed by others. The film also raises some important questions of just how one comes to grips with one's own irrationalities and what it takes to overcome them, especially in cases where one possesses skills and practical wisdom that can be turned in the wrong direction.

38. One of Ford's most famous silent films, *The Iron Horse* (1924), is a paean to the linking of East and West by the railroad and its importance in taming the West and bringing about civilization. "Civilization" as I use it here refers generally to the rule of law, rather than men, and to some regular administration of impartial justice. Its meaning does include some significant control over nature and a level of material prosperity.

39. When the truth finally unfolds and the editor of the town paper tears up his notes and is asked by Stoddard if he is going to use the story, the editor delivers the most famous line of the movie: "This is the West, sir. When the legend becomes fact, print the legend."

40. In *My Darling Clementine* the coming of civilization is only just begun. Earp settles his score with the Clantons with the precivilized form of justice, namely, clan

revenge. Earp says when help is offered to him that "this is a family affair" and even hides (though still carries with him) his marshal's badge, indicating that it is not law derived from civilization that will handle the matter, but a precivilized form of justice, clan warfare. Consequently, the qualities of character Ford admires are not yet darkened by civilization, though both films are clearly about the transition from precivilization to civilization.

41. Yet Doniphon also joins Peabody, the newspaper editor, at the dinner table during the dining-room scene, when he could have joined any other patron in the place. Peabody, besides Stoddard, is the main representative of civilization in Shinbone, and Doniphon's choice of dinner companion indicates that he is drawn in some degree to intelligence and culture.

42. The distance from civilization is humorously demonstrated when Hallie, being shown the proper way to set a table by Peabody, asks, in response to being told where the knife and fork go, whether Peabody is "superstitious or something"!

43. Obviously, "necessities" is ambiguous. Were it interpreted to mean mere biological survival, then the characters of this film and other westerns do have the "necessities." But precisely because the social order is still in flux, and also because many human goods cannot be pursued until that social order is subjected to law, peace, and prosperity, the interpretation of "necessities" offered here seems plausible. Moreover, I suspect that Aristotle has in mind the presence of a relatively significant amount of cultural wealth, since even the solitary philosopher would need both the leisure and the educational background to pursue his contemplations.

44. The issue of teleology in Spinoza is a complicated one, though Spinoza himself seems to eschew final causes (E1P16, 25, 28). Still, Spinoza, as much as Aristotle, puts the philosophic life at the center of his meaning of activity, and it is hard to imagine such a life apart from the provisions of civilization. I believe, therefore, that the notion of "reason" in both would not make them ultimately so far apart as I am currently making them here.

45. Again, I'm not referring to *all* goods, but those goods (whatever they may be) that are "necessary" for self-sufficiency as Aristotle might conceive of them plus those appropriate to one's own life plans as described by Annas above.

46. This distinction echoes one I use when referring to forms of practical wisdom in my book on prudence. There I define "ontic excellence" as "the best state or condition (accompanied by the appropriate performances) of the most perfect example of 'the thing' in question." I use "conatic excellence" as simply "exercising one's present capacities to their fullest" with the materials one has at hand. *The Virtue of Prudence* (New York: Peter Lang, 1991), 213–23.

47. It is an answer that goes way back for Ford. In the closing scene of *Stagecoach* (1939), Doc says sarcastically as Ringo and Dallas are driving to Mexico, "They're saved from the blessings of civilization."

48. We appreciate by asking this question why the philosophers may be compelled

to turn to the intellectualist solution, for it seems, as Aristotle said, the least dependent on circumstances and thus the most likely candidate for seamlessness.

49. That confusion is itself an important commentary on the relationship between the two. Interestingly, in a move that must have been deliberate on Ford's part, Pompey has trouble remembering the part of the Declaration that says, "All men are created equal"—a clear indication of Ford's recognition of the lack of equal treatment accorded African Americans.

50. As he says, "If you are true, but not in the same truth with me, cleave to your companions; I will seek my own. I do this not selfishly, but humbly and truly." *Emerson: Essays and Lectures* (New York: Penguin, 1983), 273.

51. Ibid., 279.

52. For my part, self-reliance is an individualistic form of the Socratic virtue of knowing oneself. It may be a necessary step to self-perfection, but can be exhibited prior to such perfection.

Mommas, Don't Let Your Babies Grow Up to Be Pragmatists

B. Steve Csaki

There is no reasonable argument against the (true) assertion that the ultimate American cinematic cowboy was, and remains, John Wayne. The questions of exactly why and how he and his films so captured the American psyche remain somewhat open. In fact, there are myriad aspects to this question, but I believe that there is one overarching explanation as to why John Wayne was so clearly special: he was an excellent pragmatist. I shall argue that any cowboy hero must act pragmatically and that John Wayne so embodied the true sense of the classical American pragmatist that this was one of the primary factors that enabled him to become *the* symbol of not only the American West but also of American men in general.

Since it would be impossible to cover all of John Wayne's westerns in this essay, I shall concentrate on two of his films: *Rooster Cogburn* (1975, the sequel to *True Grit*, 1969) and *The Cowboys* (1971). I choose to examine these particular films for two primary reasons. First, Wayne's persona had been perfected by the time he made these films. Second, and perhaps most obviously, Wayne is quite literally a father figure in *The Cowboys,* and so we very clearly see the attributes (in both Wayne and the boys) that a good (western/cowboy) man should possess and how they are earned by, rather than bestowed upon, a cowboy.

Pragmatism is an empirically based philosophy and, as such, experience plays a critical role in the successful application of the methodology. A pragmatic approach expands the notion of experience to include not only one's personal experience but the experiences of others as well. Thus a father figure, a library, TV, the Internet, or simple observation of others all count as types of experience that one can use to a pragmatic advantage. In western films the heroes are exemplified as role models so we ought to be able to learn from their experiences.

Before we can directly proceed to examine the films, we must at least begin a rather monstrous undertaking. In a relatively short space, a framework (however structurally slender) of what it means to be a pragmatist must be erected. This is really a twofold task. First, the pragmatic theory must be outlined and then how this theory is utilized or lived on a day-to-day basis must be explained. Once some aspects of pragmatism have been introduced, then I shall draw from the films in order both to explain additional components of pragmatism and to show that John Wayne's characters are pragmatic. Finally, once the framework of pragmatism has been completed and various examples have been examined, we can look at the films a bit more closely and see how pragmatism fits. Once the films have been examined, it will be possible to see that John Wayne's characters typically represent an excellent example of the theory and technique that is pragmatism. In fact, we shall see that these characters are not only functional pragmatists but exceptionally good pragmatists.

William James (1842–1910) offers a simple and yet gripping analogy to help us understand what pragmatism is and how it works in a series of lectures he gave in 1906–7 to explain just this issue—the meaning of pragmatism. In the second of these lectures James tells the story of a camping trip that he and some friends took. James went for a walk and returned to find that "a ferocious metaphysical dispute" had split the group into two equally opposed factions. As James puts it, "The *corpus* of the dispute was a squirrel—a live squirrel supposed to be clinging to one side of a tree-trunk; while over against the tree's opposite side a human being was imagined to stand." The person in question is trying to get a good look at the squirrel, but every time the person tries to see the squirrel and circles the tree in order to do so, the squirrel moves fast enough (in the same direction) to keep the tree in between itself and the person. Thus, the person never can see the squirrel at all. James sums up the ensuing argument in this way: "The resulting metaphysical question now is this: *Does the man go round the squirrel or not?* He goes round the tree, sure enough, and the squirrel is on the tree; but does he go round the squirrel?"[1] Of course, half the members of the camping party answer yes, while the other half say no.

Both parties look to James to settle the dispute since his vote will give either side the advantage by one. James solves the dispute by saying, "Which party is right, I said, depends on what you *practically mean* by 'going round' the squirrel."[2] James goes on to explain what he means by saying that if one *means* "around" in terms of compass directions, then of course the man goes around the squirrel. However, if one *means* "around" in the sense that you must be first in front of, then beside, then behind, and so on, then, equally obviously (since the squirrel is always facing the man on the other side of the tree), the man never does go around the squirrel. James says that nearly all of the disputants were in agreement with his solution, though a couple grumbled that he had offered only a "shuffling evasion."[3] Case solved! Here the pragmatic method is employed in order to clarify the actual question at hand and in so doing offers up a simple solution. This example is perhaps one of the simplest utilizations of the pragmatic method.

Now I, for one, can easily imagine replacing William James with John Wayne in this example. We'd need to add guns and horses, of course, but it seems to me that any of his characters would otherwise be a natural fit. Can't you just hear him saying, "It all depends on what you mean by 'round,' Pilgrim." Of course, I realize that asking the reader to imagine this scenario is hardly a compelling argument that John Wayne is a pragmatist, but it's perhaps a start. As we shall see, the example James offers actually tells a great deal more about the pragmatic method than may initially meet the eye.

First, the pragmatic method is one that is used initially only *as necessary.*[4] The meaning of this claim requires some explanation. Both James and John Dewey (1859–1952) were in agreement with Aristotle (among others) that the vast majority of human behavior is habitual in nature. The classical pragmatists[5] asserted that it is only when confronted by a problem that requires some immediate action that we are derailed from the tracks that are our usual habits. In James's example above, the simple fact that others disagree with us is enough to prompt us out of our regular routine. Disagreements, particularly powerful ones, will prompt most people to abandon habitual activity for at least some period of time.

While one might argue that the squirrel problem is clearly one that seems to require only "mental" action, it nevertheless represents a problem that requires addressing. The very fact that people have become so immersed in the argument indicates that there is need of reasonable clarification to restore the peace. With respect to it being a "mental" (versus physical) problem, as a general rule, pragmatists are opposed to dualisms of this nature. The notion that there is such a thing as thinking *as opposed to* acting is not germane to pragmatism. Au contraire, pragmatists assert that thinking is an action[6] that is utilized only in order to accomplish a goal, which in turn typically requires some sort of other action to complete.[7]

While there are a plethora of aspects and details of pragmatism that are of interest generally speaking, for the purposes of showing that John Wayne is the ultimate pragmatic hero, this particular problem-solving orientation of pragmatism is the one that I shall investigate first. After all, a western that has no problem is no western at all. Further, a hero with no adversity or obstacles that must be overcome is no hero—cowboy or otherwise. While pragmatism is a holistic philosophical methodology in the sense that it should suffice to overcome all potential problems one might encounter—ethical, economic, political, epistemological, ontological, and so on—the use of pragmatism and the pragmatic approach to solve problems and overcome obstacles that might keep one from accomplishing an important task is initially of most interest when discussing the American western film.

John Dewey refers to the particular aspect of the pragmatic method that deals with, and ultimately solves, problems as "inquiry." It is actually through the process of inquiry that we advance to the point that we can identify what initially appears as only a confused situation—more precisely, as a problem. According to Dewey, "Inquiry is the controlled or directed transformation of an indeterminate situation into one that is so determinate in its constituent distinctions and relations as to convert the elements of the original situation into a unified whole." The situation in question is any situation that one confronts that causes doubt, anxiety, or uncertainty. Dewey is very clear in his insistence that these feelings are generated because the situation itself "has these traits."[8] In other words, there is a reason (or reasons) beyond a person's state of mind that causes that person to feel doubt, anxiety, or any other feeling that might be generated in a given situation. He claims it would be "pathological" were one to feel doubt (strictly) internally where there was no "objective" reason to feel it. The bottom line here is that people simply are not comfortable in situations that are "indeterminate" in nature. These situations are in a sense profoundly unacceptable. Indeterminate situations could be confusing at best or dangerous at worst, and as we know, in westerns they nearly always are dangerous.

In *Rooster Cogburn*, in the scene in which Wolf (Richard Romancito) falls asleep when he is on guard duty and is captured by Hawk (Richard Jordan), Rooster wakes up with a start because he hears a muffled call from Wolf. This is an example of what Dewey means by an "indeterminate situation." Rooster's first reaction is (and must be), as Dewey puts it, "pre-cognitive."[9]

That is to say, it is a reaction that occurs prior to any formalized thought. He's startled and awakened. The first step in the pattern of inquiry is to establish what the problem actually is. Before Rooster can respond he must make the situation less indeterminate, at least by recognizing enough of what is actually happening to formulate an understanding of the problem. Of course, Rooster does this almost immediately as he calls out for Wolf.

Once the problem has been correctly identified, there are a couple of courses of action one can take to try to make those initial apparently disparate elements into a "unified whole." Dewey uses the terms "experimental operation" and "reasoning." Reasoning (as any philosopher can tell you) is an extremely valuable tool, but as any western aficionado can also tell you, nothing actually gets done by reasoning alone. Action is required to change any situation,[10] particularly to change it in your favor. One gains experience of what might change the situation favorably or unfavorably from having been in similar situations before and having used experimental operations with varying degrees of success.

In the beginning of *The Cowboys* we see one of the clearest instances of thought or reasoning in trying to solve a problem that we find in any Wayne film. After Wayne's character, Wil Anderson, learns that his ranch hands have all gone off to search for gold, he goes looking for anyone he can find to help him get his cattle to market. He finds no one and ends up in the saloon, where we see him thinking over the problem, and apparently coming up dry. The bartender (Slim Pickens) actually suggests hiring schoolboys for the cattle drive. Once the idea of hiring boys is adopted by Wil,[11] much of the rest of the movie revolves around "experimental operation," which will indicate whether or not this approach to solving the problem is a viable one. While we see that this particular Wayne character (like most) is better at the experimental aspect of inquiry than reasoning, still we see that he actually has employed both aspects of inquiry to deal with the problem.

Adoption of the method of inquiry specifically (or the pragmatic method more generally) results first in a realization (and later in an attitude) that holds that previous experience is absolutely essential to determining the correct course of action in any given situation. First, obfuscation must be reduced to the point that a succinct account of the situation can be established—that is, a problem is formulated. This is not as easy to accomplish as it might seem. Nonetheless, if the problem is not correctly identified, then the likelihood of a successful outcome or solution is significantly lessened. The more experience a person has, the more likely that the situation in question resembles some previously encountered situation. Whether one responded rightly or wrongly the last time, if there was a last time, that previous experience puts one at an advantage in terms of correctly establishing what the problem might be in a "novel"[12] indeterminate situation that occurs.[13] While it may occasionally be "better to be lucky than good," a pragmatist holds that it is always better to correctly utilize previous experiences than merely to be lucky.

Both *Rooster Cogburn* and *True Grit* represent fairly standard western plots. In each film Rooster is selected to go after particularly rough criminals because he is a man with "grit." Grit, an abrasive toughness, is required to take on the most vicious criminals. In both films the problem seems straightforward: locate the bad guy and bring him to justice. However, the real application of the pragmatic method is in the details. Generally speaking, a plan is made and put into motion; however, in reality the implementation of the plan is always more complex than it seems due to unforeseeable circumstances. The best and most efficient way of dealing with these difficulties that crop up is to use the pragmatic method. This is what we see in both *True Grit* and *Rooster Cogburn,* and most other westerns.

In *Rooster Cogburn* one of these unforeseen situations occurs when Rooster has appropriated the nitroglycerin from Hawk and is trying to get it back to Fort Smith. This is half of his assignment; the other half is to bring Hawk in—alive. It becomes clear that he, Wolf, and Eula will not be able to stay ahead of Hawk and his gang and at the same time retain possession of the explosives. Rooster's group comes to a river, where there is a raft to be used for crossing. Rooster realizes immediately that this raft offers the best chance to elude Hawk and his gang. Even though he hasn't had much, if any, experience with rafting through rapids, this pragmatic solution to the problem ultimately allows the group to at least put off the inevitable clash with Hawk and his gang. The speed with which Rooster is able to make these sorts of decisions makes it clear that he is an accomplished pragmatist, one who has employed this methodology many times in the past, since practicing pragmatism on a regular basis improves one's ability to use it effectively and efficiently.

The primary and pronounced difference between pragmatism and other philosophical systems (be they ultimately empirical or rational in nature) is that to be truly pragmatic one cannot accurately abstract from previous situations and experiences to produce general rules or laws that are to any significant degree *fixed.* This is because the methodology tends to mirror reality, rather than attempting to force reality to conform to its description or account of it. Given the relatively fluid methodology adopted by the pragmatists, absolutes are necessarily rejected. All established "truths" are subject to revision. This controversial claim with respect to the nature of truth required a great deal of effort by both James and Dewey to explain, and the extent to which either was entirely successful remains an open question.

While it would be much thriftier to refrain from a discussion of pragmatism's conception of truth in this chapter, it would be equally dishonest. John Wayne's characters usually get it right.[14] They manage to accomplish their tasks no matter the odds against them. It is extremely difficult to separate "being right most of the time" from somehow knowing, or at least recognizing, the "truth." So the question arises: Does a pragmatic conception of truth fit with the notion that John Wayne's characters "get it right"?

James argues, "True ideas are those that we can assimilate, validate, corroborate, and verify. False ideas are those that we cannot."[15] An idea must fit within the framework and structure of a person's life and the experiences that make up that life. If it will not fit, it cannot be assimilated. Although this notion may sound subjective and personal, it is not nearly as subjective as it sounds.[16] James does not mean that assimilation of new information is a choice. He means, quite literally, that if it is not *possible* to assimilate an idea, then that idea cannot be true.

The other three terms James employs—validation, corroboration, and verification—all rely upon past (or future) experiences and interaction with the world. However, as opposed to assimilation, these three terms are concerned with the more "objective" side of experience, including the experience(s) of others. James uses the term "agreement" when discussing all these terms, and one can also substitute the word "match" with respect to what "true" means for a pragmatist. The idea or thought that one has about any particular issue must match with what's "out there." If it doesn't (and there is no good explanation as to why), then that particular idea is likely to be false.

Since no two situations are identical, previously established "working" truths may or may not be adequate in solving new problems. This aspect of pragmatism opened it to the charge of being a completely relativistic philosophical theory (and hence very bad, morally speaking). If there are no fixed truths, how can we *know* what is right and what is wrong? Further, how can there even be a "right" and "wrong" if these notions are not fixed? Traditionally, ethical theorists have typically preferred systems that have absolutes with respect to what is morally permissible (and impermissible). For example, "Thou shalt not kill." This is certainly simple, but to apply it literally to the western would eliminate the genre. In addition, there will always be people who are immoral and don't mind breaking an absolute law. How do you deal with those people without breaking the very rules that they have broken? Of course, some western plots revolve around this very issue.[17]

In order to deal effectively with the complicated ethical issues in most westerns, a pragmatic approach to ethics is extremely practical (no pun intended). A pragmatic hero would have a general rule that said something like, "Thou shalt not kill unless I deem that the situation warrants killing." Just as with any problem, a pragmatic approach to ethical "truths" dictates that each situation is weighed individually, although past experiences are used in this weighing process. Even so, there are interesting and difficult questions surrounding any real ethical issue.

In a "good" traditional western, there is always a trespass against someone's rights. This moral violation is usually obvious to the audience. The hero must somehow "right" the situation. How the hero goes about the task is what makes the western worth watching. Does the hero simply commit the same crimes as the villain, but with "right" on his side? In *Rooster Cogburn,* we see Rooster being relieved of his duties for this very reason. Sure, he brings in the bad guys, but too many of them are brought in dead. Judge Parker (John McIntire) essentially tells Rooster that he's no different than they are when he says, "Rooster, any deputy who shoots and kills sixty-four men in eight years is breaking the law; not aiding and abetting it." Of course, shortly thereafter Rooster is rehired by Judge Parker precisely because he is the only man who can do the job, thus reinforcing the notion that although he *will* go as low as he needs to in order to bring in the bad guy, sometimes this approach is the only one that will work.

The juxtaposition of Judge Parker's courthouse in Fort Smith and the "territory" is reflective of a tension: the rationalistic, absolutist conceptions of right and wrong in terms of the written law versus the difficulty of the application of these ideas in actual situations. As Rooster tells Judge Parker (in *Rooster Cogburn*), "Well, Judge, out there in the territory they don't know about all these newfangled laws. We know it, but they don't. They're still shootin' in the same direction: at *me!*" This is the best Rooster can offer to explain his routine use of what the judge considers excessive force. In other words, if you were in those situations and you wanted to enforce the law and survive, it was essentially either kill or be killed. So, naturally from his vantage point—on paper, that is—Judge Parker has trouble differentiating Rooster's behavior from that of the criminals he is charged to bring to justice.

In general, there are subtle (or not so subtle) differences in the behavior of the hero (versus the villain) that the audience can detect. At the end of *The Cowboys,* after Long Hair[18] (Bruce Dern) has killed Wil, and the boys, with the help of the cook Jebediah Nightlinger (Roscoe Lee Browne), have buried him, they decide to take the herd back from the rustlers. Just before he died Wil asked Nightlinger to see to it that the boys got back home safely. The cowboys surprise the cook, tying him up so that he can't stop them from going after the herd. They tell him what they intend to do, and he agrees to help them make a plan if they'll untie him. Nightlinger's plan works, and they are able to retake the herd after the necessary gunfight at the end. When the dust clears, they can see that Long Hair is trapped under his horse, crying out that his leg is broken.

At this point, with Long Hair helpless, the boys have several choices as to what they can do about him. They can kill him by shooting him. They can help him get free of the horse and presumably seek "legal" justice. Or, they can choose to do nothing, which is more or less what they do.[19] Because the audience is intimately acquainted with the history of this man—the man who shot an unarmed John Wayne in the back—the boys' choice seems the right one. It's hard to imagine a Kantian or other rationalist system that would allow this response to be morally permissible, let alone right. It is precisely this convoluted ethical dimension of a western that, if thoughtfully presented, can make it a classic. However, if it is too simply portrayed, it makes the film merely another tale of revenge.

There is a critical question with regard to the role of pragmatism and the cowboys' behavior in cutting the reins. We must assume that the boys are doing their best to follow Wil's example in their behavior. If John Wayne is supposed to be a real pragmatist, then the question naturally arises: Would a pragmatic ethical approach allow for this type of justice? In other words, did they do the right thing, pragmatically speaking? This is a difficult question, but I think that one *can* answer it affirmatively.[20]

First, we know that Long Hair has been to jail already; however, the film demonstrates that he has not reformed. He lies to Wil at their first meeting. He claims that he lied because he believed that no one would hire a man who has just been released from the penitentiary. Wil tells Long Hair that the lying, not the prison time, is the reason he won't hire him.

Later Long Hair steals the herd, shooting (in the back) and killing an unarmed man in the process. Sending this individual back to jail does not seem to be a choice that will be of benefit to anyone in the long term. However, killing him outright makes it too difficult to distinguish his criminal behavior from that of the cowboys themselves. He is unarmed and helpless just as Wil was. The choice they make, handing the knife to Dan (Nicolas Beauvy), who was particularly traumatized by Long Hair, so that he can let loose the horse, is clearly a choice of vengeance. As he is dragged on the ground by the running horse, Long Hair will suffer terribly before he dies. Yet one can make the argument that Long Hair is ultimately responsible for his own fate.

How can we be sure that the cowboys made the right choice, morally speaking? Sometimes a pragmatist must wait for the data to roll in before an answer is clear. In a difficult case like this, it might take years for the cowboys to learn whether or not they made the right choice. It is possible that they might never know for certain. This is not a fault of the pragmatic method; this is the reality of the situation. Meaningful ethical issues are usually not simple, and while we desperately desire a simple answer to the problem, sometimes one is not forthcoming. Because pragmatism accepts the sometimes murky nature of these situations as part and parcel of reality, it is well suited to the moral concerns of the western.

While the ethical issues in *The Cowboys* are quite interesting from a pragmatic point of view, the plot of the film is perhaps even more so. In the beginning, it seems to involve a very simple problem that is approached pragmatically, even if the solution proves to be unorthodox. Wil's cattle need to get to market so that he can sell them and pay his bills. The only available bodies are boys from the age of thirteen to fifteen. Wil weighs the other options (none, really) and decides to use the boys after a brief test of their horsemanship skills. This appears to be a simple and straightforward pragmatic solution to a problem.

However, at some point during the cattle drive a significant shift occurs. The goal for Wil changes from getting the cattle to market no matter the cost to being a better father to the cowboys than he was to his own sons, who died because they "went bad." The audience may not realize that this shift has occurred until after Wil's death makes it obvious. Wil's failure to complete the drive is intentional to the extent that he chooses his second goal, that of showing the boys how a good man ought to conduct himself, over the first, of getting the cattle to market.

Of course, these two goals are not mutually exclusive. Had circumstances been different both could have been accomplished simultaneously. Further, it is not entirely clear that Wil made the best choices in a pragmatic sense to accomplish his goals. Clearly, he was right in hiring the boys to take his cattle to market since the boys ultimately got them there. (One has to wonder though, was it worth the life of Charlie Schwartz [Stephen Hudis], one of the boys who dies along the way?) It is not quite as clear that Wil's self-sacrifice was necessary in a pragmatic sense, but perhaps no other behavior could have made Wil's point as clearly to the boys as his willingness to die for his principles. Certainly, there are situations in which sacrificing oneself may well be the most pragmatic option available. I think that in this case we see the meeting of a generally pragmatic approach with what *appears* to be a more principle-based ethical system.[21]

Lovers of the western are familiar with the "code of the West," though it's harder to make a list of the rules that make up the code than it might seem. It might start something like this: A true hero keeps his word.[22] You don't shoot a man in the back (even if he *is* a bad guy). You give a man a chance to draw before you shoot. You care for those who can't care for themselves. And so on. However, before any more laws of the code are listed, perhaps a closer look at the application of the "code" is in order. I think we'll see that the code—while it may look like a set of absolute rules that must be followed—is actually applied pragmatically. As long as the code works in a given situation, our heroes will adhere to it, but should it prove a hindrance to the task at hand, it will be ignored. In other words, if we look closely at the heroes and their actions in western films, we'll see that there are so many exceptions to the code that it can hardly be considered an absolute set of rules at all.

For example, the "rule" against shooting a man in the back seems to be suspended once the fighting has commenced. In what is arguably John Wayne's most famous scene ever, the mounted shootout in *True Grit* when Rooster alone takes on five men, Rooster shoots two of Ned Pepper's (Robert Duvall) gang in the back after he charges past them (and they have ridden past him). As for the rule that one ought to give a man a chance to draw, in the opening scene of *Rooster Cogburn*, Rooster shoots all three criminals even though only one drew on, and shot, Rooster's deputy. In both films, Rooster is also almost as quick to lie to the bad guys as he is to "pull a cork." Simply put, Rooster adheres to the code of the West as long as it suits his needs, and yet there is no doubt at all that he is a good man—that he is heroic, in fact.[23]

John Wayne did not become a cinematic icon because the audience was willing to allow his characters to be unethical just because they were *John Wayne's* characters. This would be putting the cart before the horse, in a sense. John Wayne was able to make the audience believe that he made the only possible choices that could be right given the circumstances as they presented themselves. The choices were right not because they adhered to some set of rules, but rather because things were as right as they could be in the end. The audience understood and valued the pragmatic approach that John Wayne's characters applied so effectively, whether the problematic situation was one where the ethical concerns were highlighted or one where they were more subdued. People who watched and loved his movies imagined that they too were capable of making the right choices under duress, just as the Duke did. Audiences recognized and admired John Wayne's pragmatic skills as they were seen in his characters.

Pragmatism is not a philosophy that was invented or created by some great thinker. Charles Sanders Peirce (1839–1914) is recognized as the first person to use the word *pragmatism* to describe a problem-solving methodology that had some similarities to the scientific method, and hence he is considered the father of classical American pragmatism. William James and John Dewey[24] went on to make the term internationally renowned. Though it is associated with certain figures, pragmatism remains a description of a way of doing things rather than a detailed system that explains how things might be or should be. Pragmatism as a methodology preexists the philosophic label and has been applied for centuries. It is for this reason that John Wayne could be a pragmatist without ever being aware that he was one. He did not need to read a book, take a course, or join a group to become a pragmatist. He simply needed to use the methodology that has been described as pragmatism. His audiences did not need to do any of those things either to recognize his gift of being able to portray an accomplished pragmatist, which in truth any cowboy who could survive in the Old West, let alone prosper, would have had to have been. We need only to watch John Wayne's characters to understand how a great pragmatist would function. When we do so, it is impossible not to admire that way of acting.

Notes

1. William James, *Pragmatism* (Indianapolis: Hackett, 1981), 25.
2. Ibid.
3. Ibid.

4. This assertion requires a bit of fleshing out in order to explain what may at first glance seem incorrect. Both James and Dewey argue that we have always been pragmatic, and thus that we have always used the pragmatic method as a problem-solving methodology. So, historically speaking, pragmatism is nothing new. Hence the subtitle of James's lectures: *A New Name for Some Old Ways of Thinking.* We can trace pragmatism back to the Greeks in general and Aristotle specifically. However, it (in my view, still) has not been recognized as a methodology that can be adopted wholesale. In other words, first, we do not recognize that we regularly employ pragmatism when confronted by a problem that requires immediate attention/solution, and second, we do not understand that this very methodology (that we do use) can also be used across the board to address *any* problem, philosophical or otherwise.

5. I use this phrase to distinguish the "original" American pragmatists (Charles S. Peirce, James, Dewey, George H. Mead, and others) from later so-called pragmatists (like the logical positivists who followed them, or contemporary figures such as Richard Rorty).

6. For example, see John Dewey, *Experience and Nature* (New York: Dover, 1958), 67–68.

7. The relationship between thought and action in pragmatism is much like a Hegelian sandwich. Thought typically begets action. The result(s) of the action inspires thought and reflection. This may, in turn, generate additional actions. Any one instance of pragmatic action is assimilated as experience to be used again. The movement of pragmatism is always progressive and always goal oriented; while somewhat Hegelian in this respect, individual pragmatists differ in terms of the extent to which they see any "ultimate" end to the progress. So, unlike Hegelianism, pragmatism is not actually a teleological philosophy.

8. John Dewey, *The Philosophy of John Dewey,* ed. John J. McDermott (Chicago: University of Chicago Press, 1981), 226–27.

9. Ibid., 238.

10. Of course I realize that one can choose to do nothing—to *not* act. In this case the choice is the action. Pragmatists are antidualist.

11. He reaches this decision, at least in part, presumably because he has been forced to admit that he himself was only thirteen years old when he went on his first cattle drive.

12. Most pragmatists would agree that it is unlikely that one would encounter a completely novel situation. Generally speaking, the situations (and therefore the problems) that we encounter are not radically different from our previous experiences. There are of course exceptions to this general rule. However, these types of situations would not be commonplace.

13. If John Wayne's characters were real people, then one would naturally expect that they would learn, such that his characters in later films would react more quickly and accurately to situations. I believe that one can see in his acting that he learned how to

display this capacity or tendency in his later films. The young John Wayne typically made the right decisions, but watching the older John Wayne one *feels* that he'll be right—presumably as the result of a perceived confidence that only experience provides.

14. When I say "They get it right," I mean that they have been correct in the sense that they are not wrong, but since the issues in western films are so often moral concerns, I must also mean that they are ethically "right" as well.

15. James, *Pragmatism*, 92.

16. It is critical to keep in mind the fact that James (along with the rest of the pragmatists) rejects the notion of duality, particularly in terms of a mind/body split. Thus, just because a new idea conflicts with my previously held beliefs, this does not mean that I *cannot* assimilate it. This just means that I may not *want* to assimilate it. So, it can be true even if I don't want it to be true. For pragmatists truth is not entirely subjective, though it has subjective components.

17. While I have limited my discussion of Wayne to the later films, I would be remiss here not to mention *Angel and the Bad Man* (1947) as a film that examines this very issue.

18. Although the cast list identifies this character as "Long Hair," he introduces himself to Wil Anderson as "Asa Watts."

19. While it's literally true in the film that Dan cuts the reins, allowing the horse to get up and drag Long Hair, this outcome was inevitable. Eventually Long Hair would have tired of holding onto the reins and would have been forced to let go, letting the horse get up. Waiting for this to happen just would have been rather boring and slow for the audience.

20. The wonderful (and terribly difficult) aspect of the pragmatic approach is the fact that one could (almost) as easily answer this query in the negative. A pragmatic argument could be fashioned that the boys should have made a different choice. I leave that argument to the reader to make.

21. One can't help but think of Kant here, but actually any rationalistic system of ethics might offer up a similar outcome. While I am arguing that cowboy heroes are pragmatists, I cannot spit in the wind and claim that they do not share a code of behavior that is based on certain inalienable unwritten laws—or do they?

22. This is an extension or subset of the rule that one should be honest and tell the truth.

23. While one might argue that Rooster is an exception to the characters that John Wayne typically portrayed, I would counter that John Wayne chose to play him in two different movies and that Rooster Cogburn was one of his most famous characters. I would further suggest that we'd find similar behavior in many of John Wayne's other characters if we looked closely at them.

24. Of course I include George Herbert Mead and George Santayana as important figures in the development of classical American pragmatism.

Two Ways to Yuma

Locke, Liberalism, and Western Masculinity in *3:10 to Yuma*

Stephen J. Mexal

> Westerns . . . created a model for men who came of age in the twentieth century.
>
> —Jane Tompkins, *West of Everything*

John Locke and the Western Hero

At one of the climactic moments of the 1957 film *3:10 to Yuma,* rancher Dan Evans (Van Heflin) realizes, in the timeless tradition of countless devil-may-care western heroes, that his task has become all but hopeless. Dan has agreed to bring outlaw Ben Wade (Glenn Ford) to justice for the price of $200, money he desperately needs to pay his land debts. His job is to put Wade on the 3:10 p.m. train to Yuma, Arizona, where Wade will be imprisoned.

It is near the end of the film—when he is holed up in a hotel room with Wade and waiting in trepidation for the train—that Dan realizes he is utterly alone in his charge. The men who had originally agreed to help him have abandoned him, and Wade's seven-man "outfit" of criminals is waiting outside the hotel, nearly certain to kill Dan and free Wade the moment they leave the hotel room. Recognizing that the undertaking has essentially become a lost cause, Butterfield (Robert Emhardt), the stagecoach owner who originally agreed to pay Dan the $200, absolves him of his duty. It's just not worth it, Butterfield decides. Then, somewhat incredibly, he offers to pay him the money anyway, even though he has just released Dan from his obligations.

Earlier, Dan has declared his interest in the situation to be merely transactional. He is, he announces, "just doing this for the money" to pay his debts and maintain his property. And so, with his contractual obligations to Butterfield dissolved and his financial compensation secured, to risk death by trying to deliver Wade to the train anyway is irrational.

Yet Dan does precisely that. Declaring that he's "got to" go through with the plan, even though neither contract nor financial exigency is actually forcing him, he seems to abandon rational self-interest and familial obligation. He *must* deliver Wade to justice, he says, if only because "people should be able to live in decency and peace together." In saying this, he proclaims rational self-interest to be subordinate to a broader public good.

Tellingly, Dan links this new interest in the public good to a particular conception of masculinity. As he prepares to leave the hotel room and face seemingly insurmountable odds, he tells his wife, Alice (Leora Dana), who has come to try to change his mind, that though he has not been able to provide her with much in the way of material luxuries such as jewelry, or even necessities like ample food, he nevertheless hopes that this one moment in which he rejects economic individualism and embraces civic-mindedness will make up for his defects as a provider and a husband. Abnegative republicanism will be his legacy as a man. This final act, Dan proclaims, will be something "worth remembering" for his wife and children.

Ultimately, Dan Evans does not die, and he successfully accompanies Ben Wade to the jail in Yuma. In the 2007 remake of the film, though, the character is not so lucky. In this version, at the crucial moment when all hope is apparently lost, Butterfield (Dallas Roberts) again absolves Dan (Christian Bale) of his obligations and again offers to pay him the $200 anyway. Again, Dan turns him down. Dan then turns to his fourteen-year-old son William (Logan Lerman) and bestows manhood upon him. "You've become a fine man," he tells his son. "You got all the best parts of me." Much as in the 1957 film, Dan links patrimony to a particular conception of the good, or what he identifies as the "right." However, in the 2007 film, right action does not mean subordinating individualism to abstract notions of justice and civic responsibility. Instead, Dan renegotiates his contract. In place of the original $200, he demands from Butterfield water rights for his land and $1,000 to be given to his wife. Butterfield agrees. And though Dan asks his son to "remember that your old man walked Ben Wade to that station when nobody else would," it is clear that his real legacy of masculinity is one of property, not civic spirit. In the 2007 film, Dan Evans also succeeds in putting Ben Wade (Russell Crowe) on the train to the Yuma jail, but it is a hollow victory for a number of reasons, not the least of which is that

William is forced to watch his father die in the act of ensuring his son's right to property.

Although Dan Evans's actions at the climax of the 2007 film are motivated by his desire to provide for his dependents, it is important to note that the film conflates "family protector" with "property protector." That is to say, Dan's entire ability to care for his family is predicated on the absolute supremacy of property, a principle that forms the bedrock of atomistic individualism. And though Dan seems unconcerned with acquiring property for its own sake, the film's willingness to equate masculinity with property acquisition says much about its post–cold war politics. As a result, Dan's readiness to escort Wade to the station should not be misconstrued as a readiness to die or to be martyred for his family. Instead, the scene is better understood as a negotiation for hazard pay. Dan is undertaking an unusually dangerous job and, as a proper liberal subject, expects to be paid accordingly. Thus, while it may not be in his personal interest to die, it very much is in his interest to renegotiate his contract and attempt to complete the work. Under Dan's model of liberal individualism, ensuring property means ensuring inheritance, both of which, ultimately, sustain the untrammeled autonomy of the individual.[1]

The two films, separated by fifty years, offer an opportunity to examine the relationship between individual autonomy, property, the state of nature, and masculinity in a film genre that has long served as a repository for American fantasies about freedom and conquest. Over the course of the two films, Dan Evans and Ben Wade come to represent a changing set of ideas about American masculinity and liberal selfhood in the twentieth century. The 1957 film valorizes a masculine civic liberalism over absolute liberal autonomy, whereas in the 2007 film, with the specter of communism vanquished and laissez-faire capitalism triumphant, western masculinity ultimately means unyielding liberal individualism.

The archetypal hero of the classic Hollywood western is a figure with his roots in the political ideas of seventeenth-century philosopher John Locke. As political historian Louis Hartz writes, the political philosophy of John Locke is at the core of what has come to be called classical liberalism in America.[2] Locke believed that individuals possess a foundational and inalienable liberty. His conception of the autonomous self governed western expansion as a historical phenomenon, but it also guided the representation of liberal selfhood in fictional western narratives. That is, it shaped the development of the physical West, but also the cultural development of the *western*. And the western, of course, changes over time. Though genres can seem remarkably stable, this apparent durability is an illusion; genres seem constant precisely because they conform so effortlessly to any given historical moment. Each generation gets precisely the western it needs. Because of this, the transition from Heflin and Ford's cold war–era portrayal of Dan Evans and Ben Wade to Bale and Crowe's post-1989 representations of the same characters offers a unique opportunity to chart the Lockean underpinnings of the western myth and the evolution of masculine liberalism in America.[3]

   If the prototypical Lockean figure is masculine, capitalist, and in possession of the unswerving belief that the social good most often follows the individual good, then the two film versions of *3:10 to Yuma* offer important examples of the ways in which the western has been used to reimagine liberal selfhood. Locke explained the foundational autonomy of individuals by appealing to the language and logic of the natural world. In a premodern "state of nature," he argued, humans are naturally free. And given that the western is at least partly a fantasy about the autonomy of white males, the genre's Lockean foundations normalize white masculine privilege, justifying that privilege as the by-product of the "state of nature" found in the nineteenth-century West. As such, representations of masculinity in the fictional American West are about the conquest of the far West in the nineteenth century, but they also navigate the shifting relationship to that legacy of conquest in the twentieth. To put it another way, the 1957 and 2007 films *3:10 to Yuma* are not just about liberality, masculinity, and the West in 1884, when the films are set, they are also about how those topics are understood as historical narratives in 1957 and 2007, when the films were made. Both films, then, use western space to reconsider the "natural" foundations of Lockean classical liberalism. Ultimately, the films place individual rights and public needs into a dialectical relationship, one informed by the vagaries of their unique cold war and post–cold war historical moments.

Liberalism and the Western "State of Nature"

Liberalism in its original incarnation, what political theorists today identify as "classical liberalism," is roughly synonymous with personal freedom. It is a political philosophy that puts the individual at the center of governance. Under classical liberalism individuals are naturally autonomous, and from this simple premise—people are free—springs the entire apparatus of liberal governance. Governments derive their legitimacy from persons, and do not interfere with core liberal values such as freedom of thought and speech, the right to existence, communities bound by the rule of law, and an essential right to property. This right to property comes, like everything else, from the essential freedom of the individual. Because a person owns himself, he also owns his labor, and it is labor that creates the value that produces property.[4]

Though liberalism has its conceptual roots in a slew of Enlightenment-era thinkers such as Jean-Jacques Rousseau, Thomas Hobbes, Charles Montesquieu, and later David Hume and Adam Smith, American liberalism has most often meant the liberalism of John Locke. Laid out in his *Two Treatises on Government* (1689), Locke's ideas formed the core of what would come to be called liberality in America. Though the extent of Locke's influence and the cohesiveness of his philosophy are the subjects of perennial debate, Locke still remains the clearest expression of individual autonomy in nineteenth-century America, the period in which most westerns are set.[5]

There are a number of important reasons why Lockean liberalism explains the political philosophy of the western, but the most obvious is the centrality of nature in both the western film and in Locke's conception of the individual. Locke held that every man is self-governing, and that there is no natural or foundational political authority. Because he found the philosophical justification for this intrinsic liberality in what he called a "state of nature," and the subtext of every western film involves "civilizing" or "settling" supposedly natural spaces, Locke's governmental treatises provide a useful guide to both the western as a political text and the lasting endurance of the western in the American mind.

Land, then, is both setting and subject in the archetypal western. Land rights, water rights, and ranching politics provide the grist for most western plots, and the stark, sweeping vistas of the American West lend a crackling visual texture and mythic resonance to the otherwise quotidian dramas acted out by terse men in dusty clothes. For Locke, the natural world functioned as a sort of thought experiment, an imaginary space in which he was able to arrive at the conclusion that individuals possess a foundational liberality. What, he wondered, did the individual look like before communities or nations or political loyalties? What did the individual look like in a prelapsarian "state of nature"? For Thomas Hobbes, writing thirty-eight years before Locke, the state of nature was a state of war, a condition of perpetual anarchy that could be avoided only by subordinating the self to a strong civil government. For Locke, though, the state of nature was simply a space in which humans were naturally free. To "understand political power right," he wrote in the *Second Treatise*, "we must understand what state all men are naturally in." That natural state, he continued, is "a state of perfect freedom to order their actions and dispose of their possessions and person, as they think fit, within the bounds of the law of nature; without asking leave, or depending upon the will of any other man." Perfect freedom, though, does not mean anarchic freedom, because Locke believed that natural human liberty was partly constrained by the relative peace of the "law of nature."[6]

Locke's nature is a state of pure and perfect freedom, and does not imply a state of perpetual war. Nature, Locke clarifies, is "a state of liberty, yet it is not a state of license." Yet because the state of nature means freedom, any government is going to mean a reduction in the foundational freedoms of the state of nature and should accordingly be regarded with suspicion. As Ruth W. Grant writes, by "identifying the state of nature as the worst case, Hobbes teaches obedience to civil government. By identifying the state of war as the worst case, Locke justifies resistance." This simple hypothesis, postulating that natural space is the fount of individual freedom, delineates a perfect human liberality as well as a natural resistance to governmental authority. It also does much to explain the recurring appeal of the western in the twentieth century (after all, the genre harkens back to an earlier era of romantic individualism), as well as the role of western lands in the nineteenth-century public imagination.[7]

In the nineteenth century, the American West was widely seen as a "safety valve," a sort of regulator of socioeconomic tensions. In contrast to the entrenched class inequality in the East, the American West was viewed as an opportunity to start over, to renew the promise of American individual liberty. If resources became scarce in the East, the nation could release some of the social pressure engendered by that scarcity simply by encouraging migration west. This notion of the West as a safety valve was, of course, a myth, if a deeply attractive one. It was predicated on a vision of a frontier containing a reservoir of natural resources sufficient to fulfill the economic and political desires of all social classes. As Richard Slotkin writes, this frontier myth, which chiefly involves "the conquest of the wilderness and the subjugation or displacement of the Native Americans who originally inhabited it," has been, in the popular imagination, "the means to [the American] achievement of a national identity, a democratic polity,

[and] an ever-expanding economy." The frontier, in this mythic schema, offers a sort of reset button to civilization, a way of purifying and renewing the social contract.[8]

Although this particular ideology of the American West is indeed a myth, it is worth noting that this view of the frontier, which sustained western migration as it was enacted in the nineteenth century and reimagined in the twentieth, is also a logical outgrowth of Lockean liberalism. If persons derive their freedom from nature, then it only makes sense that persons can renew those foundational freedoms by returning *to* nature. Donald Worster calls this the "Lockean imperative," writing that because Locke's notion of property rights springs from his notion of natural freedom, then property and freedom both come from the act of developing a piece of land, "taking it out of a state of wildness and into one of cultivation." Yet in the frontier myth, actual labor is less important than abstract identification with the land. As Will Wright notes, the archetypal cowboy is defined by his honor and "wilderness identity, not by his job." Due to this romantic association of the American frontier with the Lockean state of nature, American liberal selfhood and western wilderness are always conjoined in the western genre.[9]

In both versions of *3:10 to Yuma*, the benefits of viewing the American West as a new "state of nature" accrue solely to white men. This is consistent with the nineteenth-century racial politics of "civilization." In the rhetoric of civilization, the myth of the frontier as a space where persons might renew the individualism implicit in the original liberal social contract is predicated first on the identification and elimination of "savages." That is to say, for white immigrants to be able to regard the geography of the American West as a Lockean "state of nature" requires the effacement of Native Americans and, after 1848, Mexicans.[10] As such, nonwhite persons are largely absent from both films, although in the 2007 version, Ben Wade's gang of outlaws does, somewhat perfunctorily, include a "Mexican sharpshooter and an Apache." The subtextual drama, then, becomes a de-racialized, ahistorical battle over the nature of nature. Is the American West a space of peaceful, disconnected individualism, as Dan Evans seems to believe? Or is it a space in which individual desires are allowed to run wild? "It's man's nature to take what he wants," Ben Wade declares in the 2007 film, encapsulating his position that the American West is a space for the type of hard liberalism that presumes the absolute autonomy of the individual. However, this declaration, which naturalizes excessive individualism, is notably absent from the 1957 version of the film. As such, the issue of freedom and its limits frames the evolution of *3:10 to Yuma* from a 1957 cold war drama to a 2007 post–cold war film.

Freedom and Man

Ben Wade is a charming rake. (We are meant to understand this because he delays his getaway in order to seduce a female bartender in Bisbee. Noncharming criminals, it seems, are famously indifferent to bartenders.) Clearly, the audience is meant to be seduced by him, too, as his vision of the American West is one in which individual liberty does not necessarily mean moral action. In Wade's West, crime is easy and the spoils plentiful. For him, the West represents an infinite feast for the unrestrained appetites of the atomistic liberal self.

And yet the 1957 film takes pains to emphasize the collaborative nature of his criminal threat. Wade's gang is repeatedly referred to throughout as an "outfit," a term emphasizing its disreputable collectivity. Ben Wade is a dangerous individual, but his real threat to civic order comes from the fact that he is a member of an organized cooperative whose members are working in tandem to plunder the surplus of American capitalist enterprise. During the stagecoach robbery, for example, the coach driver overpowers one of Wade's gang and, holding the man in front of him for protection, threatens to shoot him. Ben Wade pauses only briefly before shooting both the driver and his own accomplice. Later, when the men are celebrating in a bar, Charlie Prince (Richard Jaeckel), Wade's right-hand man, toasts Wade for killing an individual in order to sustain the continued existence of the group as a whole. It is beneficial, he says, to have had to "say good-bye to one of the outfit," because if they had not, it might have been "good-bye for some of the rest of us." The existence of the group trumps the rights of the individual, heightening, in the 1957 film, the threat of the western outlaw by aligning that figure with a cooperative entity. In this, the film rewrites the tropes of the western for the age of the cold war. The threat of "the outfit" is, of course, an imperfect analogy to the perceived communist threat in 1950s America. After all, Ben Wade is identified as "the boss" of the outfit, in the familiar language of the professional-managerial class, and his gang's core motivation is obviously capitalist. Yet at the film's outset, his cooperative "outfit" does present a stark contrast to Dan's atomistic liberalism. The ultimate victory of Dan Evans in the 1957 film is, in a small way, a repudiation of Ben Wade's willingness to value the rights of the group over the rights of the individual.

In the 1957 film, Dan Evans gradually moves away from hard liberalism and toward a philosophy that limits the absolute autonomy of the individual in favor of a broader civic good. A civic-minded republicanism, of course, is not incompatible with liberalism. The whole premise of Locke's political philosophy was that persons surrender particular foundational liberties in order to form a liberal civil society. By entering into social contract to become "united into one society," he wrote, each individual man must relinquish "his executive power of the law of nature" and "resign it to the public," thus forming "a political or civil society." So by surrendering absolute individual autonomy, or the "executive power of the law of nature," liberal civil society becomes possible. But because the American West was, in the nineteenth century, popularly seen as a place to renew the social contract, a large part of the fantasy of the western is the notion of a political sphere that is somehow closer to the hard individualism of the original state of nature. At the start of the 1957 film, Dan Evans is much nearer to this foundational liberalism, and it is only by the close of the film that he begins to fuse civic duty with individualism. Ultimately, his transition from hard liberalism to a soft republicanism is intermeshed with the film's ideas about the roles and responsibilities of the masculine subject.[11]

After watching Wade hold up the stagecoach in the film's opening scenes, Dan tells his wife, Alice, about the escapade and emphasizes that he took no action. He is no solitary ranger-hero, fighting with six-gun for principles that do not materially benefit him. It "seems terrible," Alice says in response, "that something bad could happen and all anybody can do is stand by and watch." At first, Dan is unswayed by this logic. Alice is evoking abstract notions of bad and good, and she feels that "bad" actions by one individual ought to require a "good" response by a second, ostensibly disinterested individual, a response that exceeds simple "watch[ing]." To this, Dan sensibly replies, "*Lots* of things happen and all you can do is stand by and watch." He alludes not only to the social responsibility of the atomistic individual (that is, he is not *obligated* to do more than "watch"), but also to the limits of individualism itself (there were seven criminals and he was one man; he could not reasonably *have* done more). Alice, though, yokes Dan's passive response not to his status as a liberal subject, but to his status as a masculine subject. Masculinity, she seems to imply, demands civic liberalism. It is not good, she says, for Dan's sons to hear that he observed a crime and did nothing to stop it. (In the 2007 film, Dan's sons actually watch the crime with him.) She ultimately connects his behavior to three topics, all of which play a key part in Locke's liberalism: masculinity, autonomy, and property. After suggesting that he is providing a poor model of masculinity for his sons, she revises the conventions of liberal autonomy, suggesting liberal individualism should not lead to selfish inaction, but rather to civic action. Because Wade has stolen private property, she suggests, he has made an implicit threat against Dan's autonomy as a liberal subject: "Dan," she finally says, "you *have* to do something. You *can't* just stand by and watch. You work so hard." This final sentence about his work as a rancher is, logically speaking, irrelevant to the matter at hand. The fact that Alice views it as relevant conveys much about the status of masculinity, property, and the civic responsibilities of the liberal subject in the imaginary West of 1950s America.

For many American liberal intellectuals in the 1950s, combating the postwar anxiety and malaise that they felt made people vulnerable to extremist politics meant recasting liberalism as something hard, virile, and masculine. As K. A. Cuordileone notes, this impulse ultimately found its apex in the Kennedy administration, which reconciled "liberalism itself with masculine virility." Yet it also had important implications for the gender politics of the era. In the 1950s liberal imagination, there was a nexus between political and sexual subversion. "Like homosexual relations," Cuordileone writes, "the practice of politics under Communism becomes transgressive." Similarly, as Robert D. Dean notes, there was a "pattern of republican 'engendered' civic virtue taken as the basis for individual political legitimacy by both Cold War conservatives and left-centrists." As a result, the 1957 *3:10 to Yuma*, like most westerns, imagines the American West as a space of freedom, a chance to renew the foundational liberal moment when autonomous individuals enter into social contract. Yet cold war politics demanded that that reimagination of liberal selfhood be not an atomistic individualism but a robust, heterosexual, masculine liberal republicanism. It was not only key that liberalism be framed as virile and masculine, it was crucial that American liberal governmentality, rather than absolute liberal autonomy, be the proper legacy of the individualism of the American West. As a result, the 1957 film is not a fantasy about unyielding liberal autonomy; it is instead a fantasy about the *surrender* of that absolute self-interest in the service of a masculine defense of the American public good.[12]

Because Ben Wade's criminal act involves usurping the liberal right to property, his crime also functions as a more general threat against liberal individualism. In overturning the rights of the individuals whose property was transported on the stagecoach, Ben synecdochically threatens the property rights of *all* liberal individuals. In this, Alice suggests, he represents a danger to liberal property generally, even though he did not threaten Dan's property rights specifically. Because Dan "work[s] so hard," he as a property owner cannot "just stand by and watch." Within the logic of the text, the best way for Dan to ensure the continued liberal right to personal property is to defend the rights of other liberal subjects, even if Dan's property was not directly trespassed upon. Because bringing Ben Wade to justice is good for the property rights of other liberal individuals, it is also, Alice suggests, good for Dan's property rights. Civic action thus becomes liberal action.

Perhaps more to the point, Dan's civic turn is also figured as the most masculine course of action, the proper task of a husband and father. Liberal individualism is used to cultivate a sense of masculine republican virtue. It is toward this civic-mindedness that Dan Evans moves over the course of the film, ultimately choosing to transport Ben Wade to Yuma even though there is no financial or contractual reason for him to do so. This transformation is never fully explained; instead, civic liberalism is uncritically framed as the best course of action and Dan, as the movie's hero, necessarily embraces that course. Getting Ben Wade to Yuma is not "right" from the perspective of an atomistic individualist, but it is "right," Alice suggests, from the perspective of a republican male interested in defending the public good. As a result, masculinity in the 1957 *3:10 to Yuma* involves a repudiation of absolute liberal individualism. But repudiating absolute individualism also means repudiating crime, as well as embracing the supremacy of private property. Being a man, by the close of the film, involves defending the property rights that come from "work[ing] so hard," and moreover embracing the seeming paradox of defending those liberal property rights by placing the interest of the public over the interest of the individual.

That is not to say that the film rejects Lockean liberalism. A key part of Locke's philosophy is the way in which autonomous individual actors come together to form communities and, in so doing, surrender some of the absolute liberality of the state of nature. Even in the state of nature, he writes, persons living under the "law of nature" must work to "preserve the rest of mankind," so long as that preservation does not come at the expense of one's own life or property. But once persons form communities—that is, once liberal*ity* becomes liberal*ism*—the absolute freedom of the state of nature is irrevocably altered. Every man, Locke writes, "by consenting with others to make one body politic under one government, puts himself under an obligation to every one of that society." Once persons have entered into social contract, the "first and fundamental" law and duty becomes "the preservation of the society, and (as far as will consist with the public good) of every person in it." Given this, one way of grasping Dan Evans's character arc in the 1957 film is as embodying a transformation from atomistic natural law liberalism to a republican liberalism that is bound to the "preservation of society."[13]

This embrace of civic liberalism is also, in the film, an embrace of a higher and more authentic masculinity. As Lee Clark Mitchell has noted, western films are obsessed with particular representations of masculinity; the genre, he writes, "allows us to gaze at men, [and] this gaze forms such an essential aspect of the genre that it seems covertly about just that: looking at men." This is surely true of the 1957 *3:10 to Yuma*, where much screen time is spent taking in Ben Wade's raffish smile or Dan Evans's soulful eyes. Yet its filmic gaze is also very much about observing particular forms of political masculinity. In the final scene of the film, once Dan has boarded the train to Yuma with Ben Wade, he grins and waves to his wife, Alice, who has observed his success. There is a complex of gazes here. As an audience, we watch Dan watch himself by watching Alice watch him. Dan knows he has succeeded as a citizen and, more important, as a man, because he has obtained the smiling approval of the woman who begged him to "do something." The accomplishment of the protagonist—that is, the simple fact that Dan has successfully put Ben on the train—is rife with political significance. Dan's achievement, ultimately, is a triumph of masculine civic liberalism.[14]

In the years between World War II and the Vietnam War, westerns served important ideological functions in the imagination of American civic masculinity by using myth to understand American imperial autonomy as well as the origins and limits of liberalism. As Stanley Corkin observes in his study of westerns and the cold war, the western normalized and justified American liberal hegemony in the middle part of the twentieth century. Westerns, he writes, "articulate the necessity of engaged heroes who morally ensure the rule of right. National interest is defined not simply by the goal of occupying contiguous lands but also by the imperative of reordering them according to a distinctly U.S. vision of civil society." In the 1957 *3:10 to Yuma*, Dan Evans most clearly becomes the film's hero at the point at which he most clearly becomes a man: when he repudiates liberal individualism in favor of a liberal civil society. In this, the film not only engages

with the age-old debate over Lockean liberalism and the proper relationship between individual autonomy and civil society, it also invokes deeply
resonant myths about American character. In doing this, it presents a virile,
masculine liberal republicanism as not only the ultimate legacy of American
individualism but also, and more important, as the finest defense against
threats to American liberal hegemony.[15]

Contract and Liberal Selfhood

The few significant differences separating the 2007 from the 1957 *3:10 to
Yuma* largely pertain to the rights and responsibilities of the masculine liberal subject, and signal much about the status of the western in the post–
cold war age. One obviously important divergence is that Dan, having been
absolved of his contractual responsibilities and told he will be paid anyway,
does *not* selflessly insist on transporting Ben Wade to the train regardless.
Instead, in the 2007 film, he uses the opportunity to negotiate for additional
payment. His first demand concerns property rights. Earlier in the film,
Hollander (Lennie Loftin), the marshal and a rival landowner who has lent
Dan money and hopes to take Dan's land as payment, has prevented water
from flowing to his property. "Before water touches your land," Hollander
tells him, "it resides and flows on mine." He is, he argues, therefore justified in doing with it as he likes. In Hollander's view, individual rights are
not oriented toward the public good or even toward fairness; instead, they
simply ensure the absolute supremacy of property. "A man has to be big
enough to see how small he is," Hollander smirks, suggesting that because
of the natural contours of the land and water, his right to property necessarily trumps any claims Dan might make. Accordingly, Dan's first step in
renegotiating his contract is to demand guarantees from Butterfield "that
Hollander and his boys will never set foot on my land again," and that his
"water's going to flow." Butterfield accedes to these new demands, as well as
to Dan's further request that Butterfield give his wife $1,000, a 500 percent
increase on their original agreement. Butterfield agrees to this, too, and it
is only at this point that Dan turns to his son and tells him that he's finally
found "what [is] right," marking his patrilineage explicitly through abstract
notions of right action and masculinity, but implicitly through the redou-
bled centrality of liberal individualism. Unlike in the 1957 film, Dan Evans
does not take Ben Wade to the train simply because it is "right," he does it
because he *gets stuff out of it.*

In the 2007 film, Dan views his contract with Butterfield as, in fact, a contract. As Brook Thomas has noted, there are a number of important links between classical liberal selfhood and the emergence of contract law in the nineteenth century. "By promising individuals equal chance to develop," Thomas writes, "contract claims to produce an equitable social harmony that has been achieved through a network of immanent and self-regulating exchanges rather than a social order imposed artificially from above." A contract, then, assumes liberal subjects. Unlike in the 1957 film, Dan Evans does not subordinate his own economic well-being to the higher claims of society; instead, he insists upon the validity and fundamentally liberal (rather than civic or republican) tenor of the original contract entered into with Butterfield. The material benefits for Dan's family are obtained through his adherence to his own status as a liberal subject. If, in the 1957 film, Dan best serves himself and his family by foregoing absolute liberal autonomy in the name of civic liberal republicanism, in the 2007 film, he aids himself and his family by holding hard and fast to his own liberal subjectivity.[16]

In another significant revision, Wade's accomplice Charlie Prince appeals to the liberal self-interest of the populace of Contention, Arizona, offering $200 to any member of the town willing to kill Dan, the sheriff, or the sheriff's deputies. Though it is in the civic interest of the town to ensure Wade's incarceration, it becomes in the economic interest of the individual townspersons to ensure Wade's escape. This potential site of tension, though, is immediately resolved, because no one is willing to put the needs of the public above individual interest, and Dan is soon dodging bullets from everyone in town. The liberal subjects of the town of Contention are citizens in name only. For both Dan and the residents of the town, it is an absolute liberal individualism, not a republican civic-mindedness, that denotes the values of the day.

Indeed, in their devotion to absolute self-interest, in the 2007 film it is the *heroes* who come closest to embodying the unyielding liberal individualism embodied by the *villain* Ben Wade in the 1957 film. And yet this exaltation of individual masculine autonomy is seemingly undone by the final moments of the film. In the 2007 version of the film, Dan Evans does succeed in putting Ben Wade on the train, but it is a hollow victory, one that occurs only because Ben Wade allows it to.

As Dan hustles him through the town, ducking bullets from Wade's gang as well as the townspeople eager to earn their $200 from Charlie Prince, Ben Wade suddenly decides he has had enough. He hurls Dan to the ground and is moments from killing him when Dan blurts that he "ain't never been no hero." His foot, Dan tells Wade, which he has long claimed was injured in an act of Civil War heroism, was in fact accidentally shot by one of his own soldiers. He says that he has been unable to tell that particular story to his sons, and as a result simply invented the story of his own war heroism. This, he suggests, is one reason why he has been so keen to escort Wade to the train—because in addition to the economic inheritance he has secured from Butterfield, his actions provide a figurative inheritance of his own masculinity. Hearing this, Wade stops choking him, thinks for a moment, says, "Okay," and then helps him to his feet.

From this scene onward, the two men work in tandem to get to the train. At the crucial moment, outlaw Wade hops onto the train of his own volition, only to watch as his own gang kills Dan Evans. Wade then exits the small train jail cell and receives his firearms from Charlie Prince. Dan's son William, who has been observing everything, rushes to his father's supine and bloody body and says, "You done it, Pa, you done it. You got him on the train." The obvious irony, of course, is that Ben Wade is not at that moment actually on the train. Yet Dan Evans dies secure in the knowledge that through his commitment to liberal individualism he has ensured his sons' inheritance. He also dies knowing he has profitably performed a sort of theater of masculinity. Even though Ben Wade is *off* the train, he was at one point successfully put *on* the train, and Dan's status as an autonomous man of action has therefore been secured. The facts that justice will not be served, that Wade will walk away, and that Dan has lost his life are somewhat irrelevant. He has performed his liberal masculinity by negotiating for more money and successfully, if temporarily, putting Ben Wade on the train.

The final moments of the film provide an odd resolution to this moral and political ambiguity. As William crouches over the body of his father, Ben Wade puts his gun belt on, thinks for a moment—as if calculating the heist spoils split seven ways, as opposed to one way—and then quickly executes every member of his gang. He then puts *himself* on the train to the Yuma jail, and the credits roll.

The abnegative masculine republicanism that characterized the end of the 1957 *3:10 to Yuma* has been, fifty years later, completely inverted. Dan's motivations stem more from the sovereignty of the Lockean liberal self than from any abstract notions of the public good. And his rhetoric of masculine duty is exposed as just that, rhetoric. Apparently, in order for Dan to establish himself as a liberal man of action it is not important to actually ensure that Wade goes to prison and that justice is served; it is sufficient to simply make sure Wade gets on the train. Whether or not he *stays* on the train is, in the eyes of Dan's son, all but irrelevant.

In this sense, the empty signifiers of masculine republicanism have replaced its substance. The 1957 film's interest in republican duty and masculine action is reproduced here only to distill that interest into a series of token symbols. Masculinity and civic spirit in the 2007 *3:10 to Yuma* are but gestures, and the thematic apex of the film is its exaltation of hard liberal individualism. The tragedy of Dan's death is softened, and his heroism assured, because he expresses a foundational liberal value of benign self-interest: he was able to derive material benefits from a contract between two liberal subjects. Unlike the 1957 Dan Evans, who claimed he was only shepherding Ben Wade "for the money," yet ultimately reveals himself to be doing it for abstract republican values of community and law, the 2007 Dan Evans is not only actually doing it "for the money," he is doing it for *a lot more money.* (And water rights.) Along similar lines, the audience's estimation of Russell Crowe's Ben Wade is shaped not only by the fact that he twice puts himself on the train to Yuma, but also by the fact that he executes his "outfit" of outlaws after they kill Dan Evans. Yet this apparent act of moral retribution is also a moment of liberal self-interest. With no one left alive to share in the spoils of the heist, the money will presumably be Wade's alone as soon as he escapes again from Yuma jail (which he has done several times before). In the 2007 film, then, the American West is upheld as a mythic "state of nature," a space of atomistic liberal selfhood where a person's first duty is to himself and his property, and civil society holds no claim on the liberty of any individual.

This was a distinct consequence of a new economic consensus after the cold war. By the turn of the twenty-first century, the threat of the "Red Menace" had become a well-faded memory, and global capitalism was widely seen as the new consensus of the age. If in 1957 it was important that the mythical frontier—the wellspring of American liberal individualism—was masculine, virile, and oriented toward the public good, then by 2007, with American capitalism facing no equivalent ideological threats, writers and filmmakers were free to reimagine the frontier as a site of absolute freedom and absolute wealth. With capitalist hegemony unimperiled, the mythic frontier could be evoked to sustain an ideology of atomistic liberalism, an ideology buttressing a new and dubious liberal right: the right to get rich.

Western Masculinity and the Cold War

It is the 1957 film that bears the closest resemblance to its source material, Elmore Leonard's 1953 short story "Three-Ten to Yuma," in which the Dan Evans character (here not a rancher but a marshal named Paul Scallen) successfully boards the train to Yuma with the Ben Wade character (named Jim Kidd). In this story, too, the narrative resolves itself in lawfulness and civic duty, but Scallen is not given the same liberal-republican narrative arc as Dan Evans in the 1957 film. Because it *is* Scallen's job to deliver Kidd to Yuma, not one he assumes for additional money, liberal self-interest and public service are fused. Though Scallen admits it was the money that initially made him become a lawman, he tells Kidd that money cannot sway him from his responsibilities to the public.

What is most significant about the two filmic reinterpretations of "Three-Ten to Yuma" is what they signal about the American West in the popular imaginations of 1957 and 2007. Much in the same way that the history of American western expansion in the nineteenth century is a political history, so also is the history of the western film genre in the twentieth century also a political history. Both films evoke a set of myths about the American West, Locke's "state of nature," and masculine freedom. But the 1957 film, born in the age of McCarthy and the House Un-American Activities Committee, takes pains to translate liberal individualism into liberal republicanism, and fuse that to a heterosexual masculine virility. Being a man, in the 1957 film, means upholding the rule of law. By the close of the film, Dan Evans's atomistic liberalism has been fully transformed into a masculine liberal republicanism, and the West has transformed from a liberal "state of nature" to a civil society.[17]

The 2007 film, in contrast, valorizes the sovereignty of the liberal subject, in the process reducing masculinity to a series of empty gestures. Unlike the abstract republican masculinity embraced by the 1957 film, here, Dan Evans's manhood is little more than a series of artful narratives that obscure the film's real vision of western selfhood: an absolute and unwavering commitment to economic self-interest. By 2007, with the cold war a fading memory and 1950s-era conformity-masquerading-as-civic-mindedness long forgotten, the western has been reimagined yet again as a cultural repository for myths about the perfect and foundational freedom of Locke's "state of nature." In the 2007 film, though, the western myth is not about purifying and renewing the social contract, it is about purifying and renewing the freedoms of the individual as that individual existed before the political technologies of civil society. If in 1957, atomistic liberalism is dissolved into the public well of republican duty, then by 2007, republican duty has been cast aside in favor of recapturing the absolute sovereignty of the Lockean liberal self, in the "state of nature" of the fictional American West.

Notes

The epigraph is taken from Jane Tompkins, *West of Everything: The Inner Life of Westerns* (New York: Oxford University Press, 1992), 17.

1. For John Locke, individual rights and property rights were indivisible, even if the individual was no longer alive to enjoy his property himself. Because of this, the right to deed and inherit property was also a fundamental liberal right. Locke devoted large sections of *The First Treatise of Government* to establishing the idea that "children have a right to succeed to the possession of their fathers' properties," a development that laid the groundwork for many of the notions of individual autonomy that emerged in the *Second Treatise*. John Locke, *The Second Treatise of Government*, in *The Selected Political Writings of John Locke*, ed. Paul E. Sigmund (New York: Norton, 2005), para. 91. Future citations of this text will refer to paragraph numbers, not page numbers.

2. Louis Hartz, *The Liberal Tradition in America* (New York: Harcourt Brace, 1955). For more on the centrality of Locke to American liberalism, see Joyce Appleby, *Liberalism and Republicanism in the Historical Imagination* (Cambridge, MA: Harvard University Press, 1992); Jerome Huyler, *Locke in America: The Moral Philosophy of the Founding Era* (Lawrence: University Press of Kansas, 1995); James Kloppenberg, *The Virtues of Liberalism* (New York: Oxford University Press, 1998); and Michael Zuckert, *The Natural Rights Republic: Studies in the Foundation of the American Political Tradition* (Notre Dame, IN: University of Notre Dame Press, 1996).

3. The year 1989 saw revolutions in Poland, Hungary, East Germany, Czechoslovakia, and Bulgaria. These political upheavals, coupled with the subsequent collapse of the Soviet Union, marked the end of the cold war.

4. From this foundational right to property comes the notion of an unfettered market, another key principle of classical liberalism. For more on the relationship between labor and property rights, see Locke, *Second Treatise*, 43.

5. For a clear overview of the current scholarly debates over Locke's role in the American political imagination, see Huyler, *Locke in America*, 1–28.

6. Locke, *Second Treatise*, 4.

7. Ibid., 6; Ruth W. Grant, *John Locke's Liberalism* (Chicago: University of Chicago Press, 1987), 72.

8. The most ardent proponent of the "safety valve" theory of western migration was *New York Tribune* editor Horace Greeley, who offered the famous slogan "Go West,

young man" as a recipe for alleviating the poverty caused by the panic of 1837. For more, see Henry Nash Smith, *Virgin Land: The American West as Symbol and Myth* (Cambridge, MA: Harvard University Press, 1950), 201–10; and Richard Slotkin, *Gunfighter Nation: The Myth of the Frontier in Twentieth-Century America* (Norman: University of Oklahoma Press, 1992), 10.

9. Donald Worster, *Under Western Skies: Nature and History in the American West* (New York: Oxford University Press, 1992), 233; Will Wright, *The Wild West: The Mythical Cowboy and Social Theory* (London: Sage, 2001), 6.

10. The Treaty of Guadalupe Hidalgo was signed in 1848, ending the Mexican-American War and ceding all of modern-day California, Nevada, and Utah, along with much of New Mexico, Colorado, Arizona, and Wyoming, to the United States.

11. Locke, *Second Treatise*, 89.

12. K. A. Cuordileone, *Manhood and American Political Culture in the Cold War* (New York: Routledge, 2005), 170, 28; Robert D. Dean, *Imperial Brotherhood: Gender and the Making of Cold War Foreign Policy* (Amherst: University of Massachusetts Press, 2001), 67.

13. Locke, *Second Treatise*, 6, 97, 134.

14. Lee Clark Mitchell, *Westerns: Making the Man in Fiction and Film* (Chicago: University of Chicago Press, 1996), 159.

15. Stanley Corkin, *Cowboys and Cold Warriors: The Western and U.S. History* (Philadelphia: Temple University Press, 2004), 10.

16. Brook Thomas, *American Literary Realism and the Failed Promise of Contract* (Berkeley: University of California Press, 1997), 3.

17. Though the McCarthy-chaired Senate Subcommittee on Investigations was three years in the past by the time *3:10 to Yuma* was filmed, and McCarthy himself died three months before the film was released, the film was unavoidably informed by the recent political climate of paranoia and lockstep republicanism.

LANDSCAPES OF GENDERED VIOLENCE

Male Love and Anxiety on the Railroad

Lindsey Collins

At President Obama's inaugural luncheon, hanging behind the president's table was Thomas Hill's *View of Yosemite Valley* (1885). Hill, a painter in the Hudson River tradition, is perhaps best known for his painting *The Last Spike* (1881), which commemorated the 1869 completion of the transcontinental railroad in Promontory Summit, Utah. Like the railroad's completion, Yosemite's preservation, decreed by Abraham Lincoln after the Civil War, was a symbol of national unity. Commenting on the significance of the painting chosen for Obama's inauguration, Senator Dianne Feinstein noted, "As a country struggled with Civil War, many Americans looked West to the dawn of a new era." Hill's painting, said Feinstein, captured "America's essence: our land of opportunity, optimism, and freedom."[1]

Though the inaugural luncheons, during which Congress formally welcomes the new president, have taken place since 1953, the tradition of choosing a specific painting for the event began only in 1985. According to the U.S. Senate's Web site, the chosen painting "reflects the official theme of each year's inaugural ceremony." The choice of a landscape is not completely new; of the seven inaugural paintings, three have been landscapes, one a depiction of the Capitol, and the others portraits: of Jefferson, Washington, and John Adams. President George W. Bush's 2005 inauguration showcased another Hudson River school painting, Albert Bierstadt's *Wind River, Wyoming* (1870), a choice meant to place Dick Cheney (with his Wyoming background) and Bush (self-fashioned as a Texan rancher) squarely within the Rooseveltian tradition of the self-made western man. Whether the inaugural paintings are rugged western landscapes like Yosemite or portraits of great American patriarchs such as Jefferson, they serve in this context the same rhetorical function: Great Men and Great Nature legitimize presidential authority and consolidate the nation.

I begin here, at Obama's luncheon, to suggest that the intertwining of masculinity, leadership, western landscapes, and the kinds of technologies that have made access to those landscapes possible comprises a narrative of national healing and progress that is still as viable and powerful, though differently inflected, as it was when Hill painted *The Last Spike*. Angela Miller has argued that classical American landscape painting has served primarily as a "retreat from history into nature": the landscapes depicted by Bierstadt, Hill, Thomas Moran, and Frederic Edwin Church are vast, awe-inspiring, and, for the most part, completely depopulated.[2] It is interesting, then, that Hill's painting, which shows a Yosemite without people, out of time and culture, is used as a national symbol specifically to anchor Obama within history, tying him both to Lincoln and to the symbolic promise of the American West. Hill's painting at Obama's inauguration is important, then, as much for what it is called upon to signify as for what it excludes: just beyond the painting's frame and Feinstein's speech is the tension between who gets left out of these landscapes (the Miwok, in this case) and who is included in the triumphant narrative of the election of the first African American president. Hill's painting and Feinstein's speech provide a means to reframe western films, particularly the ways that western films have engaged with railroads. In American painting, literature, and films, railroads have figured as a cut across rugged western landscapes, ambivalently signaling either these landscapes' imminent demise or the western dream coming to fruition. Trains and railroads created the material conditions of possibility for the "discovery" and symbolic burdening of the West, and as key elements of the representation of the West in paintings, photographs, and films, they are technologies that bring forth uneasy relationships between progress and nostalgia, masculine Anglo authority and lawlessness, and what counts as the U.S. national and natural body. The films I consider expose the strained seams of the triumphant story of the American West.

To describe how railroads in western films demonstrate both connection to and severance from highly gendered, racialized landscapes, I examine *3:10 to Yuma* (1957 and its remake of 2007) and *Tycoon* (1947). *3:10 to Yuma* is a story of failing rancher Dan Evans and his decision to help transport notorious outlaw Ben Wade to the train to Yuma prison. I consider the original *3:10 to Yuma* and its remake to illustrate the ways that trains animate masculinity and justice in western landscapes, and how issues of male homosociality, landscape, and modernity seem to have shifted in the fifty years between each version. *Tycoon* stars John Wayne as Johnny Munroe, a railroad engineer in the Andes who battles a railroad tycoon and the South American landscape to complete a tunnel project. Though many of the most familiar westerns are set in the American West, I argue that the domestication of space by the railroad is not limited to this country but is part of a broader transnational imperializing project.

As the transcontinental railroad was being completed in the late nineteenth century, this East-West orientation also produced the North-South axis as a space of desire and longing. Mexico and South America figure prominently in westerns as both hideouts for the bad guys and as the next best western frontier. When Butch Cassidy and the Sundance Kid run out of options in the West, they hop a train to Bolivia to make a not-so-clean start as bank robbers. Though its setting in South America may seem to challenge its consideration as a traditional western film, *Tycoon* provides an example of how the South becomes an imperial extension of the cultural imaginations of the American West. In American frontier ideology, looking west often also meant looking south, for expansionist discourses have long framed the South American frontier as a logical extension of the western frontier.[3]

Western films have been theorized primarily as sites of "binary battles—good versus evil, populists versus profiteers, and man versus nature."[4] Railroads and trains, however, make such binary readings difficult. Trains have occupied a central and conflicted position in westerns, as they have in American cultural imaginaries in general. As emblems of change and the abandonment of simple moral codes, they both displace and create nostalgia for the American frontier (*Johnny Guitar*, 1954) and enable lawlessness (*High Noon*, 1952) and the subsequent restoration of order (*3:10 to Yuma*). As central plot devices, railroads are multivalent and embattled. They are controlled by powerful corporations but available for resignification or robbery; they can herald progress or emasculating urbanization. If the western is supposedly about binaries of good and evil, city and countryside, cowboy and Indian, then trains, as technologies that literally move between these locations, make unsteady metaphors in films.

Rethinking trains in these films means rethinking what the West signifies and, in turn, reconsidering the ways in which the western's male hero has been understood to relate to his landscape. In *Landscapes of the New West*, Krista Comer argues that literary representations of the West have produced a western male subject with certain "spatial prerogatives." The "supremely confident, white masculinism" that dominates such representations is linked to a "particular kind of landscape perspective that operates here, that of panorama—the vast, unobstructed view from mountains and mountaintops." Such a viewpoint, one that enables mastery by fixing nature in the stable position of the bird's-eye view, "preserves what is fundamentally under assault in modernity: a place of Archimedean overview, a place that enables an unambiguous survey of a presumably stable social world."[5] Westerns embody this spatial prerogative perhaps more than any other genre, through the films' wide, panoramic shots, capturing the rugged landscape in a wide-angle lens, and the iconic masculine hero whose gaze surveys this territory. Indeed, the technologies of film and railroads worked concurrently to reinforce this paradigm. As Lynne Kirby argues in *Parallel Tracks*, a history of the silent film's development alongside the railroad, "the kind of perception that came to characterize the experience of the passenger on the train became that of the spectator in the cinema." For Kirby, "what early train travelers referred to as 'the annihilation of space and time' owed something to the effect of the panorama, an eighteenth-century invention that was the virtual reality experience of its day."[6]

Many feminist philosophers, such as Luce Irigaray, Susan Bordo, Elizabeth Grosz, and Donna Haraway, have pointed out the ways that masculinist philosophical traditions have participated in this panoramic epistemology by coding the mind as immaterial, disembodied, and male, and, conversely, the body as natural, material, and female. In this formulation, which Carolyn Merchant has critiqued forcefully, natural landscapes are the passive feminine proving ground for masculine projects of technology and progress.[7] In the films I consider, however, the landscape is unyielding and uncooperative, and the view from and of trains is not so straightforwardly panoramic, with all the identity-consolidating properties such a view confers. Rather, it is fraught with anxiety and failure, an always striving but never quite successful attempt to reconcile modernity, rationality, and masculinity. In *Tycoon* and *3:10 to Yuma*, trains make an unobstructed view difficult, if not impossible. The kinds of spatiotemporal experiences trains allow are always partial: smoke, dust, overwhelming noise, and unreliability are railroads' constant companions, even as railroads are put to the service of empire building.[8]

Railroad Histories: Anxiety in Motion

Just as the railroad changed people's relationship to time and space by shrinking the continent and providing a view of the world in motion, the railroad's financial and material presence accelerated the development of movies, another technology that altered people's relationship to time. The "motion" in "motion picture" is bound up with trains in almost every way. One important example of this relationship is San Franciscan Eadweard Muybridge's studies of photography and motion that led to films, accomplished in large part by the patronage of transcontinental railroad robber baron Leland Stanford. And there's also the motion of artists, tourists, and filmmakers on trains that carried them from East to West, which was the subject of the most popular kind of early films, and later the hub of the film industry itself.[9]

The earliest popular, nonnarrative American films, called "actuality pictures," were often made as advertisements by railroads, chambers of commerce, hotels, and boosters in Colorado and other "unsettled" western states to promote tourism and development. Andrew Brodie Smith explains, "Railroads were among the first businesses to recognize the promotional value of moving pictures. . . . A natural affinity existed between the railroad and cinema. Films made from moving trains showed off the new medium's ability to record movement and register speed."[10] In 1905, George C. Hale opened a theater that looked like a railroad car called Hale's Tours and Scenes of the World. "Ticket sellers dressed like conductors, and signs advertised excursions to exotic locations" while the train car swayed and rumbled with the film's motions.[11] Learning about the West, then, was also bound up in learning to be a good film spectator, to produce an entirely new relationship to space and time. One could experience the rumbling of the railcar in time with the film, located on a train in a different but theoretically simultaneous time and place.

The history of wilderness preservation in the American West is also deeply dependent on railroad patronage. In "Trains in the Wilderness," Kevin DeLuca argues that the Southern Pacific railroad was instrumental in helping preserve Yosemite. Even as the Californian naturalist and writer John Muir lamented its arrival, the Southern Pacific was crucial to Muir's preservation efforts. Southern Pacific executives were among first Sierra Club members, and in 1890 Muir appealed to owner Henry Harriman to help win Yosemite's federal protection. The Southern Pacific had long transported tourists and subsidized photographers and artists to record Yosemite, and in 1898 the railroad founded *Sunset* magazine as a forum for these artistic renderings. DeLuca writes, "Literally, then, through photographs, paintings, and literary essays the railroads fashioned a corporate rhetoric that promulgated park formation and wilderness preservation. . . . Promoting the spectacular wilderness scenery of the West served the twofold purpose of luring folks to ride the trains as tourists and persuading them to settle in the West as pioneers."[12] The railroad thus helped make the West available for the dream of national unity forged through bodily and natural unity. The West's representation was accomplished through the physical mobility afforded by trains and through tourism and the resulting photographic records it inspired.

This dream was not bounded by the borders of the U.S. nation, but instead gave way to what Ricardo Salvatore calls an "imperial mechanics." The possibility of a pan-American railway that would connect all the capitals of the American continent was first discussed at the 1889–90 meeting of the American republics in Washington. Though the pan-American railroad was never created, the imperial mechanics that produced a longing for a United States intimately connected to South America demonstrate the kind of "mechanical utopianism" that informs *Tycoon.*[13]

As I have mentioned, the imperial transnational ambitions embodied in trains were not unchecked utopian fantasies, but instead have been constantly accompanied by concerns about how railroad technology might change American landscape and national character. In *The Machine in the Garden*, Marx relates a story about Nathaniel Hawthorne, who in 1844 was describing in his notebook an idyllic scene in Concord, Massachusetts, when a train whistle intruded. Hawthorne wrote, "But, hark! there is the whistle of the locomotive—the long shriek, harsh, above all other harshness, for the space of a mile cannot mollify it into harmony." Marx explains how pastoral pleasure is transformed into dissonance: "Now tension replaces repose: the noise arouses a sense of dislocation, conflict, and anxiety."[14] The train is both progress and nostalgia: the pastoral ideal is tainted, but the train is the means by which one can traverse a landscape. This ambivalence registered by Hawthorne, and later by Thoreau and Emerson, is accompanied by literary denouncements such as Frank Norris's 1901 *Octopus,* in which Norris famously calls the train "the galloping monster, the terror of steel and steam . . . the leviathan, with tentacles of steel clutching into the soil, the soulless Force, the iron-hearted Power, the monster, the Colossus, the Octopus."[15]

But as Patricia Nelson Limerick and Mark Klett argue, Leo Marx's machine in the garden is about an eastern pastoral, not the failed arid landscapes of the West. As they wryly note, Marx's theory applied to the West would be better called "Abandoned Machine in the Desert."[16] In the films I consider, trains are situated somewhere between romantic ambivalence and Frank Norris's fearsome machines. Trains both threaten and consolidate national and natural masculine bodily unity. Despite the narratives of heroic masculinity and western progress that these films may offer, I argue that trains and railroads are technologies that give rise to transitional masculinities, or masculinities that must always define themselves against the specters of time, as well as gendered and racial Others, and that also expose the landscapes of the West and of the male self as landscapes of failure.

In westerns, trains create a narrative structure in which drama is produced through the elements of motion, standardized time, and violence. The earliest model for this was the Edison Company's *The Great Train Robbery* of 1903, described as the first western film, which sparked a flurry of American film production of crime films about the West. Nine minutes long, the film was based on Butch Cassidy's train robbery in Wyoming and served "loosely as a narrative model for gun-wielding crime and horse-chase retribution."[17] *The Great Train Robbery* is a productive site for thinking about how narrative, motion, film, western tourism, and train technology and the anxiety it produces come together. The film was shot in New Jersey: the four train robbers flee into a wooded area with a creek, rather than escaping into a rugged canyon or a dry, open expanse. Geographical details aside, the film transferred the popular English crime genre into the West, thus making it a viable, profitable filmic subject. *The Great Train Robbery* is "significant in its advance of narrative continuity under the auspices of the station's railroad clock."[18] Unlike *3:10 to Yuma* and *Tycoon*'s interest in individual male protagonists, the film focuses on groups—the robbers, the passengers forced to disembark from the train, and the posse recruited to pursue the criminals. But the film's final scene involves the viewer in the action when the head train robber, alone in the frame, points his pistol at the audience and fires. The film ends in a cloud of gun smoke. This scene, stunning to its contemporary audiences, suggests that the action produced by standardized, simultaneous time is inescapable. The railroad narrative inaugurated by *The Great Train Robbery* illustrates what Lauren Berlant calls "the National Symbolic," which she defines as "the technology of collective fantasy" that registers "an intense, complex, and conceptually incoherent experience of Anglo-American manhood."[19]

If films about trains produced a collective fantasy of rationalized time and justice, the railroad's insistence on standardized time also produces anxiety about successfully performing masculine duties. In *Tycoon*, Johnny Munroe cracks under the strain of completing a safe, sound railroad tunnel in his boss's time frame and before a big flood hits. In *3:10 to Yuma*, Dan Evans clutches a pocket watch in anticipation and dread of the arriving train that will take Ben Wade to prison. These narratives of masculine success are also threatened by the presence of the heroes' Others. For Johnny Munroe, it is his wife's presence in a landscape where she doesn't belong, and Chinese railroad workers are unsettling to Dan Evans's group as it transports Ben Wade through the mountains.

Lynne Kirby explains how the late nineteenth century's views of hysteria as a specifically female disease were modified by theories of male hysteria, a condition produced by increased train travel, and thus increased train accidents, which caused "traumatic neuroses" such as "railway spine" and "railway brain." These problems were supposedly more common among working-class men, surprisingly, and not the "effeminate men of the idle class." The French neurologist Charcot, an early psychological theorist, described the sufferers of this condition in an 1888 study as "those who experience in their bodies and lives the metaphor of a characteristic trait of hysteria—mobility." Kirby explains,

> If mobility of mind is one of the chief characteristics of female hysteria (the rapid ease with which the hysteric passes from laughter to tears, for example), mobility of social place is the male hysterical equivalent. . . .
>
> In a kind of mirror image of otherness, one can see that cultural displacement as massive as nineteenth-century mechanization and urbanization—railway-assisted—traumatized its victims into a condition akin to female hysteria. In other words, it "emasculated" men, and not only those men of a certain class. Women, proletarian men, tramps, and other social marginals were made to bear the brunt of the shocks of modernity. Yet, as standard-bearers of the pathologies of modern culture, these signifiers of non-middle-class men were the frightening symbols of what middle-class men were in danger of becoming as potential victims of hysteria, the psychic

disease of a modernism to which all were subject: the social and sexual Other.[20]

Though the highly rationalized, panoramic consciousness produces a colonizing subjectivity, this "train-infected consciousness" creates an inherently unstable, yet always transitional masculinity.[21] Trains in *Tycoon* and *3:10 to Yuma* seem to be narrative devices for accepting progress, mastering one's destiny, and becoming the right sort of western man. But the anxious currents in the films themselves present, in fact, a very different sort of western hero, one whose movement through failed landscapes reflects the instabilities inherent to the projects of colonialism and masculinity, an instability constitutive of the technologies of films and railroads themselves.[22]

Tycoon: Women, Nature, Trains, Trouble

Richard Wallace's *Tycoon* (1947), starring John Wayne as a railroad engineer in South America, nicely crystallizes western films' preoccupation with railroads as technologies that enable manhood, delimit industrial versus "wild," spectacular, panoramic landscapes, and protect and restore proper femininity to both women and the land. A big-budget effort by RKO, the film attempted to capitalize on the iconic status of its lead star as a western hero, even though it did not bill itself as a western per se.[23] There are, however, significant shared elements, particularly John Wayne's consolidation of masculinity vis-à-vis his effeminate foil: the hard-living John Wayne fights the excesses of wealth and corporate control embodied by the railroad's owner, Mr. Alexander (Cedric Hardwicke), a dandy in a velvet smoking jacket who paints still lifes and boasts of European travel.

Though Wayne isn't battling Indians or leading a cavalry in *Tycoon*, his masculinity is central to the film, and it is important to consider the film not as an unsuccessful nonwestern detour for the actor, but as an integral part of Wayne's body of work that links the West to the South through railroad technology. In *Tycoon*'s opening scene, railroad engineer Johnny Munroe reprimands a young South American boy who is playing at being an engineer like Johnny. After Chico (Fernando Alvarado), whose name, literally "Boy," reinscribes the film's white-brown, man-boy power differences, gets too close to the blasting and his friend is scratched by falling debris, Johnny disciplines him in front of his friends with a mock punch to the face, saying, "A good engineer doesn't get his men hurt, and if he does, he has to be punished." Chico returns to his friends, bragging, "He hit me with his fist because I am an engineer. But you, he would take down your britches and paddle your rump." South America here figures as an extension of the already closed American West, a place where (white) labor is carefully managed and valued by head engineer Johnny Munroe, and where South American boys can hope to become part of the American patriarchal family by becoming civilized, masculine adults through railroad technology.

The film's love interest, the racially ambiguous Maura (Laraine Day), is controlled by her father, Alexander the railroad tycoon, who manages her "like a railroad or a mine." In an early meeting, Johnny and Maura have a sexually charged conversation in which Johnny demonstrates, with the aid of his hat and Maura's scarf as props, how he'll ravage the landscape with dynamite and heavy machinery to complete the railroad first through the Andes and next "anywhere they want a railroad—Alaska, China, Tibet," as Maura looks on adoringly. Maura's father walks in on this scene of seduction and quickly asks Johnny to leave. The boundaries of sexual propriety have been transgressed not because of Johnny and Maura's close physical prox-imity or inappropriate flirtation, though the stodgy Mr. Alexander clearly doesn't appreciate this uninvited visitor to his daughter. The sexual conno-tations of Johnny and Maura's conversation are formed not through their bodies but through allegories of femininity and masculinity, traits rescripted as untouched female landscape changed and improved by the marvels of western male technical prowess. Maura's scarf, like the South American landscape itself, is the raw, feminine material that is ripe for empire build-ing in the Andes and at home. When his relationship with Maura becomes difficult due to her father's interference, Johnny complains to a friend as he's dynamiting the railroad's tunnel, "women trouble, trouble, women, they're all the same thing." Tunneling through the South American mountains means intimate and dangerous contact with a resistant, feminized landscape.

In Johnny's conversations with other men, there is a constant slippage between Maura and the railroad. After the tunnel collapses a third time and kills Johnny's good friend Curly (Michael Harvey), Johnny's approach to the project changes drastically. Instead of continuing to battle Alexander for safer materials for the tunnel, he forges ahead with building a bridge over the river, his original plan all along; but now he acts callously, pursuing the bridge's completion without regard for his men's safety. Even the hard-nosed Alexander becomes alarmed at Johnny's business practices; visiting the site one day, he says, "I'll give you a ninety-day extension if you like." Johnny responds, "You gave me a wedding once. Since then I've been very careful about what I accept from the Alexanders." After Curly's death, Maura accuses her father of denying Johnny raw materials, like lumber and rails, and implicates her father in Curly's death by accusing him of deliberately sabotaging the tunnel project through cheap, unsafe construction to spite Johnny, her new husband. But Maura's decision to leave Johnny and return home coincides with the tunnel's collapse, suggesting again that South America and the railroad become embodied in Maura as feminized landscapes in progress, to be brought into full womanhood by the furrowing and tunneling technologies of masculine western progress and heterosexual romance. The bridge cannot be completed without Maura's return, Chico's assimilation, and the triumph of masculine group work.[24]

In the film's final action scenes, a big flood moves down the Rio, threatening to tear down the bridge and expose Johnny's cost-cutting engineering. Having alienated all of his former white colleagues with his brash disregard for their safety, Johnny runs to the Rio in a downpour and tries to pay the local South American men to help him reinforce the bridge. After they refuse to perform such a dangerous task for any amount of payment, the omnipresent Chico follows a beaten Johnny into his house, and like a good white engineer in training, Chico distances himself from the brown workers by saying, "The men are stinkers. They will not work." Fortunately for Johnny, Maura comes home to save their marriage and tell him that his disaffected white colleagues have stepped up to perform their duty as white men and engineers. But ultimately, Johnny is not the hero, and there is no technical triumph over nature. Despite working through the night and Johnny's brave and dangerous effort to drive a train onto the bridge to weight it down and salvage the structure, when the flood hits, the middle of the bridge collapses and sends the train plummeting hundreds of feet below into the river gorge. Nevertheless, heroism happens in (white) groups of men. White men do the work—the locals are "stinkers."

Despite the film's happy conclusion—Johnny and Maura reunite, his formerly angry coworkers become supportive board members, and Alexander finds love and makes Johnny the boss again—Johnny Munroe is less an independent hero than someone deeply dependent on the capital of South America, his white labor force, and the availability of an inconstant supply of feminine nurturing. The train ultimately pitches off the bridge when the flood comes down the river, suggesting that the technical landscape ultimately fails, but Johnny is reincorporated into the folds of patriarchal capital. Though trains and tunnels fail, masculinity is given just enough to survive, even as it's shown to be just a farce. The train is conscripted into a narrative of triumphant masculinity, though the victory is fragile and the prospect of failure is constantly exposed.

3:10 to Yuma: Male Love and the Railroad Plot

If *Tycoon* is about the attempt to consolidate masculine wholeness through nature and woman, *3:10 to Yuma*, especially its 2007 remake, demonstrates the acute anxiety and scenes of violence that trains produce, only to be assuaged by male homosocial love. Though I discuss the 1957 original, I focus primarily on the remake because of the complex ways it develops the love plot between criminal Ben Wade (Russell Crowe) and rancher Dan Evans (Christian Bale).

The film's 2007 version opens with a scene that coalesces the meta-histories embedded in travel to the West: fourteen-year-old William (Logan Lerman), Dan Evans's son, lies in bed, around which are scattered dime novels, such as one called *The Deadly Outlaw,* while beside him his younger brother, Mark, who has been brought to Arizona to overcome tuberculo-sis, wheezes in bed.[25] William hears a noise outside. Hollander (Lennie Loftin), a land baron in cahoots with the railroad whom Dan owes money, has sent men to burn down the family's barn in the night. Dan limps over to the window—his leg, we learn, was partially amputated after an injury sustained fighting for the Union army—not to scare off his attackers, but to grab the gun William is holding. When Dan assures William, "I'll take care of this," William replies with contempt, "No, you won't." Even his younger son, Mark, who still believes in his father as a war hero and capable man, is dubious of Dan's ability to handle the situation:

> DAN: I'm gonna tell Hollander to make this right. I'm gonna tell him to pay for a new barn.
> MARK: Maybe we should just shoot him, like Will says.

National and familial reproduction is what's at stake in these first scenes. How can the family, the ranch, the western dream hold when William tells his father, "I ain't ever walking in your shoes"? Dan, a failing rancher in drought-afflicted Arizona, has rising debts, two young boys, one of whom is recovering from tuberculosis, and a wife to support. When notorious outlaw Ben Wade and his gang ride through Dan's property to hold up a railroad-owned stagecoach, Dan is again emasculated in front of his boys, especially William, who watches in disgust as his father lets Ben Wade and his outlaws make off with their horses. Butterfield (Dallas Roberts), a Southern Pacific executive, offers Dan $200 to transport Wade to Contention City to be put on the 3:10 train to Yuma prison. Defending this dangerous decision to accept this offer to his wife, Dan pleads, "In six months from now, everything's gonna be green. Cows are gonna be fat. We might even see the steam from the train coming over the ridge. We'll be alright. But we won't make it through the next six days if I don't do this. . . . I'm tired of the way the boys look at me. I'm tired of the way that you don't. I've been standing on one leg for three damn years, waiting for God to do me a favor. And he ain't listening." If natural landscapes are failures, beset by drought and vicious landlords, then the railroad's man-made landscapes offer possible salvation. Yet the Southern Pacific's progress narrative, the promise of its peaceful, pastoral coexistence with the green grass and healthy cattle on the ranch, also constantly undermines Dan's livelihood. Like Dan's conscription into the Union army during the Civil War, his decision to help Butterfield transport Wade isn't really a choice. The $200 the Union army pays Dan for his injured leg is too little too late, another emasculating disavowal of Dan's body, which has literally sacrificed itself for the nation. At every turn, Dan is reminded of his lack of masculine agency: his son's cutting words, his stolen horses and dying cattle, his barn that the railroad burns down, his wife's sly admiration of Ben Wade when he compliments her eyes.

In the 1957 version, Dan Evans, played by Van Heflin, is a man who has resigned himself to his bad luck. Yet despite this surrender to fate, he is portrayed as someone who still can make decisions like a man. When Dan returns home from the scene of the stagecoach robbery, his wife, Alice, questions his actions. But Dan retains his sons' admiration and respect when he replies that there's "not much else I can do." Like the drought, Ben Wade and his gang constrain the choices available to Dan. When Alice asks why he didn't do anything to stop Wade, Dan replies, "What, and get myself shot, too?" When she remarks how terrible it is that Wade killed a man on the stagecoach, Dan shrugs, "That's life—lightning can kill you. Three years of drought are killing my cattle. That's terrible, too." Van Heflin's inaction here reads like pragmatism, caution, and rationality, all hallmarks of a good western hero, versus Christian Bale's resentment, fear, and reluctance.

There are also some substantial differences between Glenn Ford's Ben Wade in 1957 and Russell Crowe's in 2007. While in the original, Ben Wade is a coy, manipulative and charming criminal, in the remake, Wade is equal parts conscienceless killer and a sensitive nature lover who sketches a hawk before slaughtering the survivors of the derailed stagecoach. Like Daniel Boone or Mary Louise Pratt's sensitive colonizer-naturalist, or "seeing-man," Wade is a romantic, well-traveled figure.[26] He romances the barmaid, promising to take her to Mexico. After their tryst he sketches her, nude and reclining, and later sketches Dan as they wait for the train's arrival in a hotel's bridal suite. And, like Natty Bumppo and Boone, Wade is attuned to the ways and plight of Native Americans.[27] One night, as his captors camp out on their way to Contention City, Wade saves Dan's life from an Apache ambush by sensing their presence, sneaking up on them as the Apache fire on the camp, and slaughtering all three of them single-handedly. Later, Wade accuses his captor Byron McElroy (Peter Fonda), a railroad merce-nary, of gunning down Apache women and children when he was working for Central railroad: "Byron acts pious. A few years ago, when he was under contract with Central, I seen him and a bunch of other Pinks mow down thirty-two Apache women and children. . . . There was young ones running around crying and screaming, no more than three years old. And his boys shot them all, then pushed them into a ditch. Some of them was still crying. I guess Byron figured that Jesus wouldn't mind. Apparently Jesus don't like the Apache." Wade is lawless, but at least he isn't a Pinkerton. His morality exists outside of structures of capital and railroad power.[28]

On one level, the film is a story about Dan Evans's almost monomaniacal devotion to masculine notions of duty, honor, and what's right, and as such he represents a clear good guy who works against Wade's badness. Dan and Wade inhabit the West in fundamentally different ways. Wade operates with a gang of devoted lackeys, while Dan struggles to command the respect of his young boys. Wade abides by the code that "it's in a man's nature to take what he wants," while Dan follows the law until his last breath. The film is set up as a struggle between these two forms of existence: lawlessness and order. In the original, this binary narrative is fairly uncomplicated. But in the remake, if the railroad is the narrative device that moves Wade toward justice, Dan toward redemption, and his family's existence toward stabil-ity, then the film reminds us that this narrative is inherently unstable. If the railroad is the path of justice, it is also the path of Pinkertons, and related to the violent slaughter of Native Americans, the exploitation of Chinese labor, and the corporate erasure of the western dream of small ranches and big, free open spaces. An unstable narrative, that is, to everyone but Dan. The narrative's movement forward in time along the railroad to the station in Contention, always anticipating its inevitable arrival for the 3:10 train, reads like a script that everyone except Dan knows he has to follow in order to become someone, to get a leg to stand on. It is this anticipatory movement itself along the railroad's narrative and spatiotemporal axis that legitimizes Dan in advance of his success, and regardless of the outcome of his dangerous task. When Dan tells William to go back home to the ranch, he says to his son, "You just remember that your old man walked Ben Wade to that station when no one else would."

Although William has begun to respect his father again, suggesting that the railroad's path to masculinity and justice is a reliable one, the film undercuts this stability by illuminating the love between Dan and Wade and the anxiety of racial difference along the railroad. After the Apache attack, Wade escapes from Dan and his group, but they find him again at a Chinese railroad work site, captured and being tortured by the white railroad engineers. In this brief but crucial scene, William locks eyes with a Chinese boy his age working in the mountain tunnels. While Dan single-mindedly pursues his captive, the Chinese boy, who is pushing an overloaded wheelbarrow down the tracks, glares at William resentfully. William returns this gaze with awe and discomfort in this scene of violence, exploitation, and racial difference. The railroad tunnel is a site in which people lay claims to different versions of morality. Boles, the railroad foreman, justifies torturing Wade because he killed his brother, while the doctor in Dan's group argues, "You can't do that, it's immoral." But Dan's version of morality isn't based on vengeance or universal humanism. Dan and the doctor shoot Wade's captors, liberate Wade, and throw dynamite in the tunnel to make their escape, illustrating that some forms of violence are more valid than others. In Dan's version, forward motion along the railroad's regime of standardized time is the only possible path to masculine honor and justice. But for this plot to work, Dan must disavow the discomfort that William feels in the presence of racial Otherness.

The film's homoeroticism also interrupts the railroad plot. From their very first encounter, Wade relates to Dan with bemused affection and indulgence. When Wade's posse scatters Dan's cattle during the stagecoach holdup, Dan asserts, "I need 'em back. They're all I got." Though he is soft-spoken, Dan's demeanor is deadly serious, as it is for the majority of the movie.

Wade's expression in this scene, however, is one of amusement and tenderness: Dan's mild assertiveness is endearing. There are stark differences in the ways that homosocial love is played out between the 1957 and 2007 versions, especially in the love triangle between Dan, Wade, and Wade's lackey Charlie Prince (Ben Foster). In the original, Wade's gang relaxes in a bar while Wade ogles the pretty barmaid. Charlie sits at the opposite end of the bar, and then leaves Wade to his seduction. When another gang member wonders where the boss is, Charlie replies, "Don't worry about him, he'll be along. He can handle that hick posse single-handed. Yah!" and rides out of town. In the remake, Charlie sits right next to Wade at the bar, noticing his interest in the barmaid. With downcast, humbled eyes, Charlie says softly, "Marshal's only half stupid. He's gonna be back soon. You're going across the border? I won't be far. I'll wait for you." Wade brushes him off, never looking at him: "Alright, Charlie."

The scenes of Wade's desire for the barmaid match those of his desire for Dan almost exactly. Though Dan doesn't get naked, both couples retire to rooms, where Wade lovingly sketches their portraits. As Dan and Wade await the 3:00 hour in a hotel bridal suite, Wade lies on his back on the bridal bed: "So this is the bridal suite. I wonder how many brides have taken in this view." If Wade is a virginal bride, he is a crafty one. He almost seduces Dan into letting him go with offers of money so that Dan can send his boys to school and be a "bona fide Arizona rancher." Though Dan is tempted, he can't consummate his masculinity and honor with Wade in the bridal suite—the pull of the railroad justice plot is too strong.

Though Dan resists being derailed by Wade's seduction, he often seeks Wade's approval, suggesting that attaining masculine legitimacy means being sanctioned not only by the railroad's model of justice but by Wade's love as well. The scenes in which Dan courts and receives Wade's approval are usually accompanied by violence, such as when Wade taunts Dan by the campfire one evening:

WADE: I imagine debt puts a lot of pressure on a marriage.
DAN: You imagine? What do you know about marriage? We can't all
    be cutthroats and thieves.
WADE: Well, I know if I was lucky enough to have a wife like Alice, I'd
    treat her a whole lot better than you do, Dan. I'd feed her better,
    buy her pretty dresses, wouldn't make her work so hard. Yeah, I
    bet Alice was a real pretty girl before she married you.

Dan has had enough: he jumps up and puts his rifle against Wade's neck, threatening to "cut him down" if he hears another word about his wife. But though Wade's insults jab at Dan's ability to be a good husband, they result in Dan being incorporated into Wade's model of masculinity and in an expression of affection when Wade smiles and says, "I like this side of you, Dan."

Another moment of intimate violence is when Dan successfully gets Wade to the station. When Wade can't convince Dan to take his money and go home, Wade begins to fully cooperate, becoming an extension of Dan's body by shooting some of Dan's would-be assassins on the way to the station. Wade demonstrates that the nature of the railroad plot is a serious joke. Wade humors Dan by allowing him to take him to the train, partially out of his love and respect for Dan, but also because he recognizes that only through Dan's death will Dan be able to earn respect in legitimate, socially sanctioned ways. Dan reveals some distance from his own plot, however, when he seeks Wade's approval. While they hunker down in the station to wait for the train, Dan tells Wade, "I ain't stubborn. . . . You said I was stubborn." Even though Wade thinks Dan is foolish for keeping his family on a dying ranch, Dan remains there so that Mark can breathe dry air and recover from tuberculosis. Wade has a confession of his own: he's escaped from Yuma prison twice. This confession has the power to unravel Dan's entire reason for being, his belief in the railroad model of masculinity and justice, yet Dan and Wade start laughing together. Dan courts Wade's approval, and Wade tells Dan that his efforts are probably in vain. Nevertheless, Wade continues to shoot at his own men to defend Dan's efforts to put him on the train.

The film's final scenes illustrate the simultaneous seriousness and fragility of the railroad plot. The train rumbles into the station, obscuring everything with its gigantic plumes of smoke and deafening engine. Close-ups of the smokestack position the train as a powerful technology that obliterates and overwhelms the human scale. Yet the train is late, hardly a model of rationalized time and justice, and since Butterfield has reneged on his offer to help Dan take Wade to the station, Wade has to put himself in the prison car. No officers of the law or railroad are there to ensure order. The train's only passengers are old men who appear to be hobos. When Charlie Prince fires fatal shots into Dan's back and then tosses Wade his confiscated pistol, Wade shoots Charlie point-blank in the heart, grabbing him by the shirt to bring the two face-to-face. Charlie's devotion to Wade violates Wade's love for Dan, which includes helping Dan follow the railroad plot to its conclusion and thereby attain masculine legitimacy.

Like Lynne Kirby, Kristin Ross tells a story of the rise of technologies of motion—trains, films, cars—that form new, panoramic ways of seeing and thereby create "l'homme disponible," or "moveable, available man (or woman) . . . open to the new demands of the market." Fueled by the "acceleration in commodity production and circulation," l'homme disponible is able to continuously "recas[t] his identity by means of continuous displacement."[29] But for Dan, railroad space and time is still a trap, though it's the only game in town.

Lauren Berlant's notion of "cruel optimism" helps makes sense of Dan's continued investment in the railroad plot. Berlant describes cruel optimism as an affective mode that arises particularly in neoliberal economies, but it is relevant to the railroad's (failed) promises of progress, rationality, and justice. Berlant defines cruel optimism as "a relation of attachment to compromised conditions of possibility," particularly for "people without control over the material conditions of their lives and whose relation to fantasy is all that protects them from being destroyed by other people and the nation."[30] Berlant continues, "What is cruel about these attachments . . . is that subjects who have x in their lives might not well endure the loss of their object or scene of desire, even though its presence threatens their well-being, because whatever the *content* of the attachment, the continuity of the form of it provides something of the continuity of the subject's sense of what it means to keep on living on and to look forward to being in the world." Ordinary life is a state of crisis for Dan, bound and imprisoned by natural time: the rains that will save his ranch will come when they come. But by attaching himself to the train, Dan emplots himself in a narrative in which motion to and along the railroad will bring security, the certitude of standardized time, and familial and patriarchal reproduction, even as Dan's faith in the railroad spells his death. Berlant writes, "Some scenes of optimism are crueler than others. Where cruel optimism operates, the very vitalizing or animating potency of an object/scene of desire contributes to the attrition of the very thriving that is supposed to be made possible in the work of attachment in the first place."[31] The film repeatedly acknowledges the hopelessness of Dan's optimism, particularly when Ben Wade's horse gallops alongside the train in the final scene, signaling his imminent (third) escape and the futility of such a powerful machine against the western outlaw. Yet Dan's sacrifice for the railroad still reads as heroism, legitimized by the indulgences of male love. Like Dan's family's ranch, the railroad plot's continuity is assured, held together by cruelty, anxiety, and love.

Notes

Thanks to Rachel Churner, Kate Coffie, John Marlovitz, and Lara Rogers for their extensive, very helpful comments and discussion.

1. U.S. Senate Art and History: Inaugural Luncheon, http://www.senate.gov/artandhistory/art/common/collection_list/inaugural_luncheons.htm (accessed January 6, 2010).

2. Angela Miller, "Albert Bierstadt, Landscape Aesthetics, and the Meanings of the West in the Civil War Era," *Art Institute of Chicago Museum Studies* 27, no. 1 (2001): 40–59.

3. When the popular nineteenth-century landscape painter Frederic Edwin Church was composing scenes of the Rockies and Sierras, he was simultaneously exhibiting his immense panoramic paintings of South America, such as his popular *Heart of the Andes* (1859).

4. Deborah Carmichael, ed., *Landscapes of the Hollywood Western: Ecocriticism in an American Film Genre* (Salt Lake City: University of Utah Press, 2006), 1.

5. Krista Comer, *Landscapes of the New West: Gender and Geography in Contemporary Women's Writing* (Chapel Hill: University of North Carolina Press, 1999), 24.

6. Lynne Kirby, *Parallel Tracks: The Railroad and Silent Cinema* (Durham, NC: Duke University Press, 1997), 7.

7. See Susan Bordo, "Feminist Skepticism and the 'Maleness' of Philosophy," *Journal of Philosophy* 85, no. 11 (1988): 619–29; Elizabeth Grosz, *Volatile Bodies: Toward a Corporeal Feminism* (Bloomington: Indiana University Press, 1994); Donna Haraway, "The Persistence of Vision," in *Writing on the Body: Female Embodiment and Feminist Theory*, ed. Katie Conboy, Nadia Medina, and Sarah Stanbury (New York: Columbia University Press, 1997), 283–95; Carolyn Merchant, *The Death of Nature: Women, Ecology, and the Scientific Revolution* (San Francisco: Harper & Row, 1980). For a good assessment of Luce Irigaray, Julia Kristeva, and Judith Butler's contributions to analyses of spatiality and political transformation, see Jenny Robinson, "Feminism and the Spaces of Transformation," *Transactions of the Institute of British Geographers* 25, no. 3 (2000): 285–301.

8. Comer (*Landscapes of the New West*) describes the ways that secondary and critical writings about western literature also tend to reproduce these kinds of spatial and masculine prerogatives. A word here about my methodology and how it relates to philosophizing westerns: in the interest of not repeating celebratory narratives of western exceptionalism, I insist upon the mutual importance of philosophical, literary, and historical approaches to western films. As a counterexample to my approach, see Peter French's *Cowboy Metaphysics: Ethics and Death in Westerns* (Lanham, MD: Rowman & Littlefield, 1997). French's writing about westerns exemplifies the problematic cordoning off of philosophy from material, historical legacies of racism in the West that produce masculinist ways of reading and legitimizing texts. French's book, which is,

ironically, about ethics in western films, takes as its subject "cowboys, gunslingers, etc.," and explicitly excludes Native Americans because they are not what French calls "the 'westerners'" (x). Furthermore, French writes, "In this book, I am interested in what is on the screen, not in what ought to be there if only some more 'sensitive guy' . . . had been behind the camera. . . . I will not be criticizing the way Westerns portray American Indians or blacks. . . . I have restricted myself to the Westerns that do not particularly feature minorities, and, in any event, I will not be using the opportunity to discuss the issues I want to raise in Westerns to reiterate those well-worn, though clearly appropriate, criticisms of the way Hollywood, until quite recently, represented minorities" (xi). French's expression of celebratory, unmarked white privilege in his introduction, accomplished through his nostalgic anecdotes about growing up in the 1940s watching the identity-shaping films in "opulent theaters," is part and parcel of his philosophical methodology, in which race, class, and gender are add-on categories (and, stunningly, not relevant "until quite recently") for reading films, and not constitutive of the films and western history itself.

9. Rebecca Solnit, *River of Shadows: Eadweard Muybridge and the Technological Wild West* (New York: Viking, 2003).

10. Andrew Brodie Smith, *Shooting Cowboys and Indians: Silent Western Films, American Culture, and the Birth of Hollywood* (Boulder: University of Colorado Press, 2003), 12.

11. Ibid., 19.

12. Kevin DeLuca, "Trains in the Wilderness: The Corporate Roots of Environmentalism," *Rhetoric and Public Affairs* 4, no. 4 (2001): 633–52.

13. Ricardo Salvatore, "Imperial Mechanics: South America's Hemispheric Integration in the Machine Age," *American Quarterly* 58, no. 3 (2006): 662–91. Also see Aims McGuiness, *Paths of Empire: Panama and the California Gold Rush* (Ithaca, NY: Cornell University Press, 2009).

14. Leo Marx, *The Machine in the Garden: Technology and the Pastoral Ideal in America* (New York: Oxford University Press, 1964), 13–14, 16.

15. Frank Norris, *The Octopus: A Story of California* (New York: Doubleday, 1901), 36.

16. Patricia Nelson Limerick and Mark Klett, "Haunted by Rhyolite: Learning from the Landscape of Failure," *American Art* 6, no. 4 (1992): 34.

17. Scott Simmon, *The Invention of the Western Film: A Cultural History of the Genre's First Half-Century* (Cambridge: Cambridge University Press, 2003), 8.

18. Kirby, *Parallel Tracks*, 55.

19. Lauren Berlant, *The Anatomy of National Fantasy: Hawthorne, Utopia, and Everyday Life* (Chicago: University of Chicago Press, 1991), 5.

20. Kirby, *Parallel Tracks*, 67.

21. Ibid., 53.

22. Ibid., 66–67. Kirby argues, "Discourses on the train's representation in film might

be said to reflect a fundamental instability common to both technologies. The instability of the railroad lies first of all in the very experience of mobility, of a passenger's being at once immobile and in rapid transit, lulled to sleep and yet capable of being shocked awake. . . . In cinema, instability is built into the basis of the filmgoing experience: the perceptual illusion of movement is tied to the physical immobility of the spectator and to the sequential unfolding of a chain of still images that constitute the basis of every film" (3).

23. Wayne's appearance in *Tycoon* comes after several B-westerns and John Ford's successful *Stagecoach* (1939), but just before his legendary status in westerns really became sedimented. Much has been written about John Wayne as an iconic western figure in both film and politics. See Garry Wills, *John Wayne's America: The Politics of Celebrity* (New York: Simon & Schuster, 1997); and James T. Campbell, " 'Print the Legend': John Wayne and Postwar American Culture," *Reviews in American History* 28, no. 3 (2000): 465–77. Campbell describes how John Wayne has been an icon for American conservatives like Pat Buchanan and Newt Gingrich (466).

24. Campbell argues, "Wayne's characters were not Indian haters, but men who 'knew' and respected Indians and were esteemed by them in turn. Yet the conclusion was the same: the Indians must give way. Indeed, it was precisely Wayne's decency, the reassuring sense of responsibility and reasonableness that he conveyed, that would make him such a potent symbol of the postwar *Pax Americana*" (" 'Print the Legend,' " 469). Campbell continues, "Befitting the exigencies of Cold War, the emphasis is less on individual valor than on teamwork, collective discipline, and the necessity of regimentation. . . . The filmic Wayne was no individualist, rebelling against a corrupt 'system'; on the contrary, he was the embodiment of the American establishment at the apogee of its power" (472).

25. Health was an important part of the nineteenth-century consumption of nature in the West. See Gregg Mitman, "Hay Fever Holiday: Health, Leisure, and Place in Gilded-Age America," *Bulletin of the History of Medicine* 77, no. 3 (2003): 600–35; and Katherine Ott, *Fevered Lives: Tuberculosis in American Culture since 1870* (Cambridge, MA: Harvard University Press, 1999).

26. Mary Louise Pratt, *Imperial Eyes: Travel Writing and Transculturation* (New York: Routledge, 1992), 7.

27. William Cronon, summarizing Richard Slotkin's argument in *Regeneration through Violence*, claims that frontier mythology is just as much about fighting Indians as it is about taking virgin land, and the ideal frontiersman is one who can balance between the savagery of the Native and the white man. Cronon argues, "The frontier hero derives his mythic status from his regenerative (but ultimately self-destructive) ability to enter wild nature and assimilate the virtues of Indian savagery to those of white civilization without becoming entangled in the corresponding vices of either." William Cronon, review of *The Fatal Environment: The Myth of the Frontier in the Age of Industrialization, 1800–1890*, by Richard Slotkin, *Western Historical Quarterly* 17, no. 2 (1986): 202.

28. Robert P. Weiss, "Private Detective Agencies and Labour Discipline in the United States, 1855–1946," *Historical Journal* 29, no. 1 (1986): 87–107.

29. Kristin Ross, *Fast Cars, Clean Bodies: Decolonization and the Reordering of French Culture* (Cambridge, MA: MIT Press, 1995), 40.

30. Lauren Berlant, "Cruel Optimism," *differences: A Journal of Feminist Cultural Studies* 17, no. 3 (2006): 21, 33.

31. Ibid., 21.

Part 2

THE CODE OF THE WEST

The Cowboy and Society

"Order Out of the Mud"

Deadwood and the State of Nature

Paul A. Cantor

> *Deadwood* is a show about how order arises out of the mud. That's what
> you see in the opening credits, and that's what you see as the story moves
> forward: men coming together out of the most limited motives to create
> something larger than themselves. Order is provisional and mysterious.
> It requires a temporary suspension of immediate concerns in the interest
> of an agreed-upon fiction about a better tomorrow.
> —David Milch, *Deadwood: Stories of the Black Hills*

Order without Law?

"John Locke" sounds like a good name for a frontier marshal in a Hollywood movie, but we do not usually associate the English philosopher with
the Wild West. Yet in his *Second Treatise of Government,* Locke speaks of
"the wild woods and uncultivated waste of America."[1] In fact, he makes over
a dozen references in this book to America, many of them specifically to
Indians (if not cowboys). Locke (1632–1704) is carrying on a debate about
the important philosophical concept of the state of nature, a debate inaugurated by Thomas Hobbes (1588–1679) in his *Leviathan,* where he also speaks
of "the savage people in many places of *America.*"[2] The third most famous
figure in the state of nature debate, Jean-Jacques Rousseau (1712–78), tells
"the story of a chief of some North Americans" in his *Second Discourse.*[3]
Evidently America was very much on the mind of the European thinkers
who contemplated the issue of the state of nature.

These inquiries into the state of nature were an attempt to conceptual-
ize the pre-political existence of humanity, life without codified laws, pub-

lic officials, or other manifestations of government power. The idea of the state of nature has thus figured prominently in modern political philosophy. Imagining human life without political institutions offers a way of analyzing the need for and value of such contrivances. One can truly say: "Tell me a philosopher's evaluation of the state of nature, and I will tell you his evaluation of the nation-state." In *Leviathan*, Hobbes presents such a horrific portrait of the state of nature as a war of all against all that he ends up endorsing any form of government, no matter how absolute, as better than none. By contrast, in creating an attractive portrait of the state of nature as idyllic, peaceful, and noncompetitive, Rousseau in his *Second Discourse* raises serious doubts about the legitimacy of civil society as an alternative, especially given its economic, social, and political inequalities. In the *Second Treatise of Government,* Locke crafts an image of the state of nature roughly midway between the extremes of Hobbes and Rousseau—less warlike than in Hobbes but more competitive and conflicted than in Rousseau. As a result, Locke's version of the state of nature allows him to legitimate political authority while still reserving the right to criticize the specific forms it takes.

If the existence of America influenced state of nature thinking in Europe, the writings of Hobbes, Locke, and Rousseau in turn influenced the political development of America. All three philosophers have had an impact on American political thinking, specifically that of the founding fathers. Locke is generally credited with being the chief theorist behind the principles embodied in the United States Constitution, such as the separation of powers.[4] Accordingly, it is not surprising that American popular culture has sometimes shown the influence of Hobbes, Locke, and Rousseau, especially in that most American of all genres, the western. This influence, whether direct or indirect, is particularly evident in the HBO television series *Deadwood* (2004–6), created by writer-producer David Milch. Widely recognized as one of the most sophisticated and artistic shows in the history of television, *Deadwood* is thoughtful, intelligent, and as close to philosophical as popular culture ever gets. Milch has been unusually forthright and forthcoming in discussing the show, in interviews, DVD commentaries, and his book about the series, *Deadwood: Stories of the Black Hills.* As a result, we have a rare opportunity—to study the philosophical underpinnings and implications of a television show as explicitly formulated by its creator.[5] At the same time, analyzing *Deadwood* helps clarify the issues at stake in the debate among Hobbes, Locke, and Rousseau about the state of nature.

Milch was attracted to the story of Deadwood, a mining camp in the late 1870s in what is now South Dakota, by a unique set of circumstances. In 1875, rumors began to spread of gold finds on Indian land in the Black Hills. Because of the U.S. government's treaty with the Sioux, this land belonged to them and was outside federal jurisdiction (as for the state of South Dakota, it did not even exist at the time). Thus the people who poured into the Deadwood camp in search of gold and other ways to make their fortune were there illegally to begin with and were not subject to any government authority, municipal, state, or federal. Almost the first words we hear in the first episode of the series come from a jailed criminal in Montana saying wistfully: "No law at all in Deadwood?"[6]

The situation in Deadwood thus allowed Milch to explore a subject he had become fascinated by during years of working on television police dramas such as *Hill Street Blues* and *NYPD Blue*—the potential disjunction between law and order: "A misapprehension that can distort one's understanding of Deadwood—and the world in which we live today—arises from the way that law and order are commonly conjoined. The phrase 'law and order' can easily create the impression that these two very different social phenomena arise from a common human impulse, or that they are somehow one and the same. Law and order are not the same. It is common for us to try to retrospectively apply the sanction of law to the things we do to maintain order. Our desire for order comes first, and law comes afterward."[7] In short, what intrigued Milch about Deadwood is how a motley group of human beings, pursuing—sometimes viciously—their own self-interest, could in the absence of any legal institutions or established government nevertheless manage to organize themselves into a community and pursue some form of common good. Or to formulate the issue another way: can human beings spontaneously arrive at rules that make possible and facilitate their productive social interaction, or are they dependent on the central authority of the state to create and enforce law and only thereby to make life in society feasible?

Thus in looking in *Deadwood*, at "an environment where," in Milch's own words, "there was order and no law whatsoever," he is raising the same question that is at the heart of state of nature thinking: how does the prepolitical existence of humanity define the parameters of political life?[8] If there can be order without law, if human beings can find ways of organizing their social life safely and productively in the absence of the state, then the state cannot claim to be the sole source of human order and must respect the independently evolved order of society. In short, the idea of order without law sets limits on state authority. On the other hand, if there can be no order without law, then the state, as the sole source of social order, can lay claim to unlimited authority, absolute power.

Al Swearengen: Nasty, British, and Short

The latter alternative is the core of Hobbes's state of nature teaching and his doctrine of absolute sovereignty. Hobbes espouses the position Milch rejects. He identifies law and order, arguing that all social order, all lawfulness in society, is ultimately the result of positive law, law made and maintained by the state. To be sure, Hobbes talks about "natural law" and the "laws of nature," devoting chapters 14 and 15 of *Leviathan* to the subject, and thus seems to allow for some kind of pre-political social order. But "natural law" quickly turns out to be a fiction in Hobbes's account:

> For the Laws of Nature (as *Justice, Equity, Modesty, Mercy* . . .) of themselves, without the terrour of some Power, to cause them to be observed, are contrary to our naturall Passions, that carry us to Partiality, Pride, Revenge, and the like. And Covenants, without the Sword, are but Words, and of no strength to secure a man at all. Therefore notwithstanding the Laws of Nature, . . . if there be no Power erected, or not great enough for our security; every man will and may lawfully rely on his own strength and art, for caution against all other men.[9]

In short, for Hobbes, natural law turns out to be unnatural ("contrary to our naturall Passions") and wholly ineffectual on its own. In his view, only by creating the Leviathan State are human beings able to achieve any kind of reliable social order, and for Hobbes an unreliable order is no order at all. Hobbes's blanket endorsement of a centralized political authority, and his basic indifference to the distinctions among the different forms authority might take, are exactly the results Milch is trying to avoid when he insists that order is separable from law and preexists it.[10]

Thus we need to resist the strong temptation to describe the vision of *Deadwood* as simply Hobbesian. To be sure, *Deadwood* is filled with violence, and one aspect that sets it apart from most television series is the fact that from its very first episode, it conditions us to believe that any character might be suddenly killed at any moment. Under these circumstances, it seems at first apt to apply to the show the words with which Hobbes famously describes the state of nature—as a state of "continuall feare, and danger of violent death; And the life of man, solitary, poore, nasty, brutish, and short."[11] People who frequent Al Swearengen's (Ian McShane) Gem Saloon may indeed find that life in Deadwood is "nasty, brutish, and short," but, aside from the obvious fact that the camp is far from poor, Milch's most basic point in the series is that human life is *not* solitary, but takes communal forms even in the absence of the state and in the midst of bitterly divisive economic and social forces. Milch rejects Hobbes's vision of the state of nature as solitary because he realizes that if community is not in some sense natural to human beings, then they will be hopelessly subject to the dictates of the Leviathan State, the artificial construct created to correct the defects of the state of nature.[12]

Nevertheless, despite Milch's fundamental difference from Hobbes, life in Deadwood shares many characteristics with the state of nature portrayed in *Leviathan*. Milch may want to show that community is natural to human beings, but he does not wish to portray it as coming easily to them. In his view, human beings must struggle to achieve community, and must overcome many potential sources of conflict to do so. On the sources of that conflict, Milch and Hobbes are in remarkable agreement. Hobbes identifies three forces that lead to the war of all against all in the state of nature: "So that in the nature of men, we find three principall causes of quarrell. First, Competition; Secondly, Diffidence; Thirdly, Glory. The first, maketh men invade for Gain; the second, for Safety; and the third, for Reputation."[13] The same array of forces is at work in Milch's Deadwood. Hobbes writes: "If any two men desire the same thing, which neverthelesse they cannot both enjoy, they become enemies."[14] That is exactly what we see happening in Deadwood, as the characters fight, often to the death, over women, as well as gold, land, and other forms of wealth and property. In addition, both Hobbes and Milch see murderous violence as arising from the radical insecurity of living without a clear government authority in place. Because any man may be attacked by any other at any time, he must forestall his potential enemies and attack them first.

Life in Deadwood continually follows this model of the preemptive strike. In season 1, episode 2, contrary to the traditional image of the honorable gunfighter, Wild Bill Hickok (Keith Carradine) draws first and shoots a man who has not yet reached for his gun, merely because he senses—correctly, as it happens—that the man meant to kill him. Many of the episodes turn on the issue of whether to neutralize an enemy by killing him before he can kill you. This issue reaches its apex on the communal level in the third season, when the "native" citizens of Deadwood, under Al Swearengen's leadership, must decide how to respond to the appearance in town of the mining magnate George Hearst (Gerald McRaney), who draws upon his great wealth to build up a private army of Pinkerton agents, which he increasingly employs to impose his will on the camp. All of Al's instincts tell him to strike first against Hearst and his army. Swearengen begs a meeting of Deadwood's elders to tell him why he should not undertake a preemptive strike while he still has a chance of defeating Hearst's continually strengthening forces.

We can readily understand why human beings fight over the same desired object or to defend themselves or to protect their family and property. But the violence in Deadwood becomes so widespread that it often seems irrational and unmotivated—men fighting, it seems, merely for the sake of fighting. But here, like Hobbes, Milch uncovers the deepest source of instability in any community: masculine pride and aggressiveness. Milch portrays Deadwood as a community of alpha males who are constantly fighting to establish their individual dominance, to maintain a pecking order in the town. Hobbes explains this situation with his typical clear-sightedness: "For every man looketh that his companion should value him, at the same rate he sets upon himself: And upon all signes of contempt, or undervaluing, naturally endeavours, as far as he dares (which amongst them that have no common power, to keep them in quiet, is far enough to make them destroy each other) to extort a greater value from his contemners."[15]

Hobbes here explains for us the fight between Swearengen and the exlawman and businessman Seth Bullock (Timothy Olyphant) that begins the second season of *Deadwood,* as well as the violent struggles between Hearst and a host of other characters in the series. This violence always seems disproportionate to its ostensible and proximate cause in some minor incident. As Hobbes puts it, men "use Violence . . . for trifles, as a word, a smile, a different opinion, and any other signe of undervalue, either direct in their Person, or by reflexion in their Kindred, their Friends, their Nation, their Profession, or their Name."[16] Because of all these sources of sensitivity, Deadwood is a powder keg of violence. Given the underlying struggle for domination in the town, the slightest incident may trigger an outbreak of murderous violence.

The Right to Property

The extent of the agreement between Milch and Hobbes on the sources of violence among human beings only highlights their more fundamental difference. For Hobbes, only the institution of the Leviathan State can end the cycle of violence in the state of nature. By contrast, *Deadwood* shows that even in the absence of government, human beings have motives for and means of limiting their violence on their own, which is another way of stating Milch's principle that order is possible without law. Here is where Milch displays his greater affinity with Locke, who, unlike Hobbes, conceives of forms of order in the state of nature. The crux of the difference between Hobbes and Locke can be seen in the issue of property.[17] For Hobbes, there is no property in the state of nature: "Where there is no common Power, there is no Law: where no Law, no Injustice. . . . It is consequent also to the same condition, there be no Propriety, no Dominion, no *Mine* or *Thine* distinct; but onely that to be every man's that he can get; and for so long, as he can keep it."[18] It is entirely characteristic of Hobbes that he views the right to property as created only by the state. If the state creates the right to property, then it can take that right away at will—a key example of what Hobbes means by the state's absolute sovereignty.[19]

By contrast, Locke argues that the right to property exists in the state of nature and thus preexists the state, or indeed any communal action: "I shall endeavour to show how men might come to have a property in several parts of that which God gave to mankind in common, and that without any express compact of all the commoners."[20] For Locke, rather than the state being the origin of property, property becomes in effect the origin of the state: "The great and chief end, therefore, of men's uniting into commonwealths and putting themselves under government is the preservation of their property."[21] Since the right to property exists prior to the state, in Locke's account, he sets limits on the state's treatment of private property. If the express end of government is to protect the right to property, it cannot legitimately seize property at will. Locke's vision of limited government, as opposed to Hobbes's absolute sovereignty, follows from his argument that the right to private property exists prior to the nation-state:

> But though men when they enter into society give up the equality, liberty, and executive power they had in the state of nature into the hands of the society, . . . yet it being only with an intention in every

one the better to preserve himself, his liberty and property—for no rational creature can be supposed to change his condition with an intention to be worse—the power of society . . . can never be supposed to extend farther than the common good, but is obliged to secure every one's property by providing against those . . . defects . . . that made the state of nature so unsafe and uneasy. And so whoever has the legislative or supreme power of any commonwealth is bound to govern by established standing laws, promulgated and known to the people, and not by extemporary decrees; by indifferent and upright judges who are to decide controversies by those laws.[22]

In contrast to Hobbes, then, Locke offers an example of what Milch means by order without law. Although Locke eventually concedes that the state is necessary to *secure* property rights, he insists that they can develop in society without the intervention of the state. This may seem like a trivial distinction—both Hobbes and Locke view the state as ultimately necessary—but if one looks at the conclusions they draw from their contrasting understanding of property, the difference is of the utmost importance. Locke's conception of the state of nature as allowing for property rights gives him a basis for evaluating different forms of government and championing those that secure property rights as opposed to those that violate them with impunity.

Locke's argument for a right to private property prior to the state grows out of his theory of self-ownership:

Though the earth and all inferior creatures be common to all men, yet every man has a property in his own person. . . . The labour of his body and the work of his hands, we may say, are properly his. Whatsoever then he removes out of the state that nature hath provided and left it in, he hath mixed his labour with, and joined to it something that is his own, and thereby makes it his property. It being by him removed from the common state nature hath placed it in, it hath by this labour something annexed to it that excludes the common right of other men.[23]

Locke's argument applies particularly to land as property. He maintains that the value of land does not reside solely in the land itself, but more importantly in what is done with it. If a man fences in and cultivates a piece of land, he thereby increases its productivity and adds to its value, and that in turn entitles him to its use and makes it his own. As Locke puts it: "As much land as a man tills, plants, improves, cultivates, and can use the product of, so much is his property."[24]

The key to Locke's defense of property rights is that he does not view the dividing up of the world into private property as a zero-sum game. It may seem that by making a piece of land his own, a man is depriving his fellow men of something. But Locke stresses the way an owner improves a piece of land by laboring on it and thereby increases the general stock of humanity. He even offers a mathematical demonstration of his point:

> He who appropriates land to himself by his labour does not lessen but increase the common stock of mankind; for the provisions serving to the support of human life produced by one acre of enclosed and cultivated land are—to speak much within compass—ten times more than those which are yielded by an acre of land of an equal richness lying waste in common. And therefore he that encloses land, and has a greater plenty of the conveniences of life from ten acres than he could have from a hundred left to nature, may truly be said to give ninety acres to mankind; for his labour now supplies him with provisions out of ten acres which were by the product of a hundred lying in common.[25]

Here is the magic of private property for Locke: if ten acres of cultivated land are more productive than one hundred acres of uncultivated, then a farmer who appropriates ten acres of land to himself will nevertheless effectively provide his fellow human beings with the benefit of at least an additional ninety acres of land. Hobbes conceives of the state of nature as a zero-sum game, a realm of scarcity in which men struggle over severely limited goods. Locke, by contrast, offers the increased productivity of private property as a way of generating a new abundance in the state of nature that works to everybody's benefit and creates a common interest in having land owned privately.

Locke and the Old Homestead

We can now see the root of the difference between Locke and Hobbes. Locke can imagine an economic order independent of the political order. Economic logic can dictate as complicated a social development as the dividing up of the world into private property, even in the absence of a government to enforce the results. Locke's argument for the priority of economic order over political is the most important example of what Milch means by order without law, and perhaps a clearer way of formulating the idea. In Hobbes's view, human beings left to themselves will simply start killing each other, and only the Leviathan State can stop them. In Locke's more optimistic view, human beings left to themselves will set to work cultivating their gardens (the killing starts much later). Locke makes his difference from Hobbes explicit: "And here we have the plain difference between the state of nature and the state of war which, however some men have confounded, are as far distinct as a state of peace, good-will, mutual assistance, and preservation, and a state of enmity, malice, violence, and mutual destruction are one from another."[26]

Milch displays his affinity with Locke on the priority of economic over political order in a pointed exchange between his two heroes in season 1, episode 4. Wild Bill Hickok has a vision of the future of Deadwood: "Camp looks like a good bet. . . . They'll get the Sioux making peace. Pretty quick you'll have laws here and every other thing." In Milch's terms, Hickok makes the mistake of viewing law as the prerequisite of all social order. Seth Bullock replies to Hickok's political vision with a more basic economic consideration: "I'll settle for property rights." In the process of laboring on a house for his family, Bullock realizes the importance of the economic foundations of society. He is not interested in grand political visions; he wants his economic circumstances clarified and determined before he will worry about political issues, and he believes that Deadwood can find ways to settle property disputes on its own.

The emphasis on property rights is the most Lockean aspect of *Deadwood* and comes naturally to a show dealing with a gold rush, where the fundamental issue for most people is staking out claims to mining territory. Milch shows that even in the absence of conventional legal institutions, Deadwood is able to evolve ways of establishing and arbitrating property rights. We learn in the first episode that a land deal in Deadwood is ratified by spitting in one's palm and shaking hands with the other party. Precisely because legal methods of enforcing contracts are unavailable in Deadwood, its citizens take the customs they have evolved for making deals very seriously. For all the force and fraud we see interfering with honest commerce in Deadwood, we still observe a basically functioning economic community, in which people can roughly rely on each other's word—or handshake—in a business deal. Since no business can take place in an environment of complete hostility and distrust, it is to everyone's advantage to observe at least a minimum of civility and probity in their dealings with each other. George Hearst is usually gruff and insensitive in his treatment of other people, but he tries to be ingratiating in his business deals, working to cover over his hostility when he concludes the purchase of Alma Garrett Ellsworth's (Molly Parker) mine: "Advancing your interest, Mrs. Ellsworth, mine, and all others, what we do here seems natural and proper" (3, 12). "Common economic interest" is about as close as we get to a definition of natural law in *Deadwood*, a definition very much in the spirit of Locke.

Deadwood even operates with a Lockean definition of property. The premise of the series is that a mining claim is yours as long as you actively work it. When Claggett (Marshall Bell), a representative of the territorial government, arrives in the camp, he makes this policy official: "The territory respects the statutes of the Northwest Ordinance, which state that a citizen can have title to any land unclaimed or unincorporated by simple usage. Essentially if you're on it and improve it, you own it" (1, 9). This passage is so close to Locke's analysis of property that, for a moment, it sounds as if he deserves a writing credit for *Deadwood*. Actually, this scene is evidence of Locke's profound influence on the development of American political institutions. The Northwest Ordinance did in fact establish this principle of land ownership precisely because the governing powers in Washington, DC, were thoroughly familiar with Locke and his arguments for private property.[27] The great American principle of homesteading, which successfully transformed millions of acres of unproductive land into productive private property, was deeply Lockean in spirit. Even if Milch was not familiar with Locke's writings on the subject, his thorough knowledge of American history led him in a Lockean direction in his treatment of the issue of property in *Deadwood*.

Commerce Tames the Alpha Male

The Lockean understanding of property in *Deadwood* points to a larger Lockean spirit in its economic and political understanding of the American West. The show reflects Locke's hope that economics might trump politics, that the peaceful and cooperative spirit of commerce might triumph over the warlike and divisive impulses of political life. As we will see, David

Milch is no friend of capitalism in the form of Big Business, and cannot be described as a champion of the free market. Nevertheless, for someone who is deeply suspicious of businesspeople, he is surprisingly open to arguments for the positive effects of commerce on human relations. In *Deadwood* commerce is the chief force that works to produce order without law. Above all, it seems to be the only force that can get the alpha males to set aside their differences, give up their fighting to the death, and work together for their mutual benefit.

The way in which economic logic can dictate social peace is most clearly evident in the career of Al Swearengen. As the owner of the Gem Saloon, he hardly seems to be a model citizen. He is involved in crooked gambling and prostitution, and we quickly learn that he is also guilty of shady land deals and runs a gang of highway robbers. He is responsible for a whole string of murders in the opening episodes. He has a hot temper and is brutal in his treatment of women and his subordinates. A perfect example of an alpha male, he seeks to dominate all around him and regards himself as the unofficial ruler of Deadwood. In short, in the early episodes he shows every sign of being the chief villain in the series and the most destructive force in the community.

Yet in the course of the series, Swearengen emerges as the chief architect of order without law in Deadwood. Of all the many alpha males in town, he is the most rational and the most able to control his emotions, especially his anger. He realizes when and where economic necessities demand that he restrain his violent impulses and work for peace. When the threat develops of Deadwood being annexed to the Dakota territory, thus becoming subject to the rule of outside forces, it is Al who organizes the influential citizens of the camp to respond to developments. One day he announces to the elders of the camp: "Be in my joint in two hours—we're forming a fuckin' government" (1, 9). He is constantly working to get the other powerful males in town to recognize their mutual self-interest and unite against their common enemies from outside the camp.

In the first season of *Deadwood,* one might well think that Milch was setting up a simple contrast between Al Swearengen as villain and Seth Bullock as hero. But the intellectual complexity of the series is evident in the way that Swearengen, the criminal, turns out to be a force for order in the community, while Bullock, the lawman, turns out to be a force for disorder. Although Bullock is genuinely good-hearted and well intentioned, he cannot control his emotions, especially his anger and his pride. Bullock is as much of an alpha male as Swearengen, and, as we have seen, their rivalry comes to a head at the beginning of the second season in a brutal fight. But it is Swearengen who realizes that they need to work together against the outside forces threatening the camp, and he swallows his pride in order to make the conciliatory gesture of returning Bullock's guns to him and thereby to solidify an alliance with a man he initially distrusted and despised. Swearengen continually struggles to calm Bullock's hot temper and to get him to act rationally in the complicated circumstances in which they find themselves. In the third season, Swearengen is willing to take calmly a terrible insult from Hearst (he chops off one of Al's fingers), whereas Bullock, provoked by mere words, hauls Hearst off to jail by the ear, thereby threatening to upset all of Swearengen's delicate negotiations with Hearst. Bullock has to learn to trust Swearengen. Silas Adams (Titus Welliver), one of Swearengen's henchmen, sums up the paradox of his character: "When he ain't lyin', Al's the most honorable man you'll ever meet" (3, 12). In the figure of Swearengen, Milch seems to be suggesting that one does not need high-minded, public-spirited motives to become a pillar of the community.

In line with Locke, then, and in contrast to Hobbes, Milch portrays how human beings, following their economic interests, can find ways to control their anger and their pride—and thus their violent impulses—and achieve forms of social order even in the absence of the state. They quickly reach the point where they themselves realize that killing each other is simply bad for business. This idea is further illustrated in the series in the role of Sol Starr (John Hawkes), Bullock's partner in a hardware store in Deadwood. Unlike Bullock, who is a lawman at heart, Starr is born and bred a merchant. He is always quoting his Viennese father, spouting maxims such as "You reduce costs buying in volume" (2, 3). Because he thinks predominantly in economic terms, Starr becomes one of the chief peacemakers in Deadwood. In the opening episodes, he labors mightily to mediate between an angry Bullock and a suspicious Swearengen. What ought to be a simple economic transaction—Bullock and Starr wish to buy land for their hardware store from Swearengen—threatens to erupt into a Hobbesian battle until Starr gets both Bullock and Swearengen to calm down and settle their differences. Generally good things happen in Deadwood when cooler economic minds prevail over the hot temper of the aggressive males in the camp. The hardware store represents the contribution commerce has to make to the Deadwood community. As Starr advertises his wares: "These are quality items. They meet these folks' needs. They're being offered at fair markup"

(1, 1). Without presenting Milch as the Milton Friedman of the western, one may note many instances in *Deadwood* of the market being portrayed as a positive force in the community. When a rival bordello opens in town, and Swearengen raises the prospect of colluding to set rates, the new madam, Joanie Stubbs (Kim Dickens), tells him: "As far as pussy, Al, we'll want to let the market sort itself out" (2, 3). In the second season, Hearst's geologist and advanceman, Francis Wolcott (Garrett Dillahunt), proclaims: "it's always preferable to allow the market to operate unimpeded" (2, 4).

To be sure, Wolcott turns out to be the creepiest villain in the series, and Milch presents the business policies he pursues on Hearst's behalf in an extremely negative light. But these policies could justifiably be described as the very opposite of the way a free market operates. Hearst is trying to buy up mining claims in an effort to create a monopoly, and doing so not by straightforward market means but instead by using force, fraud, and political influence. Hearst represents the intrusion of outside forces, on a national scale, into the local marketplace of Deadwood. Here we see Milch's distrust of large-scale business allied with the state, as opposed to the small-scale independent entrepreneurship he generally admires. And when Hearst learns of the gruesome way in which Wolcott has murdered several prostitutes, he fires him and drives him to suicide—not because of any moral outrage, but simply because Wolcott's behavior is bad for business. Many of the best outcomes in *Deadwood* happen for the "wrong" reasons—that is, not out of moral idealism but out of the apparently crudest material motives. Milch views that as characteristic of America, and a cause for celebration, not condemnation. He wants us to be clear-eyed about America and to recognize how its vices are bound up with its virtues: "None of us want to realize that we live in Deadwood, but all of us do. . . . After first recoiling in horror, we come to love the place where we live, in all of its contradictions. . . . American materialism, in all of its crassness and extravagance, is simply an expression of the fact that we have organized ourselves according to a more energizing principle than any civilization that came before us."[28] From what we see in *Deadwood*, that "energizing principle" is the market economy.

The Gold Standard

Milch's grudging respect for the material motives of humanity is reflected in his peculiar treatment of the motif of gold in *Deadwood*. Generally in American popular culture, money is viewed as the root of all evil, and the gold rush serves as an archetype of greed at its worst (think of Charlie Chaplin's great silent film on the subject). At times, gold may seem to be the central villain of *Deadwood*. Many men and women die as a result of the quest for it, or ruin their lives and destroy their families in the process. Yet in trying to give a fuller picture of the human condition, Milch insists on the way that gold can be an agent of civilization. He is well aware from his study of American history that the West would never have been settled or developed as rapidly as it was without a series of gold rushes, from California to Alaska. Gold becomes the central symbol in *Deadwood* of order without law:

> The initial transactions of gold for drink or gold for sex give rise to a more complex social order that is traced in the development of Deadwood. Everyone in town takes up a position in a social order that is based on the premise that gold has value. . . . The agreement to believe in a common symbol of value is really a society trying to find a way to organize itself in some way other than, say, hunting or killing. . . . Agreeing on this single symbol of value has allowed us to organize our individual energies on a wider scale. If we've got to barter wheat for barley and barley for shoelaces, everybody is going to fight, "I worked seven months on these shoelaces and you're going to give me one sheaf of wheat!"[29]

The evolution of gold as a medium of exchange reflects the self-organizing power of society and its remarkable ability to replace violent confrontation with cooperative and mutually beneficial transactions.

In a particularly interesting plot twist, Milch shows how gold can work to solve the bitter problem of prejudice in society, a problem of which he has been acutely aware in all his television series. The community of Deadwood is saturated with prejudices of the most noxious and virulent kind—against Indians, Jews, blacks, the Chinese, women, and many other categories. Milch clearly deplores this aspect of human behavior. He shows that economic self-interest is one of the few forces in human nature that is powerful enough to overcome prejudice. The people of Deadwood, as anti-Semitic as they are, accept Sol Starr, a Jew, once they realize that he is good for the economy of the town. Hearst's monomaniacal obsession with gold makes him a kind of monster, indifferent to the most basic human concerns, but, on the bright side, it also makes him indifferent to the color line. He employs a black cook and forces the classiest hotel in Deadwood to let her live on the premises.

He is willing to deal with her son and violate all social taboos by having a private dinner with him, only because gold is at stake between them. Milch articulates the ambivalent nature of our desire for gold:

> Yet the process of abstraction that Hearst embodies, which is symbolized in gold, is also at the very heart of what makes us human. It's the best in us, as well as the worst, and it is often both at the same time. . . . Hearst sees the power of gold . . . in the way [it] can eliminate the stickier aspects of our human particularity. That's why Hearst can befriend Odell, the son of his black chef, Aunt Lou. Odell has discovered gold in Liberia. For Hearst, the agreed-upon value of gold is the root of all civilized behavior. It mandates a calculus of utility that trumps even the most deep-seated prejudice.[30]

How remarkable to hear a television writer describe gold as "the root of all civilized behavior" and not of all evil. In the actual episode, Milch develops the point at length in a dialogue between Hearst and Odell (Omar Gooding): "Before the color [gold], no white man . . . no man of any hue, moved to civilize or improve a place like this, had reason to make the effort. The color brought commerce here and such order as has been attained." In the spirit of Locke rather than Hobbes, Hearst sees commerce, not the Leviathan State, as bringing order to human society. This insight leads to an extremely important exchange:

> HEARST: But for that gold, you'd never have sat at my table. And for the effrontery in your rising up, except that you'd showed me the gold, I'd've shot or seen you hanged without a second thought. The value I gave the gold restrained me, you see, your utility in connection with it. . . . Gold confers power, and that power is transferable. Power comes to any man who has the color.
> ODELL: Even if he is black.
> HEARST: That is our species' hope—that uniformly agreeing on its value, we organize to seek the color. (3, 7)

With all his failings as a human being, Hearst nevertheless gives the most eloquent expression of the great Lockean hope of *Deadwood*—that commerce might bring human beings together in peace by overcoming all the dark Hobbesian forces that set them at war with one another.

If human beings can evolve a widely accepted medium of exchange out of their commercial transactions among themselves—a complex task of social coordination—then they can find other ways on their own of living together peacefully and productively. Gold's importance is that it was spontaneously generated as a medium of exchange by market forces and not the result of any government action—specifically, not a paper currency made legal tender by legislative fiat and thus imposed on society from above. Milch explicitly draws a connection between gold and the spirit of Lockean liberalism in *Deadwood:*

> Yankton, the capital of Dakota territory, was a creation of the Indian agencies. It was the governmental bureaucracy, with all that that implies. When Deadwood came into being, it threw everything off. Provided with an abundant source of economic security of which any man could partake [gold], the Black Hills settlers and miners had returned to the traditional distrust of government and a renewal of pride and self-sufficiency, which the oligarchy in Yankton had never endorsed. Mining was a real industry as opposed to this sterile instrument of suppression, this paper fiction whose only real use was to steal from the Indians.[31]

As a student of American history, Milch seems to be aware that throughout the nineteenth century both government currency and treaties with the Indians were sometimes not worth the paper they were printed on. He thus views paper money as an instrument of government oppression and gold as a site of resistance to it. As such, gold is perhaps the best representative of the independence of the economic order from the political.

Town with Pity

Rousseau's understanding of the state of nature differs so radically from Hobbes's or Locke's that the *Second Discourse* can add to our understanding of *Deadwood.* One of Rousseau's distinctive contributions to state of nature thinking is his claim that natural man is characterized by the trait of pity, a point he makes in explicit contrast to Hobbes:

> There is, besides, another principle which Hobbes did not notice, and which—having been given to man in order to soften . . . the

ferocity of his vanity, or the desire for self-preservation before the
birth of vanity—tempers the ardor he has for his own well-being by
an innate repugnance to see his fellow-man suffer. . . . I speak of pity,
a disposition that is appropriate to beings as weak and subject to as
many ills as we are; . . . and so natural that even beasts sometimes
give perceptible signs of it. Without speaking of the tenderness of
mothers for their young and of the perils they brave to guard them,
one observes daily the repugnance of horses to trample a living
body underfoot.[32]

Milch is Rousseauian in his insistence that pity, fellow feeling, is innate
to humanity, and one of its most basic emotions. Compassion, particularly for the physical suffering of fellow human beings, is remarkably
pervasive in Deadwood, especially for such a rough-and-tumble camp.
What most surprises us in Al Swearengen as we learn more about him is
that this brutal man actually has a tender side, often strangely conjoined
with his cold-bloodedness. At the end of the first season, he carries out
a mercy killing of the ailing Rev. Smith (Ray McKinnon), and at the end
of the third, for what can only be described as sentimental reasons, he
cannot bring himself to kill "Trixie the whore" (Paula Malcomson) on
Hearst's orders (although he is willing to kill another one of his prostitutes as a substitute).

The outbreak of smallpox in the first season is the first occasion for Deadwood to organize itself as a community. The heroic actions to save lives on
the part of Doc Cochran (Brad Dourif) and Calamity Jane (Robin Weigert)
reflect the best side of humanity as Milch views it—a genuine concern for
the welfare of other human beings. The specific contribution of women to
life in Deadwood, especially toward the nurturing and educating of children,
reflects a Rousseauian view of compassion as essential to human sociability.
The events that truly bring the community of Deadwood together at the end
of the second season—the funeral of Seth Bullock's stepson William (Josh
Eriksson) and the marriage of Alma Garrett and Whitney Ellsworth (Jim
Beaver)—also make a Rousseauian point about the importance of domestic
sympathies to social life. There is of course a long tradition in the western
of presenting women as the great civilizing force on the frontier, and *Deadwood* follows that pattern. The building of a new schoolhouse in the third
season—an archetypal western moment—is one of the central symbols of
the growth of civilization in Deadwood.

"What Some People Think of as Progress"

The deepest way in which Rousseau is relevant to *Deadwood* is that, of the three state of nature thinkers, he is the one who has the gravest doubts about the value of civilization. Rousseau calls into question the triumphalism of the state of nature narratives in both Hobbes and Locke. They view the movement from the state of nature to the state of civil society as progress, a distinct improvement in the human condition. By contrast, Rousseau does not believe in the inevitability of the movement from the state of nature to civil society, and he is not at all convinced that this transition should be called "progress." He insists that the movement out of the state of nature, far from being a necessary development, as Hobbes and Locke present it, resulted from a "chance combination of several foreign causes which might never have arisen and without which [man] would have remained eternally in his primitive condition."[33] Moreover, Rousseau argues that even after humanity left the state of nature, its development might have stopped at a stage well short of the full-blown nation-state, and humanity would have been happier as a result.[34] Human beings in Rousseau's state of nature live in peaceful harmony, largely because they are scattered in the forests and hardly have anything to do with each other. There are no alpha males in Rousseau's state of nature, and therefore no violence and in fact no competition whatsoever. His natural men and women enjoy the peacefulness and happiness of grazing animals. In contrast to Hobbes, Rousseau views the state of nature as a realm of abundance, and in contrast to Locke, he views the development of property as generating artificial scarcities among human beings.[35]

Because Rousseau's state of nature is so much more attractive than that of Hobbes or even Locke, his writings serve as a powerful indictment of existing governments and helped to fuel modern revolutionary movements. Rousseau's state of nature offers a model of human freedom and autonomy. To be sure, Rousseau explicitly denies that the message of his work is "Back to Nature!"[36] But his political writings are devoted to the difficult task of recapturing as much of the positive aspects of the state of nature as is possible in modern civil society. He is highly critical of the way civic institutions have, in his view, distorted human nature, especially through the inequalities a modern economy creates, with its property rights and division of labor. The most famous sentence Rousseau ever wrote is the beginning of *The Social Contract:* "Man is born free, and everywhere he is in chains."[37]

Deadwood embodies a similar skepticism about the value of government and modern civilization. It may present the town's movement toward developing municipal institutions and being incorporated into the United States as inevitable, but it questions whether this truly constitutes progress, an improvement in the lives of Deadwood's citizens. In the spirit of Rousseau, Milch raises doubts about the triumphalism of the traditional western. The standard pattern of the western is the myth of the closing of the frontier, the bringing of civilization to the Wild West. Typically, a lawless community, overrun by rampaging gunfighters, must be tamed by a brave lawman or two in concert with civic-minded businessmen, a crusading newspaper editor, and a beautiful schoolmarm waiting in the wings to educate a new generation of law-abiding city dwellers.

One can hear this standard narrative of progress in the historical featurette *Deadwood Matures* included in the DVDs of the third season. The historians tell a familiar tale of the town's march toward civilization, sparked by technological developments such as the telegraph and the railroad, as well as the growth of civilizing influences such as the schoolhouse and the theater. A kind of Hegelian optimism informs these narratives—events in the West happened in the way they had to happen and no other outcome could have been better. Civilization must be good because it is what history led to. Elements of the western myth of progress are present in *Deadwood,* especially in season 3, when outside forces truly begin to transform the town. But Milch evaluates this transformation quite differently, and refuses to view it simply as progress. More than any other western I know, *Deadwood* dwells upon what is lost when a town makes the transition to civilization and becomes part of the nation-state. What is lost is freedom.

The second season of *Deadwood* begins with Al Swearengen observing the new telegraph poles going up in the town and ruefully commenting: "Messages from invisible sources, or what some people think of as progress." Al is right to be skeptical about the benefit to Deadwood of becoming connected to the outside world. Its citizens will be kept better informed of gold prices in the East, and Dan Dority (W. Earl Brown) hopes that baseball scores will now be more readily available. But the telegraph will also allow the East to exert greater control over the West, and proves in fact to be the harbinger of a federal takeover of Deadwood. The upside of Deadwood's initial isolation is its local autonomy. The bureaucratic and corporate forces that invade the town in the second and third seasons take away the camp's control of its own destiny, and have little concern for the welfare of its citizens. Politicians and businessmen eye Deadwood as a place to plunder.

The government officials who come to Deadwood are mostly looking to be bribed. With no intention of settling in the town themselves, they plan on governing it from afar, with little or no knowledge of what is actually going on there. George Hearst, as the representative of Big Business in the series, wishes to add the Deadwood camp to his far-flung mining empire. He wants to extract as much gold as he can from the Black Hills as fast as possible. At the end of the third season, he leaves Deadwood as abruptly as he arrived at the end of the second. He cares nothing about the town, speaking with contempt of the "small-mindedness and self-interested behavior that's so pervasive in this shithole" (3, 6).

During the first season of *Deadwood,* one might well think that no one could be more evil or worse for the town than Al Swearengen. It is a measure of Milch's doubts about the so-called civilizing process that by the third season, Al has become a sort of hero in *Deadwood* for leading the resistance to the outside forces trying to "modernize" the town. We certainly start rooting for him in his struggles against Hearst, and the mining magnate becomes the new villain in the series, indeed chilling us with a degree of cold-bloodedness that Al could not muster on his worst days. What are the differences between Swearengen and Hearst that make the latter the greater villain in Milch's eyes and ours? Swearengen is a tyrant, but he is Deadwood's own tyrant. As a homegrown boss, he is by nature limited in his evil. When Al kills someone, he usually has to look him—or her—straight in the eyes. In general, he has to live with the consequences of his evil deeds. Indeed, he lives among the very people he preys upon. This fact does not stop him from preying upon them, but it does moderate the way he treats them. He never kills indiscriminately. More generally, Al is a better man than his carefully cultivated public image as a cutthroat would suggest. Despite giving the impression that he is purely self-interested, he actually takes a certain civic pride in Deadwood, and from the balcony of the Gem Saloon, he secretly watches the public life of the town with a sort of seignorial satisfaction.

By contrast, in his portrait of Hearst, Milch shows all the dangers of a man who seeks to rule people as a complete stranger to them. The quality Milch associates with Hearst is abstraction. He has one goal in life—to find and extract gold from the land—and Milch acknowledges that this ability to abstract from all other considerations gives remarkable energy to Hearst's economic endeavors. But it also means that he is blind to all ordinary human concerns and tramples over anyone standing in his way. Unlike Swearengen, Hearst does not know the men he has killed and he always acts through intermediaries. He tries to keep as much distance as possible between him and the dirty deeds that make his business empire possible. For Milch, Hearst stands for the tyranny of abstraction, and symbolizes everything that is questionable about the modern nation-state, which places the seat of power remote from the communities it rules.

Deadwood begins as a small town, and the locus of small business, with impoverished men trying to make their fortunes in mining, accompanied by entrepreneurs like Bullock and Starr, who hope to make their living by providing necessary goods and services to the miners. Milch shows much that is questionable about the economic behavior that goes on in the isolation of this small town. Yet he seems to find it preferable to what happens when Big Government and Big Business invade Deadwood. As we have seen, there is something self-regulating about economic life in Deadwood, where everybody knows everybody else and people deal with each other face-to-face. It is the facelessness—the abstraction—of Big Government that Milch seems most to question. Big Business presents the same problem. Hearst represents corporate interests, and therefore Swearengen and others see no point in killing him when other shareholders in his corporation would simply take his place. Hearst's almost magical invulnerability in the third season symbolizes the implacable power of corporate—or what might be better called state—capitalism. What troubles Milch is the alliance between Big Government and Big Business that generates, and is in turn generated by, the nation-state. In the modern nation-state, power is simply too abstract and too remote from the people.

Government as a Necessary Evil

Deadwood is filled with antigovernment comments that are almost libertarian in spirit. The federal government especially comes in for criticism, because it is the furthest removed from the people it tries to rule and therefore lacks the crucial knowledge of local circumstances needed to rule well. With regard to the United States' treatment of the Indians, Swearengen sarcastically remarks: "Deep fucking thinkers in Washington put forward that policy" (1, 3). Even one of the corrupt politicians from Yankton, Hugo Jarry (Stephen Tobolowsky), speaks with contempt of the federal government, specifically its attempts to hide its own corruption and incompetence: "Washington harasses us for our difficulties in distribution to the Indians, thereby distracting the nation at large from Washington's own fiscal turpitudes and miasms" (3, 9). Jarry also complains about the ignorance of his fellow federal bureaucrats in Yankton: "They're too busy stealing to study human nature" (2, 5). Milch clearly shares his characters' skepticism about the federal government: "I'm always amazed when people say, 'Congress has adjourned and they have accomplished nothing.' A congressional term that accomplishes nothing is what the Founding Fathers prayed for. They wanted to keep the government canceling itself out, because it's in the nature of government to fuck people up."[38]

Deadwood shows how predatory government is on all levels. Nothing Swearengen can do on his own to rob the people of the camp can match the ambitious plans of the new municipal government to fleece them. The leading citizens get together under Al's leadership to raise the money to bribe officials in Yankton to let their mining claims stand. The first thing that the newly "elected" mayor, E. B. Farnum (William Sanderson), proposes is a scheme to extract money from the unwitting townspeople: "Couldn't our informal organization lay taxes on the settlement to pay the bribes?" Farnum hits the nail on the head when he defines the nature of government: "Taking people's money is what makes organizations real, be they formal, informal, or temporary" (1, 9). With government activity being epitomized by raising taxes to pay bribes, it is no wonder that politicians acquire a dubious reputation in *Deadwood*. Wolcott is the most repulsive character in the entire series, and yet even he insists on dissociating himself from the public sector: "I am a sinner who doesn't expect forgiveness, but I am not a government official" (2, 10).

Perhaps the most eloquent discourse on the nature of government in *Deadwood* is delivered by Swearengen's rival saloon keeper, Cy Tolliver (Powers Boothe), on the occasion of Yankton's attempt to question the validity of the town's mining claims: "Who of us here didn't know what government was before we came? Wasn't half our purpose coming to get shed of the cocksucker? And here it comes again—to do what's in its nature—to lie to us, and confuse us, and steal what we came to by toil and being lucky just once in our fuckin' lives. And we gonna be surprised by that, boys, government being government?" (2, 5). Despite such negative views of government in *Deadwood*, Milch seems to acknowledge its necessity, and even the idea that the town must be incorporated into the nation-state. Civilization, after all, requires some sacrifices, even of our natural freedom. In the most Rousseauian comment in the series, Swearengen tells his henchman Dority: "From the moment we leave the forest, Dan, it's all a givin' up and adaptin' "

(3, 2). But even with this concession, Milch, like Swearengen, gives a less than ringing endorsement of the power of government: "The politicians will always screw you, but there are circumstances in which we would rather have them around."[39]

This quotation from Milch seems to sum up the attitude of *Deadwood* toward government, especially the nation-state. Government is at best a necessary evil, but we must be skeptical about its claims to serve the public interest, and always remain vigilant to resist its perennial tendency to increase its power and encroach upon personal freedom. The closer power can be kept to a local level, the better. We see how Milch's faith in order without law ultimately puts him in the camp of those, like Locke, who believe in limited government, perhaps radically limited government. Whether or not one agrees with these conclusions, one must acknowledge the sophistication of the economic and political thinking that went into *Deadwood*. We have seen that the show is Hobbesian in the way that it analyzes the sources of violence in human interaction. We have seen that the show is Lockean in the way that it portrays property and the commerce that flows from its establishment as civilizing forces in society, which reflect its self-organizing power. And we have seen that the show is Rousseauian in the doubts it raises about the standard narrative of the triumph of the nation-state as progress. In combining elements of Hobbes, Locke, and Rousseau, *Deadwood* exemplifies the seriousness and thoughtfulness of the western at its best. And *Deadwood* represents the western at its very best.

Notes

The epigraph is taken from David Milch, *Deadwood: Stories of the Black Hills* (New York: Bloomsbury USA, 2006).

1. John Locke, *Two Treatises of Government*, ed. Thomas Cook (New York: Hafner, 1947), 139.

2. Thomas Hobbes, *Leviathan*, ed. C. B. MacPherson (Harmondsworth, UK: Penguin, 1968), 187.

3. Jean-Jacques Rousseau, *The First and Second Discourses*, ed. and trans. Roger D. Masters (New York: St. Martin's, 1964), 224.

4. See, for example, Thomas L. Pangle, *The Spirit of Modern Republicanism: The Moral Vision of the American Founders and the Philosophy of Locke* (Chicago: University of Chicago Press, 1988).

5. Television is a collaborative medium, and Milch himself would not claim sole responsibility for creating the whole of *Deadwood*. In the cumulative screen credits for

the three seasons the show ran, fourteen different directors and sixteen different screen-writers are named. In his commentaries, Milch makes it clear that he worked closely with the individual actors in creating the characters they were playing. Nevertheless, all the evidence suggests that *Deadwood* is essentially the product of David Milch's imagination; he maintained creative control over all aspects of the production. Therefore throughout this essay I will refer to Milch as the author of *Deadwood* in the sense in which French film theorists use the term *auteur.*

6. I have transcribed all quotations from *Deadwood* from the DVDs. I will cite them by the season number and episode number in parentheses (so that this citation would read 1, 1).

7. Milch, *Deadwood*, 121.

8. The quotation from Milch is taken from the bonus feature commentary "The New Language of the Old West" in the first season set of DVDs of *Deadwood.*

9. Hobbes, *Leviathan*, 223–24.

10. For Hobbes's basic indifference on the issue of forms of government, see ibid., 238–40.

11. Ibid., 186.

12. On the artificiality of the state, see ibid., 226.

13. Ibid., 185.

14. Ibid., 184.

15. Ibid., 185.

16. Ibid.

17. See Leo Strauss, *Natural Right and History* (Chicago: University of Chicago Press, 1953), 234–35; and Robert A. Goldwin, "John Locke," in *History of Political Philosophy,* ed. Leo Strauss and Joseph Cropsey (Chicago: Rand McNally, 1963), 492.

18. Hobbes, *Leviathan,* 188; see also 234. The word *propriety* meant the same as "property" when Hobbes was writing.

19. For Hobbes on property, see Richard Pipes, *Property and Freedom: The Story of How through the Centuries Private Ownership Has Promoted Liberty and the Rule of Law* (New York: Knopf, 1999), 32. This book gives an excellent overview of the issue of property throughout history.

20. Locke, *Two Treatises,* 134.

21. Ibid., 184. For Locke on the sanctity of property, see Pipes, *Property,* 35.

22. Locke, *Two Treatises,* 186.

23. Ibid., 134.

24. Ibid., 136.

25. Ibid., 139.

26. Ibid., 130.

27. See Pangle, *Modern Republicanism,* 308n5, where he speaks of "the truly amazing speed with which Locke's conception of property permeated and radically transformed English common law. By 1704 (six years after the publication of the *Two Treatises*!)

Locke's notions begin to appear as the standard or orthodox notions in legal commentary. I believe it is safe to surmise that Locke's influence on the legal and hence political thinking of the American colonists in subsequent years, by way of this transformation in legal thinking, was enormous."

28. Milch, *Deadwood,* 213.

29. Ibid., 41.

30. Ibid., 55.

31. Ibid., 142.

32. Rousseau, *Discourses,* 130.

33. Ibid., 140.

34. Ibid., 150–51.

35. For Rousseau's negative view of property, see ibid., 141–42, 151–52, 156–57.

36. See especially the important discussion in note i of the *Second Discourse,* 201–3.

37. Jean-Jacques Rousseau, *The Social Contract and Other Later Political Writings,* ed. and trans. Victor Gourevitch (Cambridge: Cambridge University Press, 1997), 41.

38. Milch, *Deadwood,* 143.

39. Ibid., 135.

ORDER WITHOUT LAW

The Magnificent Seven, East and West

Aeon J. Skoble

CHRIS: We took a contract.
VIN: It's sure not the kind any court would enforce.
CHRIS: That's just the kind you've got to keep.
                    —Chris and Vin, *The Magnificent Seven*

In John Sturges's 1960 western *The Magnificent Seven,* a small farming community suffering from the constant predation of a bandit gang hires seven gunslingers to defend it. This film is, of course, a remake of Akira Kurosawa's 1954 samurai epic *Seven Samurai,* in which a small farming community suffering from the constant predation of a bandit gang hires seven *ronin* to defend it.[1] Sturges and other post-Kurosawa directors of westerns (most notably Sergio Leone) were influenced by the samurai film, but it turns out that Kurosawa was himself influenced by earlier generations of westerns. So each genre can remake or borrow from the other. Why should this be successful? Separated by half a world and three centuries, it might seem odd that the same story can be told effectively in such diverse settings.

Part of what makes this work is the analogous social conditions that arose in both the post–Civil War American West[2] and feudal Japan. In both cases, areas remote from the centers of power experienced a lack of governmental administration, and this combined with other factors to produce the "gunslinger" familiar to us from westerns and the ronin phenomenon, respectively. In the American West, former soldiers from both sides of the Civil War found themselves with combat skills but no organized combat. In feudal Japan, samurai whose clans had been defeated no longer had masters to serve but were still committed to a warrior ethic. In both cases, an absence of governmental law enforcement led first to predatory raiding and then to private enforcement of law. The story, in either setting, affords an opportunity to examine the fundamental nature of authority, the justification of government, and the nature of contracts. John Locke argues that a necessary condition of entering civil society is giving up the right of private justice, but here private enforcement of law seems to be the only option. Is this, then, the "state of nature" made famous by Locke and his predecessor Hobbes? Is it an example of the "spontaneous order" made famous by Friedrich Hayek? Is it both? This essay will examine these questions and discuss how the films dramatize them. While the majority of my discussion will use *The Magnificent Seven* as a reference point, most of what I talk about is true of both films, though I will mention interesting differences as appropriate.

The basic structure of both films is the same: the bandit gang approaches the village but decides not to raid it until after the harvest. The villagers, weary of being victimized, decide that they ought to fight back, but lack the resources to do so. In the samurai film, a contingent of villagers is dispatched to a city in hopes of hiring ronin with sufficient skills to be capable of helping. The villagers are hoping to appeal to a combination of honor and desperation in the ronin—all they can offer in compensation are food and shelter. After receiving several curt refusals, they observe Kambei (Takashi Shimura) perform a heroic rescue, and, realizing he is a man of honor and virtue, they approach him. He agrees to help. In the western version, the villagers' initial plan is simply to buy guns.[3] After observing Chris (Yul Brynner) perform a heroic task with the assistance of Vin (Steve McQueen), the villagers come to the same conclusion: here is an honorable man who doesn't mind taking a risk for the sake of what he thinks is right. They ask him for help procuring guns, and he tells them that while they do not have nearly enough money to buy guns, they might be able to hire men (who would have their own guns), for here, too, out-of-work gunslingers might be willing to work for food. In both films, we then see the leader recruit additional help, and then the group goes home to make preparations to defend the village.

Why is there a problem in the first place? Why do the villages need defending? Interestingly, the banditry is primarily made possible by the same conditions that afford a solution: the existence of men with combat skills and training who have no formal combat missions to undertake and no ties to the community they happen to be living in. The Mexican bandit leader, Calvera (Eli Wallach), recognizes that the seven gunslingers hired by the villagers are similar to (if more competent than) his own men when he invites them to join him, and again later when he lets them ride off. We never hear explicitly about how the seven received their training, but it is clear that they have some, and it was not uncommon in the American West to find Civil War veterans working the ranches or seeking their fortune (honestly or otherwise). (The parallels are even more explicit in *Seven Samurai:* the bandits would have to have been in the army of some clan or other in order to have received training in swordsmanship and horsemanship.) Why would some gunslingers become bandits while others tried to find honest work? That is clearly a function of individual moral choice making on their parts, although it is exacerbated by desperation: the bandits, we're told, are close to starving. Their predatory ways are less successful than they might have thought. The gunslingers, too, are down on their luck; that's why they're willing to work for food. So the lack of money cannot *explain* the choice of banditry over honest work, although it does amplify the motivation for all the parties.

That explains why there are bandits. But why are the villages vulnerable to predation by bandits? After all, raiding farming communities is against the law. But law requires some mechanism of enforcement. The police cannot be everywhere. When asked this very question by Chris, the villagers explain that they have tried summoning the authorities, but Calvera simply waits until they leave before commencing his next raid. Similarly, in the Japanese context, the local lord who technically has jurisdiction over the area has limited numbers of samurai; he can't be expected to leave a contingent in every small farming community. So "calling the cops" is not a viable option here. And self-defense is not an option, either: the Mexican farmers think they would be incapable of fighting back, since they do not have guns and Calvera's men do, and the Japanese villagers are legally prohibited from bearing arms, as well as being untrained in swordsmanship. Hence these farming communities are essentially lawless, in the sense that their rights go unenforced. A climate has come to exist in which it is attractive to some to prey on the farmers, and there are no legal authorities that can protect them. Let us examine the various circumstances that combine to yield the "lawless" situation that calls for the presence of the heroes.

The conditions in which the farmers (in both stories) find themselves seem to represent a scenario out of Hobbes, a state of nature in which the law of the jungle prevails and might makes right. Indeed, Calvera expresses a sort of Hobbesian view when he explains that "if God didn't want them sheared, he would not have made them sheep." According to Hobbes, this unfortunate condition, in which the farmers are incapable of enjoying their productivity, is precisely why there needs to be strong centralized authority, a sovereign.[4] Only then would people cease being, or fearing, predators. But the problem isn't that nineteenth-century Mexico or sixteenth-century Japan had no sovereigns. It's that their sovereigns were not offering the farmers adequate protection against bandits. If we think of the villages as geographically isolated units of de facto anarchy, then the Hobbesian solution would be to form a state with a sovereign ruler. But actually, this would not solve the problem. For the threat to the farming community is not internal strife and distrust, it is invasion from outside the community. The internal governance of the community is not why the farmers are victims.

In fact, the villages are *not* little anarchies. They may be lawless in the sense that the laws of the political authorities are unenforceable there, but they do have governance, order. This seems to present a problem for the concept of sovereignty, at least as imagined by Hobbes. In Hobbes's theory, it is the *power* of the sovereign, not just the title, that keeps the peace and thereby ensures justice. The sovereign need not be in physical proximity, but his influence must be real, must be felt and feared, and must be capable of being enforced. In a sense, the official government of Mexico doesn't exist in this village (nor does the shogun in the Japanese village), creating a vacuum of "authority" occupied by the bandits, without consent of course. Geography therefore can play a role in the sovereign's ability to maintain order, and therefore actually be sovereign.

That's not to say that there is no "authority" in the village prior to the arrival of the predators. The social order in the farming community is one that has evolved independently of the villagers' nominal rulers. Families have been farming here for generations, and the demands of the ecosystem play a greater role than any edicts from the capital in determining the rhythms of their daily lives. In addition to the agricultural realities, the community has evolved its own social order in ways that facilitate their living together peaceably and cooperatively. The actual farm work is shown being carried out according to some plan, some strategy that is every bit as complex as the battle plans formulated by Kambei or Chris. But unlike the battle plans, which are the product of intentional design, the plan for the farming, and indeed for the farmers' social living, is not the product of anyone's intentional design, although it is of course the result of the villagers' actions and their attempts to live and work together. This is an example of what Nobel laureate Friedrich Hayek calls a "grown" (as opposed to "made") order.[5]

Hayek defines "order" generally as "a state of affairs in which a multiplicity of elements of various kinds are so related to each other that we may learn from our acquaintance with some spatial or temporal part of the whole to form correct expectations concerning the rest, or at least expectations which have a good chance of proving correct."[6] Hayek observes that every society needs to have order, and that moreover, such order will often exist without having been deliberately created. The first observation of that pair seems uncontroversial: social living depends on our having stable expectations regarding how to act and how to anticipate the actions of others. Hayek notes that part of the very function of social living is to enable us to meet one another's needs. We need other people partly because we cannot do everything by ourselves. We cannot live above a subsistence level without a division of labor. Plato makes this observation in the *Republic,* and of course economists since Smith and Ricardo have discussed the advantages of division of labor. But for society to realize a division of labor, we must be capable of cooperation, and this requires order as Hayek has defined it.

But more interesting is his follow-up observation that there are two possible sources of order: planned order and spontaneous order. Hayek notes that both biologists and economists have examined the development of orders that are not the result of deliberate planning. Spontaneous orders may also be understood as "self-generating orders" or "grown orders" or "endogenous orders," but he thinks that the most felicitous way of expressing the concept is via the English expression "spontaneous orders," for which he uses the classical Greek word *kosmos.* Similarly, planned order may be understood as "construction" or "artificial order" or "exogenous order," but is best expressed, according to Hayek, as "planned order" or "made order," for which he uses the Greek word *taxis.*

A paradigm case of planned order might be the order of a battle, such as the plans set up by Chris and his counterpart Kambei. Any organization that is the result of deliberate design is *taxis.* But what Hayek finds exciting is the "discovery that there exist orderly structures which are the product of the action of many men but are not the result of human design."[7] He cites as a relatively uncontroversial example language: there was no historical moment when some past genius invented language, yet languages do have an order. The farming villages in both films demonstrate order of just this sort, the lack of sovereign political authority notwithstanding.

Despite their functional social order, however, the farmers are vulnerable to the predatory bandits. What are their options? There already is a political authority in place, but it is one that cannot protect them. They have all the authority they need to facilitate their sociality locally. What is lacking is a reliable means of self-protection. This places the farmers in the state of nature not as it is imagined by Hobbes but as it is imagined by John Locke.[8] According to Locke, the state of nature may well allow for Hayekian evolved orders governing moral and social relations and mutually beneficial economic arrangements. But it might be subject to certain "inconveniences," among which he includes the lack of reliable protection of these orders. Thus, it's not so much that the community lacks "law," but that it lacks enforcement.

Locke argues that one aspect of joining civil society is empowering the authorities to mete out justice—members must eschew private pursuit of justice on the grounds that impartiality is compromised when it's *your* case. But in these remote farming communities, it's not clear what "society" or "the authorities" mean. It cannot mean the emperor of Japan or the Mexican (or American) president. As we've seen, these authorities cannot (or will not) protect the farmers. It isn't really a matter of "private" justice, either—the farmers want protection of their entire community from predation and theft. The remaining answer seems to be self-defense. Locke argues that all humans are naturally the owners of themselves, and therefore also of the fruits of their labor. No legitimate social arrangement can negate that. Therefore, inasmuch as it is a functioning society, the village is entitled to defend itself against attacks from the bandits. And the farmers are, it turns out, mistaken when they conclude that they lack the resources to do so.

First of all, although they lack combat training and weapons, they have resourcefulness.[9] Indeed, this is what enables the story to get going in the first place. They come up with a plan to counteract their weakness. Second of all, they're farmers. So they do have resources—food—that may be traded for other resources, in this case protection. The farmers have food but no protection; the gunslingers and samurai have weapons and combat skill but no food. The farmers can thus use trade to obtain what they need and what, in a Lockean analysis, they have every right to secure, their self-protection. Their hiring protectors is thus not contrary to Locke's injunction against private justice; it is in fact an example of Locke's prescription for remedying the inconveniences of their natural condition. They are using the resources of their society to secure their rights and protect themselves.

In both cases, the farmers show some ambivalence toward their hired protectors. In both films, the farmers are literally in hiding when the warriors arrive. Their distrust is partly paranoia, but partly, we're led to believe, based on real past experience with such people. The crucial difference is that the gunslingers or samurai who had come to town earlier were not connected to the village. They had come to prey on, or to seek refuge in, the village, but not to protect and defend it. Gradually, the farmers see that they can in fact trust the seven, and that the seven will not prey on them. In *The Magnificent Seven,* this initial ambivalence is amplified, as we see some of the villagers so afraid of the fighting, or perhaps of Calvera's retribution if the seven aren't successful, that they collaborate with the bandits to undermine Chris's plan. When Chris and the others nevertheless persist in trying to help, the last vestige of distrust is swept away, and, as in the Japanese film, the farmers realize that they can fight back, and they join in the battle.

In both films, the hired warriors face poor odds, ambivalent clients, and desperate foes. They are risking their lives to help farmers with whom they have no prior connection for very little reward. Their motives for doing so vary, but one thing they have in common is their integrity. They are as poor as the bandits are, yet they prefer to live as honestly as possible rather than as thieves.

We see their integrity in other ways also. For example, when the Mexicans first arrive in the border town, they witness a funeral procession that cannot proceed: some bigoted (and armed) residents of the town object to an Indian being buried alongside whites in the town cemetery. The funeral has been paid for, but the hearse driver refuses to risk being shot. Chris and Vin volunteer to drive the hearse, and succeed. The bigotry seems distasteful to them, but so too, and perhaps to an even greater degree, does the intimidation of the townspeople by a small number of residents. This shows us something of their character—and we see more of it in their later interactions. When the situation looks bleak in the village, and there is some talk among the seven of abandoning the mission, Chris points out that they have in fact entered into a contract with these farmers, and that, not "the law," is why they must see it through. After the exchange quoted in this essay's epigraph, Vin agrees with Chris, and there is no more talk of quitting. The gunslingers are in fact updated ronin: they have some background in honor and integrity, and even though they no longer have a "master" to serve, they still have their own sense of ethics—otherwise they, too, would have turned to banditry. Obedience to the ostensible political authorities could not compel such men to live up to their agreements—only their own existential choice to maintain their integrity could do that. Whether their code is the formalized Bushido of the samurai or the less structured one that Chris and Vin live by, these warriors are all using their honor to maintain their sense of self in the face of an apparent loss of purpose.

Here we see a cross-cultural ethical connection between the two films that parallels the cross-cultural social/political connection. Both Buddhism and existentialism can be interpreted as suggesting that there is no self apart from the actions one takes. The Bushido code isn't explicitly Buddhist, but Buddhism, particularly Zen Buddhism, was certainly an influence on the mores of the aristocratic warrior caste that eventually became codified as the Bushido code.[10] In the Bushido code, it is vitally important to pursue the good and avoid evil. A warrior who fails to do so is not truly a warrior, and hence not fully a person. A samurai may enact this through service to his lord, but what is a ronin to do? For Kambei and his comrades, honor must be maintained at all times—this is why Kambei rescued the child at the beginning of the film, and it is why all of them fight valiantly to save the village. (And, arguably, why Chris volunteers to drive the hearse.) By opposing the wicked and predatory, these warriors establish both their own honor and their own humanity. Similarly, one way of reading existentialism comes out the same way: you are what you do, so acting with valor and honor is constitutive of the honorable life, a way of avoiding "the abyss." Chris and Vin may not have read Nietzsche, but they nevertheless seem to conduct their lives according to a self-created code of ethics. Like the ronin, they are not bound in service to any particular master but are nevertheless striving to maintain their integrity because their sense of self depends on it.[11]

In both films, when the bandits are vanquished and four of the seven have been killed, life in the farming community goes on as before: the rhythms and patterns of social living and agricultural work revert to the way they had naturally become prior to interruption by bandits and warriors. In *The Magnificent Seven*, Chris says (as Kambei says in *Seven Samurai*), "Only the farmers have won. We lost. We always lose." In one sense this is true: four of their comrades died. But in another sense, one might argue that by keeping their honor and preserving the village, they achieved a victory. They reminded themselves (and us) that one does not need to have a "master" in order to have a purpose.

Notes

I am very grateful to Jennifer L. McMahon and B. Steve Csaki for their valuable suggestions and comments on this essay.

The epigraph is taken from *The Magnificent Seven*, directed by John Sturges (1960).

1. *Ronin* roughly means "masterless samurai," that is, samurai who were no longer bound to a clan or a lord, typically because the lord had been killed or deposed.

2. The village being protected in *The Magnificent Seven* is south of the border in Mexico, not in U.S. territory, but the frontier conditions in both make this fact negligible in my discussion.

3. Obviously, one big difference between the two films is the weaponry. This is not merely of aesthetic significance. In feudal Japan, not only were the samurai the only people permitted to own swords, they would be the only ones with the training to use them effectively. On the other hand, in the western setting, one could easily obtain a gun, and learning to wield the weapon was considerably easier.

4. See, for instance, Thomas Hobbes, *Leviathan* (Indianapolis: Hackett, 1994).

5. As I will explain, Hayek uses Greek terminology to further elucidate this distinction: *kosmos* for the grown or evolved orders, *taxis* for man-made orders. See his *Law, Legislation, and Liberty* (Chicago: University of Chicago Press, 1973).

6. Ibid., 36.

7. Ibid., 37.

8. John Locke, *Two Treatises of Civil Government* (Cambridge: Cambridge University Press, 1960).

9. In the Japanese movie, it turns out that the villagers actually *do* have a supply of weapons, which they had taken from murdered ronin in the past, but they literally have no idea how to use these weapons. They may also have internalized the law stating that only a samurai could go armed (which I suggest is an anti-Lockean precept, partly responsible for their predicament). In any case, functionally, the Japanese farmers are as "unarmed" as the Mexican farmers in the western.

10. A good English translation can be found in Thomas Cleary, trans., *Code of the Samurai* (North Clarendon, VT: Tuttle, 1999).

11. I should acknowledge that one of the seven, Harry Luck (Brad Dexter), does seem more motivated by financial gain than a latter-day Bushido, although he also displays personal loyalty to Chris.

FROM DOLLARS TO IRON

The Currency of Clint Eastwood's Westerns

David L. McNaron

> We thought about it for a long time: "Endeavor to persevere." And when
> we had thought about it long enough, we declared war on the Union.
> —Lone Wati, *The Outlaw Josey Wales*

Expansive in scope, geographically, historically, and thematically, *The Out-law Josey Wales* (1976) is a unique western. It has some of the best gunplay, most poignant dialogue, most colorfully vile minor villains, and most fully developed Indian characters in the genre. A film about vengeance, reconciliation, and community, *Josey Wales* extends Eastwood's western character and resolves problems in the adult western concerning the individual and the community even as it raises others. It is Eastwood's *culminating* western: to appreciate it, we must become acquainted with his others and tease out their themes.

Josey Wales, an antigovernment film, advances a sort of transcendental argument about the conditions necessary for the possibility of community.[1] These include virtues of the western hero such as self-respect, strength, and the capacity to use violence to exact vengeance or enforce rights. The film also deals in *speech*—and explores the counterfeit and genuine varieties. Consciousness heightens as Josey acquires companions and has his purpose diverted along the way, even as the landscape and times change dramatically, becoming ever more western, out of the Civil War experience, into what becomes a sprawling epic.

I will apply points from Will Wright's structural analysis of westerns in *Six-Guns and Society*.[2] In Wright's view the western hero mediates between the competing claims of wilderness and civilization, usually represented by two groups. There are four types of western plot: the classic, the vengeance variation, the transitional, and the professional. For Wright the plot types generate functions for social action in different phases of capitalistic society as well as illuminate possibilities for action in the present. John Cawelti criticizes Wright's analysis as reductionist and narrowly ideological.[3] However, an analysis is not incorrect simply because it is reductionist: each attempt must be evaluated on its merits. Wright does allow for the autonomy of culture. He selects the highest-grossing films each year for discussion but notes that big stars and big money do *not* always equal box office success. There have been spectacular big-budget/big-star failures as well as low-budget smash hits. The key is the extent to which the film's mythic structure conforms to social expectations. Wright abstracts away from particulars to provide accurate descriptions and explanations. This is a valuable strategy; however, sometimes the matter—the particulars—of a film becomes as important as the form. A prime instance is the sheer screen presence of Clint Eastwood—his physically imposing nature—and the tonal changes it has wrought. I will also draw on (pardon the pun), among others, Peter French and his thoughtful treatment of westerns in *Cowboy Metaphysics* and *The Virtues of Vengeance*.[4] Let us now turn to a discussion of Eastwood's place in the adult western.[5]

The Man with No Name

The creation of an anonymous Hollywood marketing executive,[6] "The Man with No Name" is a fitting moniker for Eastwood's characters in the *Dollars* trilogy, but the character may have begun with *Shane* (1953), the prototypical classic western. When Starret introduces himself to the Stranger, Alan Ladd's character replies: "You can call me Shane." (Compare the narrator's "Call me Ishmael" in *Moby Dick*.) Shane thus began the archetype that lasted through *Once upon a Time in the West* (1968) with Charles Bronson's character Harmonica. Actually, two of Eastwood's characters in the films directed by Sergio Leone do have proper names: Joe in *A Fistful of Dollars* (1964) and Manco in *For a Few Dollars More* (1965) (the name Manco means "one-handed" in Spanish; originally it was Monco, Italian for "monk").[7] In *The Good, the Bad and the Ugly* (1966), he is called Blondie. In what sense does Blondie qualify as the Good? He thwarts the law from carrying out a sentence on Tuco (Eli Wallach), a serious criminal, and he reneges on their partnership, abandoning Tuco in the desert. So the Good is not so good. But the Bad is *very* bad indeed, in the character of Angel Eyes (Lee Van Cleef). Tuco *is* the Ugly. Yet he becomes more sympathetic as we learn about his past. As Carl Plantinga notes, Blondie's is an "ironic 'goodness' which emerges only against a backdrop of chaotic depravity and greed."[8] After Blondie kills Angel Eyes in the final shootout, he splits his share of the gold with Tuco—something Tuco would not have done—and without leaving him literally hanging, lets him live. Maybe that's as good as we can hope for in a barren moral landscape. Such characters, which blur Wright's good/bad dichotomy, reflect an "uncertainty about values and the nature of heroism."[9]

What is distinctive about these no-name characters? They seem more myths than human beings. The Magnificent Stranger rides in from nowhere, and though strong, has a divided sort of identity. He lacks a (known) past—though we gather that past is military—and possessions other than his character and gun. Oftentimes the westerner of these films has suffered some sort of loss ("a long story" that he rarely relates).[10] But he cannot be "outside society" *simpliciter*; nor is it true that he "needs no one" (Wright's characterizations), since he knows language and depends on armaments manufacturers. Shane is a gentleman. He dances well, has exquisite manners, and is exceedingly gentle. By comparison, Joe Starret and the other homesteader males appear coarse. Shane seems the ideal husband—and father, thus the underlying psychosexual drama. At the end Little Joey, pleading for Shane to "Come back!" cries out, "Mother wants you! I know she does!" Wright's strong/weak dichotomy applies: Shane and the Rikers are strong, while the good homesteaders are weak. Of course, they could join together and stop the aggressors. One rifleman could pick off the entire group. People wanting others to fight their fights for them becomes a central concern of the Eastwood westerns. Shane's skill with a gun is an ultra-refinement of civilization, a fact that complicates the simple equation between the hero and wilderness so popular in the secondary literature. But let's be clear: Shane's *aretē* is gunfighting. Following Wright, *Shane* is a classic western, while the Leone films reflect the professional plot, in which heroes seek financial gain.

As Little Joey says, Shane is "so good." But with the arrival of Eastwood the western hero is transformed into a morally ambiguous figure, an antihero. Perhaps the "heroes" of these films represent what Harvey Mansfield calls "manly nihilism."[11] On this view, men legislate whatever values are realized in the world, since no objective values exist. The goodness of the hero is reduced in the professional plot generally. Why then do we favor some as heroes? Wright claims that in the professional plot we are simply more sympathetic to some characters than others, period. But no western antihero would ever do what Edward Fox's consummate professional assassin does in *Day of the Jackal* (1973), that is, kill the woman he slept with simply to eliminate someone who can identify him. Though not amoral, the western hero was never a do-gooder altruist. He doesn't draw first, but he finds his completion in the act of violence, which can be "graceful, aesthetic, and, even, fun."[12] The hero's violence is generally treated as redemptive and restorative. Shane becomes true to himself once again by strapping on his gun and taking on Wilson and the Rikers.

After Joe observes the cruel scene at the beginning of *A Fistful of Dollars,* he simply rides off. Eastwood stated he'd always wanted to do that in a western.[13] However, Joe gives away his money to the family and enables them to flee. Eastwood was responsible for the dialogue in this scene. Leone had Joe making a long-winded explanation when the woman asks why he is doing this for them. Joe replies, with characteristic westerner brevity: "Because I knew someone like you once and there was no one there to help."[14] The western is spare,[15] especially in the hero's distrust of language.[16] As for the people he helps, the weak are merely weak, no better because of their innocence.[17] In fact, their lack of strength enabled the bad thing to happen to them in the first place.

Perhaps the spaghetti westerns performed an experiment in moral reduction, to see how much goodness could be drained from heroes and still have them retain that status.[18] Eastwood reveled in the new role: "I was one of the people who took the hero further away from the white hat. In *A Fistful of Dollars,* you didn't know who was the hero till a quarter of the way through the film, and even then you weren't sure; you figured he was the protagonist, but only because everybody else was crappier than he was. I like the way heroes are now. I like them with strengths, weaknesses, lack of virtue."[19] French lists several kinds of false courage: one is Torrey's foolhardy bravado in *Shane.* Kane in *High Noon* (1952) seems the truly brave man; he is less certain in his abilities with a gun than a Shane or Manco, and acts for a noble purpose: to save the town (from itself). But which is better, true courage or the "false courage" of professional confidence?[20] To answer a question with a question, which is more likely to keep one *alive*—and protect those one loves?

Bud Boetticher, fuming over the Leonesque direction of *Two Mules for Sister Sarah* (1970), said, "My men have become tough for a *reason.*"[21] By comparison, the heroes in the Anthony Mann and Leone westerns are morally ambiguous and act somewhat mysteriously, for their *own* reasons, usually unstated. Supplying the reason is precisely where Boetticher goes wrong.[22] The true adult western deals in shades of gray, not black and white. It also elevates style above moral considerations. According to Schickel, "Clint's work for [Leone] always suggested that when there are no reliable values to resort to, heroes must fall back on personal style."[23]

However morally ambiguous the antihero is, he still has virtues, including self-control, strength and style, and a sense of justice. In Aristotle's ethics self-control (*sōphrōsyne*) and moral insight (*phronēsis*) are master virtues. The good person possesses all the excellences of character. Excellence is uncommon, since there are many ways to miss the target and fall short of a virtue, and only one way to hit the bull's-eye and achieve it. For Aristotle the conclusion of a practical syllogism was an action. The morally perceptive person "sees" how to act. This seems consonant with the westerner's ability to see what should be done and act accordingly. As J. B. Books says in *The Shootist* (1976), "Some men hesitate. I won't."

Nietzsche endorsed strength and style as virtues. He denied Plato and Kant's attempts to know reality "in itself" and base moral values on this metaphysical foundation. According to Nietzsche's perspectivism, the value judgments "good and bad" were basic for master morality, while "good and evil" characterized slave morality. The aristocratic person bestows the appellation "good"—meaning noble, proud—on himself. He uses "bad" to refer to what is other: the common, base, or weak. But the person of slave morality designates the powerful other as *evil*. He then declares himself good by contrast. This leaves such "virtues" as humility and meekness, as well as an altruistic conception of morality, to count as "morality in itself," whereas this stance reflects only a certain perspective or form of life. Thus Nietzsche thought a "slave rebellion in morals" had occurred, in which Christianity stood ancient aristocratic value judgments on their head. He sought to "revaluate values" and restore master morality.[24] The person of master morality will be perceived as evil. "Yes, he's suave, confident, and charismatic. But what really makes every man want to be 007 is that he's dangerous."[25] The western hero often shares qualities with those he opposes and thus appears inexplicable or evil to the weaker parties.

Concerning style, we might say the western agrees with Nietzsche against Kierkegaard and places "the aesthetic level" above "the ethical level" (and certainly above the *religious*). Kierkegaard thought the ideal order of progression was from the aesthetic to the ethical to the religious. For Nietzsche, the higher person transcends the religious and ethical stages to the aesthetic. Further, it's not so much what one does as who one is that matters in westerns. We are willing to grant greater moral latitude to the hero. This is in keeping with both Aristotle's and Nietzsche's ethics, which stress character and self-development over principles of right conduct.

However morally ambiguous he is, the western antihero always falls on the good side of the good/bad dichotomy. It is interesting to consider Eastwood's remarks above about the hero in light of his negative reaction to the later Leone films, in which his character's importance would be diminished.

"Not a Symbol": *Hang 'Em High* and the Rule of Law

In the script for *Hang 'Em High* (1968), Eastwood found "a certain feeling about injustice and capital punishment" that intrigued him. In this, his first American western, Eastwood remarked that he would "not be a symbol, but a rather troubled figure, questioning both his own motives and those of the system he served."[26] In *Hang 'Em High* Eastwood played Jed Cooper, a man cut down from a lynching tree by a passing marshal (Ben Johnson). The perpetrators were "just men," upstanding members of the community, who mistook Cooper for the murderer of their friend. A local sheriff, Calhoun, who has a "bad back" (lazy, weak-willed, morally shallow), intercedes on the men's behalf and tries vainly to protect them against Cooper. The film is a variation on the vengeance and transition plots. The hero seeks vengeance, but does so through the offices of law; *part* of the community is villainous.

The film makes an excellent case for the rule of law. Cooper forgoes vengeance and agrees to work for the judge in the Oklahoma Territory, where nineteen marshals and one judge are responsible for seventy thousand square miles. But the legal order comes at a price. The stench of justice pervades its administration: literally, in the overcrowded stinking jail, metaphorically in various ways. Crucial distinctions from the point of view of justice are overlooked. The law is arbitrary in the acts it criminalizes, such as forbidding whiskey peddling but allowing prostitution. It imposes the death penalty for a variety of offenses. It violates a rule of justice—that only those who commit a wrongful act should be punished for it—by employing the murder/felony rule, still found in a number of states. The judge sentences to death two misguided young men who fell in with a violent older outlaw,

Miller (Bruce Dern), to rustle cattle. Miller committed the murder yet all three face the gallows. Cooper saves them from a lynching in a near-repeat scenario of his own lynching. However, Cooper finds the judge's *legal* hangings equally repugnant, a carnival-like atmosphere surrounding a mass hanging, Christianized, with whitewashed gallows. Nevertheless, the law does bring killers to justice. In so doing it replaces vigilantism, which is wholly lacking in impartiality and evidence-sifting ability.

The western takes place either during a time prior to a fully functioning legal order or during its lapse: a period marked by a rough transition. In *Hang 'Em High* Eastwood plays the western hero as lawman. The judge adduces utilitarian arguments for using people "as kindling in my fire of justice." If the law doesn't hang them, the next time a cattle rustling occurs, people will say, "Hang 'em, and hang 'em high." Cooper must perform a limited role in the system. Justice is the sole province of the judge until the arrival of statehood, when "no one man can call himself the law." The rule of law, though imperfect, is preferable to seeking vengeance. Judicial hanging makes people just as dead, but, as the judge says, there's a difference between being lynched and being judged. Cooper and the judge pass the badge back and forth during their arguments. So, the film *is* about a symbol—the badge: much is gained, and much lost, in the transition to the mechanical system of justice it represents.

In a brilliant move, this western lawman reappears in contemporary times, carrying an enormous revolver, as Detective Harry Callahan in the Dirty Harry films. The society is a legal order, though one in which crime has become rampant and in which there exists a general breakdown of respect. Crime has been given permission—it flowers in an ethos of 1960s narcissism disguised as antiauthoritarianism. The legal system, which impedes the police officer's functioning and bestows all rights on criminals, becomes the villain. The western situation reemerges in uncivil society. How can the hero walk the line between extrajudicial violence and adherence to an ineffectual system? In the sequel, *Magnum Force* (1973), Harry says—as if in response to the censure *Dirty Harry* received—to the vigilante police officers who confront him with the now-infamous "You're either with us or against us": "I'm afraid you've misjudged me." Why?

A fair guess is because Callahan is acting in good faith to protect life in emergencies, not to carry out extrajudicial punishment for its own sake, although it *appears* that he dispenses substantive justice.[27] In homage to *High Noon,* Callahan tosses his badge into the water at the end of *Dirty*

Harry, the legal system having failed the citizenry. Although the morality of westerns is usually deontological, the only arguments the judge in *Hang 'Em High* and Callahan in *Magnum Force* can muster against vigilantism are utilitarian. If we let them do it this time, what will they do—whom might they kill—the next time? This leaves open the possibility that such acts are justifiable in individual cases.

In Between with Joe Kidd

Despite its undeservedly low reputation among critics (for example, Leonard Maltin and Richard Schickel) *Joe Kidd* (1972) is a well-wrought western that nicely illustrates the in-betweenness of the western hero. The film is notable for its detestable subcharacters, one on one side, one on the other: parallel sociopathic creeps. Joe is bailed out of jail by a ruthless land baron (Mr. Harlan, played by Robert Duval) bent on hunting (literally) a land-reform revolutionary named Luis Chama (John Saxon) to protect his six hundred thousand acres and stop Chama, who is "stirring up the Mexican population." Harlan seeks out Joe on the strength of his reputation as tracker and (former) bounty hunter. Joe initially declines, but upon returning to his ranch finds his workman wrapped cruelly in barbed wire, retribution for Joe's having dispatched another nasty associate of Chama's he met while in jail on a minor, erroneous charge. Sheriff Bob Mitchell, a thickheaded but well-meaning imbecile, put him there.

When Joe returns to the hotel to accept Mr. Harlan's offer, the loutish "associate" Lamar (Don Stroud) tries to block his way and Joe pulls him down the stairs by his belt buckle, hilariously sending him tumbling. Joe accepts Harlan's offer for personal reasons—Chama, he supposes, has wronged him or someone close to him—and in ignorance of the nature of Harlan and his men, who turn out to be cold-blooded killers. The film exposes the flawed, human side of causes. Chama's idealistic girlfriend becomes disillusioned when she discovers his baser side. He brings her along, he says, "for cold nights and when there is nothing else to do, not to hear you talk." Chama is willing to let others die for him. Kidd is in between. He takes the legal way out in the end, convincing Chama to turn himself in ("straight up or draped over a saddle") and plead his case in court. But Chama has tried this approach and failed. The land titles he depended on conveniently disappeared in a courthouse "fire." The judge in the U.S. Territorial Court is hardly inclined to think that "land grants signed by the king of Spain or the emperor of Mexico" will hold up against deeds on file with the court. But in its way the rule of law prevails, although with a good measure of assistance from a neutral party ensnared neither by ideology nor desire for gain. (Well, he does get the girl in the end.)

Resurrecting the Mythic with a Vengeance: *High Plains Drifter*

In the eerie vengeance western *High Plains Drifter* (1973), Eastwood's mythic character found its ultimate expression. He has no name or mortal existence whatsoever and materializes out of nowhere. But he cuts a striking figure in his dusty range coat sitting atop a dappled horse. The townspeople gawk at him with blank incomprehension as he rides into town, as if they'd never seen a man before, being, as *they* are, mere simulacra of human beings. Here we find the Magnificent Stranger at his most menacing. The whore Callie Travers (Marianna Hill), who intentionally crashes into him in the street, even says, as though she were the town itself projecting, "From a distance you'd even pass for a man." The Stranger seems to be the reincarnation of the town's murdered marshal, Jim Duncan, or his avenging angel. He is certainly the spirit of vengeance and purveyor of a creed that people should face their fears and stand up for themselves. He crosses out "Lago," the name of the town, and scrawls "Hell" in its place.

Hell is moral cowardice, exemplified by the venal hypocritical townspeople who stood by and watched as their marshal was bullwhipped to death by killers hired by the town to protect its interest in illegal ownership of the silver mine, which the marshal was in a position to expose. The scene, recalled in flashbacks, is reminiscent of the murder of Kitty Genovese in New York. She was stabbed to death in front of dozens of onlookers who did precisely nothing.

The townspeople are bigots. They refer to Mexican residents as "Mex," and treat the Indians in the general store with contempt. Yet they claim to be "good Christian people" whose motto is to "forgive and forget." It is quite evident that they do not practice what they preach. They hold grudges, for example, beating up the midget for his newfound status as mayor. The Stranger treats the Indians to blankets and jars of candy for the children in his first act once given "a free hand in this town"—the price tag for the cowards' unwillingness to defend themselves—in exchange for protecting it against the killers, soon to be freed from prison. The hotel owner delivers a mercenary utilitarian argument for killing the marshal: "For the good of the many. That's progress." Rachel, his wife, as if invoking Kantian deontology or natural law theory, replies: "What's the price of a human life?" According to Kant's categorical imperative, we ought never to treat a rational being merely as a means. Persons, unlike things, possess moral dignity as ends unto themselves and ought to be treated with respect. The theory of natural law, while teleological, holds that human lives are incommensurable. We ought never to perform a cost-benefit analysis that trades off individual lives for the sake of a greater good. Rachel tells the Stranger, "You're a man who makes people afraid, and that's dangerous." He replies, "Well, it's what people know about themselves inside that makes them afraid."

This film also presents a scathing critique of religion, positively heaping scorn on it. When the Stranger orders the people to paint the town red, one asks, "Even the church?" to which he replies, "I mean especially the church." The preacher hides behind fine words about brotherly love that belie his ignoble motives. As the Stranger leaves town, the midget says, "I never knew your name." "Yes, you do," he replies.

Enter Josey Wales

The Outlaw Josey Wales is a vengeance/transition western with a twist: government, rather than "society" or the community, becomes the villain. Josey, the hero, not the past-less drifter of classic westerns, comes with a backstory: his family has been killed by Union redlegs from Kansas at the outbreak of the Civil War. The audience knows his motivations, which are apolitical: he joins the Confederate forces to avenge the murders of his wife and son. The war concludes in montages while the credits roll. The film's action begins with the deception at the holdouts' surrender to Union forces, a senator and Josey's commander, Fletcher (John Vernon), having brokered the deal for "full amnesty." All but Josey accept. Fletcher sees redlegs in the camp—"the worst enemies these men have got"—commanded by Captain Terrill (Bill Kenny), who led the murder raid on Josey's farm. During their oath-taking the Rebs are mowed down by Gatling gun fire. Josey rides in and prevails in a gunfight, escaping with a mortally wounded young soldier, Jamie (Sam Bottoms). They ride off to take refuge in the Indian Nations. Later, as Jamie lies dying, he sings a song, "The Rose of Alabama," whose sweetness resonates throughout the film, becoming its musical signature. Unbeknownst to them, Fletcher, who, along with Terrill, survives, was not party to the betrayal. The senator charges Fletcher to "hound this Wales to kingdom come. . . . Send him to hell." Fletcher replies that Wales will be waiting for them there. Fletcher is never really "with" the pursuers; he ridicules Terrill along the way for constantly underestimating Josey. In his flight from Terrill, Josey takes on a number of dispossessed individuals whom he rescues, somewhat unwittingly, including an elderly Cherokee man, Lone Wati (Chief Dan George), a young Navajo woman, Little Moonlight (Geraldine Keams), an elderly Jayhawker woman, Grandma Sarah (Paula Trueman), and her "odd" granddaughter, Laura Lee (Sondra Locke), and a "mangy redbone hound."

Josey's relation to the Indian characters is one of the most important aspects of the film. The scene is this: we see an elderly Indian in a top hat exiting a cabin. He aims a rifle at Josey's horse galloping through a glade. Josey, standing behind the Indian (Chief Dan George), cocks his pistol and says, "Howdy. My name is Josey Wales." "Howdy. I have heard of that name." The Indian says he has heard that there was reward money coming to anyone who would kill him. Josey says, "Seems you were looking to gain some money here." "I was looking to gain an advantage. I thought you might be someone who would sneak up on an Indian." "It's not supposed to be easy sneaking up on an Indian." The humor begins a tonal shift in the film, some sort of rising consciousness. Lone explains that as the "civilized tribe," the Cherokee have now become easy to sneak up on. "The white man has been sneaking up on us ever since." Josey turns away and wryly replies, "Seems like we can't trust the white man." He then falls asleep, after listening politely for awhile as Lone drones on with a long-winded but revealing story about his trip to Washington and the government's betrayal. The Union took the Cherokee's lands, saying they would not be happy there, and forced them onto the Trail of Tears where Lone's woman and two sons died. His speech shows the government's hollow words, which culminate in "Endeavor to persevere."

Robert Sickels comments: "Both men have lost their families to the forces of the Union, and that turns into a bond, thus reversing the situation in *The Searchers*."[28] True, but the main point of the exchange is different. Josey's sardonic response indicates he has caught Lone uttering an empty abstraction. Josey hardly seems a "politically correct Ethan Edwards." His response exposes a victim's statement that lacks force or "iron." Throughout the film Josey and Lone verbally play off one another and take turns saying too much and having the other walk away. The film explores speech generally, and in particular genuine versus counterfeit varieties.

The following columns contain examples of genuine and counterfeit speech from the film.

Counterfeit Speech	Genuine Speech
	Fletcher (at the surrender): "You said regular federal authorities would be handling this."
The senator: "Captain Terrill *is* a regular, federal authority now."	
"Fletcher, there's an old saying, 'To the victors belong the spoils.'"	
	"There's another old saying, Senator: 'Don't piss down my back and tell me it's rainin.'"
	(During massacre): "Damn you, Senator. You promised me those men would be decently treated."
"They *were* decently treated. They were decently fed, and they were decently *shot*."	
Terrill: "Doin' right ain't got no end."	
	Granny Hawkins: (Laughs contemptuously.) Earlier, to Josey: "I say that big talk's worth doodly-squat."
Carstairs (the ferryman): He curries favor with each side and sings "Dixie" and "The Battle Hymn of the Republic" "with equal enthusiasm, depending on the company."	
The Carpetbagger: He touts his panacea of an elixir, which just happens to equal the cost of a ferry ride.	
	Josey: "Works wonders on just about everything, huh?" (Spits on his lapel.) "How is it with stains?"
(After the ferry crossing): "There is such a thing in this country called justice."	
	"Well, Mr. Carpetbagger, we got somethin' in this territory called a Missouri boat ride."

Lone (quoting U.S. politicians): "You boys sure look civilized" (dressed up like Lincoln). "Endeavor to persevere."

"And now the white man is sneaking up on me, *again*."

Josey: "Guess we can't trust the white man."

Carpetbagger (words to Lone Wati in Texas town about the benefits of his elixir): "For those who can't handle their liquor."

Lone: "What's in it?"

"Well, I don't know . . . various things. I'm only the salesman."

"You drink it."

"What do you expect from a nonbeliever!"

Bounty hunter: "You're wanted, Wales."

Josey: "Reckon I'm right popular."

"Man's got to do something to make a living nowadays."

Josey: "Dyin' ain't much of a livin', boy."

Grandma Sarah (to Lone): "We're sure gonna show them redskins tomorrow. No offense meant." Lone: "None taken."

Lone: "They won't miss you. Maybe they'll forget you."

Josey: "You know there ain't no forgettin'."

Josey (beginning a flaccid explanation): "Sometimes trouble just follows a man . . ."

(Lone walks away, leaving an empty doorway.)

Lone (to Grandma): "Yawee, we're really gonna show these palefaces somethin'. No offense." Grandma Sarah: "None taken!"

Josey: "I guess everybody died a little in that damn war."

The senator's words are full of equivocations. Grandma Sarah's overblown words about Josey having been a "murdering bushwhacker on the side of Satan" and her son Tom Turner as having "served proudly with Senator Jim

Lange's Redlegs on the side of justice" are not treated contemptuously and should not appear in the counterfeit column. Some of her remarks are factually mistaken, but honestly spoken. She alters her views in light of experience. The Carpetbagger's words are moralistic but he's a crook and a bigot. Terrill, a murderer and plunderer, wraps himself in zealotry.

All of Josey's and Ten Bears's words to each other are genuine; they hold the iron. Each year Ten Bears (Will Sampson) meets with the generals: they make promises and he is pushed farther back. Now he will move no more. The fateful encounter between Josey and Ten Bears encapsulates the political theme of the film. Josey rides into Ten Bears's camp, to die with him or to live with him: "Dyin' ain't so hard for men like you and me. It's livin' that's hard, when all you've ever cared about's been butchered and raped." Josey continues: "Governments don't live together; people live together. With governments you don't always get a fair word or a fair fight. Well, I've come here to give you either one, or get either one from you." He offers his "words of death" and "words of life" and promises Ten Bears numerous things in exchange for peace.

> TEN BEARS: These things you say we will have, we already have.
> JOSEY WALES: That's true. I ain't promising you nothin' extra. I'm just giving you life and you're giving me life. And I'm saying that men can live together without butchering one another.
> TEN BEARS: It's sad that governments are chiefed by the double tongues. There is iron in your words of death for all Comanche to see, and so there is iron in your words of life. No signed paper can hold the iron. It must come from men. The words of Ten Bears carry the same iron of life and death. It is good that warriors such as we meet in the struggle of life . . . or death. It shall be life.

What of Josey and Ten Bears's enthymeme: "Only when there is iron in a person's words of death can there be iron in that person's words of life"? What does this mean, and is it true? True strength is honest in word. Verbal commitments that issue from weakness might fail to hold up. The Union lied, cloaking its deadly purposes—like the Gatling guns—under deceptive words. Government is treated differently in the film than men. Men put themselves at risk to guarantee their side of the bargain. But governments can remain aloof and make empty promises.

COMMUNITY

The distinction between genuine/counterfeit speech corresponds to authentic/false kinds of community. This bears some analogy to Plato's political philosophy. Plato exposed parallels between various psychologies and philosophies and corresponding types of regimes. For instance, the Sophists' outlook and method of argumentation, the *eristic,* correspond to regimes in which appetites are the "ruling element." In the dialogue *Gorgias,* Socrates defines rhetoric, like cookery and makeup, as a branch of one pursuit: flattery. This branch reflects a certain type of politics: a foul and ugly politics that aims at pleasure and gratification, not the good. Rhetoric is an imposter art (*technē*). True arts carry an expertise or knowledge, while false ones foster belief without regard to knowledge, pleasure without regard to what is really good. In the film counterfeit, flattering speech implies deceptive government serving exploitative, criminal purposes.

Robert Sickels views *Josey Wales* as reflecting 1970s liberalism in light of its views on Indians and multicultural community. While I don't wish to deny this as an element of the film, there is a tension between this interpretation and the film's strongly antigovernment thrust. Liberalism embraces the state. But Josey and Ten Bears thoroughly distrust government for its deceit and duplicity. When *Josey Wales* was made, the United States had just emerged from the Vietnam War, Watergate, and the civil rights struggle. Despite that movement's legal victory and forced social reforms, government failed to alleviate racial enmity and produce social harmony. How will we live together in a pluralistic society? *Josey Wales* is not so much a liberal film as a questioning of political assumptions. The state alone cannot secure peace and justice: living together is a human affair. It requires individuals of a certain sort, who are capable of entering into honest agreements—and backing them up. The unfolding logic of the Eastwood western culminates in *Josey Wales.*

The pact that Josey and Ten Bears form to establish peace between their communities is founded on the words of men who possess the strength to guarantee life or death, a bargain one cannot get from government. This echoes the westerner's hatred of lying and raises the specter of a community in which self-respecting individuals do not forswear violence. In *Once upon a Time in the West,* Cheyenne (Jason Robards) tells Jill McBain (Claudia Cardinale) not to count on Harmonica staying: "You don't understand, Jill. People like that have something inside . . . something to do with death." Loss is at the center of the western hero's identity. Anything that denies its reality is a lie. But *Josey Wales* implies that the hero rides back to a community of persons whose lives are marked by the knowledge loss bestows, who have demonstrated their ability to defend themselves and others. Such a community differs radically from those in *High Noon* and *High Plains Drifter.* The Indians are strong and independent characters, not mere obstacles for the hero. They are "persons of substance," to use English Bob's (Richard Harris) words from *Unforgiven,* though he spoke them in a very different context.

The western generally and *Josey Wales* in particular demonstrate points about knowledge, understanding, and identity. What is known is knowable, in principle, by anyone. An Italian can understand the most American of art forms. A white southerner can understand an Indian. Nor is it necessarily about what side one is on. In the montage sequence we see Josey and his men presiding over hangings; it is possible they committed injustices in their lust for vengeance. Likewise, Josey befriends Grandma Sarah, the mother of redleg Tom Turner, and understands that Turner must have been a fine man. Grandma takes sides against the redlegs who attacked her home, and sees what they—or this faction of them—are like after all, and thus finally comprehends Josey's point of view. Ten Bears understands the meaning of Josey's spitting: an expression not of contempt but of confidence and indifference to danger. And we understand that he understands; and so on. Josey doesn't at first understand Moonlight's language—Lone translates—but he comes to understand, and like her, very well. Little Moonlight says early on that she in a way belongs to Josey because he saved her, which he denies. In the end, though, as in *Breakfast at Tiffany's* (1961), people do belong to one another. Community is possible because understanding is possible: cultural solipsism is false.

So, membership in a community need not consist merely in staying true to one's "own kind" (as Josey says in his brief eulogy of Jamie), if that is construed in some narrow way. In the final analysis, it is people of integrity—of any age and of any ethnic, regional, or linguistic variety—who are to be counted among the western hero's own kind. The individualism of the western gives way a little bit in this film, which looks beyond drifting to living a settled life. But we can bargain away too much in the social contract. Government cannot be trusted to hold up its end; nor can it ameliorate human conflict.

VENGEANCE

Having made peace with the Comanche, Josey must square accounts with Terrill. But Terrill's posse awaits him. "You're all alone now, Wales," Terrill says. "Not quite," replies Lone from the window. Josey wins the battle with the help of his partners inside the house, who follow the get-tough advice Josey gave them in case the Comanche attacked. A wounded Josey rides off in hot pursuit of a wounded Terrill. When he finds him, alone outside a barn, he walks toward him, pulling the trigger on each empty chamber of four pistols, "killing" him over and over as Terrill flinches. Josey holsters his weapons and looks at Terrill with a self-satisfied grin. Has Josey's desire for vengeance been satisfied—has he given Terrill the choice of life or death? Terrill draws his sword. Josey turns it against him and runs him through.

French argues that vengeance is justified under certain conditions, one being that the vengeance seeker wishes his act to communicate the wrongness of the perpetrator's transgression. According to French, "The call to forgive is the call to forswear resentment, and that is the call to relinquish one's self-respect. . . . The westerner would prefer to remain unforgiven and unforgiving, rather than to accede to the Christian's code."[29] Compare the ending of *Once upon a Time in the West,* when Harmonica and Frank (Henry Fonda) have their duel. It is Frank who comes to Harmonica, seeking knowledge. When Frank asks what it is that he wants, Harmonica answers, "Only at the point of dyin'." Frank replies with "I know." After the draw, Frank shot through the heart, Harmonica reveals who he is by jamming his harmonica between Frank's teeth. Frank seems to nod in recognition before falling dead in the dirt, much as Harmonica had "died" the day Frank orchestrated the bizarre hanging of his brother. It may be that ultimately Josey doesn't feel he needs to kill Terrill, that he has made his point already, and Terrill forces him to act in self-defense. Some people can acquire the knowledge that vengeance can bestow only a posteriori.

RECONCILIATION

The final scene occurs back at the Lost Lady Saloon. Josey enters to find Texas Rangers taking an affidavit from Rose and one of the men stating they witnessed Josey's death at the hands of five pistoleros in Mexico. Fletcher is there, emerging from shadow. Something about his face when he was with the posse earlier in town, framed by a window, indicated he had broken completely with Terrill. Fletcher addresses Josey indirectly as "Mr. Wilson," the name his friends called him inside to protect his identity, observing the blood dripping onto Josey's boot. Fletcher doesn't believe that "no five pistoleros could kill Josey Wales." He thinks he's still alive, and will go down to Mexico to look for him. "And then?" asks Josey. Fletcher says he's got first move—"I owe him that"—and he'll "try to tell him the war is over." Josey reckons so, pauses, and adds, "I guess we all died a little in that damn war." Enough said.

In the ending Josey rides off wounded in Shane-like pose; but probably toward "the valley," instead of the mountains. The valley in *Josey Wales* now symbolizes a community based on words that hold the iron. *Josey Wales* ends on a note of reconciliation, healing, and hopefulness. Josey may have even killed Tom Turner, whose daughter he will likely marry. From death comes life. Rose had said of Josey, "Oh, he is dead. Dead, all right." Josey and Fletcher seem transformed or reborn. Through the crucible of war and strife they have worked through to a place of earned forgiveness where they can live with themselves—and thus with others.

Implications for the Western

"The crowd," Kierkegaard wrote, "is untruth." When responsibility is abandoned or diffused throughout a group or organization, bad things happen.[30] But *Josey Wales* illustrates that not all communities are crowds. The western offers complex moral dilemmas and an array of characters for reflection. Violence in the western serves as metaphor for confronting conflict and moral cowardice in our own lives. Wright is right. Westerns show how individuals have opportunities for courageous action now, in (mostly) settled society, by exercising nerve and boldness, having a sense of decency and justice, and giving style to their character.

While there are numerous explanations for the demise of the western—changes in racial and gender consciousness, as well as the genre perhaps having simply run its course[31]—this fact bears notice. Adulthood and seriousness are no longer the ideals they once were. The United States during the era when westerns flourished was, though flawed, both more innocent and more mature. The 1960s replaced the ideal of adulthood with a counterideal of perpetual adolescence. My parents' high school yearbooks from the late 1930s are filled with pictures of students who look like men and women. Isn't the purpose of child rearing to raise children to become adults? It's hard to make a western today. Its sensibility has all but vanished. Although the genre has enjoyed something of a revival, most attempts since *Unforgiven* have been failures: "westernlike" or pseudo-westerns. Exceptions include *Lonesome Dove* and *Deadwood*. Leone thought that faces were all-important: do any of our male actors look enough like men to carry westerner roles? There is more violence in society today than in the heyday of TV westerns, World War II series, and mock-violent cartoons, and a rise in incivility is apparent.[32] Clearly, the way to instill virtue in children is to raise them on the likes of *Have Gun, Will Travel, Rawhide, Combat!* and *The Bugs Bunny Show*.

The inspirational western characters are killers, but there is iron in their words and deeds. They have a certainty about themselves, of their potency and being equal to their task—as well as awareness of their limitations, which a person's got to know. Harvey Mansfield, who maintains that women, too, can be manly, writes: "Manliness seeks and welcomes drama and prefers times of war, conflict, and risk. Manliness brings change or restores order at moments when routine is not enough, when the plan fails, when the whole idea of rational control by modern science develops leaks. Manliness is the next-to-last resort, before resignation and prayer.[33] The ancient Greeks said that while other cities produced poems and statues, Sparta produced men.[34] So does the western, by showing people of integrity—men like Josey Wales and women like Little Moonlight—who are worthy of emulation.

Notes

I would like to thank Professors Jennifer L. McMahon, B. Steve Csaki, and Stephen Levitt for their insightful comments on earlier drafts of this essay.

The epigraph is taken from *The Outlaw Josey Wales*, directed by Clint Eastwood (1976).

1. A transcendental argument attempts to prove a proposition by showing that its truth is necessary for something else that we already know or assume. Kant famously answered Hume by arguing that a number of "synthetic *a priori*" truths—that concern, among other things, the concepts of number, space and time, and causality—whose existence empiricists like Hume had denied, are presupposed by the fact that we do have sense experience of a world.

2. Will Wright, *Six-Guns and Society: A Structural Study of the Western* (Berkeley: University of California Press, 1975).

3. John Cawelti, *The Six-Gun Mystique*, 2nd ed. (Bowling Green, OH: Bowling Green State University Press, 1984), 9.

4. Peter French, *Cowboy Metaphysics* (Lanham, MD: Roman & Littlefield, 1997); Peter French, *The Virtues of Vengeance* (Lawrence: University Press of Kansas, 2001).

5. I have omitted from my discussion *Pale Rider*, with Eastwood's no-name character. While it contains interesting elements, it is mostly a poor remake of *Shane*.

6. See Richard Schickel, *Clint Eastwood* (New York: Knopf, 1996), chap. 5.

7. Ibid., 139.

8. Carl Plantinga, "Spectacles of Death: Clint Eastwood and Violence in *Unforgiven*," *Cinema Journal* 37 (Winter 1998): 73.

9. Cawelti, *Six-Gun Mystique*, 13.

10. The quotation is from *Shane*. An exception is Henry Fonda's character in *The Tin Star*. He reveals to the greenhorn marshal that he turned to bounty hunting after the town he marshaled for allowed his wife and child to die.

11. Harvey Mansfield, *Manliness* (New Haven, CT: Yale University Press), chap. 4.

12. Cawelti, *Six-Gun Mystique*, 16.

13. Quoted in Schickel, *Clint Eastwood*, 145.

14. Schickel writes of this incident: "Leone, however, remained dubious until Clint at last won him over with a different argument: 'OK, Sergio, look. In a B movie we tell everybody everything. But in a real class-A movie we let the audience think.'" Ibid., 146.

15. Cf. James Stewart's comments confirming this in his interview included on the DVD of *Winchester '73* (Anthony Mann, 1950).

16. I have benefited from discussions of this and many other points about westerns with my colleague Professor Darren Hibbs.

17. Pauline Kael writes that "the scattered weak are merely weak." Quoted in Schickel, *Clint Eastwood*, 140.

18. Schickel writes: "Leone and his several writing collaborators had scraped away the western's romantic, poetic and moral encrustations, leaving only its absurdly violent confrontational essence." Ibid., 138.

19. Robert E. Kapsis and Kathie Coblentz, eds., *Clint Eastwood: Interviews* (Jackson: University Press of Mississippi, 1999), 43.

20. See French, *Cowboy Metaphysics*. French distinguishes true courage from three kinds of false courage: first, behaving bravely to gain honors or to avoid punishment or degradation; second, the courage of experience, the "impression of courage" displayed by professional soldiers or gunmen, and shared by Eastwood's spaghetti western characters and "most of the other gunfighting westerners" (113); and third, spirited temper, the sort of emotion displayed by William Munny in *Unforgiven*, the preacher in *Pale Rider*, and James Stewart's characters in the Anthony Mann vengeance westerns (114).

21. Quoted in Schickel, *Clint Eastwood*, 226.

22. I owe this point to my friend Rick Scarborough.

23. Schickel, *Clint Eastwood*, 226.

24. French argues that one of the main themes of the western is the westerner's opposition to the "feminized Christianity" of the easterner, especially in their views of vengeance and death.

25. Michael Dirda, "James Bond as Archetype (and Incredibly Cool Dude)," *The*

Chronicle of Higher Education online, http://chronicle.com, June 20, 2008 (accessed June 20, 2008).

26. Quoted in Robert Schickel, *Clint Eastwood,* 186.

27. See Karl B. Klockars's interesting article "The Dirty Harry Problem," reprinted in John Arthur and William H. Shaw, eds., *Readings in the Philosophy of Law,* 4th ed. (Upper Saddle River, NJ: Pearson/Prentice Hall, 2006), 284–91.

28. Robert C. Sickels, "A Politically Correct Ethan Edwards: Clint Eastwood's *The Outlaw Josey Wales," Journal of Popular Film and Television* 30 (Winter 2003): 223.

29. French, *Virtues of Vengeance,* 21.

30. For a famous study of this phenomenon, see Stanley Milgram, *Obedience to Authority* (New York: Harper & Row, 1974).

31. See Sickel, "A Politically Correct Ethan Edwards," for a discussion of possible explanations.

32. See my forthcoming article for a discussion of civility: " 'Quiet . . . *Please!'* Reflections on Golf and Civility," in *Golf and Philosophy* (Lexington: University Press of Kentucky, 2010).

33. Mansfield, *Manliness,* ix.

34. The attribution of this saying to citizens of other *poleis* is to be found *somewhere* in Steven Pressfield's historical novel about the battle of Thermopylae, *Gates of Fire* (New York: Bantam, 1999).

THE DUTY OF REASON

Kantian Ethics in *High Noon*

Daw-Nay Evans

Besides receiving numerous Academy Awards and making the American Film Institute's list of the top ten westerns of all time, *High Noon* (1952) is the most requested film by American presidents.[1] In his autobiography *My Life,* former president Bill Clinton writes:

> I saw a lot of movies, and especially liked the westerns. My favorite was *High Noon*—I probably saw it half a dozen times during its run in Hope, [Arkansas], and have seen it more than a dozen times since. It's still my favorite movie, because it's not your typical macho western. I loved the movie because from start to finish Gary Cooper is scared to death but does the right thing anyway. When I was elected President, I told an interviewer that my favorite movie was *High Noon.* . . . Over the long years since I first saw *High Noon,* when I faced my own showdowns, I often thought of the look in Gary Cooper's eyes as he stares into the face of almost certain defeat, and how he keeps walking through his fears toward his duty. It works pretty well in real life too."[2]

Clinton's remarks highlight the central theme of this essay and of Kant's moral theory, namely, doing the right thing requires us to do our duty despite any unintended or negative consequences that might follow. In this essay, I argue that Marshal Will Kane (Gary Cooper) is Kant's ideal moral agent.

Kant's Moral Theory: Good Will and the Concept of Duty

In his *Groundwork of the Metaphysics of Morals* Kant argues that the most basic requirement for doing the right thing is the possession of a good will. You have a good will if you are internally motivated to act in accordance with what you know you ought to do. In Kant's view, a good will is "good without limitation" and "good in itself."[3] Having a good will precedes attaining happiness or any of the virtues and is an end in itself, rather than a mere means to acquire some other good (4:393–94). To have a good will one must carry out moral obligations befitting a rational being. All human beings have the ability to be rational ones; however, some choose to do what is socially acceptable instead of what is morally right. As rational beings whose actions spring from a good will and thus from duty, we should seek to do what reason dictates rather than what our instincts desire (4:395–96). For example, Kant argues that we have a duty to nurture our natural talents rather than letting such "talents rust" by engaging in "idleness, amusement, [and] procreation" (4:421–24).[4] Reason, then, is a practical faculty whose aim is to both cultivate a good will and ensure that we will engage in right conduct by governing the operation of that will (4:396).

As mentioned above, we have to be morally motivated in the right way to do our duty and thus be able to claim that our actions have moral worth. Before delving into what it means to act from duty, it's crucial to know what it means to fall short of doing so. In Kant's view, actions that include "lying, cheating, [and] stealing" are contrary to and directly conflict with duty (4:397). Be that as it may, there are three conceptions of moral motivation that are in conformity with duty, but are not done from duty (4:397–98). According to Kant, only actions done from duty can have moral worth. First, there are actions that conform with duty but ones we have no immediate desire to perform ("one pays [one's] taxes not because [one] likes to but in order to avoid penalties set for delinquents, one treats [one's potential voters] well not because one really likes them but because [one] wants their votes when at some future time [one] runs for public office, etc."). Second, there are actions that conform with duty and that we have an immediate desire to perform ("one does not commit suicide because all is going well..., One does not commit adultery because [one] considers [one's partner] to be the most desirable creature in the whole world, etc."). Finally, there are actions that accord with duty but are contrary to some immediate desire we might have ("one does not commit suicide even when [one] is in dire distress, one does not commit adultery even though [one's partner] turns out to be [exceptionally disrespectful], etc.").[5] These last actions are the only ones of the three conceptions of moral motivation that have moral worth, because they not only conform with duty but are actually done from duty (4:399). To be sure, Kant argues, "[If one] does the action without any inclination, simply from duty; then the action first has its genuine moral worth" (4:398). In short, all three conceptions of moral motivation challenge us to be the kind of morally righteous beings Kant argues we have the potential to become.

THE SUPREME PRINCIPLE OF MORALITY

After determining how one runs afoul of doing the right thing by engaging in actions that only conform with duty, I will now give an account of what Kant calls the "supreme principle of morality" to determine what it means to act from duty. In his preface to the *Groundwork*, Kant claims that the text is "nothing more than the search for and establishment of the *supreme principle of morality*" (4:392). Kant also refers to this principle as the categorical imperative and the moral law. As laws and imperatives tend to do, this principle obligates us to act in a manner consistent with what reason commands. Specifically, reason commands us to abide by principles rather than consequences. To deliberate about the consequences of one's actions, Kant holds, is to use means-end reasoning as the sole criterion for right action. In so doing, consequentialists focus on a particular means to achieve a particular end. This type of reasoning is based on experience and, for Kant, one's experiences are an insufficient means to determine right action (4:407–9; cf. 4:416). Such experiences are subjectively contingent, while the categorical imperative is objectively necessary (4:415–20). Subjectively contingent actions cannot establish an objectively necessary and morally obligatory principle such as the categorical imperative. To sum up, particular actions cannot demonstrate that something is universally good.

As an alternative to the means-end reasoning of the consequentialist, Kant emphasizes reasoning about the categorical imperative as an end in itself. In other words, we should adhere to the categorical imperative because it is a creation that is distinctively human, namely, our ability to choose right actions over wrong ones.[6] In order to accomplish this task, Kant offers us three formulations of the categorical imperative (4:421; cf. 4:429, 440). The first formulation, the Formula of Universal Law, demands that one "act only in accordance with that maxim through which you can at the same time will that it become a universal law" (4:421).[7] A maxim, Kant holds, is a "subjective principle of volition" (4:401). To be clear, maxims are thoughts formulated as statements that precede those actions to which they directly correspond. The second formulation, the Formula of Humanity, instructs one to "act so that you use humanity, whether in your own person or in the person of any other, always at the same time as an end, never merely as a means" (4:429). Finally, the third formulation of the categorical imperative, the Formula of Autonomy, directs one to abide by the principle that views the "will of every rational being as a will giving universal law" (4:431; cf. 4:439–40).[8]

One example will suffice to explain all three formulations of the categorical imperative simultaneously. There is a severe financial crisis, and you must borrow money from a friend to survive. As far as your unsuspecting friend is concerned, you have every intention of repaying your debt within one week; however, the maxim you formulate to yourself is as follows: "I will make a false promise to my friend to acquire her money." In other words, you have made a false promise to receive money you have decided never to repay. In so doing, you have violated all three formulations of the categorical imperative.

First, you have formulated a maxim that cannot become a universal law binding for all rational beings. According to Kant, all maxims should be formulated in a manner such that every rational being could conceivably act on the same maxim. Yet, if the above maxim were to become a universal law, it would create, according to philosopher Christine M. Korsgaard, "a straightforward logical contradiction in the proposed law of nature. One might argue, for instance, that universalization of the maxim of false promising would undercut the very practice of making and accepting promises, thus making promises impossible and the maxim literally inconceivable."[9] For that reason, your action does not arise from duty and certainly has no moral worth. Second, by asking a friend for money you have no intention of repaying you have, in effect, used your friend as a means to your own end, thus violating the Formula of Humanity. By deceiving your friend in this way, you have demonstrated that you have no respect for her humanity. Third, you have failed to act autonomously. To be autonomous, you must formulate maxims that can become universal laws. An autonomous agent is one who is morally motivated to do her duty because she knows it's the right thing to do. On the other hand, one who has chosen to disregard the directives of reason is motivated by his own desires or external influences to do things that conflict with or are contrary to duty. Indeed, Kant argues that when we follow these motives, we act pathologically, namely, in accordance with motives that are not fundamentally human. Instead of abiding by the principle of autonomy, those motivated by their own desires or external influences abide by the principle of heteronomy. Kant explains: "If the will seeks the law that is to determine it anywhere else than in the fitness of its maxims for its own law giving of universal law—consequently if, in going beyond itself, it seeks this law in a property of any of its objects—*heteronomy* always results" (4:441). To put it briefly, one's will is heteronomous rather than autonomous when one permits someone or something other than oneself to give one the moral law.

Welcome to Hadleyville: "Do Not Forsake Me, Oh My Darlin'!"

Kant's moral theory is a fitting lens through which to analyze *High Noon,* particularly when one considers the circumstances surrounding the city of Hadleyville and the choices of its citizenry. Although Marshal Kane has just married his Quaker bride Amy (Grace Kelly), the news that Frank Miller (Ian MacDonald) and his minions are returning to Hadleyville brings an end to the festive occasion. Arguably, what is more troubling than the return of Frank Miller is the reaction of Hadleyville's citizens themselves. Almost no one, with the exception of a drunk named Jimmy (William Newell) and a fourteen-year-old kid named Johnny (Ralph Reed), wants to assist the marshal with the very unenviable task that lies ahead. Kane searches in vain for volunteers to help him fend off the Miller gang. He visits the courtroom, the church, the Ramirez Saloon, and the barbershop, only to discover that many of those who were initially willing to do the right thing have now been persuaded to do otherwise. Indeed, it's not only members of the general public who wish to circumvent their moral duties, but also the marshal's own friends, colleagues, and even his new wife. Judge Percy Mettrick (Otto Kruger), former marshal Matthew Howe (Lon Chaney Jr.), and Hadleyville mayor Jonah Henderson (Thomas Mitchell) are sympathetic to Kane's plight on a personal and professional level, but wish he would forget about Frank Miller and concentrate on his future as a husband and storekeeper. As the man who originally sentenced Frank Miller to prison, Judge Mettrick is concerned for his own life and thus is eager to leave Hadleyville. The arthritic former marshal is disillusioned by what he views as a defective legal system, the financial instability that plagues a lifetime civil servant who upheld justice, and his own physical infirmity. Of the three, Mayor Henderson has the best understanding of and appreciation for Marshal Kane's dedication to the moral law. He tells his constituents that Kane is the best marshal Hadleyville has ever seen and that they need to do the right thing. Even so, the mayor then proceeds to convince them that the financial interests of the city outweigh what they owe themselves as rational beings. His impromptu speech privileges financial gain over morality. In Kant's view, this is equivalent to having no interest in morality. As previously mentioned, morality requires us to act in accordance with the moral law rather than the kind of consequentialist reasoning that characterizes the mayor's proposal. All in all, his moral intuitions were correct; however, he permitted external factors to deter him from the path of right action. In so doing, he failed Kant's test to determine whether his actions have moral worth.

Given her commitment to pacifism, Amy thinks it best that she and the marshal depart Hadleyville promptly to begin their new life together. Her decision is shaped by both her religious views and the danger the Miller gang poses to her and her new husband. Despite her allegiance to Quakerism, Amy is, at least at one point during her conversation with Helen Ramirez, ready to reject morality altogether if only it will bring an end to all forms of violence. From a Kantian standpoint, neither one's religious doctrines nor one's personal anxieties about the human condition are an appropriate means for determining right action. In the realm of morality, Amy's loyalty should have been to her own capacity for moral reasoning. Had she relied on her own rational nature to guide her actions rather than her religious beliefs, Marshal Kane would not have had to wait until the final moments of his skirmish with the Miller gang for his wife's support. They would have both independently reached the conclusion that the right course of action is to postpone their matrimonial bliss, stay in Hadleyville, and confront the Miller gang regardless of the consequences.

Besides Amy Kane, Marshal Kane's deputy sheriff Harvey Pell (Lloyd Bridges), as well as his former lover Helen Ramirez (Katy Jurado), make questionable moral decisions. Far from being concerned with his duty as one of the two deputy sheriffs of Hadleyville, Harvey Pell is preoccupied with careerism and his own jealousy.[10] Pell struggles, more or less unsuccessfully, to negotiate the space between being Marshal Kane's friend, his subordinate, and the current lover of the marshal's former lover Helen Ramirez. To contend with these unruly emotions, Pell turns not to the categorical imperative but to alcohol and, in his drunken stupor, instigates a fight with Marshal Kane. Even if he has not convinced the majority of the Hadleyville citizens that he is a suitable replacement for Kane, he has nevertheless deceived himself about the matter. That is to say, Pell is convinced that his actions arise from duty when, in actuality, his actions only conform with duty. This is confirmed when one considers the means-end reasoning he employs as a justification for resigning from his post as deputy sheriff. Pell warns Kane that without a proper recommendation for the job as the new marshal of Hadleyville he will leave Kane to deal with the Miller gang on his own. With fifty-eight minutes until Frank Miller's arrival to take his revenge, Pell relinquishes his badge and gun belt. It never occurs to him that by abiding by the supreme principle of morality—that is, by simply doing what he knows he ought to do—he would very likely convince the towns-people and Marshal Kane that he is an autonomous agent whose actions have moral worth. Unfortunately, he is unable to stand up for himself or the townspeople when it counts the most.

Besides being romantically linked to Marshal Kane and Deputy Sheriff Harvey Pell, Helen Ramirez is Frank Miller's former lover. After Frank was arrested and sent to prison by the marshal (supposedly for life), Helen had a love affair with Kane. Following a brief deliberation, Helen reasons that there are no benefits to being in town once Frank Miller returns, especially since he might very well know of her previous relationship with the man responsible for depriving him of his freedom. For Kant, doing the right thing is not a cost-benefit analysis. Contrary to consequentialist philosophers such as John Stuart Mill, Kant is uninterested in a "creed which accepts as the foundation of morals 'utility' or 'the greatest happiness principle' [and] holds that actions are right in proportion as they tend to promote happi-ness; wrong as they tend to produce the reverse of happiness. By happiness is intended pleasure and the absence of pain; by unhappiness, pain and the privation of pleasure."[11] Helen's tentative desire to escape Frank's rage over her past deeds would allow her to avoid the embarrassment and guilt one is sure to feel in a face-to-face confrontation with a jilted lover. More impor-tant, she would also avoid the seemingly unavoidable emotional and pos-sibly physical abuse to be had at the hands of Frank Miller. In addition, she helps Ed Weaver (Cliff Clark) by selling him her remaining interest in the general store. By doing so, Helen would have brought about the "greatest happiness" for all those affected by her actions. Despite the allure of some of these consequences, neither Helen nor her would-be defenders should view them as good reasons for abnegating her moral obligation as a rational being to do the right thing.

As previously mentioned, Kant claims there are actions "that are already recognized as contrary to duty even though they may be useful for this or that purpose; for in their case the question whether they might have been done from duty never arises, since they even conflict with it" (4:397). Following

Kant, it seems uncontroversial that Frank Miller's desire to exact revenge on Marshal Kane and those whom he considers responsible for sending him to prison is one that "never arises" from duty. To be sure, a maxim based on Frank's thirst for revenge is, like the maxim of false promising discussed earlier, doomed to fail. A maxim of action based on revenge can be willed, but one cannot will that a maxim of revenge become a universal law binding for all rational beings. In other words, one can formulate, if one so chooses, maxims whose content would bring about contradictory results if willed not only by oneself but also by other similarly situated rational beings, but such actions have no moral worth.

MILDRED'S SUPPOSED RIGHT TO LIE

Mildred's (Eve McVeagh) choice to lie to Marshal Kane about the where-abouts of her husband, Sam (Henry Morgan), directly conflicts with what she knows she ought to do. Despite the fact that she acts at the behest of her husband, the motivations underlying her actions are just as immoral as those of the Miller gang. Mildred had a choice between (1) telling Marshal Kane a lie to spare her husband moral guilt; or (2) telling Kane the truth, thus putting Sam in a very agonizing position. Mildred's dilemma is similar to issues that arise in a dispute about the conditions under which lying may be warranted. Kant addresses the matter in his 1797 essay *On a Supposed Right to Lie because of Philanthropic Concerns*.[12] In the essay, Kant responds to an article written by Benjamin Constant, a Swiss-French liberal philosopher, in which the latter claims that we have a duty to tell the truth as long as such truth telling does not bring harm to the one who has a right to hear it. Constant criticizes Kant for arguing that we have a moral duty to tell a murderer who knocks at our door the whereabouts of his intended victim, a friend who is hiding in our house. In Constant's view, then, Mildred does the right thing by lying to Kane about Sam leaving for church without her. Although Marshal Kane is no murderer, Sam is certain that he will be killed in a shootout with the Miller gang if he answers the door himself and agrees to assist the marshal. Strangely, after having his wife lie for him, Sam blames her for his inability to take moral responsibility for his own inaction.

Not surprisingly, Kant disputes Constant's analysis and therefore we can extrapolate the conclusion he would likely reach regarding Mildred's actions. Kant's reply to Constant involves moving the debate from talk of truth to that of truthfulness: "Truthfulness in statements that cannot be avoided is the formal duty of man to everyone, however great the disadvantage that may arise therefrom for him or for any other" (4:426). Regardless of whether Sam would have taken his last breath that day in a gunfight with the Miller gang, Mildred should have been honest with the marshal. We must uphold our duty to truthfulness rather than truth, because talk of truth gives the false impression that truth is a personal artifact to be disclosed or concealed on a whim. Kant claims that truth is not a "possession" to be "granted to one person and refused to another" (4:428–29). Mildred has a duty to be truthful and the marshal has a right to her honesty. Also, Mildred's duty to truthfulness is an "unconditional" one. Kant's stance is unequivocal: "To be truthful (honest) in all declarations is, therefore, a sacred and unconditionally commanding law of reason that admits of no expediency whatsoever" (4:427). If she is actually dedicated to truthfulness, then she cannot tell the truth only in advantageous circumstances that serve as a means to her desired end. She has to tell the truth even when truth telling could do "harm" to herself or her husband (4:428). Mildred was only thinking of her husband when she lied, but as Kant sees it, "Whoever tells a lie, regardless of how good his intentions may be, must answer for the consequences, resulting therefrom even before a civil tribunal and must pay the penalty for them, regardless of how unforeseen those consequences may be" (4:427). Assuming the marshal was killed by Frank; Ben Miller (Sheb Wooley), Jack Colby (Lee Van Cleef), and Jim Pierce (Robert J. Wilkes) went on a rampage through Hadleyville terrorizing its mostly timid citizens; and Frank had his way with Kane's widow, Amy; Mildred Fuller would have far more to contend with than merely an angry husband had these potentially tragic events transpired.

MARSHAL WILL KANE: DEAD MAN WALKING

Ultimately, the protagonist of *High Noon*, Marshal Will Kane, is Kant's ideal moral agent. To begin with, the marshal's moral intuitions are quite different from those of the other townsfolk, his friends, and even those of his wife, Amy. For this reason, they do not understand him. Amy claims that she does not want to wait to find out if she will be a "wife or a widow"; his friends think he is foolhardy to risk losing the new life that awaits him for, as Judge Mettrick puts it, "a dirty little village in the middle of nowhere"; the townspeople view his seeming stubbornness as harmful to the city; and his other colleagues and friends have abandoned him. Arguably, there has to be something more profound than one's professional duties as a marshal that justifies putting one's life in danger when one has so much to lose. He explains to his wife that he will not be run out of town by the Miller gang.

In fact, the marshal states: "I never run from nobody before." He knows that "they'll just come after us. Four of them and we'd be all alone on the prairie." Despite his reasoning, Amy proposes moving to an out-of-the-way township that will be difficult for the gang to locate. For the marshal, standing up for what's right takes priority over one's marriage, friendships, and even the interests of the city he is charged with protecting. In other words, his moral intuitions produce an obvious distinction between professional duties and moral ones. His professional duties are those of a marshal of Hadleyville, while his moral duties arise from his autonomy as a rational being who shows respect for the moral law.

There are several ways in which Kane displays respect for the moral law. As we learned earlier, the first formulation of the categorical imperative, the Formula of Universal Law, tells us to "act only in accordance with that maxim through which you can at the same time will that it become a universal law." From the beginning to the end of the film, the marshal's actions are guided by a maxim of standing against lawlessness. The marshal's maxim can be articulated as follows: "When morally unjust threats against my life are made by outlaws, I will stand against them to achieve justice regardless of the consequences to my person, my friends, and my family." This is the maxim in its subjective form. Since maxims and the universal law are not synonymous, one has to inquire as to whether the maxim in its subjective form can be stated objectively. In its objective form the maxim reads as follows: "When morally unjust threats are made by outlaws, everyone will stand against them to achieve justice regardless of the consequences to their person, friends, and family." It still has to be considered whether or not the marshal's maxim can be willed to become a universal law. If it can pass the test of universalizability, then it can be said to have moral worth. And indeed, the marshal's maxim is universalizable. One could certainly imagine a world in which others stand against the moral injustice of outlaws whose moral norms include assaulting innocent people, rape, robbery, and murder.

The marshal's maxim of standing against lawlessness can also be viewed from the perspective of the second formulation of the categorical imperative, the Formula of Humanity. Again, it states that we should "act so that you use humanity, whether in your own person or in the person of any other, always at the same time as an end, never merely as a means." When we treat others as ends in themselves rather than as a means to an end, we show them respect as rational beings. This principle holds not only when dealing with others but also when dealing with ourselves. The marshal's actions satisfy both requirements. Regarding others, he does not attempt to deceive anyone. That is, he never tells Amy they could simply elude Frank and everything will work itself out; he never tells Herb he has more special deputies than he actually has (which are none); he never tells Deputy Sheriff Pell he will recommend him for a job he does not think the deputy deserves; he never makes use of sophistic arguments to dissuade patrons at the Ramirez Saloon or the church from their skeptical concerns; he never takes advantage of the sincerity of people such as Jimmy the drunk and fourteen-year-old Johnny; he never tries to manipulate what remains of Helen Ramirez's affection for him as a means to call off the Miller gang; and he does not come up with a clever ploy to inveigle Mildred as a means to determine whether or not Sam is actually home and, as a result, lure him out of hiding. Had he engaged in such consequentialist reasoning, the marshal may have benefited greatly. Be that as it may, his actions would not have had moral worth. Regarding showing respect for himself, the marshal never lies to himself about what he is doing. Even so, he does have moments of weakness and even admits to Pell that he is scared. His fear may have less to do with indecisiveness and more to do with the marshal's own explanation: fatigue. It would be difficult to argue that the marshal is indecisive about his moral duty when he is steadfast in his commitment to what he knows to be right.

By choosing not to deceive others, we show them respect and give them the opportunity to exercise their autonomy as rational beings. Kant reformulates the categorical imperative to reflect this idea when he argues, in his Formula of Autonomy, that we should treat "the will of every rational being as a will giving universal law." The marshal is the lone Kantian in Hadleyville. He is the only person who gives himself the moral law such that he can will maxims that are universalizable. The marshal's ability to be a moral agent is due to his autonomy and his autonomy is due to his rational nature. To elaborate further on what it means to be autonomous and how autonomy itself is possible, Kant tells us that there are two types of freedom. Positive freedom is freedom to act as an autonomous rational being who gives oneself the law. Negative freedom is freedom from external influences. As an autonomous moral agent, the marshal has *freedom from* doing things others would like him to do as well as *freedom to* do what he considers to be morally necessary. In doing so, the two types of freedom logically entail each other. For example, the marshal decides to stay in Hadleyville to confront Frank Miller when he could very easily have made Amy happy and ridden out of town in their horse-drawn carriage. By making the choice he does, he is exercising his freedom to do the former, while, at the same time, exercising his freedom from doing the latter.

As an autonomous moral agent who formulates maxims that are universalizable, the marshal is, as I have been arguing, Kant's ideal moral agent. As such, he should view himself as part of a "systematic union" of rational beings who give themselves the moral law. Kant writes: "A rational being belongs as a *member* to the kingdom of ends when he gives universal laws in it but is also himself subject to these laws" (4:433). For this reason, the marshal has to picture himself as a member of a hypothetical community in which rational beings formulate maxims that are universalizable and from which, Kant tells us, "he can appraise himself and his actions" (4:433). By utilizing the kingdom of ends as a thought experiment, the marshal can judge whether or not he is living up to the moral demands of the categorical imperative.

In the end, *High Noon* not only presents us with an exemplary Kantian moral agent in the character of Marshal Kane but also shows us how difficult it is to be one. On a daily basis we are confronted with, among other things, an internal battle with our own desires, unsettling moral dilemmas, plain bad luck, and pressure to conform to social norms. For these reasons, it's worth repeating the words of former president Clinton with which this essay began: "When I faced my own showdowns, I often thought of the look in Gary Cooper's eyes as he stares into the face of almost certain defeat, and how he keeps walking through his fears toward his duty. It works pretty well in real life too." Perhaps, like Clinton, we also can learn from Marshal Kane, Kant's ideal moral agent, about how to keep our heads high and moral character intact when we face what appear to be insurmountable difficulties that lie at the heart of human experience.

Notes

1. Hugh Davies, "High Noon Is Tops with Film-Loving Presidents," *Daily Telegraph,* August 5, 2003, http://www.telegraph.co.uk/news/worldnews/northamerica/usa/1438073/High-Noon-is-top-with-film-loving-presidents.html (accessed April 16, 2009).

2. Bill Clinton, *My Life* (New York: Vintage, 2005), 20–21.

3. Immanuel Kant, *Groundwork of the Metaphysics of Morals,* trans. and ed. Mary J. Gregor (Cambridge: Cambridge University Press, 1998), 4:393–94. All references to Kant's works throughout this essay are based on the Prussian Academy's edition of his

complete works. Subsequent references to this work will be given parenthetically in the text.

4. This is an example of what Kant calls an imperfect duty. Kant makes a distinction between perfect and imperfect duties. Perfect duties are proscriptive; that is, they tell us what we ought not to do. Imperfect duties are prescriptive; they tell us what we ought to do.

5. I owe these examples to James Ellington's notes in his translation of Kant's *Grounding for the Metaphysics of Morals*, 3rd ed. (Indianapolis: Hackett, 1993), 10–11.

6. As Kant makes clear, the moral law is objective. Maxims are the only feature of Kant's moral theory that are subjective.

7. A variant of this formulation is called the Formula of Natural Law. It requires one to "act as if the maxim of your action were to become by your will a universal law of nature."

8. Kant also refers to this formulation as the Principle of Autonomy. A variant of this formulation is called the Formula of the Kingdom of Ends. It requires one to "act in accordance with the maxims of a member giving universal laws for a merely possible kingdom of ends." I discuss this variant in the last section of the essay.

9. Christine M. Korsgaard, introduction to Kant, *Groundwork*, xix.

10. Despite the fact that he himself is also a deputy sheriff, Herb (James Millican) tells the marshal to seek out additional assistance to handle the Miller gang. When the marshal is unable to secure such assistance, Herb concludes that he cannot risk putting his life in danger since he has a family.

11. John Stuart Mill, *Utilitarianism*, 2nd ed. (Indianapolis: Hackett, 2001), 7.

12. This essay appears as a supplement to Ellington's translation of the *Grounding for the Metaphysics of Morals*, 63–67. For the facts surrounding the origin of this essay and a quite illuminating analysis of Kant's reply to Constant, I am indebted to Roger Sullivan's *Immanuel Kant's Moral Theory* (Cambridge: Cambridge University Press, 1989) 173–77.

Part 3

Oᴜᴛʟᴀᴡs

Challenging Conventions of the Western

THE COST OF THE CODE

Ethical Consequences in *High Noon* and
The Ox-Bow Incident

Ken Hada

A common perception associated with the classic western suggests characters welded to their notions of right judgment, characters who will not deviate from their code of honor, regardless of consequences. The honor implied in such deliberate devotion to duty is characteristically celebrated, at least on the surface, in the acts and speeches of typical heroes. It follows that the unyielding posture of the hero suggests a certain understanding of ethics. A strong hero is committed to his course of action because he sees the necessity to choose in a particular way, as the right thing to do, regardless of public opinion or even the law. However, a close examination of two important western films, *High Noon* (Fred Zinnemann, 1952) and *The Ox-Bow Incident* (William Wellman, 1943), might lead to the conclusion that the films undermine the very codes set up by the leading voices in those films. This essay, following the neo-Aristotelian ethics of contemporary philosopher Martha Nussbaum (1947–),[1] will demonstrate that an unflinching devotion to an absolute code is challenged and undermined by the greater context of the films themselves. Such subversion is primarily demonstrated by the tremendous personal cost paid by the hero, family structures, and finally society at large as a consequence of following the codes. Ironically, in the most unfortunate situations, injustice may result from a blind absolute devotion to a perceived code of duty. Given these concerns, *High Noon* and *The Ox-Bow Incident* illustrate that a qualified understanding of duty seems worthy of consideration. As will be demonstrated, Nussbaum's position suggests that literature (I include films in this category) is essential to moral philosophy because it fleshes out the consequences of holding various theoretical positions.

Immanuel Kant and Duty

If a sense of duty is common in westerns, and if western characters are judged to be heroic in part because of their stubborn allegiance to a code of conduct, then it is worthwhile to consider why this has become formulaic in our popular culture, particularly in the western genre. What is the ideological foundation upon which this notion rests? Though several factors, no doubt, contribute to this psychological stance, a primary influence may be found in the philosophy of Immanuel Kant (1724–1804). One of history's most prominent philosophers, Kant is famously associated with the notion of duty. For Kant, duty is absolute, a virtue associated with rational, willful, good men. Kant's ethics of duty has a singular emphasis, and thus it overrides claims of utilitarian ethics (acts based on the maxim of what produces the most good for the most people) and disputes the concerns of empiricism.[2] For Kant, morality is a matter not of analyzing the situation, but rather of applying the law. For him, "A good man is one who acts on the supposition that there is an unconditional and objective moral standard holding for all men in virtue of their rationality as human beings."[3]

Kant's view of duty represents an ideal, one that helps to affirm the Enlightenment ideal of rational man making right choices on the basis of objective knowledge. Much of the social context for a western hero may be associated with Manifest Destiny, a concept popularly realized in the nineteenth century when Americans felt that the expansion of the West and Southwest was divinely ordained. In order for this sense of destiny to become manifest, however, two significant challenges had to be overcome. First, room had to be made for new Americans moving west, settling on the ancestral lands of native peoples. Second, in these territories where expansion occurred, often there was competition for resources and land. Many of these places tended to be lawless vacuums where victimization could occur. In these contested places and situations, popularized in western films, it became necessary, then, perhaps even natural, that there be someone strong enough to rise to the level of hero, someone able to bring a sense of order to the often chaotic world of the American West. In fact, much of the conflict so dominant in American westerns features an idealized, rational hero in conflict with opportunistic antagonists who live only for material gain and sensual pleasure—enemies who justify their behavior simply on the basis that they are strong enough to get away with their lawless deeds.

Kant's idealism provides a foundational absolute for so-called civilized humanity, and his insistence that duty is necessary, even to the sacrifice of self-interest, seems to be a notion that western heroes routinely attempt to imitate. Typically, a western hero seems to be motivated by a sense of "oughtness." He feels honor-bound to live according to some sense of duty that becomes codified within a culture. For Kant, duty is a supreme calling, an action that a good man must take regardless of the cost to his self-interest or happiness.[4]

Kant's famous formula, the categorical imperative, argues that one "ought never to act except in such a way that [one] can also will that [one's] maxim should become a universal law."[5] Any action must pass this test in order to be ethical. He asks: "Can you also will that your maxim should become a universal law? Where it cannot, it is to be rejected, and that not because of a prospective loss to you or even to others, but because it cannot fit as a principle into a possible enactment of universal law."[6] Though western heroes frequently exhibit this absolutist position, other ethical philosophers take exception to these absolute and universal aspects of Kant's ethics.

Nussbaum: Particulars, Social Context, and Emotion

Moral duty, as frequently expressed in westerns, is familiar and appealing to audiences. We expect the code of the hero to be in play. We expect it to be challenged by dishonorable antagonists in the conflicts of the plot, but we also anticipate it will be upheld in some honorable manner. Assumed in this formula is the expectation of justice. Routinely, a western hero affirms the ideals of justice even if he must go beyond the parameters of law for justice to be realized.

The lack of ambiguity, the clear call to sacrificial duty on the part of the hero, is appealing to audiences. Part of the appeal is the visceral delight audiences experience watching the bad guy reap what he has sown. Audiences may suspend reality and vicariously participate in the final overcoming of injustice. In this process, a predictable, unambiguous code is comforting. A clear call to sacrificial duty is celebrated, yet it is often true that the results are not as clean as the formula might predict.

Martha Nussbaum claims that despite its appeal, a Kantian approach to moral duty is insufficient, precisely because of the generality of the categorical imperative. She interprets and contemporizes Aristotle, applying his ethics to fiction and society. Her view concerning moral inquiry calls for a particularized, contextualized, and social approach. Following her lead, one might well conclude that an absolute allegiance to duty can in fact bring about injustice. Duty ethics may neglect individual concerns said to be served by the would-be hero bound to his absolute code. Moreover, since Kant's call to moral duty does not allow for exceptions, particular nuances may be overlooked. Such an appeal to duty may in fact sacrifice anyone or anything for absolute principle. In certain western films, a call to duty may sacrifice the well-being of the individual hero and related family and societal members, and may even cause (at least indirectly) injustice to occur in the guise of moral duty.

Nussbaum, following Aristotle's lead, argues that Kantian ethics are not sufficiently just because they fail to do justice to particulars.[7] Because there are no exceptions to the Kantian imperative, there can be no sensitivity to context, such as when individuals struggle with ethical dilemmas found in race, class, and gender relations. Nonetheless, a rational, absolutist ethic persists in western films, and is often presumed to be ideal. Upon examination, however, it is possible to understand that the tension between an Enlightenment ideal and frontier conflict results in a tremendous price for the one committed to an idealistic code. The price is evident in any number of popular westerns, including *Lonesome Dove* (Simon Wincer, 1989), *3:10 to Yuma* (James Mangold, 2007), and the recent *Appaloosa* (Ed Harris, 2008). In each of these films, significant reflection occurs on the part of the heroes about the ultimate worth of living by an absolute devotion to honor. Similar reflection and uncertainty are also found in westerns set in the twentieth century, such as *Lonely Are the Brave* (David Miller, 1962), *Legends of the Fall* (Edward Zwick, 1994), and *All the Pretty Horses* (Billy Bob Thornton, 2000). Here, too, in these more modern extensions of the previous era, the heroic ideal is assumed. In each film, despite the appeal of the hero types, the audience is left with profound doubt concerning the value of their idealistic postures. In so-called postmodern westerns that employ antiheroes or intentionally subvert the notion of honor, films such as *The Wild Bunch* (Sam Peckinpah, 1969), *Unforgiven* (Clint Eastwood, 1992), and *No Country for Old Men* (Ethan and Joel Coen, 2007), the notion of absolute honor is either parodied or reduced to complete ineffectiveness by certain important characters. If we were to recognize the continuing influence of the western in contemporary areas of popular culture, for example, the military code demonstrated in *A Few Good Men* (Rob Reiner, 1992), there, too, we would see the lingering effect of misplaced honor.

Nussbaum identifies and expands upon three dimensions of Aristotle's attack on absolute rationalism: "An attack on the claim that all valuable things are commensurable. An argument for the priority of particular judgments to universals. A defense of the emotions and the imagination as essential to rational choice."[8] Contrary to the absolutist approach, Nussbaum argues that not every ethical inquiry or situation has the same value. Some choices are more important than others when considering action based on moral motivation. All consequences are not equal, nor are the assumptions of motive, perception, or expectations similar in all participants. And, as is usually precluded in a rationalist system, the emotions, not just reason, should determine moral choosing.

Nussbaum's understanding of moral duty requires a relative and practical social component rather than an absolute ideal.[9] What good does it do to uphold a code of honor in an attempt to be morally correct if that very code causes oppression or injustice to others in a related context? The collateral damage to those directly involved and to those peripherally affected should also be considered, rather than appealing stoically and stubbornly to an idea and willfully refusing to consider mitigating, conflicting circumstances. Her starting point for ethical inquiry begins with the question: "How should one live?"—which is quite different than the Kantian question: "What is my moral duty?" Nussbaum argues that the Kantian question "assume[s] that there is a sphere of 'moral' values that can be separated off from all the other practical values that figure in a human life." She contends that one who chooses morally does so based on practical concerns. An act of choosing, she argues, is not a priori; it is not based on motives intrinsic to humankind (as Kant believes). Rather, its foundation lies in concert with a concern for one's "own practical ends." She argues that people making moral choices

> do not inquire in a "pure" or detached manner, asking what the truth about ethical value might be as if they were asking for a description of some separately existing Platonic reality. They are looking for something in human life, something, in fact, that they themselves are going to try to bring about in their lives. What they are asking is not what is the good "out there," but what can we best live by, and live together as social beings? Their results are constrained, and appropriately constrained, by their hopes and fears for themselves, their sense of value, what they think they can live with.[10]

A critical tension exists, then, between the supposed oughtness sensed by important figures in many western films, and how the undoing of that value, resulting from idealistic presuppositions and implications, violates the very clarity assumed by the moral code. Since humans are capable of rational deliberation, a rationalist, idealistic approach to ethics is often presumed, but the simplification of human rationality fails to consider the broader, complex constitution of human behavior. An ethics based on this broader understanding becomes, in the end, a preferable, more just conclusion.

"I've Never Run Before; I've Got to Go Back"

High Noon is, for many people, the ultimate western. In the film, an aging Will Kane (Gary Cooper, in an Oscar-winning role) marries his Quaker sweetheart (Grace Kelly) on the same day he resigns his duties as sheriff. At the celebration among his friends, Kane is declared to be a free man. Before the newlyweds can leave, however, word arrives that Kane's nemesis, Frank Miller (Ian MacDonald), has been released from prison and is to arrive on the noon train and join his gang to seek revenge against Kane, who was responsible for sending him to prison. Kane is assured by the elders of the town that everything will be fine, that they can handle the situation. Kane is free to go. In fact, he is encouraged to leave by his former employers and constituents. Technically, the town is no longer his responsibility. A potential conflict in this town is not his fight anymore.

Surely the lasting appeal of this movie is grounded in Sheriff Kane's defiance against criminals bent on revenge. Kane has the easier option of leaving town and avoiding conflict, yet when he is just a few miles out of town the plot reverses itself. Deep in troubled thought, Kane stops his carriage, turns around, and returns to town, determined to meet one last challenge. He cannot leave town knowing of Frank Miller's presence there. As he explains to his protesting wife: "I've never run before. I've got to go back." He believes that Miller would just follow them anyway, so it is better to confront him and be done with it. Kane's refusal to run, his stoic appeal to duty, then, becomes the primary theme that drives the movie. This ultimate hero, honor-bound to uphold justice, renounces pleasure as well as safety to defend a town that no longer employs him. Kane's sense of duty is absolute.

Apparently Kane assumes the town really needs him and truly wants his protective leadership, but back in town, he is surprised and disappointed to discover that no one will help him. This fact leads Kane to recognize the dilemma confronting him. Despite his disappointment and the resulting intensified anxiety, he chooses to face the Miller gang anyway—alone—

regardless of potential cost. For Kane, his personal safety and the well-being of the town are one and the same, but his fellow citizens, in refusing to help him as he had anticipated they would, apparently do not read the situation in that manner.

Despite the kind gestures of those attending his wedding ceremony, evidently there is no unanimous affection for Kane, though people grudgingly recognize that he was a good sheriff. In fact, several of those whom he served seem almost happy to see him desperately squirm under the imminent threat. Some feel that he is acting out of fear; others believe he is simply vindictive. No one, friends, enemies, or detached bystanders, believes that his efforts will have a positive outcome. Kane's sense of duty, however, is undeterred. On this fateful Sunday morning, he appeals to citizens in the saloon and in the church. In both places, he is met with a resistance that seems to be motivated by fear and a desire for self-preservation, but is rationalized as right by the individuals involved. The response of the citizens forces Kane's hand, and in a Kantian sense of duty, he chooses to stand alone despite personal cost. Kane's solitary and heroic stand is dramatically pronounced when one of Kane's enemies, one of the Miller brothers, is toasted in the saloon. His popularity is strikingly contrasted with disapproval and even disdain for their former sheriff. The official deputy, Harvey (Lloyd Bridges), is overcome with jealousy of Kane. His contrasting image is demonstrated in several ways in the film. The opposite of Kane, Harvey craves attention and material reward though he is a coward and has no real sense of moral duty. As the clock hauntingly ticks toward high noon and the arrival of the train, Kane's resolve is galvanized, though the chances of survival for this aging lawman seem remote.

Kane risks his life, and to his way of thinking, he is not acting out of petty self-interest. He is desperately trying to guarantee the safety of this town. He cannot distinguish his personal conflict with Miller from the good of the community. Presumably, he might also feel personal obligation based on the assumption that he is responsible for bringing danger to the town. Sheriff Kane's decision, then, illustrates Immanuel Kant's sense of moral obligation, namely, the rational duty to act on the basis of the categorical imperative and not on the basis of self-interest. Even if death is likely, one is bound to exercise one's sense of the absolute. Kant does recognize one's duty to preserve one's own life, but such self-preservation is secondary, not primary, and properly speaking is not a moral concern. One may protect one's life "in *conformity* with duty, but not from the *motive* of duty."[11] In the case of Sheriff Kane, the motive of duty, protecting a town and preventing a criminal from revenge, calls him to risk his happiness and his life. In this unfortunate instance, duty does not conform with self-preservation, so the motive of duty takes precedence.

In the end, his new wife breaks her religious vow of pacifism and shoots one of the gang members in the back, helping Kane survive. But at what cost? In the concluding scene, Kane throws the official sheriff's star in the dirt, suggesting his disgust for his fellow citizens who failed to act. But this act also suggests self-contempt, frustration that this day had to occur at all. It is appropriate to ask why so many citizens in the town are disinclined to help Kane. Why do so many of them hold some type of grudge against Kane? Could it be that his absolutist ethics have caused unnecessary strife and division? At least this much is certain: there is no celebration in his triumph over Miller. The hero maintains his status, as demanded by his code. He acts heroically, but clearly he is dissatisfied with the whole process of trying to do right, of trying to protect people who won't help themselves.

"I'll Have No Female Boys Bearing My Name"

In *The Ox-Bow Incident*, a similar homage to absolute duty is evident. It could be argued that despite the personal and familial toll, Kane's actions in *High Noon* generally help a society, and that a sense of justice results. In *The Ox-Bow Incident*, however, clearly an absolute sense of duty leads to a gross injustice. In this story, a herd of cattle is stolen, which is a hanging offense. Circumstantial evidence points to three unsuspecting cattlemen who have recently purchased a herd. The circumstantial evidence stirs a mob mentality. The sheriff and judge are not immediately available, so citizens decide to take matters into their own hands. Refusing to wait for the official representatives of law and order, they form a vigilante posse, but in their rush to judgment three innocent men are hanged.

Contrary to Kane's dilemma in *High Noon*, in which he could not find any legitimate help against Miller, in *Ox-Bow*, the citizens are all too eager to involve themselves in a misguided, vigilante posse. The mob comes to order only when Major Tetley (Frank Conroy) arrives on the scene. Before Tetley's arrival, Arthur Davies (Harry Davenport), a merchant, speaks passionately against the hastily and illegally formed posse, but it is Tetley who provides authoritative leadership to the mob. Based on his clearly articulated rational sense of duty, he demands that the vigilantes be functionally democratic.

He requires that the men listen to a variety of arguments before proceeding with the hanging. Most citizens do not resist Tetley; they are either afraid of him or they are convinced in their own minds that the accused are guilty and feel that the hanging is right and necessary.

Tetley convinces his fellow citizens in no small part because of his appeal to honor. In his diatribes he emphasizes the duty of this citizen posse to hang these cattle thieves, despite the arguments against rushing to judgment. More than once he is sarcastically referred to as "God-Almighty-Tetley"—yet in his attempt to play God, that is, to administer final justice, clearly he fails in what Nussbaum refers to as the particulars of a situation.

Even if Tetley had been proven to be right and the three suspects truly had been guilty, several violations of others occur in this miscarriage of due process. Foremost, the end does not justify the means. In his fervor, Tetley viciously attacks anyone who doubts the process he has initiated or questions the tactics of how to pursue the accused men, or even those who simply want more than circumstantial evidence before hanging them. What is true of Tetley is also true of several others in the posse. When mob action occurs, the collective attitudes and acts of individual members who fear being labeled as dishonorable only cause the chaos to be increased exponentially. In other words, idealistic allegiance to a code deteriorates into an indulgent rampage to pacify egos propped up by a false ideology. To be fair, Tetley's behavior is not the sort of duty that Kant endorses. Tetley's actions may well demonstrate Nietzsche's view that reason is a tool of the will, not an autonomous entity. Kant is aware, however, that human will can be put in the service of self-interest. With Tetley, the problem seems to be that self-interest and emotion may masquerade as reason. Another uncomfortable possibility is that Tetley honestly thinks that he is being reasonable and fair and in fact *not* operating on the basis of self-interest. Whether he is hiding his true intentions or whether he is simply blinded by his allegiance to an absolutist code, in either case, the same unfortunate miscarriage of justice results. This possibility of enabling injustice or even the failure to fully appropriate actual justice, inherent within a limited, codified behavior, is precisely what concerns Nussbaum.

Tetley posits himself as just and fair, allowing for things to be done "regular" in accordance with what the judge would approve (had the judge been available). He prides himself on his ability to cross-examine the three accused men. In a methodological manner, he considers the defendants' claims before dismissing each one based on his understanding of contrary evidence. His matter-of-fact method terrorizes the defendants, humiliates the handful of riders who disagree with his tactics, and even irks the members of the posse who are eager to hang the accused. Nonetheless, Tetley successfully argues that as leader of the posse, he is doing what the majority of the community desires and demands. Ironically, it is his view that his manner and process protect them all against anarchy.

Among Tetley's several flaws, one of the most grievous is his harsh relationship with his son Gerald (William Eythe). He forces his son not only to ride with the posse against his will, but also to actively participate in the details of executing the men. Whenever Gerald falters, Major Tetley is quick to insult his son in front of the other men. It is his futile attempt to make his son into a masculine authority worthy of typical western iconography, and to eradicate what he believes to be his son's weak, feminine traits. Of course, his parental approach comes crashing down when his son later kills himself. Tetley's manner with Gerald has proved to be an ongoing sacrificial rite to protect his own public image, an image polished with the blood of honor. In the end, facing the devastating consequences of this projection, Tetley kills himself, suggesting that his public demeanor of strength belied a desperation deep within. Perhaps no clearer picture could be painted of the potential perils associated with the blindness of one obsessed with honor in an absolute, idealistic sense.

Tetley assumes a false dichotomy, pitting a skewed view of masculinity against anything that does not fit the prototype, such as women, minorities, or men who are physically weaker or who lack the taste for blood that Tetley seems to enjoy. Secure in his code of honor, he mistakes neighbors for subordinates, and like all arrogant types who cling to false notions of honor, he is apparently blind to the extent of his hubris, all the while suppressing his self-destructive inclinations or transferring them onto weaker victims, like the three men unjustly hanged or like his son. The result of Tetley's action is darker than that of Sheriff Kane, yet his methods illustrate the frightening potential inherent within an absolute, rational methodology. Nussbaum argues: "Frequently a reliance on the powers of intellect can actually become an impediment to true ethical perception, by impending or undermining those responses." Reason can become a "dangerous master" because of its "incomplete perception."[12]

Tetley's character must also be considered within the context of his most outspoken critic, Arthur Davies. The physical and emotional contrast between the two principals is significant. Tetley is cool and calculating while

Davies is emotional, though not irrational. Both men appeal to their fellow riders as a jury, each trying to convince the others of the rightness of his position. Finally, in a gesture of democracy, in mocking deference to Davies, Tetley allows a majority vote, but as he predicted, most of the riders are too intimidated to vote against him, despite a growing uncertainty about the ugly business before them. Davies offers a different approach, one that is not absolute, not preoccupied with honor for honor's sake in a detached, forensic sense. Rather, he is capable of reading the particular situation even as he understands the varying levels of potential guilt. As Nussbaum's discourse suggests, Davies is informed—and, more important, cautioned—by emotions, rather than driven by abstract ideology. She states, "Emotions may after all in many cases be an invaluable guide to correct judgment. . . . [The] general and universal formulations [like Kant's categorical imperative] may be inadequate to the complexity of particular situations . . . immersed particular judgments may have a moral value that reflective and general judgments cannot capture."[13] Admittedly, Davies is not absolutely certain of the guilt or innocence of the accused, but in his thoughtful deliberations, clearly he finds it more humane and just to err on the side of caution. His honor, to use that term, demands that the men not execute the accused until every lead has been thoroughly—that is, empirically—investigated and verified. Tetley and most others are quite satisfied that they have enough evidence and that the process of investigation has been sufficiently fair. Unfortunately, the line between honor and vengeance is drawn too finely, too fine to be of practical use in a democracy. Tetley and his eager comrades should cause us to consider the contaminating effect of lust for power emerging within the call to duty.

The unjust hanging validates some of Nussbaum's concerns about absolutist duty-bound ethics. First, consider the notion of commensurability. All three men who are hanged are considered equals in their transgression, but the dialogue in the film clarifies that mitigating situations should be considered. One old man is nearly senile. Another is openly defiant, while the third is heartbroken by the fact that his wife and children will suffer. One is the boss of the outfit, who either paid for the cattle or ordered them to be stolen. Tetley's view assumes they all are equal coconspirators. Tetley's honor-bound pursuit of these men, likewise, casts a wide net against women, his son, and the black minister. Also, consider the emotion of Davies. Ironically, like western iconic heroes, he has the courage to stand alone, yet his convictions do not stem merely from a detached code that threatens to simplify the nature of law and order. Rather, they are alive and arise out of the complex situation before him. He derives his conclusions not merely from a sense of duty, but from a careful and deliberate reading of the particulars of the situation. In Nussbaum's words, the "universalizable does not . . . determine every dimension of choice."[14]

High Noon and *The Ox-Bow Incident* suggest another important, often overlooked consequence of living strictly by code. When something goes wrong, that is, when the ideal formula fails in a complex, real-life situation, scapegoating the hero becomes an easy way for citizens to deny their individual responsibility. It is too easy to blame Kane or Tetley or others of their kind, when, in fact, a democracy would demand justice on the part of all its citizens. Perhaps an absolute allegiance to honor and duty lends itself to scapegoating because the code is easily recognizable and unequivocally associated with the actions of the supposed isolated hero, whereas a social question raised by Nussbaum would emphasize a communal approach toward the responsibility of discovering and implementing justice.[15]

The western hero, bound to his sense of duty, is so entrenched in our popular culture that it routinely recurs in films such as *A Few Good Men*. In this film, two Marines are court-marshaled for the death of a fellow soldier. Their defense is that they obeyed the code of honor intrinsic to their unit. In the end, the code is proven to be not only ineffective but also destructive and unjust. At the conclusion of the trial, one convicted Marine (James Marshall), relying on his indoctrination into an absolute code, exclaims: "What did we do wrong? We did nothing wrong." His friend, superior officer, and fellow dishonorably discharged Marine (Wolfgang Bodison) answers him: "Yeah, we did. We were supposed to fight for the people who couldn't fight for themselves." In this film, clearly, the allegiance to a code not only fails to fulfill any possible intention of justice, it significantly contributes to injustice. Lest anyone think such a discussion is merely academic, even a casual understanding of recent political debate concerning water-boarding, Abu Ghraib, and detainees at Gitmo should remind us of the consequences of attempting to substitute the implementation of a code for true justice.

Concluding Questions and Implications

Ethical choice is rarely easy. Determining the right course of action out of several possibilities or truly knowing the role self-interest plays in a choice can be perplexing. It is precisely because of such difficulty that the complexities involved in ethical inquiry should be all the more appreciated rather than simplified.

Questions remain, however, concerning the role of honor. Moral courage is necessary, but is a heroic posture always admirable? How do we determine the line between bravery, courage, and heroism and pride, vindictive foolishness, or immorality posing as a legal process? Bertrand Russell (1872–1970), like Nussbaum, argues that the consequences of moral choice (not merely abstract principles) must be considered. He, too, doubts the practical efficacy of a pure Kantian ethic. He argues, "Kant . . . states emphatically that virtue does not depend upon the intended result of an action, but only on the principle of which it is itself a result; and if this is conceded, nothing more concrete than his [categorical imperative] maxim is possible. . . . If taken seriously, it would make it impossible to reach a decision whenever two people's interest conflict."[16] In the case of Will Kane, we will never know what might—and more important, what might not—have happened had he moved on with his newly married life and avoided the conflict with Miller. As the film's text says, Kane believes that Miller would have pursued him, but that is not absolutely certain. It could be argued that his dramatic return to town is, in effect, a preemptive act that in fact keeps the old conflict alive. Given his isolation, Kane seems forced to act as he does, but it is to be remembered that his return to the town contributes directly to this life-or-death showdown. His return to face Miller is not completely devoid of self-interest.

Perhaps a satisfying balance to this discussion can be found in the lessons that fiction teaches. David Novitz (1945–2001), in *Knowledge, Fiction and Imagination*, explains that fiction informs its audiences of various types of knowledge, including propositional, factual events, practical skills of survival and coping, acquiring values and new perspectives on familiar dilemmas or new perceptions regarding aspects of our environment.[17] Most important, and very much in line with the traditional Aristotelian idea of catharsis and pathos, Novitz suggests that fiction teaches empathetic knowledge: "Fiction enables its readers to acquire beliefs about, indeed knowledge of, what it feels like to be in certain complex and demanding situations."[18] Empathy for individuals within complex situations may be the highest good fiction can offer. Perhaps fictive situations provide at least some semblance of understanding for one who resorts to a code to demonstrate honor. In the two films discussed here, the results of moral choosing offer a strong contrast. Kane's decision, it could be argued, turns out with some degree of satisfaction (though it is debatable what degree and kind of satisfaction finally is established). Tetley's action, of course, represents gross injustice. Yet, as I have attempted to demonstrate, both Kane and Tetley operate from a similar assumption of duty. Given the stories, it is certainly easier to sympathize with Kane rather than Tetley, but, more important, perhaps it would be well to consider Novitz's claim of empathy. How might any one of us act when faced with a perceived threat to our personal and communal well-being? It is this fact of potential misperception and shared human vulnerability, however, that argues most persuasively for Nussbaum's approach to contextualized ethics. We must consider the possibility that our leaders, even we ourselves as individuals in a functioning democracy, potentially run the risk of unnecessary trauma, oppression, or miscarriage of justice by relying all too readily on a seductive, one-dimensional approach when faced with moral choices.

Notes

I am grateful to Jennifer L. McMahon for her insight and commentary on this essay. Any shortcoming in the essay remains my responsibility.
    1. Martha C. Nussbaum, *Love's Knowledge: Essays on Philosophy and Literature* (New York: Oxford University Press, 1990).
    2. H. J. Paton, "Translator's Preface," in Immanuel Kant, *The Groundwork of the Metaphysics of Morals*, trans. H. J. Paton (New York: Harper Torchbooks, 1964), 8. Paton writes: "An exclusively empirical philosophy, as Kant himself argues, can have nothing to say about morality: it can only encourage us to be guided by our emotions, or at the best by an enlightened self-love."
    3. Ibid.
    4. For Kant, the good exercise of the will must be "apart from any further end" (*Groundwork of the Metaphysics of Morals*, 64). The highest moral worth occurs when one "does good, not from inclination, but from duty" (66). "The prescription for happiness is, however, often so constituted as greatly to interfere with some inclinations, and yet men cannot form under the name of 'happiness' any determinate and assured conception of the satisfaction of all inclinations as a sum.... When the universal inclination toward happiness has failed to determine his will, ... what remains over ... is a law—the law of furthering his happiness, not from inclination, but from duty; and in this for the first time his conduct has a real moral worth" (67).
    5. Ibid., 70.
    6. Ibid., 71.
    7. Nussbaum, *Love's Knowledge*, 55.
    8. Ibid.

9. Ibid., 139. Nussbaum writes: "[Ethical consideration] cannot . . . in any way be cut off from the study of the empirical and social conditions of human life; indeed, ethics, in Aristotle's conception, is a part of the social study of human beings."

10. Ibid., 173.

11. Kant, *Groundwork of the Metaphysics of Morals*, 65.

12. Nussbaum, *Love's Knowledge*, 81.

13. Ibid., 182.

14. Ibid., 39.

15. Though it is beyond the scope of this essay, one might consider the notion that the dedication to absolute principles can itself be read, in some instances, as born of the desire to scapegoat, specifically, the desire to avoid personal responsibility from moral decision making. If one has a code to fall back on, one can always say that one's moral assessment was made on the basis of the code. Any criticism can then be deflected by virtue of the fact that in effect, the decision was of the code, not of the self.

16. Bertrand Russell, *A History of Western Philosophy* (New York: Simon & Schuster, 2007), 711.

17. David Novitz, *Knowledge, Fiction and Imagination* (Philadelphia: Temple University Press, 1987). Similar emphases of fiction and social ethics are implied in Nussbaum's *Love's Knowledge* and in Wayne C. Booth's *The Company We Keep: An Ethics of Fiction* (Berkeley: University of California Press, 1988).

18. Novitz, *Knowledge*, 120.

"BACK OFF TO WHAT?"

The Search for Meaning in *The Wild Bunch*

Richard Gaughran

The Year of the Bunch

Much has been written and said about Sam Peckinpah's *The Wild Bunch* (1969) and the way it departs from the western genre in its violence and in its disruption of expectations concerning the moral stature of its heroes. The most sympathetic characters in the film, to be sure, are outlaws who do their share of killing and more, to paraphrase a line from the film. In fact, they do *a lot* more than their share. However, the disturbing aspects of *The Wild Bunch* should not cause viewers to dismiss the film as dishing up gore for its own sake, labeling Peckinpah "Bloody Sam," as some have done.

In fact, the philosophical movement that has come to be called existentialism, with roots in the nineteenth century but most fully articulated in the twentieth by writers such as Jean-Paul Sartre and Albert Camus, opens ways of understanding Peckinpah's violent masterpiece. The film, to be sure, is disturbing. But its unsettling qualities suggest a world that has become unhinged in the ways existentialist thought asserts and to which it provides a response. As philosopher Gordon Marino puts it in his anthology of existentialist writers, "The existential movement is a response to the disenchantment of the world, that is, to the sense that the history and social structure of the world are not God-sanctioned." Marino further points out that the movement's popularity can perhaps be attributed to "the abattoir of the twentieth century."[1]

To lay a foundation for examining the ways existentialist thought aids our understanding of *The Wild Bunch,* it is useful to examine the era in which the action of the film takes place, since the political and cultural changes of the time were cataclysmic, reverberating around the world, and these transformations impinge upon the film's view of human identity, human freedom, and the characters' options.

Most westerns are set in the second half of the nineteenth century. Viewers expect the stars to be riding on horses, not in cars. The railroad appears often within examples of the genre, of course, and steamboats are likewise permissible. But no automobiles, and certainly no airplanes. Peckinpah's masterpiece takes place not in the nineteenth century, however, but in 1913. And it prominently features an automobile, just as does the director's follow-up, *The Ballad of Cable Hogue* (1970), in many ways a comedic counterpoint to *The Wild Bunch*.[2] Furthermore, the appearance of the automobile in the earlier film occasions a brief discussion among members of the Bunch about airplanes, with Pike Bishop (William Holden) declaring that "they" plan to use them in "the war."[3]

This reference to war implies that these new machines possess destructive power. Indeed, the cars that appear in both *The Wild Bunch* and in *The Ballad of Cable Hogue* are instruments of harm. The car in *The Wild Bunch* drags the battered Angel (Jaime Sanchez) through Agua Verde, and in the later film Hogue (Jason Robards) is fatally injured when a car rolls over him. Machines represent a serious threat to human life as it has been lived till this time. Cecilia Tichi, commenting on the rise of new technologies in this period, says, "Machine technology . . . sometimes comes to represent uncontrolled, destabilizing power."[4]

Peckinpah introduces the automobile in *The Wild Bunch* quite suddenly, without preparing the audience. Paul Seydor cogently comments on the director's impulses in this regard: "The filmmaking itself is . . . made to convey what it must have felt like to see this strange thing for the first time. No one prepared the people in this village for the automobile—suddenly it was there, and suddenly life was different."[5] It may be more than coincidence that 1913, the year of the action of *The Wild Bunch*, was also the year that Henry Ford first introduced the moving assembly line for the manufacture of automobiles.[6] It was also the year the Lincoln Highway was dedicated, the first highway to link the nation's two coasts.[7]

The period that provides the setting for *The Wild Bunch* introduced more than technological change, however. The Mexican Revolution was at a crucial stage; the film itself depicts members of the Wild Bunch as playing a role in the conflict. On another continent, war was rapidly changing national boundaries on the Balkan Peninsula. And war on an even greater, unprecedented, scale was imminent, with Gavrilo Princip's 1914 assassination of Archduke Franz Ferdinand about to ignite the First World War.

(The appearance of German advisors in Agua Verde encourages viewers of *The Wild Bunch* to think of the impending war.) Within a few years, great empires—the Austro-Hungarian, the Ottoman—would cease to exist, and the Bolsheviks would seize power in Russia.

Accompanying these technological and political transformations were new ways of thinking, new philosophies. Karl Marx spearheaded just one of these. Although Marx had written in the previous century, his ideas concerning economic determinism and the progression of history found a foothold in the 1910s. The ideas of Charles Darwin, another nineteenth-century thinker, were being digested in this period, presenting a challenge to the traditional understanding of human origins. Sigmund Freud, for his part, presented compelling but disturbing new ways of understanding the internal world of the individual. His central work, *The Interpretation of Dreams,* though it had been published in German over a decade earlier, appeared in English for the first time in the year of the Bunch: 1913.

There were also important new artistic developments in this period— again, more threats to the established order. In 1913, while members of the Bunch were shooting up south Texas and northern Mexico, in Paris Igor Stravinsky presented his *The Rite of Spring* for the first time. This shocking departure from traditional musical form was met with hostility from critics and the audience; the police were finally called to quell a riot.[8] In New York, again in 1913, the infamous Armory Show art exhibition took place, provoking ridicule and abuse in speech and print. The show included works such as Marcel Duchamp's *Nude Descending a Staircase,* scandalous not for showing the naked female body, but for seemingly being devoid of any form other than a cascade of numerous flesh-colored geometrical shapes—far different from traditional depictions of the human body.

In 1913, the *modern* was being born.

This barrage of changes, these new ways of thinking about the universe and a human being's place in it—or lack of place in it—resulted in a general feeling of anxiety in American lives. Tichi appropriately uses terms such as "agitation, restlessness, frenzy" to describe the "undisciplined, destabilizing energies loosed throughout American life."[9]

"Maybe a Few Hymns Would Be in Order"?

This dizzying assortment of changes accompanied, if not caused, changes in traditional religious and spiritual orientation, with concomitant disruption to views of morality. In the 1880s Friedrich Nietzsche—a precursor of twentieth-century existentialists—declared "God is dead," meaning, of course, not that God had once existed and then expired but that "the belief in the Christian God has ceased to be believable." Writing in the late nineteenth century, Nietzsche acknowledged that this realization had not yet come to the masses, but soon, he wrote, in "the coming century," a new dawn would reveal a free horizon, "even granted that it is not bright."[10] If there is no God, then there is no *Truth,* at least not one with a capital T: "To acknowledge untruth as a condition of life: this clearly means resisting the usual value feelings in a dangerous manner; and a philosophy that risks such a thing would by that gesture alone place itself beyond good and evil."[11]

Nietzsche refers to this new state of affairs as "dangerous," because without God, or without an agreed-upon set of moral standards such as those established by Christianity, values, or *truths* in the lowercase, derive from the individual alone, opening up any number of possibilities: "The dangerous and uncanny point has been reached when the greatest, most diverse, most comprehensive life lives past the old morality. The 'individual' is left standing there, forced to give himself laws, forced to rely on his own arts and wiles of self-preservation, self-enhancement, self-redemption. There is nothing but new whys and hows; there are no longer any shared formulas."[12]

In this context, a close look at the opening scenes of *The Wild Bunch* reveals just how thoroughly the film discredits traditional religious belief and observance. In particular, Christianity and Christian pieties are subject to parody and ridicule. For one thing, the film opens as the Bunch rides into Starbuck, a curious name for a town in south Texas, given that the town also seems to bear the perhaps older name San Rafael, a name inscribed on a building shown in the opening sequences. The name Starbuck seems strange, until one recalls that Starbuck is chief mate on the *Pequod* in Herman Melville's *Moby-Dick.* He is the representative Christian man, the resident democrat, embodying ideals said to derive from God. But the self-righteous Starbuck is ultimately ineffectual, and he must submit to—and die under—a more primitive form of authority wielded by Captain Ahab. Likewise, this sleepy town in south Texas is ill equipped to handle pitiless power and unrestrained grasping, whether exercised by Pike and his men or by Harrigan (Albert Dekker) and his railroad.

Still, Christian references and imagery abound in Starbuck. The South Texas Temperance Union is engaged in a tent meeting as the Bunch rides in, and the film's opening credits roll against the cutting back and forth between this meeting, presided over by Mayor Wainscoat (Dub Taylor), and the advance of the outlaws. Two philosophical approaches are juxtaposed: one Christian and traditional, one lawless and adrift, searching for new meanings with which to fill the void. Those who attend the tent meeting are uniformly old, or if not, then they look old. Their time has passed, and the film's irreverently comic treatment of this meeting, with the self-righteous mayor intoning a pledge that his audience tries unsuccessfully to repeat, underscores the ineffectual nature of this set of values. When Pike suggests that his men fall into step with the marching Temperance Union, Dutch Engstrom's (Ernest Borgnine) incredulous reaction again emphasizes the film's point that traditional belief and observance have been rendered obsolete. He reacts with an impish giggle. Crazy Lee's (Bo Hopkins) mocking march with his hostages, to the tune of "Shall We Gather at the River," has a similar effect.

To further emphasize the point, one of the bounty hunters, Coffer (Strother Martin), sports a cross around his neck. But in place of Christ's body he has fastened a bullet. Coffer has taken the central symbol of one set of values and defaced it to signify a new reality. This new reality announces itself with the command Pike Bishop delivers just as the opening credits end and the director's name is about to flash on the screen: "If they move, kill 'em!"

It becomes clearer as the film continues that moving is the Bunch's modus operandi. The outlaws, now diminished in number, retreat across the desert, along with a member who, shot in the face, can no longer see to ride. After briefly expressing his desire to persevere, he despairs, pleading with Pike to "finish it." After Pike complies, he poses a question to the others: "You boys wanna move on? Or stay here and give him a decent burial?" He pauses before the word *decent*. Then he spits it out, almost contemptuously. Pike is asking the others to choose between his pragmatic decision to keep moving without delay and a traditional response to death, namely, Christian ritual. When Tector Gorch (Ben Johnson) refers to their dead comrade as "a good man" who deserves respectful treatment, Dutch intervenes with the appropriate sarcasm: "Maybe a few hymns would be in order, followed by a church supper. With a choir." The world of 1913 is no longer the world of nineteenth-century poet Robert Browning's character Pippa, who sings, "God's in his heaven— / All's right with the world!"[13] Any meaning will have to come from a different source, namely, as mentioned earlier, the individual, upon whom the responsibility for all values now rests.

A problem arises, or a danger, to again use Nietzsche's language, in that actions originating from a purely subjective source might be destructive, even murderous. Since life is absurd, an individual might decide upon any action at all, shrugging off traditional qualms with a simple "Why not?" Sartre refers to this seeming difficulty by quoting Fyodor Dostoyevsky's character Ivan Karamazov: " 'If God didn't exist, everything would be possible.' That is the very starting point of existentialism."[14]

"Those Days Are Closin' Fast"

The members of the Wild Bunch, however, are not thoroughly nihilistic. They too cling, albeit tenuously, to values from the past. Tector's impulse to dignify his fallen comrade's death with a ritual, for example, reveals that a vestige of belief remains. And Pike in particular often forcefully professes his belief in certain values and a code of behavior that springs from those values. After he stops Tector from dispatching Freddie Sykes (Edmond O'Brien), who has become an annoyance to the impatient Gorch brothers, Pike delivers a speech: "When you side with a man you stay with him. And if you can't do that you're like some animal. You're finished. *We're* finished. All of us."

Pike himself, however, demonstrates how difficult it is to remain faithful to such a code. The scene that follows finds him riding alongside Old Man Sykes, who starts a conversation by referring to Pike's speech: "Hey, uh, that was a mighty fine talk you gave the boys back there about sticking together." He then asks about his grandson, Clarence "Crazy" Lee: "Say, back there in Starbuck, how'd my boy do?" A flashback to the scene in Starbuck then interrupts the conversation between Pike and Sykes, forcefully underscoring Pike's betrayal. In Starbuck Pike gave Crazy Lee the meaningless task of guarding a small group of citizens and abandoned him to die, seemingly forgetting about him—or, perhaps, deliberately using this situation as a way of eliminating this mentally unstable and therefore unreliable member of the gang.

Sykes's reminder of the values that Pike has just espoused comes just before the reminder that Pike hasn't really been living by these values. The expression on Pike's face in this scene communicates awareness of failure to live by his own codes. Yet he feebly attempts to excuse himself, saying to Sykes, "Why didn't you tell me he was your grandson?" He is saying, in effect, I may not be living by my own rules, but I could have resorted to favoritism or nepotism if I had only known.

But the abandonment of Crazy Lee is only one of Pike's failures. In fact, Pike will abandon Sykes himself—the very person he defended with his sticking-together speech—after the old man is wounded in the leg, a wound recalling Pike's own injury. Moreover, Pike and his men are running from a posse of bounty hunters because of Pike's previous abandonment of Deke Thornton (Robert Ryan), revealed, again, in flashbacks. Pike's former partner was captured and sent to prison after Pike reassured him that a knock on a door signaled nothing more than the delivery of champagne, not the law. He proclaims his certainty with a boast: "Being sure is my business!" But he is being careless, not sure, just as he is careless in getting wounded in the leg and getting his lover Aurora (Aurora Clavel) killed by her husband, again an event revealed in flashback.[15]

To reiterate, Pike *knows* he has failed in these instances. He tells Dutch about the loss of Aurora and how he was wounded—and viewers see the flashback to the episode—just as the outlaws are riding off to rob an army supply train. After talking about Aurora, Pike abruptly says to Dutch, "This is our last go-round, Dutch. This time we do it right." His resolute tone here functions as a confession of past failures and an expression of his determination to make amends. Yet, as we shall see, he will be careless again, and he will abandon another member of his close circle, Angel—a failure addressed only in the bloody climax of the film.

Pike's failures deserve further scrutiny. To be sure, he fails to live up to his code. But the code itself has been rendered obsolete. It belongs to a previous era, the "Old West," and the code is probably best exemplified (within the Peckinpah canon, at least) in the character Steve Judd (Joel McCrea) from *Ride the High Country* (1962), who, nearing the end of his life, says, "I want to enter my own house justified." The manner in which Peckinpah chose to film Judd's death in that earlier film is telling. The fallen hero sinks slowly to earth, like a setting sun, finally dropping below the screen. In this manner the film suggests that the myth of the Old West has died, and with it a set of values—if that era and its values ever existed in the first place. As critic Richard Whitehead says, *Ride the High Country* "is not only a celebration of the myth, it is also a requiem."[16]

Significantly, when we first see Deke Thornton—played by an actor with considerable experience in old-style westerns—he is waiting in ambush on a Starbuck rooftop, but he has dozed off, his aged, wrinkled face seeming to belong to an old man taking his afternoon nap rather than to a seasoned outlaw or bounty hunter. The leader of the bounty hunters, the members of the Temperance Union, the members of the Bunch—they are *old*, out of time. After the botched robbery in Starbuck, Old Man Sykes pointedly reminds the Bunch of the passing of time: "You boys ain't gettin' any younger." Pike then acknowledges the fact: "We gotta start thinkin' beyond our guns. Those days are closin' fast." But the doors to those days are not closing; they are closed. Only the speeches and gestures remain. As Paul Schrader says, "The Westerners of *The Wild Bunch* have only the remnants of the code. They mouth many of the familiar platitudes but the honor and the purpose are absent."[17]

Several of the discussions among members of the Bunch reveal a group of men groping in the dark for meaning, as they engage in debates, albeit laconic ones, about values. One of the most pointed of these occurs after Sykes is shot by one of Thornton's men. Dutch curses Thornton, to which Pike replies, "What would you do in his place? He gave his word." When Dutch dismisses this consideration because Thornton gave his word to a railroad, Pike stands by his absolutist position: "It's his word." He has no answer to Dutch's impassioned relativistic response: "That's not what counts; it's who you give it to!"

Peckinpah's previous films similarly address the theme of adhering to one's word. In *Ride the High Country*, Gil Westrum (Randolph Scott) tempts Steve Judd by saying, "You gave your word to a bank. The deal doesn't count." In this case, Judd doesn't budge. His word is his word, and standing on it will keep him justified as he enters his "own house." In the follow-up to *High Country*, *Major Dundee* (1964), Captain Tyreen (Richard Harris) keeps his word to Dundee (Charlton Heston), a man he despises. In *Dundee*, however, the ground has shifted somewhat, since Tyreen's adherence to the code is complicated, as Deke Thornton's is, by a practical consideration: in both cases the keeping of one's word keeps the character out of prison, and in Tyreen's case most likely saves him from execution for the murder of a guard. In *High Country* the code remains in place, though relativist doubts lurk just over the horizon; in *Dundee* these doubts have begun to erode the code; by *The Wild Bunch* the erosion is complete, as Pike has no response to Dutch's statement other than to internalize its implications, squinting his eyes and tightly pursing his lips.

Dutch and Pike engage in a similar exchange about values when the outlaws sit at a table in Agua Verde, within sight of General Mapache (Emilio Fernandez). Dutch says the general is nothing more than a common bandit, "grabbing all he can for himself." When Pike jokes, "Like some others I could mention," referring to himself and his men, Dutch takes offense, again trying to make relativist distinctions: "Not so's you'd know it, Mr. Bishop. We ain't nothin' like him; we don't *hang* nobody." Here again, the characters are searching for moral clarity. Dutch's point is arguable, of course. Pike and his men may not hang people, but they do plenty of indiscriminate killing, beginning in Starbuck and ending in Agua Verde. So the debate is unresolved, just as is the discussion of whether the inviolability of one's word changes with the context.

But the unresolved nature of the debate is precisely the point: in this world no one can be certain what's right and what's wrong, whether one action has any more meaning than another. Seydor, in his intricate study of Peckinpah's marriage of form and content in film, mentions the frequent explosions, the collapsing bridges, the race against lit fuses and the like, as literal, concrete examples of what happens on an abstract plane. He paraphrases W. B. Yeats: "It is a world where things really do fall apart and the center does not hold for very long."[18] It is, in short, the world as Nietzsche describes it: "this mad chaos of confusion and desire."[19] Seydor further suggests that the unstable nature of Peckinpah's film world, on the concrete and abstract planes, speaks to an uncertain worldview: "The multiple perspectives that are the organizing principle of his films suggest a mind dissatisfied with all absolutes, discontent with all certainties, disinclined to settle upon any simple explanations."[20]

"You Have No Eyes"

Besides these pointed debates concerning moral issues, the dialogue of *The Wild Bunch* often involves disputed interpretations of the objective world, further implying that reality is uncertain, the world unstable. After the failed robbery in Starbuck, the outlaws meet at their rendezvous point to discover that they have robbed the railroad office of simple washers. But at first one of them, Tector Gorch, believes they are silver rings. For a brief moment he sees what he wants to see. But Tector's vision gives him a less optimistic interpretation of Mexican vistas when the outlaws approach the Rio Grande. Angel, for his own subjective reasons, sighs, "*Mexico lindo,*" to which Tector's brother Lyle (Warren Oates) says, "I don't see nothin' so *lindo* about it," with Tector chiming in, "Just looks like more of Texas far as I'm concerned." Angel counters, "Ah, you have no eyes," both a romantic's defense of his homeland and the film's suggestion that reality is purely subjective.

In effect, when these characters question each other about the nature of the world and its possible meanings, they implicitly illustrate Sartre's notion of "forlornness," which results, he says, from the awareness "that God does not exist and . . . we have to face all the consequences of this."[21]

Individuals cannot refer to meanings provided beforehand, since there is no one outside of them to provide them: "If God does not exist, we find no values or commands to turn to which legitimize our conduct . . . we have no excuse behind us, nor justification before us." Explaining existentialist philosophy's emphasis on the subjective nature of reality, Sartre continues, "The existentialist does not think that man is going to help himself by finding in the world some omen by which to orient himself. Because he thinks that man will interpret the omen to suit himself."[22]

The Wild Bunch's characters illustrate the uncertain nature of their interpretations in various other exchanges, some of them seemingly mundane, and these exchanges further underscore the film's general atmosphere of instability and uncertainty. When Deke Thornton and his men arrive at the river crossing and stare across into Mexico, Thornton, learning that Agua Verde is the closest substantial settlement, asks Coffer, "What's in Agua Verde?" Coffer replies, reasonably, "Mexicans. What else?" Coffer no doubt deliberately mishears the intent of Thornton's question for the sake of humor, but the exchange again hints that meanings are uncertain, words themselves fluid.

Similarly, characters often misunderstand or misread what they are seeing, and sometimes they act upon these misunderstandings. When Angel shoots Teresa (Sonia Amelio), Zamorra (Jorge Russek) demands, "Why did he try to kill His Excellency?" When members of the Wild Bunch uncouple a section of the army supply train, the bewildered army officer, who slept through the robbery, concludes that "the railroad deputies have robbed the train." Because Thornton and his men (the deputies in question) leave the train before the army contingent does, the officer makes a faulty assumption. He, too, has no eyes. In the ensuing gun battle, the misunderstanding becomes lethal, as the bounty hunters/deputies briefly turn their guns on the pursuing army. "You stupid bastards! Why did you fire at those soldiers?" asks an incensed Thornton afterward. His men lack an adequate answer. Viewers, however, are left with the realization that the world has become unmoored and that reality is unfixed. Individuals have a limited field of vision, and their knowledge of the world around them is greatly restricted. They see only what they are able to see or what they want to see. Indeed, reality has never been absolute, but the modern era brings this realization to the fore. As Sartre says, meaning does not originate from outside the individual. Instead, "it can only come from subjectivity."[23] As Peckinpah has remarked, referring to his characters in *The Wild Bunch*, "In a land for all intents and purposes without law, they made their own."[24]

Angel is the one member of the Bunch who consistently clings to a set of beliefs, and he finally dies for them. His very name suggests connections to an invisible realm, and his *"Mexico lindo"* quickly reveals his romanticism, if not his chauvinism. As the scene shifts to Mexico, particularly as the Bunch visit Angel's village, Angel's character comes into clearer focus. We learn that he idealizes women, viewing them, notably his Teresa, as chaste and incorruptible. When he learns that Mapache has killed his father and that Teresa willingly left with the general, he is especially concerned that Teresa's purity might be compromised. The village elder, Don Jose (Chano Urueta), diagnoses Angel's idealism: "To him Teresa was like a goddess, to be worshipped from afar. Mapache knew she was a mango, ripe and waiting!"

In the steam bath scene in Agua Verde, Angel's belief system collides with the other outlaws' plans. He is unwilling to rob the supply train and thereby supply guns to the Mexican army, his people's enemy. Dutch, who previously expressed sympathy for the revolutionary cause Angel supports, here mocks his friend, saying, "Noble, noble, very noble." When Sykes then reminds Angel that he had no qualms about participating in the bloodletting in Starbuck, Angel says, "They were not my people. I care about my people, my village, Mexico!"

Needless to say, Angel's beliefs and his resulting actions put the Bunch in considerable danger in Agua Verde. His shooting of Teresa could easily have gotten him and all his companions killed. His insistence on redirecting some of the stolen guns to his village eventually does get him killed, and it provides the catalyst for the film's climactic bloodbath. But it is a mistake to conclude, as critic Michael Bliss does, that *The Wild Bunch* ultimately sanctions Angel's beliefs. Bliss argues, "It should be apparent that through our final identification with the Bunch, the film virtually compels us to accept these ideals, thus making us over in its own image."[25] On the contrary, Angel's beliefs are unrealistic regarding women, as we've seen. Furthermore, Angel's privileging of his family, his village, and his country—however customary and widespread similar allegiances might be—still derives from an arbitrary, invented value system.

"Let's Go!"

To be sure, some of Angel's fellow outlaws express nostalgic sympathy for his worldview. Dutch wants the cause of Angel's villagers to succeed—mostly, it seems, because he sees the repulsive contrast in Mapache and his kind. And

Pike, especially, harbors notions of hearth and home. He says he wanted to marry Aurora, and in the bathhouse scene he argues that Angel should get over his qualms about assisting Mapache by using his cut to buy distant ranches for his villagers. Yet even in this scene, Pike, when challenged by Angel to consider what he would do in Angel's situation, says, "Ten thousand cuts an awful lot of family ties."

Angel's ideals, in fact all ideals or notions of absolute value, are most forcefully undercut fairly early in the film, on the night of the Starbuck debacle, as Dutch and Pike talk and sip whiskey while lying in their bedrolls. Pike declares, "I'd like to make one good score and back off." Dutch poignantly asks, "Back off to what?" The answer to this question comes in the form of approximately ten seconds of palpable silence, as the camera cuts from face to perplexed face. Clearly, these men are asking themselves about ultimate meanings, about what's possible in the world in which they find themselves. For a few seconds, they gaze into the abyss.

Pike seems to assume, with his "back off," that an a priori ground of meaning exists, whether it involves buying a ranch and raising a family, supporting a revolution that will lift villagers from sadness and deprivation, or ascending to a home on high reserved for those who remain faithful to God. But the times in which they live, as well as experience, show the Bunch that no fate has been predetermined. God is dead, and the characters of *The Wild Bunch* demonstrate through their actions that they know that this is true, whether they say so or not. There is nothing to affirm except that humans exist on the earth. There are no answers to the question *why* except ones human beings provide for themselves. And when members of the Bunch commit themselves to action by saying "Why not?"—as Pike and Lyle do at different key moments—they acknowledge that no ground of absolute value exists. Sartre puts it this way: "All possibility of finding values in a heaven of ideas disappears along with Him [God]; there can no longer be an *a priori* Good, since there is no infinite and perfect consciousness to think it. Nowhere is it written that the Good exists, that we must be honest, that we must not lie; because the fact is we are on a plane where there are only men."[26]

Thornton's frustrated declaration to his incompetent, undisciplined men ("egg-suckin', chicken-stealin' gutter-trash") about the Wild Bunch—"We're after *men,* and I wish to God I was with them"—takes on new resonance in this context. Thornton has this wish partly because his former partner and his men still have choices left to them, whereas Thornton has been given an ultimatum by Harrigan ("thirty days to get Pike, or thirty days back to Yuma"), and Thornton has sealed the ultimatum with his "word." In effect, Thornton has freely chosen to have limited choice, and Harrigan himself implies that such is the case when he worries that his "Judas goat" might exercise other options in running off with the other bounty hunters or in rejoining the Bunch. "You'd like that, wouldn't you?" he says to Thornton, who acknowledges that he would but that his "need" takes precedence over his desires. Nevertheless, he remains envious of the Bunch, of whom Pike can say with some justification, "We're not associated with anybody."

In their fireside conversation about backing off, Dutch and Pike are merely talking. But talk or good intentions count for nothing in a universe that provides no ground for meaning. Only in action can they affirm meaning. As Sartre puts it, "Action is the only thing that enables a man to live."[27] Robert Culp, in an appreciation of Peckinpah published shortly after release of *The Wild Bunch*, echoes this theme:

> Finally, in the least creature on this earth, only the quality of his behavior is important to survival, to establish intrinsic value. That's all there is. The rest is literally only talk. And talk is a trick of the mind, not very reliable: The Bunch spits in death's eye (for us), embraces the final knowledge of every man (for us), that he must at the end go down alone and must do it well. They don't talk about it, they just do it. For us. . . . All that Sartre and Camus have done from their massive, agonized intelligence, Peckinpah attempts empirically from his guts.[28]

The Wild Bunch announces the theme of action very early, in a remark by an official in the Starbuck railroad offices that the Bunch is about to rob. The scene provides no context for the remark, no information about the person to whom it is addressed. Rather, the film includes this speech, delivered before the final opening credits, solely to announce a theme. The official is scolding an employee: "I don't care what you meant to do; it's what you *did* I don't like."

Furthermore, the film repeatedly reminds viewers of this theme of action in the refrain "Let's go!" Pike barks it out more than the other characters do, but Thornton and Coffer use it, as does even Mapache, albeit in Spanish. In this brief exhortation, the characters establish themselves as Camus' rebels, those who recognize their absurd condition. They reside in a world without intrinsic meaning. Death is the only certain future. Yet the rebel refuses to surrender. "Rebellion," Camus says, "is one of the essential dimensions of man. It is our historic reality. Unless we choose to ignore reality, we must find our values in it."[29] Peckinpah's instincts, or his deliberations, were correct in having the phrase spoken in isolation, brief and undiluted by longer speech. (Admittedly, Pike adds, " . . . you lazy bastard" on a couple of occasions.) Walon Green, Peckinpah's cowriter of *The Wild Bunch*, has commented on the brevity of the phrase: "That was the place in the film for a speech, you know, that's where the guys should've said what their whole thing was about. . . . It did just say 'Let's go,' and it was really Sam's direction that made the line work."[30]

The line works, as Seydor has said, because it expresses Peckinpah's notion of character, which "views people not as fixed and limited but as fluid and dynamic." Furthermore, the line encapsulates the Bunch's "fundamental dialectic, which is drawn not between life and death, but between movement and death defined as stasis."[31] If we think back on the good citizens of sleepy Starbuck, we can see them as in stasis. Harrigan might not be far wrong in referring to the place as he does, and his barnyard imagery includes a reference to the citizens' penchant, not for action, but for speech and speechifying (for example, the Temperance Union meeting): "How long do you think anybody in this manure pile could keep his mouth shut?"

Not all the occurrences of "Let's go!" have equal force. Some of them are evasions, as is Pike's "Why not?" in reference to choosing a romp with Agua Verde whores rather than the pursuit of further attempts to rescue Angel. He offers to buy him from Mapache but then doesn't insist when the general refuses to part with him. Earlier, before the Bunch returns to Agua Verde for the last time, Dutch reveals that Sykes has said the Bunch should go after Angel. Pike dismisses that suggestion quickly: "No way in hell." He clearly would like to free Angel from being tortured, but, as we have seen, intentions have no meaning. Only actions count. An external reality will not provide Pike with authentic meaning. He can't hope for outside intervention, any more than he can expect a retreat to Agua Verde will solve the problem of Deke Thornton's pursuit. Pike's inaction with regard to Angel reveals the hollowness of his earlier code speech about loyalty to those with whom one sides. Sartre argues against quietism, "the attitude of people who say, 'Let others do what I can't do.'" He then approvingly imagines the words of those with the opposite view: " 'There is no reality except in action. . . . Man is nothing else than his plan; he exists only to the extent that he fulfills himself; he is therefore nothing else than the ensemble of his acts, nothing less than his life.' "[32]

Sartre's words here clarify Pike's enigmatic remark to Dutch during their fireside chat about backing off. When Pike refers to plans for new heists, Dutch reminds him, "They'll be waitin' for us," referring, of course, to those empowered to carry out the law. Pike replies, "I wouldn't have it any other way." Dutch's answer doesn't come until the close of their talk, as the two are drifting into sleep: "Pike? I wouldn't have it any other way either." Their position expresses more than mere machismo. They implicitly know that only in testing themselves in action can they bring themselves into being.

Pike, as we have seen, is haunted by accumulating acts of carelessness and, in particular, his abandonment of those with whom he has sworn to stand. By the time he reaches his final decision—whether to confront Mapache over the fate of Angel—his options have narrowed. True, he has gold buried in the desert. He could presumably ride out of Agua Verde without being stopped. But such a choice would be an evasion, a further postponement of his need to claim genuine meaning for his life, to create a unified center. As Seydor pointedly says, "Walk away, his life's a fraud; stay and fight, his life is over."[33] Camus speaks about those who reject traditional structures of meaning because they don't honestly address the human condition: "There is not one human being who, above a certain elementary level of consciousness, does not exhaust himself in trying to find formulas or attitudes that will give his existence the unity it lacks. . . . This passion which lifts the mind above the commonplaces of a dispersed world, from which it nevertheless cannot free itself, is the passion for unity. It does not result in mediocre methods to escape, however, but in the most obstinate demands."[34]

The many repetitions of "Let's go" throughout the film prepare us for Pike's choice and for the decisive utterance of the phrase. Pike pays a whore, leaves her chambers, and confronts the Gorch brothers, who are haggling with a whore in an adjoining room. "Let's go!" he says. The Gorches look at each other, saying nothing, but they evidently fill in the blanks. "Why not?" Lyle says, thereby giving his and Tector's assent. Likewise Dutch, outside the door idly whittling a stick, says yes to this decision, this created meaning, simply by exchanging a smile with Pike and repeating one of his patented giggles. As Walon Green has said, these exchanges require little speech, and on film the moment is perfect. It's time for decisive action, not talk.

This crucial decision does not proceed from the Bunch's agreeing to a preordained system of meaning, nor are these men reclaiming obsolete frontier codes. Instead, by heroically marching to their deaths they are paradoxically choosing life over death, spitting in death's eye, as Culp says. It is true that the revolutionary cause and that of Angel's village benefit from the bloodbath that decimates Agua Verde. Presumably, Angel's people now have not merely one case of the stolen rifles with which to advance their aims but all sixteen. And scores of their enemy perish. But the four men who confront Mapache, his troops, and the German advisors are not thinking about balancing an arms race, or about revolution and other abstract principles. They intuitively realize that absolute value does not exist, but they know they have failed Angel, just as they failed in similar ways in the past. They express not revolutionary zeal in this moment but "fidelity to the human condition."[35]

In this decisive year, the year in which traditional systems of meaning have been put on trial and have been found wanting, the members of the Wild Bunch recognize the absurdity of the human condition, but they say "Let's go!" They refuse to surrender to the deathward drift. They no longer resort to deceit or evasion. Instead they act, albeit belatedly. Their tragic choice constitutes a creative act that asserts authentic meaning. They act, and in acting they create values where none existed before, creating, as Sartre says, "an image of man as [they] think he ought to be."[36] They address a question Camus raises: "Is it possible to find a rule of conduct outside the realm of religion and its absolute values?"[37] As an answer, the members of the Bunch decide to be fully human themselves and to make a stand for humanity.

Notes

1. Gordon Marino, introduction to *Basic Writings of Existentialism*, ed. Gordon Marino (New York: Modern Library, 2004), xiv. Peckinpah, it should be noted, was versed in the writings of Sartre and Camus. See David Weddle, *"If They Move . . . Kill 'Em!"* (New York: Grove, 1994), 73–74.

2. John M. Gourlie most pointedly refers to these films as companion pieces, saying, "These two films constitute Peckinpah's *Iliad* and *Odyssey*" (115). See his "Peckinpah's Epic Vision: *The Wild Bunch* and *The Ballad of Cable Hogue*" in *Sam Peckinpah's West: New Perspectives*, ed. Leonard Engel (Salt Lake City: University of Utah Press, 2003), 115–27.

3. It's not clear exactly which war Bishop means. The Mexican Revolution is unfolding before his eyes, but the Second Balkan War was also raging at this time, in which

planes saw limited use. He's also only about a year away from the outbreak of World War I, which would see extensive use of warplanes. Is Pike predicting WWI?

4. Cecilia Tichi, *Shifting Gears* (Chapel Hill and London: University of North Carolina Press, 1987), 52.

5. Paul Seydor, *Peckinpah: The Western Films—A Reconsideration* (Urbana and Chicago: University of Illinois Press, 1997), 186. Like many writers on Peckinpah's films, I find Seydor's analyses and insights to be first-rate on almost every aspect of the director's struggles and achievements. Among other things, his discussion of the different versions of *The Wild Bunch* is authoritative, and he is instrumental in bringing to market the 1996 DVD of the film, the 145-minute "director's cut."

6. Michael Adas, *Machines as the Measure of Man: Science, Technology and Ideologies of Western Dominance* (New York: Cornell University Press, 1989), 409.

7. Brian Butko, *Greetings from the Lincoln Highway: America's First Coast-to-Coast Road* (Mechanicsburg, PA: Stackpole, 2005), 6.

8. See Peter Hill, *Stravinsky: The Rite of Spring* (Cambridge: Cambridge University Press, 2000), 30–32.

9. Tichi, *Shifting Gears*, 43.

10. Friedrich Nietzsche, *The Gay Science: Book V*, in *The Portable Nietzsche*, trans. and ed. Walter Kaufman (New York: Viking, 1954), 447.

11. Friedrich Nietzsche, *Beyond Good and Evil: Prelude to a Philosophy of the Future*, trans. Judith Norman (Cambridge: Cambridge University Press, 2001), 7.

12. Ibid., 159.

13. Robert Browning, "Pippa Passes," in *Poetry of the Victorian Period*, 3rd ed., ed. Jerome Hamilton Buckley and George Benjamin Woods (Glenview, IL: Scott, Foresman, 1965), 184.

14. Jean-Paul Sartre, *Existentialism and Human Emotions*, trans. Bernard Frechtman (New York: Philosophical Library, 1957), 22.

15. The flashbacks, sacrificed in the abridged versions of the film, are necessary for the establishment of the theme of desertion, and they are indispensable for understanding character motivations, particularly for understanding how Deke Thornton finds himself in deadly pursuit of his friend. For a thorough discussion of the flashbacks and their importance, and for his decisive argument in favor of the 145-minute version of the film, see Seydor, *Peckinpah*, 151–63.

16. Quoted in Paul Schrader, "Sam Peckinpah Going to Mexico," in *Doing It Right: The Best Criticism on Sam Peckinpah's "The Wild Bunch*," ed. Michael Bliss (Carbondale: Southern Illinois University Press, 1994), 18.

17. Ibid., 24.

18. Seydor, *Peckinpah*, 201.

19. Nietzsche, *Beyond Good and Evil*, 6.

20. Seydor, *Peckinpah*, 204.

21. Sartre, *Existentialism and Human Emotions*, 21.

22. Ibid., 23.

23. Jean-Paul Sartre, *Being and Nothingness,* trans. Hazel E. Barnes (New York: Philosophical Library, 1956), 539.

24. Quoted in *Sam Peckinpah Interviews,* ed. Kevin J. Hayes (Jackson: University Press of Mississippi, 2008), 41.

25. Michael Bliss, *Justified Lives: Morality and Narrative in the Films of Sam Peckinpah* (Carbondale: Southern Illinois University Press, 1993), 107. Anyone studying Peckinpah's films, in particular *The Wild Bunch,* has reason to be grateful for Bliss's work, and his anthology of criticism on *The Wild Bunch* is invaluable. In my judgment, however, his Neoplatonist reading of this film, which sees it as a contest between materialistic and idealistic worldviews, is derived from making too much of the Bunch's idyllic exit from Angel's village and the scene's reappearance at the close of the film.

26. Sartre, *Existentialism and Human Emotions,* 22.

27. Ibid., 36.

28. Robert Culp, "Sam Peckinpah, the Storyteller, and *The Wild Bunch,*" in *Doing It Right: The Best Criticism on Sam Peckinpah's "The Wild Bunch,"* ed. Michael Bliss (Carbondale: Southern Illinois University Press, 1994), 8–9.

29. Albert Camus, *The Rebel: An Essay on Man in Revolt,* trans. Anthony Bower (New York: Vintage, 1991), 21.

30. Green's comments are given in a voice-over on Paul Seydor's documentary *The Wild Bunch: An Album in Montage,* which is included with the 1996 DVD of *The Wild Bunch.*

31. Seydor, *Peckinpah,* 194.

32. Sartre, *Existentialism and Human Emotions,* 31–32.

33. Seydor, *Peckinpah,* 169.

34. Camus, *The Rebel,* 262.

35. Ibid., 290.

36. Sartre, *Existentialism and Human Emotions,* 17.

37. Camus, *The Rebel,* 21.

No Country for Old Men

The Decline of Ethics and the West(ern)

William J. Devlin

"You Can't Help but Compare Yourself against the Old Timers"

The "Wild West," as depicted in the cinematic genre of the western, is "wild" not only in the sense that it is portrayed as an untamed land of lawlessness, but also in the sense that the films present us with a variety of "wild" but colorful characters, some of whom are considered notorious, while others are treated as role models. From charismatic individuals and brave groups of pioneers who sharply depict moral dispositions in their pursuit of law and order to villains, bandits, and gangs of outlaws who seek to challenge such order, the western ethos is built on stories of moral duty, friendship, loyalty, and camaraderie. "Good guys" like Marshal Will Kane (Gary Cooper) in *High Noon* (1952) and Shane (Alan Ladd) in *Shane* (1953) exhibit rugged masculinity and moral commitment. They are courageous and righteous, strong in their firm belief in justice and morality, and ready to save the day (and the town) from evildoers. Their moral qualities are clearly emphasized by their polar opposites: the "bad guys." Villains, gunslingers, cruel mercenaries, and greedy gold hunters—from the cold and selfish Jack Wilson (Jack Palance) in *Shane* to the powerful Coy LaHood (Richard Dysart) in *Pale Rider* (1985)—pose as the moral counterparts to the heroes, as they are driven by their own selfish desire for power.

Together, these two kinds of characters suggest that there is one overarching theme to the characters of the western genre. Namely, they are either good or bad; they are either heroes or villains. They either terrorize a small community of families striving to live the American dream, or they are called to heroically save it. In short, the moral poles of good and bad in the western cinematic society are very clearly defined. The lines are clearly drawn so that the viewer can easily see who is good, who is bad, and the reasons for such a distinction.[1]

This moral framework helps to provide stability and order to the western film. With the dualism between good and bad implicit in the film, the narrative is able to interweave these two components in such a way that the good always triumphs over the bad. But we find that notions of the hero, the villain, the narrative, and hence the moral framework and the stability of the western film are shattered in the Coen brothers' *No Country for Old Men* (2007). In this chapter, I argue that when we examine this film as an example of the western genre, we will find that *No Country for Old Men* demonstrates a decline, or decay, of the traditional western ideal. First, there is decay, in the sense that the old western style of living has come to an end. Second, there is decay in the sense that the moral map that was used in the traditional western narrative has faded, leaving viewers without a clear moral compass to determine what is right and wrong, thereby forcing the western tradition to collapse into moral nihilism. I will show how this decline takes place by examining two of the central characters in the film, the hero, Sheriff Ed Tom Bell (Tommy Lee Jones), and the villain, Anton Chigurh (Javier Bardem), looking at how their characters develop in a way that is expressive of the decline of the western genre.

The Moral Frontier: Mapping Out the Terrain of Good and Bad in the Western Narrative

Films of the western genre have at least three central features that help to make them properly western films. First, each film has a hero who displays morally good qualities. The hero is the good guy who always makes the right decision, can always be understood as acting with moral justification, and always saves the day through his actions. Second, each film has a villain who serves as the antagonist to the hero. The villain is the bad guy who acts from selfish motivations and desires, can always be understood as acting immorally, and is always thwarted by the hero. Finally, each film follows a narrative in which the confrontation between the hero and the villain, between good and bad, is inevitable, and the hero triumphs in the end. My analysis of *No Country for Old Men* will show that this film, as a neo-western, degenerates each of these key ingredients of the western film. But in order to see how the Coen brothers' film achieves this, it is important to examine each of these features more closely.

Let us start with the first ingredient of the western film, the hero who always does the right thing, whose actions are morally justified, and who ends up saving the day. Here we can use the film *Shane* as a paradigm case. Shane, the hero, rides into a small community of homesteaders in Wyoming, where he discovers that the settlers are in a battle with a cattle baron, Rufus Ryker (Emile Meyer), who is trying to force them off their land. Shane decides to defend the ranchers against Ryker and his henchmen—gunslingers he has hired to help bully the homesteaders off their land. But Shane's decision to do what is right (defend the ranchers) develops only gradually in the film, in the course of four separate encounters with Ryker and his gang in the local saloon. First, he is confronted by Ryker's henchman Chris Calloway (Ben Johnson); Shane walks away. Second, he is again confronted by Calloway, and this time Shane fights and wins. Third, Shane is challenged by five of Ryker's henchmen, and Shane chooses to fight all five, holding his ground well (reflecting his skills as a fighter) until Ryker jumps into the fray and helps his gang subdue him. It isn't until Joe (Van Heflin) intervenes to help Shane that the two together are able to hold off Ryker and his men. Finally, Shane kills both Ryker and Jack Wilson, thereby ending the battle between Ryker and the homesteaders.

Ultimately, we can say that Shane did the right thing and saved the day. But what makes his actions to fight Ryker and his gang moral? How do we justify his actions as good and thereby see Shane as the hero? There are at least two moral theories that are important for us to examine, not only to help explain Shane's moral worth as the hero of the film, but also to see the moral degradation in *No Country for Old Men*. The first theory is known as virtue-ethics.

Presented by Aristotle (384–322 BCE), virtue-ethics is a system of normative ethics that is concerned primarily with the acquisition of virtues, such as courage, modesty, temperament, and so on, designed to promote the good life. Following Aristotle, we can say that virtue is "a state of character concerned with choice, lying in a mean, i.e., the mean relative to us, this being determined by a rational principle." In other words, it is a state of character that involves the individual making a decision to act, with the correct decision leading to the action that is the moderation or "mean between two vices, that which depends on excess and that which depends on defect."[2] For example, the character trait of courage is considered a virtue when it is exemplified in an action that lies in between two extremes: the excess of courage (recklessness) and deficiency, or lack, of courage (cowardice). Using Aristotle's example of courage, we can use virtue-ethics to trace Shane's development in acquiring the virtue of courage. In Shane's first encounter, where he is bullied out of the saloon, Shane does not defend himself. Rather, he leaves the saloon quietly, without any fuss. Following virtue-ethics, this can be treated as an example of cowardice. Shane acted with a deficiency of courage: he had an opportunity to defend his and the homesteaders' honor, but he chose not to. Shane grows into his role as the virtuous character by the second encounter, when he chooses to fight Calloway. Then, when Shane confronts the five members of Ryker's gang, he decides that he must fight. Even when Joey (Brandon DeWilde) begs him to not fight, pleading, "But Shane, there's too many," Shane decides that he must still perform the courageous act: "You wouldn't want me to run away, would you?" Furthermore, Shane is courageous in his showdown with Ryker and his gang. Even though he is outnumbered, and even though he is risking his life, Shane is not reckless, since he is aware of his own abilities and the abilities of his enemies. He thus acts with the virtue of courage when he decides to confront the villains alone, without the assistance of Joe. From the perspective of virtue-ethics, then, Shane is the good guy of the film who saves the day because he grows into his role of courageous hero.

On the other end of the moral spectrum is deontological ethics, most famously presented by Immanuel Kant (1724–1804). Deontology is a system of ethics that maintains that an action is considered good or bad in and of itself, without any appeal to the consequences or ends to which that action may lead. For Kant, an action is considered to be good so long as it conforms to, and is motivated by, our moral duties or specific moral obligations, such as being honest, developing one's talents, helping others in need, and so on. To help determine our moral duties, Kant introduces a principle to guide our decision making, which he refers to as the categorical imperative. The most famous formulation of this imperative states that "I should never act except in such a way that I can also will that my maxim should become a universal law." That is, you should follow your personal, or subjective, volition for action (your maxim) only if it is an action that everyone can follow at the same time (a universal law). If your maxim cannot be rationally comprehended as a universal law, it is morally prohibited.[3] Following Kant, the deontologist would examine Shane's actions according to whether or not they are good in themselves. In Shane's first encounter with Calloway, Kant would argue that Shane fails to follow his moral duty, which is to defend the homesteaders. But in the remaining three encounters with the gang in the saloon, Shane acts morally since he chooses to defend the homesteaders. From the deontologist's perspective, Shane is a morally good person because his decision to fight is not only in accordance with his duty, but his motivation stems from his duty. Shane does not look at the consequences of his actions as his motivation to act. Even in the final showdown with Ryker and Wilson, Shane confronts his enemies fully aware that his decision to follow his duty may lead to his death. In this sense, then, the deontologist can accept Shane as the moral hero insofar as he recognizes his moral duties, is motivated to follow such duties, and finally acts accordingly.

Whether we look at Shane's actions from the moral theory of virtue-ethics or of deontology, we can understand that he is the good guy of the film, insofar as he does what is right and these right actions can be explained as having moral worth. But the goodness of the good guy must also be understood and measured against his counterpart, the bad guy. The villain is the second ingredient essential to the western, and we can see this exemplified in Shane's counterparts, Ryker and Wilson. Ryker fits the paradigm of the powerful businessman. He is motivated by an unconditional drive for power, which is represented in his unadulterated desire to acquire land, even if that land is owned by the innocent and wholesome homesteaders. Meanwhile, Wilson fits the paradigm of the other kind of villain—the cold-hearted, rough and tough, skilled gunslinger who is hired by Ryker to help drive out the homesteaders.

Ryker and Wilson are considered the villains of the film because we can understand their actions as immoral. First, from the analysis of virtue-ethics, neither individual exemplifies virtuous characteristics. Ryker's actions are driven by an extreme drive for excessive power and wealth. He doesn't choose a moderation of such acquisitions, and therefore exemplifies the vice of excess. Likewise, Wilson exemplifies the vice of excess insofar as he callously guns down a rancher in cold blood. Here, Wilson acts with recklessness. Second, in the deontological analysis, both Ryker and Wilson are immoral insofar as neither acknowledges his moral duties, either in motivation or in action. Both choose to ignore their moral duty to help those in need (the homesteaders), and instead choose to act according to their own greedy ends: Ryker seeks power obtained through land, no matter what the means, while Wilson seeks power obtained through killing others, whether they are innocent or not. Finally, we can generally see that both are immoral characters in the sense that they follow a position known as moral egoism. According to moral egoism, one's actions are rooted in one's self-interests. Ryker acts as an egoist insofar as all of his actions are centered on his selfish desire for power. It is this unconstrained drive for power that leads Ryker to hurt the lives of the homesteaders. Wilson, too, acts according to his own self-interest. Driven by money and his reputation as a notorious gunslinger, he is ready to kill anyone around him, so long as he gets paid and accrues the power of notoriety.

Every western has the ingredients of a hero and a villain. But these ingredients, even together, cannot meet the criteria of a western film without the third ingredient: the narrative that weaves the hero and villain together for a showdown. There is a general structure that western films follow in this respect, in one form or another. First, the western film moves forward with a moral dilemma, typically brought out through human situations. In *Shane*, the dilemma is presented in the context of the war between Ryker and the homesteaders. The homesteaders are represented as good, innocent families seeking a better life for themselves through hard work and honest living. Ryker and his gang are represented as immoral and evil individuals who act only out of selfishness. Second, we find that the hero must face this moral dilemma and determine how to act. Shane is represented as the lone rider who comes upon this dilemma, and though he initially backs down from defending those in need, he eventually comes to see that the right thing to do is fight Ryker and his gang. Third, in many westerns, there is an occasion when the hero and the villain meet—this occasion serves as the precursor to the ultimate showdown. For instance, Shane meets both Ryker and Wilson several times. When he runs into Ryker in the saloon, Ryker is impressed with Shane's fighting skills. He offers Shane double the pay that Joe is paying him (which, unbeknownst to Ryker, is nothing), but Shane refuses. Likewise, Shane meets Wilson on Starrett's ranch. There, while Ryker and Joe debate, Shane and Wilson confront each other, stare eye to eye, each without saying a word, but each aware that they will have a showdown in the future. Finally, as suggested, every western has a final showdown between the hero and the villain, a showdown that will leave the villain dead and the hero triumphant. The hero must be able to save the day so that the moral dilemma is finally resolved and all is set right in the western country. We see such a showdown at the end of *Shane*, when Shane kills Ryker and Wilson. Even though he himself is shot, he wins the shootout, tells Joey to let his mother know that "everything's all right and there aren't any more guns in the valley," and rides off into the night. The western narrative is thus able to weave the hero and the villain(s) of the film together in such a way that good always triumphs over evil.[4]

There's an Old Sheriff in Town

Having carefully explored three essential ingredients of the western films, we can now examine how *No Country for Old Men*, a film set in Texas in 1980, deconstructs the western genre by shattering each of the ingredients, one by one. The film opens with a narration of the traditional western hero, portrayed by Sheriff Ed Tom Bell. Bell relates the following about himself and his life in the West: "I was sheriff of this county when I was twenty-five. Hard to believe. Grandfather was a lawman. Father too. Me and him was sheriff at the same time, him in Plano and me here. I think he was pretty proud of that. I know I was. Some of the old-time sheriffs never even wore a gun. A lot of folks find that hard to believe. I always liked to hear about the old-timers. Never missed a chance to do so. You can't help but compare yourself against the old-timers. Can't help but wonder how they would've operated these times." Here, Bell acknowledges that he is part of a tradition—and not simply that of generations of lawmen in his family. From the view of the western genre, Bell is part of the tradition of generations of western heroes. Like his forefathers, Shane, Blondie, Ringo Kidd, and the like, Bell is a good guy. Bell recognizes both traditions, as he honors those heroes (in his case, the "old-time sheriffs"). Like Joey in *Shane*, he looks up to the hero as a role model. We can even say that Bell himself has become such a hero in his life insofar as he has carried out his moral duties as sheriff since he was a young man.

But it is now 1980, and times have changed in at least three significant ways. First, the western frontier is no longer characterized as the "Wild West," where the land is unpopulated and unsettled, power-hungry tycoons dominate the innocent, and legal order is yet to be established. Second, though the "Wild West" has been "tamed" in one respect, the modern West has a new breed of lawlessness. As Bell explains in his opening narrative:

There's this boy I sent to Huntsville here a while back. My arrest and my testimony. He killed a fourteen-year-old girl. Papers said it was a crime of passion but he told me there wasn't any passion to it. Told me that he'd been planning to kill somebody for about as long as he could remember. Said that if they turned him out he'd do it again. Said he knew he was going to hell. Be there in about fifteen minutes. I don't know what to make of that. I surely don't. The crime you see now, it's hard to even take its measure.

In other words, the moral framework of the West—or the country, or the world—is changing. The traditional western framework that contained innocent and wholesome westerners striving to live out the American dream, typical villains driven by greed and power, and the heroes who fought for what is right, is fading. The villains, or the criminals, act in such a way that the traditional hero cannot make sense of their criminal behavior. While the traditional villains, such as Ryker or Wilson, are immoral and clearly "bad guys," we can understand them because their actions are rational. We can see their actions are based on moral egoism, measured by their own self-interests. But in the world of *No Country for Old Men*, the "bad guys" act irrationally. They don't even act with criminal passion. As such, Bell cannot comprehend the enemies he should be confronting as the hero of today—for him, "it's hard to even take measure."[5]

Third, the hero of the West has grown old. Bell is no longer a young, twenty-five-year-old sheriff, ready and willing to act according to his moral duties with courage and without hesitation, not regarding the consequences. Instead, he is now weary and cautious: "It's not that I'm afraid of it. I always knew you had to be willing to die to even do this job—not to be glorious. But I don't want to push my chips forward and go out and meet something I don't understand. A man would have to put his soul at hazard. He'd have to say, okay, I'll be part of this world." Though the western frontier has been tamed so that towns have been settled and cities have developed, a new kind of wildness has now spread and ravaged the world. Bell, part of the tradition of the "old-timers" in the western genre of film heroes, is confused as to how to handle this new immoral wildfire, because he cannot understand the motives the villains today act upon. In other words, he cannot get into the mind of the current villain—he cannot fathom the depths of evil that exist in the West—and therefore, he is now hesitant about abiding by the traditional moral justifications that underlie the actions of the hero.

We can see these changes unfold in the film, as Bell investigates and follows the trail of Chigurh. He initially exhibits similar traits to the western hero. He still rides a horse as he's investigating the crime scenes. He still wears the white hat. Similar to Marshal Kane in *High Noon*, Bell acts according to his duty as sheriff to fight the bad guys and defend the innocent citizens of the western community. For instance, aware that Llewelyn Moss (Josh Brolin) is in danger, he meets with Llewelyn's wife, Carla Jean Moss (Kelly McDonald), telling her that Llewelyn "needs help, whether he knows it or not." This example further suggests that, like his western counterparts, he acts with wisdom. Highly experienced with trailing the bad guy, Bell is sharp enough to put the pieces of this criminal puzzle together. However, though his experience and wisdom are part of his moral worth as the hero of the film, they are also his downfall. Since Bell relies on his ability to know the villain, he is at a loss when he cannot understand him. This lack of comprehension is caused by his method of analyzing the bad guy from the traditional framework of the western genre; as such, Bell is unable to even imagine the horrors of the new bad guy.

When Bell manages to put together the pieces to track the criminal, it is done only incidentally. For instance, Bell is able to infer that Chigurh uses a cattle gun to kill his victims only after he reflects on how one used to slaughter livestock. This method reveals that Chigurh dehumanizes his victims, treating them as animals to be brutally slaughtered. As such, there is a cold detachment to his character. But such revelations don't inspire Bell to carry out his moral duty as sheriff; rather, they haunt him so that he is afraid to confront Chigurh. The more Bell learns about Chigurh's "methods," the more frightened he becomes, as he sees how horrible Chigurh's actions really are. Though he recognizes the horror, he remains in the dark as to completely understanding his enemy. As he tells Sheriff Roscoe (Rodger Boyce), Chigurh is a "ghost" to him, one who represents the "signs and wonders" of the horrors of today's world. And thus Bell remains afraid. This fear of the unknown is encapsulated when Bell returns to the El Paso Motel, the crime scene where Moss was killed. There, Bell steps up to the motel room but hesitates to open the door (knowing not only that Chigurh was there, but that he may still be in the room) with a fear reminiscent of a child's terror of the boogeyman. Bell is drawing up the courage required to face his greatest fear—the fear of that which he does not understand, the fear that his ghost will gun him down and take his life. Though Bell is courageous enough to eventually enter the motel room, there is no confrontation with Chigurh, and Bell decides to retire from his role as sheriff. As he tells his friend, former deputy Ellis (Barry Corbin), he retires because he feels "overmatched" and "discouraged." In other words, Bell acknowledges that the country has changed, and though in his youth he had the moral integrity to be "willing to die" in performing his duty as sheriff, he has now come to terms with the idea that he doesn't really want to be part of this world.

Bell thus walks away. His final opportunity for confrontation is like Shane's first. While Shane grows and develops into a moral hero, Bell has to face the loss of his moral integrity. Though he swore an oath to uphold the law, and though he promised Carla Jean that he would protect her husband, he fails on both counts. He walks away from a live case, and he arrives just a bit too late (perhaps slowed down by his age) to save Moss. Bell is no longer courageous like Shane, no longer a real deputy of the law like Kane. Bell, the hero, has grown old and cannot make sense of the world today, and so he cannot carry on with the same courage and proud dedication to his duties as the heroes of the western genre. But this aging, this idea of growing old, is not simply physical—it is also a metaphorical and philosophical claim about the moral impetus behind the western genre. The moral messages of heroes and role models of the western genre are now inapplicable to today's standards. The world has changed so drastically that the hero of yesterday can no longer survive as the hero. Whether it be Bell, or Shane, or Kane, or another, *No Country for Old Men* tells us that this world, this country, today is no longer a place for the western hero.

"He's a Peculiar Man": The Face of the New Villain

Just as the hero of the western genre has changed in *No Country for Old Men* (in the sense that he can no longer do the right thing), so, too, has the villain changed. Perhaps the most striking change between Chigurh and the villains of the old westerns is that Chigurh cannot be understood. While it is true that the traditional villain is immoral and we don't like him for acting that way, we can still understand him. We understand him as selfish, greedy, driven by money and power. This is the first characteristic of the traditional villain from which Chigurh unchains himself. We know he does bad things, but we cannot understand why he does them. In the film, several different people characterize him differently because he is so elusive. He is "a ghost," "a homicidal lunatic," "a loose cannon," and the "ultimate badass." And yet none of these labels seem to fully capture the essence of Chigurh.

Perhaps the closest analysis of Chigurh's character in the film is presented by Carson Wells (Woody Harrelson). As we learn from Wells's meeting with his boss (Stephen Root), the man who hired Chigurh in the first place, Wells is familiar with Chigurh: "I know him every which way." From Wells's perspective Chigurh is "a psychopathic killer" as dangerous as the "bubonic plague." More important, as he tells Llewelyn, he is "a peculiar man," in the sense that "he has principles . . . principles that transcend drugs and money. He's not like you. He's not even like me." Wells's analysis provides us with an insight into Chigurh's character as the villain of *No Country for*

Old Men. Let's take the last point first—Chigurh is not like Wells. But who is Wells? Wells is a hired hand sought by a wealthy businessman, a perceived "gunslinger" who is driven by self-interest and the thirst for money. We can see these characteristics during his visit to Llewelyn, where he offers to save him from Chigurh for money: "Look. You need to give me the money. I've got no other reason to protect you." In short, Wells is the traditional villain of the western genre, in the spirit of Wilson from *Shane*. As such, he is the closest to Chigurh's character, and so thinks that he knows him.

But ultimately, not even Wells completely understands the face of the new villain. In Wells's final scene, he attempts to persuade Chigurh to spare his life by offering him a deal: Wells will let Chigurh know where the money is if and only if he lets him live. But Chigurh has no interest in making such deals. The traditional villain of the western genre would take such a deal (as we imagine Wilson did to work for Ryker), as it serves his own greedy egotistical self-interest. But Chigurh is not the traditional villain; in fact, he suggests to Wells that such a justification for one's actions is ultimately a poor way to make decisions: "If the rule you followed brought you to this, of what use was the rule?" This line of thinking, however, is foreign to Wells, and we find that he, too, really doesn't understand Chigurh. He refers to him as "goddamn crazy," and when Chigurh misunderstands him to be referring to "the nature of this conversation," Wells replies, "I mean the nature of you." In Wells's last moments, we find that not even he, the personification of the traditional western villain, understands this new villain. But Wells does understand himself in light of this new villain. As he pleads with Chigurh to take the deal he's offering him, Wells refers to himself as just a "day trader." Here, the image of the traditional villain is deflated. In today's world, the bad guy of the western genre is an immoral businessman, nothing more. He's just in it for the money. All he can do is keep giving Chigurh the same pitch—he can keep the money, and Wells will just "go home." But of course, this method of reasoning with Chigurh, the new villain, fails, leaving Wells dead in cold blood.

Chigurh's decision to murder both Wells and his own "boss" reveals two things about Chigurh. First, Chigurh's character as the villain shatters the traditional notion of the villain in the western genre. He literally kills the two characters of the film who represent the traditional villain: Wells as the hired gunslinger and the "boss" as the immoral business tycoon. Second, as suggested in the previous paragraph, Chigurh's actions cannot be understood as moral egoism. Wells is correct to say that he has "principles that transcend drugs and money." But these principles are twisted in the sense that although he acts with moral consistency (to a degree), he applies this consistency in horrible ways. For instance, upon killing his boss, Chigurh explains to his boss's accountant (Trent Moore), that the boss was wrong to hire more than just Chigurh to look for the money, since "you pick the one right tool," and then rely only on that tool. Another example of Chigurh's principled reasoning occurs when he offers a deal to Llewelyn. Chigurh tells Llewelyn: "So this is what I'll offer. You bring me the money and I'll let her [Carla Jean] go. Otherwise she's accountable. The same as you. That's the best deal you're going to get. I won't tell you you can save yourself because you can't." Llewelyn implicitly refuses this offer. Chigurh thus tracks down Carla Jean at her mother's home and tells her that though he has no reason to hurt her, "I gave my word. . . . Your husband had the opportunity to remove you from harm's way. Instead, he used you to try to save himself." Together, these two scenes provide us with an insight into Chigurh's twisted moral consistency. First, Chigurh does not appeal to money or power as the greatest end for which one should strive. Second, Chigurh does not appear to be acting purely out of self-interest. By murdering his boss and Carla Jean, he gains nothing for himself. These two points help us to see why the traditional villain couldn't make sense of Chigurh. His actions are not motivated by what normally drives the bad guy; he is not selfish and egotistical. Third, Chigurh's own justification of his actions doesn't appeal to the consequences that are produced; rather like Kant's deontology, he justifies his actions insofar as they are "good" in themselves. He kills his boss on the principle that his boss made a wrong decision. He did not stick with the one right tool, and so this bad decision entails the act of Chigurh murdering him. Likewise, Chigurh admits that there is nothing he gains from killing Carla Jean. But he must do it because he gave his word. That is, he made a promise, and, as Kant would argue, we are morally obligated to keep our promises (whether we like it or not) because it is part of our moral duty. Thus, Chigurh seems to be morally consistent insofar as he follows a deontological line of reasoning to justify his actions.

Chigurh's deontological reasoning helps to place him on a new level of immorality. To an extent, his actions are grounded on what appear to be moral principles, similar to the moral justifications made by the hero of the western genre. But when the bad guy of the film uses the good guy's line of reasoning, the polarity between good and bad begins to weaken. This polarity is weakened even further by Chigurh's other twisted behavior: flipping a coin to determine whether or not his next potential victim lives or dies. The "coin-flip scenario" occurs twice in the film on separate occasions: Chigurh invites the gas station attendant in one scene and Carla Jean in another to "call it" when he flips a coin. The threat of what's at stake is obvious to the viewer and obvious to Carla Jean (though not to the attendant): correctly calling the coin means that Chigurh will not kill the person, while incorrectly calling it entails the person's death. Here, Chigurh's behavior implicitly suggests two important points about his beliefs. First, at the moment his potential victim calls the coin toss, he believes that his victim has a fifty-fifty chance of living (or dying). Second, Chigurh believes that he himself is not responsible for the outcome. We can infer this from his conversation with the attendant, as he tells him: "You need to call it. I can't call it for you. It wouldn't be fair. It wouldn't even be right." With this, Chigurh is acknowledging that since this is a life or death decision, it is only morally right for the person whose life is at stake to roll the dice of chance. Furthermore, Chigurh cannot make the call because he would then be held accountable insofar as he chose what would lead to the attendant's life or death. By abstaining from calling, Chigurh detaches himself from the situation and its results. Carla Jean sees this reasoning in Chigurh and attempts to challenge his move to distance himself, as she tells him, "The coin don't have no say. It's just you." But for Chigurh, it is not his say at all, as he tells Carla Jean, "This is the best I can do . . . [because] I got here the same way the coin did." As such, Chigurh portrays himself as a disinterested force, free from accountability.

Together, these two points suggest a further point about Chigurh's use of the coin flip, namely, he introduces the philosophical issue of moral luck into the equation of evaluating an individual's behavior. According to Thomas Nagel (1937–), moral luck occurs "where a significant aspect of what someone does depends on factors beyond his control, yet we continue to treat him in that respect as an object of moral judgment."[6] For example, suppose we have two cases of drivers that are identical in nearly all respects: both are driving down a road and run a red light due to a brief lapse of focus. But let's suppose further that in one case, the driver hits a child crossing the street as he runs the red light, thereby killing the child; meanwhile, in the other case, there is no child crossing the street. Both drivers have equal responsibilities as drivers and both are guilty of lapsing in their duty to pay attention as they drive. But we would like to say that the first driver is also responsible for the death of the child, even though the fact that the child happened to be crossing the street at the exact same moment when the driver failed to focus is something that was out of the driver's control. Instead, it was bad luck.

Since moral luck concerns conditions that are beyond one's control, we may wonder how one can be held morally responsible for such conditions. One way to respond to the notion of moral luck is to treat those conditions as restrictions to moral evaluation. From this perspective, as Nagel explains, we have a "view which makes responsibility dependent on control" and which thereby concludes that the phenomenon of moral luck "is absurd."[7] That is, we need to eliminate those chance occurrences from our moral evaluations or judgments of individuals, as they are not responsible for those conditions. This response to moral luck is Chigurh's response. By offering his potential victims the coin flip, Chigurh sees himself as introducing a chance occurrence into the equation. Their fate is now a matter of luck, and since it is only a matter of luck, he does not see himself as morally accountable for his actions, whether they are to murder the person (because he or she made the wrong call) or to let the person live (because he or she made the right one). Chigurh is thus a disturbing character who twists the notion of the villain in the sense that he utilizes some of the moral justifications traditionally used by the hero, and he introduces the notion of luck and chance occurrences into his decision making, thereby negating, in his own estimation, any moral responsibility for his actions.

"You Can't Stop What's Comin'": A Nihilistic Country

The distortion of the first two ingredients of the western film, the moral decay of the hero and the moral complexity of the villain, contributes to the distortion of the third ingredient, the traditional narrative in the western genre. *No Country for Old Men* begins in a similar vein as the traditional western in the sense that what sets the film in motion is a moral dilemma. But this initial dilemma is not a dilemma that Bell, the hero, faces; rather it is a dilemma that Llewelyn faces: should he return to the scene of the botched drug deal to give the dying Mexican water? His decision to do the right thing and help a person in need helps to pull Llewelyn into the world that Bell ultimately decides to leave. Bell's moral dilemma doesn't arise until the end of the film: having failed to save Llewelyn, and having learned more about the villain, should he choose to have the final showdown with Chigurh and try to save the day? Ultimately, Bell says no. Instead of giving himself the hero's triumphant ride off into the sunset, Bell retires and heads home (much like Moss, the traditional villain, wanted to do). Thus, by failing to follow the hero's path in the traditional western framework, the character of Bell brings into question the moral simplicity embedded in the classic western. It is not the case that good will always triumph over the bad. Furthermore, Bell never meets his enemy face-to-face: there is no meeting prior to a showdown, and there is no showdown. The closest we get to a cinematic image of the two figures being brought together for the precursor to the showdown occurs in Llewelyn's trailer. There, Chigurh sits down, drinks milk, and stares at the turned-off television, allowing the viewer to see his dark silhouette. A brief time later, we find Bell doing the exact same thing—sitting down, drinking milk, and staring into the television so that we see his dark silhouette. The traditional meeting will not take place in the normal sense of the word; rather, at best, it will occur through passing images on the TV screen.[8] Meanwhile, the closest we get to a showdown occurs during Bell's nonconfrontation with Chigurh in the El Paso Motel room. Though dreadfully afraid, Bell enters the room alone. Like Shane, he does not call for backup; he does not bring in a posse or the cavalry. For that moment, he is like the lone hero. But he is older. He has fear in his eyes, and he hesitates. And, in the end, it is his fear that wins out, compelling him to avoid any future opportunities to have the real final showdown with Chigurh.

By eliminating the three central ingredients of the western film, *No Country for Old Men* shatters both the moral framework and the stability that westerns have provided us. First, the moral framework is dismantled in the sense that duality between the ideal good figure and the ideal bad figure has been erased. The hero is no longer a hero. At worst, from the traditional standards of the hero, he is a coward who could not stand up to the lone villain. At best, he is a former hero who has grown old and is now unfit for this new world of lawlessness and chaos. Of course, if he is unfit, then the film begs the question of who could fight the villain. Who could be a new hero? The closest we have to a hero is Llewelyn, but even he doesn't live up to that ideal because not all of his actions are morally justifiable. For instance, he never once considers giving up the money. He has at least two opportunities to give up what does not rightfully belong to him. The first opportunity occurs when Wells offers to help him handle Chigurh. But whether it is from greed (in wanting the money for himself) or excessive pride (in wanting to kill Chigurh himself), Llewelyn rejects the offer. The second opportunity, to hand the money over to Chigurh, will not save his own life but will save his wife's. And so, whether it is from greed, his pride, or the love of his own life, he once again refuses to give up the money. Ultimately, it is his excessive pride and inflated conception of his strengths that lead to his death. Unlike Shane, Llewelyn is outmatched, and so he mistakes his recklessness in wanting to fight Chigurh and the Mexicans as a sign of his own courage.[9] The villain, meanwhile, is now more horrible, more twisted, and more disturbing than ever before. Rather than acting out of selfishness, Chigurh is detached from his own self-gain. He sees himself as a tool, guided by moral principles that dictate what he ought to do. But such principles, though deontological in spirit, can be understood only in the context of chance, so that Chigurh can absolve himself (at least in his own eyes) of any personal moral responsibility for his actions.

Second, the stability of the western film collapses in the sense that we lose the order of the western narrative that provides us with the happy ending in which good triumphs over evil. In *No Country for Old Men,* without the final showdown between the hero and the villain, good cannot triumph. And so we see that the good either is killed (Llewelyn) or runs away (Bell). But does this mean that evil triumphs over good? Not necessarily. Bad guys, such as Wells and Chigurh's boss, are killed, but it takes an even worse person to do it. Though that may seem to suggest that in the end evil wins, the film ultimately suggests something even worse: what is good and what is bad is all a matter of chance. Whether it is the attendant who lives by correctly calling the coin flip, Carla Jean who dies, Bell who ends up not confronting Chigurh, or Chigurh getting into a car accident—all of these events occurred by some degree of chance. This suggests that the question of good versus bad is no longer a significant question since these values can no longer be applied to individuals. We can no longer apply the terms "good" and "bad" to the "guys" opposing one another—and this shatters the order we recognize and assume in every western film. This leads to nihilism in the western frontier. As Friedrich Nietzsche (1844–1900) explains, nihilism occurs when one infers "that there is no meaning at all"; "everything lacks meaning." According to nihilism, life and the world are meaningless because there are no inherent structure, stability, order, or framework to them. As such, all the values that were once held to be significant are now seen as empty. Or, as Nietzsche puts it, "The highest values devalue themselves."[10]

We can see the sense of nihilism opening up toward the end of *No Country for Old Men* when we compare the dialogue between Bell and Ellis to the dialogue between Shane and Joey in *Shane.* After Shane has saved the day, Joey pleads with him to stay. But Shane explains that he can't since "a man has to be what he is. . . . Can't break the mold." Even though he tried to break the mold, he found it didn't work for him. Instead, the moral framework remains intact: "Right or wrong, it's a brand. A brand sticks. There's no going back." But this moral framework has branded him as the hero of the film. The discussion Bell has with Ellis is much darker. Ellis, an old man in a wheelchair (which we can infer was caused by a criminal who shot him as deputy), learns that his shooter died in prison. When Bell asks him, hypothetically, what he would have done if the criminal had been released, Ellis cynically responds, "Nothin'. Wouldn't be no point to it." He explains to Bell, "All the time you spend tryin' to get back what's been took from you, there's more goin' out the door. After a while you just try and get a tourniquet on it." That is, Ellis suggests that there is no meaning, no value, to our actions in life. Acting according to moral justifications of justice, duty, courage, and so on is pointless. Further, as Bell explains his feelings of being "overmatched," he is disturbed by the thought that God hasn't helped him: "I always thought when I got older God would sort of come into my life in some way. He didn't." For Bell, God's presence in his life would help him to see his life as meaningful; without God, Bell falls into nihilism and is discouraged. Finally, Ellis summarizes the situation to Bell: "What you got ain't nothing new. This country is hard on people. Hard and crazy. Got the devil in it yet folks never seem to hold it to account. . . . You can't stop what's comin'.'"

Ellis concludes with a nihilistic evaluation of the West. The country is "crazy" in the sense that it is irrational. Those who were once seen as good and heroic are now old and feeble, unable to uphold the standards of morality that were ingrained in the traditional western genre. Meanwhile, those who are lawless today have become more maniacal, more twisted, making the villains incomprehensible in their behavior. As such, the West is now a world where there is no rhyme or reason, and those within it are never held accountable. It has become a country without meaning and without any inherent value. The country, in short, has collapsed into nihilism.

Notes

1. Perhaps the most salient depiction of these moral lines can be found in the film *The Good, the Bad, and the Ugly* (1966). First, we have "the good," Blondie (Clint Eastwood). He doesn't need a name—his actions, his look, his measured speech, his entire essence stand for nothing but good (at least, "good" as the western genre understands it). Second, we have "the bad" in Angel Eyes (Lee Van Cleef). He, too, doesn't need a

name. Dressed in black, his demonic eyes and his greed (which is essentially no different than that of the other characters) are associated with torture, and his entire essence
is summed up as "the bad." Finally, there's Tuco (Eli Wallach). He is the only one with a
real name, the only one who is too weak and stupid to be either good or bad. He's "sitting on the moral fence," as it were. Hence, his indecisiveness, his lack of integrity and
of a clear and cohesive moral stand earn him the soubriquet "the ugly." But even if there
are ugly characters in classic westerns (and there are!), their ugliness is defined only in
light of the polarized reality of good versus bad.

   2. It is important to note that Aristotle maintains that there are certain actions
and dispositions that do not admit of a mean between vices, but are instead always
immoral. Such actions include murder, adultery, and theft. See Aristotle, *Nicomachean
Ethics: The Basic Works of Aristotle*, ed. Richard McKeon (New York: Random House,
1941), book 2, chap. 6, p. 959.

   3. Immanuel Kant, *Grounding for the Metaphysics of Morals* (Indianapolis: Hackett, 1993), 7–15. For both a further presentation of Kant's deontology and an analysis
of such moral themes in *High Noon*, see Daw-Nay Evans's chapter in this volume, "The
Duty of Reason: Kantian Ethics in *High Noon*."

   4. It is interesting to note that Shane may have actually died due to his decision to
confront Ryker and Wilson. In *The Negotiator* (1998), Lieutenant Danny Roman (Samuel
L. Jackson) debates with Lieutenant Chris Sabian (Kevin Spacey) about whether the final
scene of *Shane* depicts Shane's death after his showdown with Ryker and Wilson.

   5. Another example of Bell's bewilderment regarding today's villains occurs as he
tells Wendell (Garret Dillahunt), "My Lord, Wendell, it's just all-out war. I don't know
any other word for it. Who are these people? I don't know. Here last week they found
this couple out in California they would rent out rooms to old people and then kill 'em
and bury 'em in the yard and cash their Social Security checks. They'd torture them
first, I don't know why. Maybe their television set was broke. And this went on until,
and here I quote, 'Neighbors were alerted when a man ran from the premises wearing
only a dog collar.' You can't make up such a thing as that. I dare you to even try. But
that's what it took, you'll notice. Get someone's attention. Diggin' graves in the back-
yard didn't bring any."

   6. Thomas Nagel, "Moral Luck," in *Mortal Questions* (Cambridge: Cambridge University Press, 1979).

   7. Ibid., 26. See also Bernard Williams, "Moral Luck," in *Moral Luck* (Cambridge:
Cambridge University Press, 1982), 31.

   8. It may be the case that the Coen brothers are saying more with Chigurh and Bell
as images on the TV screen; perhaps these two scenes serve as a cinematic reminder
that the classic westerns are films. That is, they provide us with a narrative of good versus bad, and good always triumphs. But, as *No Country for Old Men* attempts to show,
this traditional narrative is too simplistic and so fails to capture the moral complexities
and subtleties of life.

9. It is interesting to note a further reason why Llewelyn is not the hero of the film in the traditional sense. He is akin to the normal member of a western community, such as Joe, the homesteader, in *Shane*. Like Joe, Llewelyn is trying to make a good life for himself and his wife. Unlike Joe, however, he is not purely moral, and he is neither weak nor hopeless. But the playing field has been leveled so that the hero and the homesteader are no longer different by the degree of their moral character. The homesteader was originally seen as good but weak, and so had a lesser degree of moral strength compared to the hero. Llewelyn displays heroic features because he stands up for himself, but it is his own ego that leads to his downfall.

10. Friedrich Nietzsche, *The Will to Power*, trans. Walter Kaufmann and R. J. Hollingdale (New York: Random House, 1967), book 1.

THE NORTHWESTERN

McCabe and Mrs. Miller

Deborah Knight and George McKnight

An End-of-Genre Western

Set near the Pacific Ocean in a heavily forested, frequently overcast corner of Washington State that is alternatively rain-soaked and muddy or snow-covered and cold, Robert Altman's *McCabe and Mrs. Miller* (1971) is not a classic western in the way that, say, John Ford's *My Darling Clementine* (1946) and George Stevens's *Shane* (1953) are classic. The setting is a first clear indication that *McCabe and Mrs. Miller* differs from classic westerns. Gone are the familiar landmarks we conventionally expect to see, the open wilderness and frequent wide-angle shots of a sun-drenched landscape. Nothing is to be seen here remotely like Utah's Monument Valley (John Ford's *She Wore a Yellow Ribbon*, 1949) or the scenic grandeur of Wyoming's Grand Teton Mountains (*Shane*) or the Nevada desert landscape in *The Stalking Moon* (Robert Mulligan, 1969). *McCabe* is an end-of-genre western, a film made toward the end of a variety of different but related stories that had celebrated the settlement of the American wilderness within this most central genre of American filmmaking. The classic western tells the story about expansion westward.[1] *McCabe* tells what happened when the idealization of western expansion and the mystique developed around the figure of the western hero faltered in the late 1960s and early 1970s. This is not a film centrally featuring cowboys, soldiers, sheriffs, or homesteaders, or the need to protect the new and developing community from incursions from lawless individuals, cattle barons, or Native Americans. It is not a film whose central protagonist has a clear moral commitment to the community he is either already a member of or that he enters in order to take on duties such as enforcing the law or defending the innocent. *McCabe* is set in the extreme northwest, not the open west of the classic western, and the central characters and conventional features of the classic western as a genre have been completely rethought by Altman, who not only directed the film but cowrote the screenplay.

The westerns that emerged after World War II were ultimately tales of moral optimism developed around moral conflict between western heroes and those who challenged them (*My Darling Clementine*). During the 1950s, westerns were much more morally cautious, introducing protagonists with questionable pasts such as we find in *The Gunfighter* (Henry King, 1950) or *The Naked Spur* (Anthony Mann, 1953). At this time, too, we find protagonists with possibly morally objectionable plans of action directed toward the future, although, in the end, these protagonists came through with morally laudable conclusions to their endeavors (*The Searchers*, John Ford, 1956). The group of films that we place in the category of "the end-of-genre western" are those in which the initial values of the classic western, even though challenged to some degree by the late-classic westerns of the 1950s or early 1960s, have broken down. While there were end-of-genre westerns made prior to *McCabe*, for instance, *The Left Handed Gun* (Arthur Penn, 1958), as well as since *McCabe*, notably a group of films from Clint Eastwood's *Unforgiven* (1992) through to the Coen brothers' *No Country for Old Men* (2007), Altman's film merits attention for at least three philosophically interesting reasons. First, *McCabe* is a western in the ironic mode. Thus, it asks us to look at what Northrop Frye, developing ideas central to Aristotle's *Poetics,* might have called the mythos of the classic western from a very different perspective.[2] Second, it asks us to align ourselves with characters who are marginal in classic westerns. McCabe (Warren Beatty), for example, is the antithesis of a Wyatt Earp (Henry Fonda in *My Darling Clementine*) or an Ethan Edwards (John Wayne in *The Searchers*). Earp and Ethan are heroes; McCabe is not. The western as a genre has featured whores principally in secondary roles from early days—consider Dallas (Claire Trevor) in *Stagecoach* (John Ford, 1939) or Chihuahua (Linda Darnell) in *My Darling Clementine*. Mrs. Miller (Julie Christie), by contrast, is not a secondary character at all but a protagonist in her own right, yet hardly the nurturing and virtuous female protagonist of the classic western, such as Clementine Carter (Cathy Downs) in *My Darling Clementine* or Marian Starrett (Jean Arthur) in *Shane*. Third, this is a film that manifests its ironic perspective aesthetically as well as narratively. In particular, and as we often see in Altman's oeuvre, key aspects of the film's style—including its general stylistic self-consciousness, its use of wide-screen, the sound track featuring several haunting songs by Leonard Cohen[3]—contribute to the philosophical significance of irony in this film.

Our focus, then, is on the aesthetics of the western as well as the central ethical themes that characterize, in particular, the classic and late-classic westerns. There has been a lively debate in philosophical aesthetics in recent years centering around the ethical criticism of literature and other works of narrative fiction. Martha C. Nussbaum and Wayne C. Booth have been two of the most committed proponents of ethical criticism. Nussbaum focuses on the major novels of Henry James, for example, *The Golden Bowl*, in her *Love's Knowledge*.[4] Booth likens our relationship with authors to a kind of morally beneficent friendship in *The Company We Keep*.[5] Interestingly, neither gives particular attention to works that are ironic—or, if it were claimed that James occasionally writes from an ironic perspective, this is a feature of his works that Nussbaum does not address. Yet irony is, arguably, a moral position. It is a position of detached and reflective scrutiny that readers or viewers are invited to share. Irony occurs when the moral axis of a work or genre has collapsed, where the moral compass has fallen away. This is the situation for the characters and actions of *McCabe and Mrs. Miller* with respect to the classic western. And this is why the film has to be examined in relation to the classic westerns that are organized around clear and normative moral axes. Nussbaum's ambition is to extol literature that makes us "finely aware and richly responsible," hence her focus on the works of authors such as James.[6] Irony doesn't work this way. Despite its seeming preference for works of so-called high literature and its general disregard of generic fictions, ethical criticism might claim that the heroes of the classic westerns could serve as models of laudable moral action. There is nothing about the character of McCabe to be lauded from a moral perspective. But that is really the point about creating a western in the mode of irony. Nussbaum says, prophetically, that "obtuseness and refusal of vision are our besetting vices."[7] *McCabe and Mrs. Miller* shows us obtuseness and the refusal of vision, most obviously through the character of McCabe himself. We are not asked to condone the lack of any moral basis for individual or community actions. We are asked to think about the implosion of the moral vision conventionally at the heart of the western.

The Mythos of the Classic Western: Narrative Conventions and Generic Motifs

Frye, and following along from him, Paul Ricoeur,[8] adopts the term *mythos* from Aristotle to designate the overarching plot structure characteristic of particular generic works of narrative fiction. Aristotle, of course, was interested in dramatic tragedy. His *Poetics* has come down to us as something of a handbook for the creation of successful and coherent Greek tragedies.[9] But as Frye and Ricoeur both note, the plot structure—the mythos—Aristotle derived from the tragedies of his time is something we can also abstract from other works of generic fiction. In particular, and this is a point on which Aristotle, Frye, and Ricoeur would all agree, the western as a narrative genre must be considered first in terms of plot structure. Only then can we consider the role played by the characters who participate in plot action.

As a means of identifying the mythos of the western, we begin with a survey of some key features of the classic western—features that serve as ironic reference points for *McCabe*. And by "classic," we mean those films that have emerged as classics, as examples of the western film as art.[10] These are the films by the likes of Ford and Stevens and not, for instance, the B-westerns featuring actors such as Tex Ritter and Roy Rogers. The governing mythos of the classic western has several recognizable features: the figure of the male hero who helps bring order to the often lawless West, the tale of progress in the expansion westward, the beginnings of settlement and the establishing of community, and a plot that ultimately leads to a confrontation between good and evil, namely, between those who defend and those who threaten the order and stability of the community. The classic western hero represents justice and morally appropriate action, and in the end acts to protect members of the community from lawless villains, even if in some cases he is initially reluctant to involve himself in local troubles. Consider Wyatt Earp, who agrees to become sheriff of Tombstone only after his brother's murder, and even Ethan Edwards, although Ethan's relationship to these key aspects of the classic male hero's character is darker and less obviously "heroic" than Earp's.

Some of the binary oppositions around which classic westerns are traditionally constructed have just emerged: hero/villain, good/evil, lawful community/lawless wilderness.[11] Another binary opposition at the heart of classic westerns occurs in the depiction of central female characters. Again citing *My Darling Clementine*, we see the opposition between the proper and virginal Clementine and the often unscrupulous, disloyal, and sexually available saloon girl Chihuahua. When it comes to the representation of gender, in other words, classic westerns tend to uphold moral conventions and gender norms characteristic not so much of the time the films are set but the time the films are made and initially exhibited.[12] Chihuahua's death might be sentimentalized, but it is the whore who dies, not Clementine, the nurse who will become the first schoolteacher in Tombstone.

The classic western frequently begins with a protagonist (usually male and often alone) located in or initially identified with a wilderness landscape.[13] Such scenes establish the male protagonist as someone separate from community or home, as self-reliant and self-sufficient, as someone who may eventually be of help to the emerging community but who is uneasy about becoming integrated into it. The protagonist's identity is quickly established in relation to courage, skill with weapons, and a reputation from the past: for instance, he is known as a former soldier, sheriff, or gunfighter. The protagonist emerges, so to speak, from the landscape into a community. Sometimes, the community is represented as little more than a few isolated farms (*The Searchers*), although we see the settlers join together in the search for Debbie (played first by Lana Wood then by her older sister Natalie Wood) and Lucy (Pippa Scott). Sometimes, it is the disorder of a young frontier town (*My Darling Clementine*). Sometimes, it is represented by a group of homesteaders who band together to go into the town that has no law and is controlled by a self-interested cattle baron (*Shane*). By contrast, the action of *High Noon* (Fred Zinnemann, 1952) takes place within a settled town. The only problem is that the townspeople are moral cowards, unwilling to help or defend their departing marshal Will Kane (Gary Cooper), who is being hunted by gunmen. A significant point here is that in virtually all cases in the classic western, the central male protagonist's actions will involve commitments to the fledgling community as well as the need to take action for personal reasons to avenge lawlessness: the slaughter of Ethan's brother and his brother's family; the murder of Wyatt's brother, James (Don Garner), by the Clantons; Shane's sense of personal responsibility for the well-being of the Starrett family when Joe Starrett (Van Heflin) decides to confront Ryker (Emile Meyer) and the gunfighter Wilson (Jack Palance). In *High Noon*, even though he is no longer marshal, Will Kane returns to the town, having left after his marriage, knowing that Frank Miller (Ian MacDonald) and his men will eventually hunt him and his new bride, Amy (Grace Kelly), down. Even in a western where a community is yet to be established and settlement is little more than a stagecoach junction or an isolated railway station, such as in *The Stalking Moon*, Sam (Gregory Peck) offers to protect Sarah (Eva Marie Saint), a former Apache captive, and her half-Indian son against the threat of the renegade Apache leader Salvaje (Nathaniel Narcisco). The actions of the classic western protagonist have a clear ethical dimension to them.

Finally, and significantly, the narrative closure of the classic western typically involves the hero's triumph over adversity and the successful completion of his goal: Ethan exacts revenge against Scar and rescues his abducted niece; Wyatt avenges the death of James and also the death of Chihuahua during the shoot-out at the OK Corral; Will Kane and his bride face and kill Miller and his men when the townsfolk fail to help; Shane kills the Ryker brothers and Wilson, the villains who have been trying to run the Starretts and other settlers off their homesteads; and Sam kills Salvaje, who has left a trail of innocent victims in his attempt to find his son. In each of these classic westerns, with the exception of *The Stalking Moon*, where there is not yet an established community, the protagonist pointedly does not remain in the community he has defended. The very qualities that make these protagonists able to act on behalf of the community against those who threaten its stability make them finally unable to integrate themselves into it. So Wyatt, Will Kane and his bride, and Shane ride off at the end of these films. In one of the most striking closing shots in the history of the genre, having rescued his niece Debbie and brought her to the Jorgensens' farm, Ethan stands at the farmhouse doorway. For this extended take, the camera is positioned inside, with the inside of the house in darkness and Ethan silhouetted against the bright sky in the door frame. The closing shot is a reference back to the opening shot, which establishes the film's polarities: inside/outside, home/wilderness, and family/the outsider. Rather than crossing the threshold, Ethan turns and walks away as the door swings slowly shut. In sum, regardless of the stage of development of the community in the western, action to ensure order and some form of justice lies finally in the hands of the central hero, who acts out of a sense of moral right although he is finally never integrated into the community.

Earlier it was mentioned that the classic westerns to which *McCabe* is a calculated and ironic response have achieved the status of film art. This is not to minimize the fact that, like their cousins, the B-westerns, classic westerns are members of a genre, and are to be understood in terms of the use to which governing generic conventions are put. In this section, we have outlined several of the most central generic conventions of the western.

These conventions include identifiable characters, recognizable patterns of narrative action, a range of generically relevant locations, and conventions of narrative closure. There are four more thematic plot-points characteristic of the genre that bear mentioning. Combined, the way these generic conventions are implemented will tell us a great deal about the moral/ethical perspective of the particular film in which they appear.

The first plot-point or thematic motif concerns what we refer to generally as the threat to innocence. This threat can take a variety of forms. An obvious example occurs in *Stagecoach,* in which a newborn baby is inside the coach attacked by Indians while it makes its way across the desert. Another version is the death of the innocent, as we see in the murder of Wyatt's younger brother, James, by the Clantons. Yet another version is the violation of innocence, which is a theme central to *The Searchers,* since plot action involves not just the murder of Ethan's brother, Aaron (Walter Coy), and the rape and murder of Ethan's sister-in-law, Martha (Dorothy Jordan), but also the abduction, rape, and murder of Ethan's niece Lucy, as well as the abduction into sexual servitude of Ethan's other niece, Debbie, at the hands of "Scar" (Henry Brandon), the Nawyecky Comanche chief Cicatrice. In *The Stalking Moon,* Salvaje's killing of innocent victims during his search for his son includes the Mexican family who are Sam's only neighbors. The threat to innocence in the western represents the loss of order and stability when it occurs early in the narrative or underlines the threat of lawlessness that precedes the final shoot-out.

The second thematic motif to mention is the funeral or graveyard scene. Deaths happen often in classic westerns—deaths of villains, certainly, but also deaths of ordinary citizens at the hands of villains, and of course deaths of characters who count, whether literally or metaphorically, as innocents. These latter are the cases of interest. In its classic formulation, the graveyard scene or burial scene embodies the particular western's statement of moral idealism. In *Clementine,* the moral idealism is captured by Wyatt's words over the grave of James when he looks forward to a time when "kids can grow up safe." This is important not only in itself, but also because it foretells Wyatt's desire to eliminate the lawless element that killed James and to restore to the community the innocence that was lost with James's murder. In *Shane,* Torrey's (Elisha Cook Jr.) funeral is set on a hilltop with the lawless town in the distance. From this vantage, the settlers at the funeral can see the smoke from the farm of Lewis (Edgar Buchanan) and his family, who were about to leave the valley, which Ryker's men have set ablaze, causing Lewis to decide to remain in the community and, with the promise of help from his fellow settlers, to rebuild. Things are somewhat different in *The Searchers*. There, at the funeral of his brother, sister-in-law, and their younger son (the whereabouts of his nieces Lucy and Debbie not yet having been discovered), Ethan disrupts the Reverend Captain Samuel Clayton (Ward Bond), saying, "Put an amen to it!" Ethan's point in walking away from the funeral is that time is valuable if he is going to search for his nieces, and the niceties of a public observance come second to finding his nieces and avenging his dead family members.

The third additional motif to mention is the depiction, in the classic western, of romantic love. Interestingly, romantic love—within appropriate social boundaries, of course—is a sign of socialization and settling into the community. Wyatt attends a church dance early in *Clementine*, where he asks Clementine (whom he addresses as "Miss Carter") to dance. Despite his awkward dancing style (reminiscent of how Henry Fonda dances in Ford's *Young Mr. Lincoln*, 1939), it is clear that the two are interested in one another. At the end of the film, Wyatt promises Clementine that he will return to Tombstone, where she stays on as the schoolteacher, but nevertheless rides out of town to visit his father. In *Shane*, following the shoot-out, Shane rides out of the valley back into the mountains where we first saw him and does not return to the homestead, where there is obviously a strong mutual attraction between him and Mrs. Starrett. In *The Searchers*, a main reason for Ethan not to stay is that his true love, his sister-in-law Martha, is dead. But the future of the wilderness community can at least look hopefully toward the forthcoming wedding of Ethan's nephew, Martin (Jeffrey Hunter), to the Jorgensens' daughter, Laurie (Vera Miles).

The final point about the thematic significance of community in the classic western underlines the spiritual dimension of expansion and settlement. Whether it is an isolated homestead or a developing town, the essence of the community involves selfless and future-oriented cooperation among settlers and citizens. That said, community is often defined by what is absent or by what has yet to be achieved. For example, in *Shane*, Joe Starrett foresees "a town and churches and a school." In *The Searchers*, Mrs. Jorgensen (Olive Carey) talks about Texicans being "way out on a limb. This year and next. Maybe for a hundred more. But I don't think it will be forever. Some day this country's gonna be a fine good place to be." The symbol by which this community is represented in many classic westerns is the church, even when, as we see in *Clementine*, it is still under construction. The dance mentioned earlier occurs as part of the first social gathering to raise money to finish the construction of Tombstone's church even though it does not yet have a regular preacher. One of the settlers, John Simpson (Russell Simpson), leads the singing of the hymn "Shall We Gather at the River" as well as playing fiddle for the dancing. Even when there is no church, the western has often celebrated how spiritual and moral values have been part of the settlement of the West and the establishment of a law-abiding community. In a telling conjunction of the spiritual and the civic in *The Searchers,* the Reverend Captain Samuel Clayton both leads the Texas Rangers and officiates at funerals and weddings ("Shall We Gather at the River" is sung at both the funeral and the interrupted wedding ceremony). He also observes proper behavior on all occasions, from not permitting alcohol during the wedding ceremony to allowing the attacking Comanche Indians to carry out their dead and wounded unhindered during a break in the fighting. In *Shane* we again see a conjunction of the civic and the spiritual during the Independence Day celebration at one of the homesteads. With the American flag flying in the background, the homesteaders sing the hymn "Abide with Me," dance to the folk song "Goodbye, Old Paint," and in a more comic moment tease the former Confederate soldier Torrey with a few bars of "Dixie." As in *My Darling Clementine,* the civic and the spiritual is bound into family and more particularly into personal and community relationships. The homesteaders in *Shane* also celebrate Joe and Marian Starrett's wedding anniversary just as the settlers make way for "the marshal and his lady fair" in *My Darling Clementine.* Even in westerns with an established town setting, such as *High Noon,* the church remains a symbol of community. Following the opening credits, we see three gunmen ride into town on the right side of the image, with the church prominent on the left side. When Will Kane seeks the support of the community he goes to the Sunday service, although the townspeople fail him—again underlining the need for the western hero to demonstrate the courage and moral will to defend the community.

The Western in Ironic Perspective

The optimistic classic western—our central examples have been *My Darling Clementine* and *Shane*—are, narratively speaking, examples of what we, following Northrop Frye, call the master genre of romance. The narrative structure of the classic western is that of a quest, with a hero who sets out to accomplish some goal that is both a social and a moral good. Many later and darker westerns—our example is *The Searchers*—are explicitly quests. Ethan and Marty's search to find Debbie and punish Scar lasts, literally, for years, and takes them all over the American Southwest and also north into Colorado. Central to the quest plotline is the basic ambition of turning the western desert into a garden, making the community safe from internal or external threats, and introducing key civilizing aspects to the lawless frontier, notably law enforcement (the sheriff or marshal), religion (the church and its preacher), and education (the schoolteacher). What the classic western is not, even in its darker moments, is ironic. *McCabe and Mrs. Miller* is a self-consciously ironic examination of the paradigmatic conventions and motifs of the western. We have already discussed the film's setting in Washington State. Let us turn to the central protagonists.

That *McCabe* is a western presented in the ironic mode might not be initially apparent to viewers. This is partly because the film might not initially look like a western at all. The rain-soaked forest, through which a hooded man dressed in an oversized fur coat rides a horse, muttering to himself, while on the sound track Leonard Cohen sings the melancholic "The Stranger Song," is obviously not how westerns typically present themselves. Rain and mud and overcast hillsides are not the sorts of markers that western viewers typically expect. Nor do we conventionally find mutterers transformed into western protagonists. The rider enters a small town very much under construction, as is the town's church, which is the first structure we see as he approaches. Once inside the town (later identified as Presbyterian Church), the rider shakes off his huge fur coat, dismounts, and takes out of a box being carried by his saddle pony a bowler hat, which he carefully puts on. Then, in a long shot filmed from inside the door of Sheehan's Saloon and Hotel, the initial social center of the community, the man who will shortly be identified as McCabe walks through the dark and muddy town center, across a wooden footbridge, and into the bar.

As might be expected, the arrival of a stranger arouses the interest of many at Sheehan's, including Sheehan (Rene Auberjonois) himself. Questions about whether the stranger is wearing a gun are quietly voiced by those in the bar. Putting together bits of information while McCabe sets up a game of poker with the locals, Sheehan is led to believe that the stranger is none other than John "Pudgy" McCabe, the man who shot Bill Roundtree. McCabe never confirms or denies Sheehan's guess. Virtually no one in the bar has heard of either John McCabe or Bill Roundtree, but Sheehan insists that the card player is McCabe and that he has "a big rep." Trying to draw him out, Sheehan suggests that McCabe is a gunfighter. McCabe replies, "Businessman, businessman." So while we seem to have here the convention that establishes McCabe's reputation as a gunfighter, he is unwilling to acknowledge who he is. Invariably, the classic western hero's identity and reputation are enhanced by his subsequent actions, but McCabe's actions will continually raise doubts about his reputation. The film's genuine gunman, Butler (Hugh Millais), will eventually declare of McCabe, "That man never killed anyone!"

What do we learn about McCabe in the opening sequences of the film up to the arrival of Mrs. Miller? Several things, none of them remotely likely to identify him as a western hero. He is vulgar. He drinks to the point of drunkenness. He is incompetent in his various professional undertakings, as is obvious from the brothel he sets up in three canvas tents, not to mention his inability to even fathom how to organize and manage his prostitutes. When Mrs. Miller arrives, it is clear that, as she says, she is a whore and knows a lot about whoring. (We see her twice, briefly, inside the brothel in Bear Paw where McCabe goes to buy "chippies," as he calls them.) She will be the organizer and the manager of the new brothel. Compared to Mrs. Miller, McCabe is shown not only to be a bad businessman—his saloon is mostly always empty—but also to be singularly unimaginative. She sees the potential that Presbyterian Church offers for a whorehouse with proper linen and high-class girls brought in from Seattle. McCabe seems not to have thought beyond buying the most unfortunate whores available from the brothel in Bear Paw. If all this were not bad enough, McCabe doesn't even have the vision of Sheehan, who is himself represented as being not particularly bright. Yet even Sheehan can anticipate the day when Presbyterian Church might have not two saloons, but four or more. He has the foresight to propose striking up a partnership with McCabe to ensure that anyone who opens a saloon after the two of them is forced to give them a cut of the profits. In response to Sheehan's proposal, McCabe can offer only the inane remark that "if a frog had wings, he wouldn't bump his ass so much" before having to intervene as one of his psychologically frail prostitutes attacks a client with a knife.

The first main arc of narrative action, then, runs from McCabe's arrival in Presbyterian Church to getting his tent brothel up and running. The second main arc begins with the arrival of Mrs. Miller on the steam engine with Ida (Shelley Duvall), the mail-order bride sent for by Bart Coyle (Bert Remsen). Archetypally speaking, Ida is the virgin and Mrs. Miller is the whore, but ultimately both women understand that if they are to have livings at all, it will be as the result of an exchange for sex. With Mrs. Miller's arrival, the town's central institution shifts from being Sheehan's saloon to McCabe and Mrs. Miller's whorehouse. The church, after which the town is named, seems to be the only building under construction with which no progress is made, short of lifting the cross to the top of the steeple during the film's most beautiful sequence, as McCabe brings the Bear Paw whores to town while on the sound track Leonard Cohen sings "The Sisters of Mercy."

Conventionally, while the saloon might in some westerns be a place for relaxation and interaction with fellow settlers or townspeople, the moral epicenter of the community is the church and if there is no physical church, then in the ceremonies that are related to the church, including weddings and funerals. The church is central even if, as we see in *Clementine*, it is in such early days of construction that it is little more than a floor and the framework for the steeple. Nevertheless, in *Clementine*, the church represents the unifying aspects of the community. It combines the personal, the civic, the social, the spiritual, and the patriotic (as seen, for instance, by the flags flying on the framework for the steeple). There is even community support in the final shoot-out, as the settler John Simpson, who presides over the gathering at the church, and the mayor (Roy Roberts) serve as decoys for Wyatt's brother, Morgan (Ward Bond) and Doc Holliday (Victor Mature) as Wyatt walks to the OK Corral, adding a civic and a spiritual sanction to the gunfight. The church serves no such function in *McCabe*. It is a mere shell, and the minister, Mr. Elliot (Corey Fisher), is an unnervingly cold, awkward individual, unable to converse with the townspeople even when he has to make his way through Sheehan's crowded bar to the small store at the back to buy food. (In a lovely moment, Sheehan's door is thrown open and someone shouts, "Close the goddamned door," only to see who has come in and then sheepishly add, "Evening, Reverend.") The place of relaxation, fellow feeling, conviviality, and social cohesion is the whorehouse. While the social dance takes place at the church in *Clementine*, it takes place at the whorehouse in *McCabe*.

Earlier it was mentioned that McCabe couldn't be more different from classic western heroes like Earp and Ethan. Shortly after Mrs. Miller's arrival, and due to her initiative, McCabe can boast not only a saloon (although McCabe notes at one point that he hasn't sold a bottle of whiskey all day), but also a bathhouse and a whorehouse, and at least the two businesses run by Mrs. Miller are turning a profit. None of the heroes we have considered—Earp, Ethan, Shane, Will Kane, or Sam—is motivated by profit. They represent clear moral positions with respect to other characters and ongoing narrative action. They are each on moral quests. McCabe, however, represents no clear moral stance or position, and is certainly not on any sort of moral quest. The western heroes have a lively sense of the various threats that will confront them. McCabe has no comparable sense, since he simply does not understand how vulnerable he is when, as shortly happens, bigger corporate interests see what he has accomplished and want to buy him out.

Worse yet, McCabe does not have the imagination to recognize the economic imperative of big business in the settlement of the West. In its ironic perspective, *McCabe and Mrs. Miller* offers a dark vision of expansion in which a fledgling community is overtaken by institutional capitalism. The Harrison Shaughnessy Mining Company represents the expansion of big business at the expense of small businessmen and entrepreneurs like McCabe and Sheehan. It also represents the lawlessness of the frontier, since what big business cannot achieve by negotiation, it achieves by force. Two of the mining company's representatives, Eugene Sears (Michael Murphy) and Ernie Hollander (Antony Holland), come to Presbyterian Church to buy McCabe's holdings. McCabe is simply foolish trying to impress them with his jokes and one-liners. For instance, after Sears introduces himself, McCabe quips, "I'm Roebuck. Who's watching the store?" Understandably, Sears and Hollander dismiss him as a "smart ass," especially after the story McCabe tells about the frog that is swallowed by an eagle, a story that ends with the punch line, "You wouldn't shit me now!" While they say that they understand he is "the town's leading citizen," they see clearly that he lacks their sophistication and their ability to negotiate. While trying to work out a better offer than Sears and Hollander are authorized to endorse, McCabe makes a serious social gaffe by trying to entertain them at the whorehouse. That they have already bought out Sheehan's holdings ought to cause McCabe to take seriously the nature of their offer, but he does not, claiming he has already received a better offer from "Monkey Ward," that is, Montgomery Ward, the mail-order store chain. He also fails to recognize the threat of violence barely concealed in the offer to buy his holdings, violence that will become evident when, to McCabe's surprise, Sears and Hollander simply leave, turning the matter over to the company's hired gunman, Butler, and his associates. Even Mrs. Miller realizes immediately the risk McCabe runs by not capitulating to the deal proposed by Sears and Hollander. In amazement at his recklessness, she exclaims, "You turned down Harrison Shaughnessy? You know who they are?" And then she adds, "You better hope they come back. They'd as soon put a bullet in you as look at you."

The evening Sears and Hollander arrive in Presbyterian Church, they witness the attack on Bart Coyle, whose funeral, which takes place after Sears and Hollander leave, is the next major turning point of the narrative. On a hillside, with the townsfolk in attendance and the whores leading the singing of the hymn,[14] the minister conducts the service in a fast, flat voice devoid of feeling or conviction. Mrs. Miller, from several yards away, intently scrutinizes Coyle's widow, Ida, sizing up her possibilities as a future whore. Ida returns Mrs. Miller's look, and not long later she takes up her new place in the whorehouse. During the funeral, McCabe—who has been edgy since the departure of Sears and Hollander—sees a horseman approach in the distance. Thinking this is a gunman sent to resolve the situation with Harrison Shaughnessy, McCabe goes up to him. Stylistically, this is set up as if McCabe is about to participate in a classic showdown confrontation, with McCabe preparing his gun. It turns out not to be a gunman at all, but a youthful cowboy (Keith Carradine) in an oversized hat, who tells McCabe that he's heard about "the fanciest whorehouse in the whole territory up here." He adds, "It's so long since I had a piece of ass!" The solemnity of the traditional graveside scene in the classic western is thus totally disrupted, while at the same time, the absolute centrality of the whores and the whorehouse to the community of Presbyterian Church is underlined.

McCabe, as it happens, has not been wrong to anticipate the arrival of gunmen representing Harrison Shaughnessy. The leader, Butler, is a bear of a man, and looks even larger in an oversized fur coat. He dwarfs McCabe, but also confounds him. McCabe offers him a cigar and Butler counters, "Have one of mine." As might have been anticipated, McCabe still doesn't understand the precariousness of the situation he has put himself into. Thus, he wrongly believes that Butler and his men have come to continue negotiations. They have not. As Butler wryly puts it, "I don't make deals." Shortly after this, in a moment that captures forcefully the motif of the death of the innocent, Butler's teenage gunman, the "Kid" (Manfred Schulz), deliberately murders the young cowboy who, from his arrival in Presbyterian Church, has spent his entire time running around the whorehouse, and is simply looking to buy a pair of new socks, having worn his threadbare.

The brutal murder of the cowboy, who has been deliberately lured into drawing his gun by the Kid, brings into sharp focus both the potential violence of the men hired by Harrison Shaughnessy and the lack of a sheriff or anyone representing the law in Presbyterian Church. The idea of the law, so prominent in classic and late-classic westerns, is represented in *McCabe* by a lawyer (William Devane) whom McCabe visits after he is told that Sears and Hollander have left Bear Paw. Representing himself as someone who can help the "little guy," including McCabe, the lawyer talks about his own future as "the next senator from the state of Washington" and how he can imagine that he and McCabe will sit down to dinner with William Jennings Bryant. The lawyer's rhetoric is filled with the idealism of western expansion, for example, "When a man goes into the wilderness and with his bare hands gives birth to a small enterprise . . . I'm here to tell you that no sons of bitches are going to take it away from him." He also offers words of reassurance: "Harrison Shaughnessy. They have stockholders. Do you think they want their stockholders and the public thinking their management isn't imbued with fair play and justice, the very values that make this country what it is today?" Less than reassured, McCabe can only respond, "Well, I just didn't want to get killed."

The classic western often ends with a final shoot-out. Something rather like this happens in *McCabe,* but it is stripped of any suggestion of a heroic showdown in which the protagonist faces his antagonists face-to-face. The shoot-out in *McCabe and Mrs. Miller* pits McCabe against Butler and his associates, who are hunting him in order to kill him, while also featuring the church and its minister (who conventionally represents the moral and spiritual center of community), as well as most members of the community, but it brings them together in a quite surprising manner. Taking place unconventionally in a heavy snowstorm, the shoot-out occurs at various locations throughout Presbyterian Church, ironically highlighting the growth of the town and the fresh-cut lumber of the new bridge and the buildings that have replaced the tumbledown shacks we saw when McCabe first arrived. Seeking a vantage point, if not a refuge, in the church, which stands isolated from the town, McCabe finds the interior not a place of worship but a dark space cluttered with tools, wagon wheels, the minister's bed in a corner, wood shavings and bits of discarded wood. It is quite clear that no one in Presbyterian Church attends church. In addition, McCabe is confronted by the minister who, now carrying McCabe's shotgun and acting without any sign of charity, forces him out with the words, "This is God's house," ignoring McCabe's pleas for his safety. An unexpected consequence is that the minister, who is holding McCabe's gun, is shot by Butler when he kicks open the church door. In turn, the minister drops the lamp he is holding, starting a fire in the church. Alerted by the call, "Fire! Fire! The church is on fire!" and a later cry, "Jesus Christ, the church is on fire!" the majority of the townspeople, including the whores, work together to save the church they do not attend.

Again, in an unconventional representation of the traditional shoot-out, where the classic western hero traditionally faces the villains in a face-to-face confrontation, the final shoot-out is crosscut with shots of the townspeople, who are completely unaware of McCabe's circumstances while they are fighting the fire. And while there may be suspense in McCabe's attempt to elude his enemies, McCabe's actions and the deaths of Butler and his accomplices are all unheroic. McCabe is simply running for his life, and will ultimately die alone. Butler's gunman the Kid is shot in the back although he wounds McCabe before falling into the tub in the bathhouse where he drowns. Butler's other gunman, known as "Breed" (Jace Van Der Veen), is shot in the back and dies in the snow. Wounded, and at the very moment that he appears to have found an isolated shack where he can take refuge, McCabe is shot in the back by Butler, and then slides down a snow-covered slope. Butler, making his way through thigh-deep snow, stands above the prostrate figure of McCabe who, unexpectedly, raises his hand and shoots Butler in the forehead with a derringer, the gun he reportedly shot Bill Roundtree with. If our expectation was that the townspeople would discover McCabe's plight and save him, it is not fulfilled, as everyone is totally caught up in the celebration after putting out the church fire, unaware of the fate of the minister and the fate of McCabe, who dies from his wounds, completely alone and increasingly covered by the falling snow. The final sequence of shots intercut the body of McCabe, now without his bowler hat and with his face obscured by snow and the warm, red glow of Mrs. Miller's face as she lies drifting into oblivion in the opium den, as on the sound track Leonard Cohen sings, "Traveling lady, stay awhile, until the night is over. I'm just a station on your way, I know I'm not your lover." The final extended shot of McCabe's body represents not only his death but also Altman's way of delineating the death of an ideal of moral action as well as the death of a symbolic triumph over lawlessness and evil that the genre had heretofore invested in the western hero.

Notes

1. We are indebted to earlier film critics who drew attention to the western as a genre, notably Jim Kitses, *Horizons West* (London: Thames & Hudson, 1969); and Jim

Kitses, "The Western: Ideology and Archetype," in *Focus on the Western*, ed. Jack Nachbar (Englewood Cliffs, NJ: Prentice-Hall, 1974), 64–72.

2. Northrop Frye, *Anatomy of Criticism* (Princeton, NJ: Princeton University Press, 1957).

3. Leonard Cohen's songs are linked thematically with various characters in the film. "The Stranger Song" is identified with McCabe. "The Sisters of Mercy" is identified with the "chippies" McCabe brings back from Bear Paw. "Winter Lady" is identified with Mrs. Miller at the end of the film.

4. Martha C. Nussbaum, *Love's Knowledge: Essays on Philosophy and Literature* (Oxford: Oxford University Press, 1990). See also Martha Nussbaum, "Exactly and Responsibly: A Defence of Ethical Criticism," *Philosophy and Literature* 22 (October 1998): 343–65.

5. Wayne C. Booth, *The Company We Keep: An Ethics of Fiction* (Berkeley: University of California Press, 1988). See also Wayne C. Booth, "Why Banning Ethical Criticism Is a Serious Mistake," *Philosophy and Literature* 22 (October 1998): 366–93.

6. Nussbaum, " 'Finely Aware and Richly Responsible': Literature and the Moral Imagination," in *Love's Knowledge*, 148–65.

7. Ibid., 148.

8. Paul Ricoeur, *Time and Narrative,* 3 vols., trans. Kathleen McLaughlin and David Pellauer (Chicago: University of Chicago Press, 1984, 1985, 1988).

9. Aristotle, *Poetics*, trans. Kenneth Telford (Chicago: H. Regnery, 1961).

10. We include *The Stalking Moon* with acknowledged classic westerns such as *My Darling Clementine* and *Shane* because we believe it deserves retrospective consideration for canonical status.

11. See Kitses, "The Western," 65–66, for an earlier mapping of thematic dichotomies in the classic western.

12. See Gary Heba and Robin Murphy's essay in this volume, "Go West, Young Woman! Hegel's Dialectic and Women's Identities in Western Films."

13. See Shai Biderman, " 'Do Not Forsake Me, Oh, My Darling': Loneliness and Solitude in Westerns"; and Douglas J. Den Uyl, "Civilization and Its Discontents: The Self-Sufficient Western Hero," both in this volume.

14. The hymn sung at the burial scene is "Asleep in Jesus," by Margaret Mackay, published in 1832. The whores begin singing with the second line of the first verse: "Asleep in Jesus! blessed sleep / From which none ever wakes to weep / A calm and undisturbed repose / Unbroken by the last of foes."

Part 4

ON THE FRINGE

The Encounter with the Other

Savage Nations

Native Americans and the Western

Michael Valdez Moses

Todorov and Columbus: The Indian as "Other"

It is a commonplace of contemporary film criticism that Native Americans have historically been ill served by the American western, a genre in which they have been misrepresented and demeaned.[1] For those who regard an honest and impartial portrayal of historically oppressed minorities as a moral if not an aesthetic imperative, the American western will offer little in the way of spiritual uplift. But if the American western fails to offer an objective ethnological depiction of indigenous peoples (assuming that such a thing were both possible and desirable), it nonetheless invites a philosophic consideration of the problematics of alterity, an analysis of the ways in which cinematic representations of the cultural Other have been invented and manipulated, and an examination of the various political ends to which those representations have been put.

In his seminal work, *The Conquest of America: The Question of the Other,* the Bulgarian-born French philosopher and literary theorist, Tzvetan Todorov (1939–) investigates "the discovery the self makes of the other" by means of a historical and philosophical analysis of "the Spaniards' perception of the Indians" during the century that followed Columbus's first voyage in 1492.[2] Todorov notes that Columbus's attitude toward the Indians veers between two incompatible views. At times the explorer describes them as perfectly good: beautiful, virtuous, generous, peaceable, brave, and entirely innocent; at other times he depicts them as supremely wicked and cowardly, fabulously cruel and violent, given to all manner of vices, especially lust, greed, and thievery. Columbus conceives of the Indians either as perfect prelapsarian Christians and potentially ideal Spanish subjects or as corrupt and debased creatures, natural slaves who must be dealt with by force and systematic coercion. According to Todorov, Columbus

> either conceives the Indians (though without using these words) as human beings altogether, having the same rights as himself; but then he sees them not only as equals but also as identical, and this behavior leads to assimilationism, the projection of his own values on the others. Or else he starts from the difference, but the latter is immediately translated into terms of superiority and inferiority (in his case, obviously it is the Indians who are inferior). What is denied is the existence of a human substance truly other, something capable of being not merely an imperfect state of oneself. These two elementary figures of the experience of alterity are both grounded in egocentrism, in the identification of our own values with values in general, of our *I* with the universe.[3]

Todorov offers a theoretical explanation of Columbus's incompatible representations of the Indians: "How can Columbus be associated with these two apparently contradictory myths, one whereby the Other is a 'noble savage' (when perceived at a distance) and one whereby he is a 'dirty dog,' a potential slave? It is because both rest on a common basis, which is the failure to recognize the Indians, and the refusal to admit them as a subject having the same rights as oneself, but different. Columbus has discovered America but not the Americans."[4]

For Todorov, a fully humane relationship between the Self and the (exterior) Other depends upon the willingness of the Self to accept both the equality and the difference of the Other. "On the ideological level . . . we are trying to combine what we regard as the better parts of both terms of the alternative; we want *equality* without its compelling us to accept identity; but also *difference* without its degenerating into superiority/inferiority. We aspire to reap the benefits of the egalitarian model *and* of the hierarchic model; we aspire to rediscover the meaning of the social without losing the quality of the individual."[5]

For Todorov, the mere acceptance by the Self of the equality of the Other is not sufficient to establish a properly humane and just relationship between them, for egalitarianism may easily slide over into an insistence that the Other is or should become identical with the Self, that the Self and the Other must share identical values. In his analysis of the controversy in 1550 at Valladolid between two sixteenth-century priestly scholars, Bartolomé de Las Casas, who famously argued on behalf of the rights of the Indians, and his intellectual adversary, the philosopher and theologian Ginés de Sepúlveda, who maintained that the Amerindians were naturally and culturally inferior, and hence could be legitimately enslaved and violently coerced into accepting the Catholic faith, Todorov points out that Las Casas's defense of the Indians crucially depends upon his representation of them as devoid of all defects: the Indians are models of humility, patience, peaceableness, and obedience, singularly free of cupidity, in short, "veritable Christians." Although Todorov explicitly praises Las Casas for his efforts to treat the Indians with greater humanity and justice, he nonetheless faults him for his idealized (mis)representation of the Indians, which, from an ethnographic point of view, is even more unsatisfactory than Sepúlveda's, and paradoxically, no less complicit in the colonial efforts of the crown and the church to subject the native peoples of the New World to Spanish imperial rule and the Catholic faith. He writes, "We must acknowledge that the portrait of the Indians to be drawn from Las Casas's works is rather poorer than that left us by Sepúlveda: as a matter of fact, we learn nothing of the Indians. If it is incontestable that the prejudice of superiority is an obstacle in the road to knowledge, we must also admit that the prejudice of equality is a still greater one, for it consists in identifying the other purely and simply with one's own 'ego ideal' (or with oneself)."[6]

Todorov notes that the originality of Las Casas's defense of the Amerindians "proceeds from the fact that he attributes the 'valued' pole to the other and the rejected pole to 'us' (the Spaniards). But this inverted distribution of values, incontestable proof of his generosity of spirit, does not lessen the schematism of his vision."[7] Las Casas offers no more accurate an understanding of the Other, since he merely inverts Sepúlveda's moral evaluations of the Spaniards and Indians; for Las Casas, it is the Indians who are the true Christians and the Spaniards the demonic savages.

In what follows, I shall argue that representations of Native Americans in the Hollywood western have much in common with those generated by the sixteenth-century Spaniards whom Todorov criticizes: such wildly inconsistent conceptions of Native Americans, for all their apparent differences, are almost always (egocentric) projections of the culturally delimited and historically specific values and desires of both the makers of Hollywood westerns and their (chiefly American) audiences. But in contradistinction to many contemporary critics of racial stereotyping of Indians in American westerns (and in accord with Todorov's critique of Las Casas), I will also maintain that the (mis)representations of Native Americans in the Hollywood western are as likely to be exaggeratedly "positive" and idealized as "negative" and degrading. As Jonathan Rosenbaum has pointed out, the American western almost never "assumes [or] addresses Native American spectators."[8] The fact that Hollywood westerns have not historically been aimed at a Native American audience (which would at best comprise a negligible percentage of any film's projected market) necessarily suggests that the chief cultural importance and primary ideological function of their portrayals of the American Indian often have little to do with modern America's attempt to discover, control, or relate to its "exterior Other," the Amerindian.[9]

Even when Hollywood westerns have manifested a conscious desire to revise and compensate for earlier unenlightened portrayals of the Native American in American cinema, the cultural and ideological energies of these films have typically been directed elsewhere. To put this in a more provocative fashion: given that the near annihilation of the indigenous populations and the widespread (but by no means complete) destruction of Amerindian culture that accompanied the imperial expansion of the American regime westward was completed before the advent of the Hollywood western, misrepresentations of "Indians" in the American western were hardly necessary to ensure the hegemonic subordination and political marginalization of those native peoples who managed to survive. Subsequent attempts to correct these misrepresentations likewise had less to do with altering or improving the Native Americans' material conditions or social status than with *other* cultural and political objectives deemed more pressing. Accordingly, I argue that the varied (but always constructed) portrayals of Native Americans in the Hollywood western, whether idealized or demonized, served a variety of often contradictory and mutable ideological and cultural aims, chief among them the critique of perceived defects and shortcomings of modern American society.

In what follows I discuss several films: a postwar western "classic," *Fort Apache* (1948), the first in John Ford's so-called Cavalry Trilogy; three "revisionist" westerns from the 1970s, *Little Big Man* (Arthur Penn, 1970), *A Man Called Horse* (Elliot Silverstein, 1970), and *The Return of a Man Called Horse* (Irvin Kershner, 1976); and two new-wave westerns from the 1990s, *Dances with Wolves* (Kevin Costner, 1990) and *Dead Man* (Jim Jarmusch, 1995). While focusing on the cultural significance of the historically specific representations of Native Americans in these films, I also aim to place their varied and contradictory portraits of the American Indian within a larger western literary and philosophic tradition concerned with how the "civilized" is to be defined with respect to the "savage" or the "barbarian."

Postwar Fordism and New Deal Savages

If many film critics have insisted that the American western consistently portrays the American Indian in a negative light, a number of prominent cultural historians of the genre have insisted that its long history reveals a striking number of exceptions, not least the early silent classic *The Vanishing American* (George Seitz, 1926) based on Zane Grey's novel.[10] In any event, there is general agreement that the Hollywood western, which had been mainly a "B-film" genre before World War II, assumed greater complexity and depth in the postwar period, an accomplishment credited in large measure to the efforts of John Ford. Defenders of Ford argue that among the director's contributions to America's only homegrown cinematic genre is a more informed and sympathetic portrayal of the American Indian (at least when compared to prewar Hollywood films). For if Ford had portrayed Geronimo's warriors as mere savages intent on killing the white protagonists in *Stagecoach* (1939), in his 1948 *Fort Apache,* the director presented the Apache people as not only the outraged victims of illiberal and high-handed federal government policy, but also as the military superiors of the U.S. Cavalry's elite West Point–educated officers.

In a crucial scene in *Fort Apache,* Captain York (John Wayne) explains to his commanding officer, Lieutenant Colonel Thursday (Henry Fonda), that the Apache "uprising" (the refusal of the Indians to stay on the reservation) is due to their ill treatment and exploitation by a chartered U.S. government agent, Silas Meacham (Grant Withers). York explains that Apache women have been "degraded" and that the Indians have been regularly "cheated" in their commercial dealings and knowingly corrupted by Meacham's illegal sale of whiskey. Sold shoddy goods and denied their proper rations of food, the Apache have become desperate. Given the failure of the U.S. government to honor the terms of its treaty with the Indians, and the malfeasance and dishonesty of the government's representative, the Apache are justified in taking up arms. In fact, it is Meacham himself who has (illegally) supplied the Apache with the very rifles that enable their rebellion. In a later scene, the Apache chief, Cochise (Miguel Inclán), tells Colonel Thursday that his people will return to the reservation peaceably, provided Meacham is removed as government agent. Cochise insists that the Apache have only looked "for protection" from "the great white father" in Washington, DC, and have resorted to arms only when that promised protection was not forthcoming. Colonel Thursday's high-handed dismissal of the Apache's reasonable demands—Thursday insists that the Indians agree unconditionally to return to the reservation or face immediate attack—and his gratuitous public insult of Cochise (Thursday tells the Apache leader he is "without honor") reinforce the view of the Apache (and Ford's audience) that native "rights" are being arbitrarily violated by both civilian and military representatives of the U.S. government. In sum, Cochise and his people demand justice, while Meacham seeks personal profit, and Thursday proclaims that the Apache have only the "right" to obey.

The corruption, dishonesty, and injustice of the American government are matched by the manifest incompetence of its commanding military officer at Fort Apache. "Thursday's Charge," the ill-conceived attack on Cochise's warriors that leads to the gratuitous massacre of Thursday and many of his men, becomes in the newspapers and commemorative paintings of the "battle" another legendary example of the outstanding bravery of the U.S. Cavalry. In the final scene of the film, a reporter comments that Colonel Thursday, a Custer-like figure, "must have been a great man" and a "great soldier." York, like Ford's audience, knows better. Colonel Thursday, however courageous in his last moments, was every bit the "martinet" whose ignorance of local conditions in the field, overweening professional ambition, and ill-founded faith in the superiority of "classroom" tactics learned at West Point contributed directly to the near annihilation of his troops that provides the dramatic climax of *Fort Apache*. Ford dramatizes Thursday's unfounded presumption that, as an elite graduate of the U.S. Military Academy, he has nothing to learn from the field-tested officers and soldiers on the frontier whom he commands. Thursday repeatedly fails to heed considered advice from his staff (most pointedly Captain York), knowingly manipulates and misleads his officers (allowing York to negotiate with Cochise in good faith even while the colonel plans a "surprise" assault on the Apache), and places his own glory and professional advancement before the safety of his own men. Ford's unflattering portrayal of Colonel Thursday doubtlessly stems in part from his experience as a documentary filmmaker serving in the armed forces during World War II. Having shot thousands of feet of footage during the war, Ford came to share the ordinary GI's skeptical view of the incompetence and self-interested motives of the ranking military brass. *Fort*

Apache, like Ford's contemporaneous war films such as *They Were Expendable* (1945), offers a populist perspective, in which the real, if unsung, heroes are the enlisted men and junior officers often needlessly sacrificed by conceited and vainglorious senior commanders.

Colonel Thursday chronically underestimates the military skill of the natives. Captain York informs Thursday that the Apache have regularly beaten the Sioux and Cheyenne. Captain Collingwood (George O'Brien), whom Thursday relieves of command, warns the colonel that the U.S. Cavalry has been bested in six previous campaigns against the Apache. Because he dismisses out of hand the notion that a ragtag band of "savages" is to be taken seriously as a military adversary, Thursday blunders his way into a debacle. Though no graduate of West Point, Cochise proves to be Thursday's superior when it comes to field tactics; whereas the colonel's troops are nearly annihilated, Cochise's braves incur few casualties. Moreover, while Thursday treats the Apache leader contemptuously, Cochise proves an honorable soldier sensitive to the niceties of "civilized" warfare: after the defeat of Thursday's troops, the Apache leader publicly returns the captured company "colors" to (his trusted friend and adversary) Captain York.

Ford's portrait of Cochise as a man of principle, resolute courage, martial ability, unyielding honor, and magnanimity fits neatly into a long tradition in modern Western culture of the celebration of the "noble savage." The concept is customarily taken to originate with Rousseau's *Second Discourse on the Origin and Foundations of Inequality among Men,* although as we shall see, Rousseau conceives of "the savage" as a creature more pacific and independent than warlike and civic-minded.[11] However, the eighteenth-century philosopher Adam Ferguson, sometimes referred to as the "Scottish Rousseau," provides an apt characterization of this archetype in his most influential work of political philosophy, *An Essay on the History of Civil Society.* "If the savage has not received our instructions, he is likewise unacquainted with our vices. He knows no superior, and cannot be servile; he knows no distinctions of fortune, and cannot be envious; he acts from his talents in the highest station which human society can offer, that of counselor, and the soldier of his country. Toward forming his sentiments, he knows all that the heart requires to be known; he can distinguish the friend whom he loves, and the public interest which awakens his zeal."[12]

According to Ferguson, "the virtues" among "all simple nations" (including the Native American tribes) are "contempt of riches, love of their country, patience of hardship, danger, and fatigue."[13] Savage people most admire fortitude and courage, while despising the commercial arts.[14] Though they will follow a successful chief into battle, and honor his martial skill, rude nations are, by Ferguson's account, fundamentally egalitarian, admitting "of no distinctions of rank or condition," or at any rate of no fixed distinctions.[15] Though blessed with fortitude, these savages are nonetheless addicted to war, easily divided, unsophisticated, uncultured, and liable to face defeat in battle by better-organized opponents and more advanced civilizations. As much as Ferguson admires his virtues, the Savage is ultimately only a remote proto-type of the modern republican citizen-soldier. Rude nations must undergo a long political education. Only through the rough travails of political his-tory do they pass from the "savage" to the "barbarian" state and then to the condition of "polished nations."[16] While Ferguson argues on behalf of good laws, a demanding civic education, and active participation in public life as the necessary basis for a free republican citizenry, he remains wary of even the best and most gifted of political leaders. Rulers, especially successful ones who seek the public good, are likely to augment their power, and in so doing threaten those very civic virtues and political freedoms they initially aimed to protect and preserve. According to Ferguson, "Liberty is never in greater danger than it is when we measure national felicity by the blessings a prince may bestow, or by the mere tranquility which may attend on equi-table administration."[17] Political liberty cannot be guaranteed by a profes-sional army, by well-made laws and institutions, and much less by capable leaders who promise freedom. Ferguson insists, "Liberty is a right which every individual must be ready to vindicate for himself, and which he who pretends to bestow as a favour, has by that very act in reality denied."[18] If the "polished" citizen of the modern republic is to retain his liberty, something of his original savage independence and martial fortitude must remain.

Ferguson's typology of savage society helps to sharpen the contrast between the simple martial and civic virtues of Cochise, devoted to the preservation and welfare of his people, and the commercially and profes-sionally self-interested characters of Meacham and Thursday. Throughout his *Essay*, Ferguson warns against the potentially enervating and corrupting effects of a modern commercial ethos. For Ferguson, excessive love of gain and an unhealthy tendency in modern society for the material self-interest of individuals to prevail over the public good threaten to undermine the basis of a free society; a people overly interested in their commercial well-being are inclined to be servile and ill prepared to defend their liberties when a political crisis requires of them heroic self-sacrifice.[19] Ford certainly doesn't portray Thursday, much less his officers, as lacking in bravery (if anything, Thursday is recklessly courageous), but he strongly suggests that the corruption that bedevils relations between the Apache and the government arises from the latter's collusion with Meacham, whose greed and financial corruption precipitate the Apache uprising. Moreover, Ford implies that Thursday's failings stem from his willingness to risk needlessly the lives of his men for the sake of professional advancement and the prospect of a more glamorous military posting. Ferguson insists that in savage societies, the paramount goal of a chief is not a chivalric conception of honor but "the preservation and increase" of the members of the tribe; consequently, "the American [by which Ferguson means the Indian] rates his defeat from the numbers of men he has lost, or he estimates the victory from the prisoners he has made; not from his having remained the master of a field, or from his being driven from a ground on which he encountered his enemy."[20] Although Thursday is courageous, his dramatic last stand needlessly sacrifices both his life and those of many of his men in a vainglorious attempt to salvage his personal honor.

As noted, Ferguson highlights the essentially egalitarian basis of "rude nations"; the savage virtues are linked explicitly in Ferguson's account to an unwillingness to bow down before others: the savage "knows no superior, and cannot be servile." In contrast to the fundamentally egalitarian spirit that prevails among rude nations, Colonel Thursday insists upon the privileges of his rank and demands public displays of homage and obedience not only from Apache, civilians, rank-and-file soldiers, and friends, but also from his staff of fellow officers. To be sure, Thursday is never in violation of military protocol, nor does he exercise greater authority than that to which his rank entitles him. But Ford's unflattering portrait of Thursday, an inveterate social snob, reminds his audience that the structure of the army is at odds with a popular American democratic sensibility. Thursday's military blunders stem in no small part from the fact that he neither brooks criticism nor accepts guidance from the common soldier or lower-ranking officer, even when their combat experience and knowledge of the local theater are greater than his own.

The reading we have pursued of *Fort Apache* invites a consideration of the larger cultural significance of Ford's 1948 western. Despite its celebration of savage independence and martial valor, Ford's portrait of the much-aggrieved Apache Indians, betrayed and exploited by a civil and military administration that fails to keep its promise to protect and provide for the native population, ultimately depends for its moral and dramatic effect upon the questionable premise that the Apache would (and should) be perfectly content to live on the reservation, if only the federal government were a better steward of its wards. In keeping with the "New Deal" ethos that characterizes many of Ford's films in the 1930s and 1940s, *Fort Apache* suggests not that paternalistic government is *inherently* flawed, but rather that the American government of the late 1940s needs to make good on its promise to manage the lives of its citizens. For all their differences over how the Apache uprising should be handled, Captain York and Colonel Thursday are in agreement that the Indians must be returned to the reservation where they can be looked after by civilian and military authorities. If the Apache are morally justified in challenging federal authority, it is only because incompetent government agents and rapacious business interests have abused their powers and mismanaged the domestic affairs of the reservation. Neither Cochise nor the members of his war council (which includes Geronimo) ever suggests in Ford's film that the incarceration of the Apache on a desolate strip of federal land is at odds with a traditional Indian way of life or inconsistent with a native conception of freedom and autonomy. In fact, Ford's film treats Cochise and the Apache sympathetically precisely insofar as they remain willing to lay down their arms if Thursday will only replace Meacham and see that business dealings on the reservation are more rigorously regulated. The "untamed" ferocity of the Apache is thus merely the flip side of their docility. Rebels against the U.S. government, the Apache would be the most peaceable, long-suffering, and obedient of peoples, if only they were given adequate rations, forbidden access to firearms, and prohibited from imbibing strong liquor. In sum, Ford's Indians are an image of "the common people" as envisioned by New Dealers of the 1930s (although the Apache are not credited with sufficient self-control to handle the end of prohibition). In the end, Ford's native peoples are not in essential respects much different from Las Casas's conception of the docile and virtuous Indian.[21]

Ford's portrait of the civil and more especially the military government in *Fort Apache* is likewise a reflection not of a radical (or conservative) critique of those institutions, but rather a kind of populist plea for their reform. In the final scene, York, now promoted to colonel, has taken command of Fort Apache and is about to embark on a major campaign against the recalcitrant Indians. But unlike the insolent and overbearing Thursday, he is steeped in the language and lore of the local tribes and intimately familiar with their military tactics and strategies. To be sure, he likes and admires Cochise and the Apache, and we know that they admire and trust him in return. But for all that, he is as determined as Thursday to see that the Apache are forcibly removed to the reservation. It is hinted that York is also a graduate of the U.S. Military Academy, and he promises to be a better commanding officer than Thursday in no small measure because he *knows and fraternizes with* the rank-and-file soldier, just as he *knows and socializes with* the Apache. But at the end of the film, what we see is not a demonstration that York is a more effective officer in the field, but instead an exhibition of his masterful manipulation of the press. Offered a chance to explode the myth of the "great man," the late Colonel Thursday, York allows the popular legend to stand and uses the interview to propagandize on behalf of the U.S. Army. Albeit a much shrewder and media-savvy commander than his rash and overbearing predecessor, York is no less convinced that the Indians must be forced to accept the sovereignty of federal authority, regardless of the costs to the soldiers and native peoples on the frontier. One might say that *Fort Apache* reflects Ford's liberal reformist and populist conception of America. In this view, America emerged from the Great Depression and overcame its adversaries in World War II in spite of the machinations of corrupt business interests and the incompetence of an antiquated and hidebound East Coast political and social elite. In this powerfully mythic version of American history, the Republic (indeed the West itself) is saved through the forbearance and courage of the common man, who, for all his patriotic love of personal liberty and individual autonomy, has the good sense to put his trust in the paternalistic governance and superior political skills of his new "populist" leaders.

The Sixties Generation: Savage Nobles and Indian Hipsters

If John Ford's *Fort Apache* implicitly expresses a postwar populist view of the Native American as the common man, who threatens to become a violent menace to civil order if his rights are contravened by a corrupt financial or authoritarian political elite, but who, if properly fed, housed, clothed, regulated, and policed by the "great white father" will be a willingly obedient and docile subject of the state, then the revisionist westerns of the early and mid-1970s represent the American Indian as a countercultural ideal. The cinematic image of the Native American that emerges in the wake of the cultural revolution of the 1960s is less akin to Adam Ferguson's primitive proto-"republican" warrior than it is to Rousseau's idealized description of the "savage" in the *Second Discourse* or to the free-spirited "solitary walker" of his *Reveries.*

According to Rousseau, the savage or barbarian (he uses these terms interchangeably) occupies a happy middle stage or "just mean" in the historical development from the state of nature to civil society:

> Although men now had less endurance, and natural pity had already undergone some attenuation, this period in the development of human faculties, occupying a just mean between the indolence of the primitive state and the petulant activity of our amour propre, must have been the happiest and the most lasting epoch. The more one reflects on it, the more one finds that this state was the least subject to revolutions, the best for man, and that he must have left it only by some fatal accident which, for the sake of the common utility, should never have occurred. The example of the Savages, almost all of whom have been found at this point, seems to confirm that Mankind was made always to remain in it, that this state is the genuine youth of the World, and that all subsequent progress has been so many steps in appearance toward the perfection of the individual, and in effect toward the decrepitude of the species.[22]

Rousseau waxes eloquent in his celebration of the simple life of the savage:

> So long as men were content with their rustic huts, so long as they confined themselves to sewing their clothes of skins with thorns or fish bones, to adorning themselves with feathers and shells, to painting their bodies different colors, to perfecting or embellishing their bows and arrows, to carving a few fishing Canoes or a few crude Musical instruments with sharp stones; In a word, so long as they applied themselves to tasks a single individual could perform, and to arts that did not require the collaboration of several hands, they lived free, healthy, good, and happy as far as they could by their Nature be, and continued to enjoy the gentleness of independent dealings with one another; but the moment one man needed the help of another, as soon as it was found to be useful for one to have provisions for two, equality disappeared, property appeared, work became necessary, and the vast forests changed into smiling Fields that had to be watered with the sweat of men, and where slavery

and misery were soon seen to sprout and grow together with the harvests.[23]

To be sure, the Native Americans (chiefly the Cheyenne and the Yellow Hand Sioux) portrayed in *Little Big Man, A Man Called Horse,* and *The Return of a Man Called Horse* don't precisely conform to Rousseau's description of the savage. For one, the Cheyenne and Sioux comprise tight-knit and highly evolved communities. The native tribes of these films do not suffer from the anomie, alienation, and loneliness that characterize the "white" societies that their protagonists, Jack Crabb (Dustin Hoffman) and John Morgan (Richard Harris) reject. Lord John Morgan rejoins the Yellow Hand tribe in America because he finds the formal rituals of aristocratic English society—foxhunts, church services—oppressive and meaningless. In an early scene in *The Return,* Morgan abandons his companion (an unnamed fiancée) at the chapel during a Sunday service and returns to the vast emptiness of the ornate sitting room in his country house. The camera zooms to a close-up of the elegantly attired but obviously agonized Morgan, who lets loose an existential howl of rage and dread. In the very next scene he tells a servant he will go back to America. Though the tone of *Little Big Man* is rather more satiric and mock-heroic, its image of white society is hardly more appealing; it consists of a dysfunctional assemblage of gamblers, drunks, snake-oil salesmen, bombastic puritanical preachers and their sexually hypocritical wives, paranoid gunslingers, prostitutes, dishonest and bankrupt merchants, and vainglorious soldiers, a mere aggregate of isolated and self-interested individuals with no lasting ties to one another, much less an organic sense of community. By contrast, the Cheyenne of *Little Big Man* and the Yellow Hand Sioux of *A Man Called Horse* and *The Return of a Man Called Horse* welcome the white heroes into small organic communities founded upon intricately complex ties of blood and marriage and unified by common religious rituals and social customs. While white society is comprised almost entirely of alienated individuals and loners, the Native American tribe is an extended *family*: though merely adopted by the tribe, Jack regards Old Lodge Skins (Chief Dan George) as his beloved "grandfather," while seeming to bear the separation from his biological sister, Caroline (Carol Androsky), with equanimity and even indifference. Though both Crabb and Morgan initially become members of their respective tribes as a consequence of being taken captive in an Indian raid, ultimately each comes to embrace the choice of the "dropout" who rejects "respectable" bourgeois society for a walk on the wild side.[24]

All three revisionist westerns portray the simplicity and indeed the relative poverty of the Native Americans: a small handheld mirror, one of Morgan's gifts to the Yellow Hand tribe, is considered by its members an unheard-of luxury. But in the tradition of Rousseau, this simplicity is presented as one of the most appealing features of savage society. Visually, the identification of the white protagonists, Crabb and Morgan, with the "simple" lifestyle of the Indians is most clearly established by their rejection of the sartorial fashions of "uptight" white society and their adoption of native dress. Often appearing in little more than an animal-skin loincloth and headband, the trimly muscular and well-tanned Morgan, with his long flowing blond hair, is at once the consummate brave and quintessential hippie. Manifesting a countercultural rejection of modern commercial and consumer society, these revisionist westerns celebrate the antimaterial ethos of the Native Americans. In a pivotal scene in *The Return*, Morgan tries to convince the chief of a neighboring tribe to join with the Sioux to resist the encroachments of white settlers who have come to take possession of the land; the chief angrily dismisses Morgan's request; he knows that no one can "own" the land, so clearly Morgan must be a liar. It is no accident that the native tribes presented sympathetically in *The Return of a Man Called Horse* are nonmaterialistic communitarians who cannot conceive of the private ownership of land, while those tribes who work for and trade with the white trappers are depicted as corrupt traitors to their race. Though contemporary economic historians have exploded the myth that Native Americans had only a communal sense of property ownership, the Indians of the revisionist western remain within a Rousseauian utopia in which "property" is a crime.[25]

As presented in revisionist westerns of the 1970s, Native American life subsumes the energies and allurements of the contemporaneous sexual revolution. Ostensibly faithful to an ethnologically accurate depiction of the alternative sexual mores of Native Americans, *Little Big Man* and *A Man Called Horse* are clearly meant to titillate their 1970s audience. Morgan's first dalliance with Running Deer (Corinna Tsopei), features soft natural lighting, luxurious animal-skin rugs, and Corinna Tsopei's carefully shaved and amply endowed physique. The love scene seems more akin to a Hugh Hefner fantasy than a gritty and anthropologically scrupulous depiction of Sioux tribal customs of the 1820s. Likewise, the local sexual politics of the Yellow Hand tribe approximates those of a free-love commune: Black Eagle was Red Thorn's "first man," but she has married Yellow Hand, only to take up again on a sometime basis with Black Eagle after he is rejected by Running Deer, who prefers to give herself to Horse (John Morgan). *Little Big Man* takes comparable liberties in its presentation of the sexual rites of the natives. Though his "grandfather," Old Lodge Skins, tells Jack that "human beings" (as the Cheyenne call themselves) take only one wife, Crabb nevertheless ends up with four. After many Cheyenne braves have been killed by U.S. troops, Crabb's Indian wife, with the ever-so-fashionable 1960s moniker of "Sunshine" (Aimée Eccles), urges him to take on her three widowed sisters as additional wives. Suggestively, they don't need food or protection, simply sexual gratification. In a seriocomic scene, Jack dutifully drags himself about his tepee and satisfies each of his new wives in turn while the pregnant Sunshine cheerily goes off to bear Jack's son in the woods. Nor is sexual liberation just for the straights among the Cheyenne; Younger Bear (Cal Bellini), who dresses in squaw's clothes and affects a lisp, puts in an appearance for gay liberation when he proposes that Jack take him as his "wife." While anthropological evidence would suggest that the Cheyenne did maintain a ritualized role for homosexual males within the tribal structure, the film's selective attention to this practice is no accident; it reflects a desire to criticize contemporary "straight" society as sexually repressive and intolerant.

If the Native Americans of the revisionist western do not routinely use drugs (other than tobacco), they are nonetheless blessed by the most vivid hallucinations and visions. Old Lodge Skins tells Jack about his dreams, which, no matter how outlandish, invariably come true. In the most famous scene of *A Man Called Horse*, during a violent initiation ritual in which Morgan is suspended for a prolonged period from ropes attached to his body by means of horn (or bone) blades forcibly inserted behind his pectoral muscles, the white-man–cum-Indian is granted a vision of his destiny. His hallucination takes the form of a psychedelic montage in which Morgan sees in quick succession images of a bald eagle descending, a white buffalo charging across the plains, himself and Running Deer running naked through a stream in order to embrace each other, a mounted chief with a feathered war bonnet and lance, and finally an image of himself facing a powerful wind that blows away his western clothes to reveal him in loincloth and headband. The vision is accompanied by a voice-over, spoken in Morgan's voice, but purportedly providing a mystical message of greeting from Tatonka, the divinity of the Yellow Hand Sioux, identified as the "spirit of the buffalo." This montage provides one of the most embarrassing scenes in the film, conjoining almost every cliché of the 1960s counterculture in a sequence that, at just over a minute, is at least sixty seconds too long. But the montage reveals as vividly as any scene in the film that the "view" of the Indian in the revisionist western is often less an image of the historical Native American of the nineteenth century than of the countercultural rebel of the 1960s who drops out of white bourgeois society in order to find his roots, get his head together, and live free.

One final but especially significant way in which these revisionist westerns comment upon America of the late 1960s and early 1970s is by means of a dramatic conflation of the plight of the Indians with that of the Vietnamese. Such an identification of Native Americans with a foreign adversary was nothing new in the history of the Hollywood western; the Apache of Ford's *Rio Grande* (1950)—which appeared just months after MacArthur's Inchon invasion—would appear to stand in for the North Koreans and Chinese. Lieutenant Colonel Kirby Yorke (John Wayne), anticipating (if not echoing) the pronouncements of General MacArthur, bitterly resents official U.S. policy that prevents him from crossing the Rio Grande (the Yalu River) to pursue the Apache bands that have taken refuge in bases in Mexico (China). But in the case of the revisionist westerns of the early and mid-1970s, when we meet the enemy, "they are us." In one of the most talked about and fiercely debated scenes in *Little Big Man*, Lieutenant General George Armstrong Custer leads his troops in the slaughter of the Cheyenne people at their winter camp at Washita River. During this scene, the U.S. Cavalry troops under Custer's command indiscriminately kill Indian women and children along with unarmed braves before shooting the Indian ponies and setting fire to the tepees (thus ensuring that the Cheyenne will have the utmost difficulty surviving the winter). This scene, in which Jack's wife, Sunshine, and their child are mercilessly shot to death by a U.S. soldier, is based on a real historical incident that took place on November 27, 1868: the "Battle of the Washita," as the U.S. National Park Service officially refers to it, or the "Massacre of Washita River" as Native American activists and antiestablishment historians are wont to call it. The incident still provokes considerable controversy and not all the facts are agreed upon (in a grimly ironic twist, Custer himself appears to have overestimated the number of Cheyenne and Arapaho killed at Washita River as a way of ingratiating himself with his superior, General Sheridan, while native witnesses insisted that far fewer of their number were killed than officially reported by the army); but the historical "massacre" or "battle" nonetheless generated a political firestorm even in the 1870s. However, what is significant about this violent scene as presented in *Little Big Man* is the way in which Custer's attack is meant to evoke an atrocity that occurred one hundred years later, the My Lai massacre of March 16, 1968, in which U.S. Army soldiers killed several hundred Vietnamese civilians, including women, children, and elderly individuals, along with their animals, before setting fire to their dwellings.[26]

No doubt the makers of *Little Big Man* hoped to win sympathy for the contemporary plight of the American Indian and to correct an all-too-sanitized popular understanding of the settlement of the American West that prevailed at the time. But just as certainly, the dramatization of the Washita River massacre is more pointedly meant as an antiwar statement at a time when the Vietnam War was still raging. A case can be made that Arthur Penn and his screenwriter, Calder Willingham, exaggerated the carnage at Washita River, occluded the official government pretext for Custer's attack on the Cheyenne and Arapaho encampment (Indian war parties had attacked white settlements, killing women and children), and failed to make mention of the fact that Custer released his Indian prisoners (a large number of women and children whose lives were spared in the assault). Likewise, one can question *Little Big Man*'s portrait of the Cheyenne as essentially peace loving: recalling the early days of his "captivity" among the Indians, Jack Crabb insists that the form of war preferred by the Cheyenne is "counting coup," a ritualized form of combat in which the brave closes on his opponent and strikes but does not kill or wound him (the objective being to prove one's bravery and humiliate the adversary). Though such ritualized forms of combat surely were part of Native American culture, Jack's characterization of Indian warfare is nonetheless misleading, as his grandfather's subsequent display of a war trophy—the scalp of a fair-headed opponent—vividly attests. But surely such objections about the historical accuracy of the film would miss the contemporary significance of Arthur Penn's depiction of the terrible violence done to these cinematic Cheyenne, who serve as symbolic stand-ins for their ill-fated civilian counterparts at My Lai.

To be sure, the two *Man Called Horse* films dwell at length on the intense cruelty and violence of Native American life. But the latter film also hints at an implicit identification between Native Americans and the Vietnamese. In *The Return*, John Morgan organizes the ragtag remnants of the Yellow Hand tribe into an effective guerilla force. Relying chiefly upon women and young boys as combatants, employing only primitive or improvised weapons, and depending upon the successful infiltration of the enemy camp, Morgan launches a successful raid upon the fort of the white trappers who have invaded the land and set themselves up as an occupying power. If *Little Big Man* protests against the atrocities committed by American forces in South Vietnam, *The Return of a Man Called Horse* slyly invites its audience to exult in the heroic exploits of the Viet Cong.

Dances with Wolves: Revisionism Redux

Winner of seven Academy Awards including one for "Best Picture," *Dances with Wolves* (1990) was hailed as marking the revival of the American western and offering a new, more sympathetic representation of Native Americans. Whatever its technical merits, Costner's film breaks little new ground in its portrayal of the American Indian, and is rather more derivative of earlier westerns, especially *A Man Called Horse* and *Little Big Man,* than fans and early reviews sometimes acknowledged. Like the revisionist westerns of the 1970s, *Dances with Wolves* takes a dim view of white society; like Jack Crabb and John Morgan before him, Lieutenant Dunbar (Kevin Costner), another loner, flees the horrors of the white world (specifically the carnage of the Civil War, which pits one American against another) to find peace and a more spiritually satisfying existence among the Plains Indians (the Sioux). The organic wholeness of Native American tribal society—its social rituals and elaborate customs, its intimacy and communal spirit—contrasts sharply with the dishonesty, financial chicanery, ignorance, brutality, political oppression, militarism, and madness—manifested in the figure of Major Fambrough (Maury Chaykin), who commits suicide—that typify white American society. As in *A Man Called Horse* and *The Return of a Man Called Horse,* it is a *white* hero whose intervention in Indian affairs saves "his" adoptive people from the depredations of their enemies, both the hostile Pawnee and the U.S. Army. *Dances with Wolves* thus highlights one of the less progressive motifs of the earlier revisionist westerns, the ultimate dependence of the Native Americans on their white saviors. Without the foresight, access to new (mainly military) technologies, greater knowledge of the political world, and personal courage of Morgan and Dunbar, the Sioux would not fare so well (though we know they are doomed in the long run). In this respect Dunbar, like Morgan before him, fits easily into a well-established romantic literary tradition that dates back at least as far as Walter Scott's *Waverley* and continues through Conrad's *Lord Jim,* in which a beleaguered and "backward" people (the Highland Scots, the islanders of Patusan) turn to their adoptive white son from the modern world to protect them from imperialistic enemies and interlopers.

What *Dances with Wolves* adds to the formula of the revisionist western are slightly more up-to-date gestures toward the causes of feminism and environmentalism. To be sure, the women of the Yellow Hand tribe in *A Man Called Horse* choose their men (and may choose to leave them), but the ethos of the Sioux in the earlier film is still decidedly masculine and martial; one proves oneself worthy of leadership through extraordinary acts of martial bravery and physical courage. While the tribal elders of the Lakota Sioux in *Dances with Wolves* are still the leading braves, one is struck by their unusual sensitivity to the emotional needs of their women. Though captured as a child (suggestively, by Pawnee braves, not Sioux) and presumably raped and then sold to the Sioux, Stands With A Fist (Mary McDonnell) seems utterly unaffected by her ordeal; indeed, she seems perfectly at home among the Sioux, who treat her with the utmost delicacy and respect. Though he is fully authorized as her adoptive father to dispose of the marital fate of Stands With A Fist when she is widowed, Kicking Bird (Graham Greene), the nominal chief of the tribe, is eager to look the other way when she takes up with Dunbar, even though her affair violates the traditional tribal customs governing mourning (and presumably dishonors the memory of her husband). Masculine pride, tribal rites, and ancient custom unproblematically give way before the romantic yearnings of an independent woman.

The environmental note is struck during a scene in which Dunbar helps to save the Sioux from hunger by locating a herd of buffalo (one among many scenes in *Dances* borrowed directly from the *Man Called Horse* films). But the tribal hunt of the buffalo is pointedly contrasted with a scene depicting the aftermath of a gratuitous and wasteful slaughter of bison by a passing group of white settlers. Interested only in their hides and horns, the whites leave the plains littered with the bloody and rotting corpses of the animals. Unlike the Sioux, who hunt the buffalo to survive, and who conscientiously use every part of the few bison they kill, the whites are interested only in the profits they make from the sale of hides. Unlike their environmentally conscious Native American counterparts, the white pioneers prove poor conservators of land and wildlife alike.

If *Dances with Wolves* often offers an early-1990s remodeling of themes already well established in the revisionist westerns of the 1970s, it also makes more concessions to the popular pro-market mood of the 1980s. In a comic scene depicting his slow acculturation to the ways of tribal life, Dunbar suddenly becomes the teacher rather than the student of the benighted Sioux. He pointedly schools one of the leading Sioux in the fundamental principles of private property; the impetuous brave must learn not to claim Dunbar's hat (lost on a battlefield) as his own. Instead, he must learn to "trade," an English word Dunbar introduces into Sioux dialect with the official public approval of Kicking Bird. In Costner's film, the anticommercial and anticapitalist energies of the revisionist western have ebbed, as has the enthusiasm for the freewheeling sexual lifestyles of the late 1960s. Unlike Jack Crabb, Dunbar (which is to say, Kevin Costner, the romantic leading man of *Bull Durham* [1980]—he of the long, deep kiss) doesn't sleep with several "wives" at one go in a feat of sexual bravado—indeed, he doesn't even take up with a non-white squaw. There will be no interracial romance in this version of Native America. Instead, Dunbar respectfully courts the only white female in the tribe, Stands With A Fist, a woman of an appropriate age and experience, who will become his wife. *Dances with Wolves* thus offers its audience the vicarious romance of "going native," but in Costner's new age western, the romance is very sensible and "straight." A nice white (and mature) couple, both of whom have earlier failed in an attempt to end their lives, learn to love again, having undergone a therapeutic experience that only extensive travel and immersion in a foreign and exotic culture can provide.

Coda: *Dead Man*—"West of Everything"

Jim Jarmusch's 1995 "post-western," *Dead Man,* radicalizes the revisionist western, once more lending it an edginess that filmmakers of the late 1960s and early 1970s strove to bring to the genre (Alejandro Jodorowsky's 1970 cultish "acid" western, *El Topo,* comes to mind).[27] As one of the film's most astute critics, Jonathan Rosenbaum, has argued, *Dead Man* can be read as "one of the ugliest portrayals of white American capitalism to be found in American movies," indeed, one might say that it offers one of the most scathing critiques of modern American society in general.[28] The only truly independent and non-Hollywood western here considered, *Dead Man,* for all its heavy-handed anticapitalist and antiestablishment vehemence, offers a novel and distinctive view of the Native American, one that is by no means predictably politically correct. It remains to be seen whether a Native American director will be offered (or be interested in) the chance to make a big-budget Hollywood western in the future.[29] In the meantime, one might look to *Dead Man* for a distinctively novel portrait of the Native American.

The ostensible hero of the film, William Blake (Johnny Depp), having been mortally wounded in the hellish mining town of Machine during an early scene in the film, travels westward across frontier America with a bullet in his chest, accompanied for much of his journey toward death by his Native American counterpart, Nobody (Gary Farmer), a half Blood and half Blackfoot Indian. Nobody had been captured as a boy and taken to England, where, before he returned to America, he read (and memorized) the verse of William Blake. Nobody mistakes the character played by Depp for the "real" William Blake, and takes the dying man under his wing, guiding him toward his final demise near a Makah village on the coast of the Pacific Northwest. Labeled a liar (He Who Talks Loud, Saying Nothing) by both Blood and Blackfoot, Nobody is an outcast from both his mother's and father's tribes. Jarmusch has characterized Blake and Nobody as "two guys from different cultures who are both loners and lost and for whatever reasons are completely disoriented from their cultures."[30] Nobody ultimately arranges to borrow a canoe from the members of a Makah village on the Pacific coast, in which he places the expiring Blake and sets his friend adrift toward the setting sun, sending him, in a phrase made famous by Louis L'Amour, "west of everything."[31] As he launches Blake on the final stage of his mortal quest, Nobody is shot and killed by the bounty hunter Cole Wilson (Lance Henrikson), who has tracked Blake from Machine to the Pacific coast. In that same instant Nobody also succeeds in shooting and killing his assailant.

Dead Man reprises many of the criticisms of modern Western (particularly American) society featured in the revisionist westerns of the 1970s. In the opening sequence of the film, in which William Blake travels westward by train, we witness an episode in the ongoing U.S. government campaign to exterminate the herds of buffalo on which the Plains Indians depend; the train fireman (Crispin Glover) tells William Blake that a "million [buffalo] were killed last year alone."[32] Nobody's recounting of his life story to William details the systematic mistreatment, dehumanization, and attempted genocide of the American Indian by white civilization. Having been taken captive by British soldiers as a boy, Nobody has been caged and exhibited to white crowds in Europe like some sort of exotic animal.[33] Upon his return to America, Nobody comes across Native American villages laid waste by whites: in two scenes in the film we see the smoking ruins of an Indian village (complete with the charred body of one of its murdered inhabitants). Nobody explains to William Blake that missionaries and traders have deliberately spread diseases such as smallpox and consumption to the Indian population by means of infected blankets.[34] Accordingly, Nobody comes to see in Blake an avenging angel or (to employ a key phrase from Jarmusch's screenplay) a "scourge of God." Nobody not only leads William Blake on his journey toward the next world, but also encourages him to become a "killer of white men." By the film's end, Blake has fulfilled the destiny Nobody prophesizes for him: he has killed Charlie Dickinson (Gabriel Byrne), two federal marshals—Lee (Mark Bringleson) and Marvin (Jimmie Ray Weeks)—a fur trapper (Todd Pfeiffer), a trading-post missionary (Alfred Molina), and two other unnamed men at the same trading post.

Jarmusch's depiction of a Native American making use of a white man as the instrument for wreaking violence on white civilization reverses the historical and cinematic stereotype of the "good" Indian made use of by white settlers and soldiers to tame the "bad" (that is, rebellious) Indians. (The heroic Navajo cavalry scout decorated in the final scene of Ford's *Rio Grande* provides a typical example of this older stereotype.) *Dead Man* systematically works through an extended series of cultural role reversals to achieve its dramatic effect. In Jarmusch's film it is the white man (Cole Wilson), not the Indian, who proves to be the cannibal. The Indian who ominously looms over the wounded white man and thrusts a knife into his chest is not a savage killer, but his would-be healer and spiritual savior (Nobody is trying to remove the bullet from William's body). It is not the oral culture of the Native American but the literate one of the white man that proves untrustworthy and undependable—as the train fireman tells Blake, with respect to the written contract he's received from Dickinson Metal Works, "I wouldn't trust no words written down on no piece of paper." It is not the idolatrous faith of "heathens and Philistines" (to cite the words of the trading-post missionary) that proves to be a religion of debauchery and death, but rather Christianity, which supplies the ideological justification for all manner of dishonesty, thievery, sexual rapacity, racism, and murder. Quite often, Jarmusch works these role reversals to comic effect. It is Nobody, the Indian, who has trouble telling one white man from another. In his account of his travels on the east coast of the United States and Canada, it is white, not Native American, civilization that turns out to be nomadic and unsettled: "Each time I arrived at another city, somehow the white men had moved all their people ahead of me. . . . Each new city contained the same white people as the last. And I could not understand how a whole city of people could be moved so quickly." And in one of the slyest and subtlest role reversals of all, Jarmusch turns on its head the long-established (though now roundly denounced) tradition of whites playing the parts of Native Americans in "red face" by casting Johnny Depp, whose grandfather was a Cherokee Indian, in the role of the "stupid fucking white man," William Blake.[35]

Jarmusch's telling contrast between white and Native American societies (to the advantage of the latter) and his inversion of their respective worth is brought home by two parallel scenes, one occurring early and one late in *Dead Man*. In the first scene, Blake, a newly arrived stranger in town, makes his way through the main street of Machine. In the second, William, once more a recently arrived stranger, but this time aided by Nobody and accompanied by the leading men of the tribe, slowly makes his way through the main street of a Makah village. A number of individual shots are "matched" in the two sequences, giving the impression that Blake is undergoing two versions of the same "event." Tellingly, in Machine the main street leads to the hellish and brooding Dickinson Metal Works factory, a version of the poet William Blake's "satanic mills," the chimney of which belches smoke into the air. Though he is as far west as the train will take him, Blake finds that the blight of modern industrialism has preceded him; there is no pristine "frontier" for him to discover out west. In the words of Nobody, the white man's "stench precedes him." But in the Makah village, the main street leads to a beautifully adorned and wonderfully crafted communal lodge where the elders of the village meet to discuss Blake's fate. The streets of Machine feature drunks, prostitutes servicing their clients in broad daylight, any number of menacing and well-armed toughs more than willing to gun down a stranger who looks their way, a forlorn mother and child, and seemingly endless piles of bones, skulls, and animal hides, many of them mounted ostentatiously on the sides of buildings as trophies. In the Makah village, though the Indians are evidently poor and the streets muddy and grim, the inhabitants don't greet Blake with hostility (but rather with something like curious indifference). Instead of being threatened, ridiculed, and summarily driven away at gunpoint from the factory where he was promised work, Blake is helped along his way (he can't walk on his own) and is welcomed by the leading men of the Makah village who grant the foreign stranger the gift of a sea canoe that will carry him to his final destination. While the streets of Machine appear to be a kind of open-air charnel house filled with the remains of the dead, those of the Makah village (which do sport more than a few animal bones) also display the rudiments of simple barter and native crafts (we see textiles being made and grain traded). Suggestively, in the Makah village, a mother holds her child to her breast, whereas her white counterpart in the earlier scene in Machine leaves her baby to swing in a cradle and has no direct physical contact with her child. Most importantly, the streets of the Makah village prominently feature well-tended Indian "burial" grounds and gigantic totem poles, artistic representations of tribal heritage and identity, as well as symbols of a functioning religious life and of ongoing, intimate, and extensive relations with ancestors. No sign of a church or of religious or spiritual life is evident in Machine.

One might note that in Machine Jarmusch evokes the cinematic style of early German expressionist films (this is especially true of the camera angles and obliquely cantilevered sets of the interior of the Dickinson Metal Works), while in the Makah village the none-too-steady handheld camera gestures toward Italian neorealism.[36] The contrasting cinematic styles of the two scenes emphasize that while Machine represents a modern white civilization characterized by aggression, industrial blight, alienation, and the culture of death, the Makah village, for all its relative poverty and bleakness, is a "primitive" place where "real" communal relations, spiritual and religious practices, familial relations, and intimate human contact are still of vital importance. Machine may be the place where Blake is *killed,* but the Makah village is the place where he *comes home to die.*

Like *A Man Called Horse,* Jarmusch's "post-western" dramatizes the transformation of a white man into someone resembling an idealized Native American. Blake and Nobody's journey westward is more than a physical ordeal, it is also a spiritual quest. Nobody plays Indian shaman and sage to Blake's well-meaning but uncomprehending white "outlaw." *Dead Man* thus combines the revenge story with the spiritual quest narrative. Blake plays both the spiritual quester who seeks enlightenment *and* the revenger who scourges the white race for its crimes against the Indian people. Nobody plays the Mephistophelian mentor who teaches his student how his "poetry will now be written in blood." But he also acts the role of the spiritual guide who, Virgil-like, leads the "poet" on a Dantesque journey back to the other world, which is also his homeland: "I will take you to the bridge made of waters, the mirror. Then you will be taken to the next level of the world. The place where William Blake is from, where his spirit belongs. I must make sure that you pass back at the place where the sea meets the sky." This spiritual quest is punctuated by the ceremonial use (what Nobody poetically terms "the loving ways") of peyote. In a critical scene, Nobody ingests "the food of the great spirit." When Blake asks to take part, Nobody refuses, telling him he's not yet ready: "The powers of the medicine give sacred visions which are not for you right now." Nobody's hallucinations allow him to see Blake as a skeleton, a dead man. Nobody shortly departs with Blake's eyeglasses, painting his friend's face with ritual marks and blessing him: "May the Great Spirit watch over you, William Blake." Though Blake doesn't partake of "grandfather peyote," without his eyeglasses and suffering from hunger and his festering wound, he soon has his own visions: he sees the faces of Indians in the dark woods, Indians who appear to turn into harmless forest animals (though Blake later sees evidence that they've ambushed whites in the woods).[37] When Blake comes across a dead fawn shot through the neck, he uses the animal's blood to add to the ritual marks upon his face and curls up next to its body to sleep. Blazoned like an Indian, he sleeps peacefully in the bosom of nature.

This bizarre, idiosyncratic, and improvised "ritual" seems to mark the point at which Blake enters into a kind of quasi-spiritual communion with Native America. Blake's transformation, however, is not completed until journey's end, when, shortly before he expires in the sea canoe, he finds himself newly dressed in the clothes of the Makah people, complete with fur cap, animal-skin robes (the latter decorated with the images of whales and dolphins), bead necklace, and a locket featuring the portrait of an Indian.

It's worth considering in what ways Blake's transformation differs from those of his predecessors such as Crabb, Morgan, and Dunbar. In the first place, he does not fully enter into the tribal life of the Indians—he never becomes a member of the Makah (or any other tribe). Moreover, his metamorphosis requires the assistance of a "native" agent who is never dependent upon Blake. Neither Nobody nor the inhabitants of the Makah village ever ask *anything* from Blake (except tobacco—something exchanged as a token of friendship). They remain entirely independent from him; his entry into the spirit world is effected by them, but it is a gift freely given, with nothing asked in return. Unlike his white cinematic predecessors of the revisionist western, Blake will never be the hero or leader of an Indian tribe. Finally, Blake's transformation is made possible only because he is dying. What he learns from Nobody is not *how to live* but *how to die*. There will be no triumphant masquerade of Indian life by a white man, only the enacting of an improvised ritual that enables Blake to find his way to the next world. Indeed, Blake's partial miscomprehension of this ritual provides welcome seriocomic relief even in the film's final tragic scene. When Nobody tells the supine Blake, who lies amid cedar branches in the sea canoe that it is "time to go back to where you came from," William responds, "You mean Cleveland?" Jarmusch suggests that Native America has something to offer to white America, even if the latter does not quite understand what it is or how to "use" it. But if Nobody's tears as he watches Blake float away in the ebbing tide can be trusted, it is a gift from a native heart untainted by the "white man's metal."

The simultaneous deaths of the seemingly ill-matched and often mutually uncomprehending Blake and Nobody (another in the long line of white-native tandems beginning with James Fenimore Cooper's Natty Bumppo and Chingachkook) play off a number of archetypal motifs of the western: the tragic end of the hero who has nowhere left to roam, the end of the vanishing American, the end of the frontier, the death of the western itself. But what is particularly suggestive about the relationship between the two is that they meet as cosmopolitan individuals who, "alienated" and exiled from their respective peoples, form a relationship, however fraught with mutual incomprehension, that is haunted by—but not ultimately determined by— their respective "social constructions." Nobody, for all of his ancient wisdom, mystical insight, linguistic facility, and native lore, is no mere representative of a traditional and unchanging way of life. Like his white counterpart, he remains on the margins of the life of the Native American tribes with which he comes in contact. A speaker of Blackfoot, Cree, Makah, and English, Nobody is a polyglot, multiethnic cultural hybrid. What is perhaps most impressive about his verbal facility is his astonishing capacity to "naturalize" the verse of the English romantic poet William Blake to make his poetry seem as if it were rooted in the Native American soil. Briefly annoyed with William's (Depp's) chatter, he responds: "The eagle never lost so much time as when he submitted to learn from the crow." On another occasion he tells his friend, "Don't let the sun burn a hole in your ass, William Blake. Rise now and drive your cart and plow over the bones of the dead." As Jonathan Rosenbaum puts it, "According to the film's alchemy . . . the poetry of Blake becomes a form of Native American wisdom."[38] Unlike even his most sympathetic Native American cinematic predecessors, Nobody does not represent the ways of *a people,* even less *his own people* (whether for good or evil). Instead, he stands forth as a refreshingly *individual* character who selects and mixes his cultural (and aesthetic) values from the many different peoples among whom he has lived and from the far-flung lands where he has wandered. He is intended, as Jarmusch puts it, to be not a stereotype but "a complicated human being."[39] Like his counterpart, William Blake, He Who Talks Loud, Saying Nothing is a kind of misfit, an exceptional and unique individual who must constantly invent himself anew. His friendship with

Blake is founded not upon the unvarying traditions or sacred ways of a collective, but rather upon his imaginative capacity to bridge the cultural divide between them through his own inventions and idiosyncratic creations. If his white friend has the name of a poet, he has the heart of one. Little wonder that no one knows what to call him—he is an Other, a Nobody.

If *Dead Man* in the end does not fully achieve the philosophic goal that Todorov sets for the representation of alterity—to portray the Other as both *equal* and *different*—(and what film could?), it nonetheless marks an advance upon earlier representations of the Native American in the western by virtue of its portrait of the Indian (*and* his white brother) as an *individual* rather than as merely an instance of a racial and cultural collective. Nobody is quite unlike any other "major" Native American character found in earlier cinematic westerns. His distinctiveness derives not so much from Jarmusch's more accurate or favorable representation of an Indian character as from the director's attempt to depict Nobody as free to fashion his own identity as he sees fit. Much like the Irish-Jewish hero of Joyce's *Ulysses*, Nobody represents his people not because of his stereotypical "native" character but because of his atypicality, his idiosyncrasies and unique qualities. In the end, Jarmusch's affecting portrait of the friendship of the red man and white man depends not upon their finding common ground between their peoples but upon their proto-philosophic willingness to meet and converse with each other outside the political boundaries and cultural traditions of their respective societies. By virtue of individualizing his protagonists, who cease to be pure types or ideal representatives of white and Indian society, Jarmusch has advanced the American western into new territory and pushed the frontier of the genre ever so much farther westward.

Notes

1. For two revisionist critiques of the representation of Native Americans in the American western, see Jacquelyn Kilpatrick, *Celluloid Indians: Native Americans and Film* (Lincoln and London: University of Nebraska Press, 1999); and Jonathan Rosenbaum, *Dead Man* (London: British Film Institute/Palgrave Macmillan, 2000).

2. Tzvetan Todorov, *The Conquest of America: The Question of the Other* (Norman: Oklahoma University Press, 1984), 3–4.

3. Ibid., 42–43.

4. Ibid., 49.

5. Ibid., 249.

6. Ibid., 165.

7. Ibid.

8. Rosenbaum, *Dead Man*, 18.

9. One of the surprising things about the Hollywood western is how infrequently the genre deals in any central or meaningful way with Native Americans. In such American "classics" as *High Noon, Shane, Gunfight at the O.K. Corral, My Darling Clementine, The Man Who Shot Liberty Valance, 3:10 to Yuma, Bad Day at Black Rock, The Wild Bunch, The Magnificent Seven, Butch Cassidy and the Sundance Kid, High Plains Drifter, Pale Rider,* and *The Outlaw Josey Wales,* Native Americans are completely or almost entirely absent. The same is true of many of the best-known "contemporary" cinematic revivals of the American western: *Unforgiven, Wyatt Earp, Tombstone, The Assassination of Jesse James by the Coward Robert Ford, All the Pretty Horses, No Country for Old Men,* and *3:10 to Yuma.*

10. For example, the comments of Christopher Frayling, a cultural historian, and Scott Eyman, the biographer of John Ford, in "The Western," an episode of the UK television documentary series *Film Genre* (Jason Wright, 2002).

11. Rousseau does not in fact use the term "noble savage" in *The Second Discourse.*

12. Adam Ferguson, *An Essay on the History of Civil Society* (New Brunswick, NJ: Transaction, 1980), 186; however, for Ferguson's qualification that American savages, like the ancient Greeks, do not observe the niceties of chivalrous conduct, see 201–3.

13. Ibid., 78.

14. Ibid., 95, 93.

15. Ibid., 83–84, 88. Ferguson specifically offers the Iroquois as an illustration of a proto-republican, egalitarian social organization.

16. For Ferguson, "the barbarian" marks a developmental stage beyond the savage. The transition from savagery to barbarism is characterized by a shift from a nomadic to a settled existence, and from hunting and gathering to agricultural production and the development of elaborated property rights. Whereas Amerindian peoples are "savages," the medieval Germanic and Gaulic peoples who conquered Rome are "barbarians."

17. Ibid., 269–70.

18. Ibid., 266.

19. Ibid., 92–93, 145, 150, 160, 186–87; however, Ferguson's views of the commercial character of modern societies are more complicated than I've indicated, and less unqualifiedly negative than those of Rousseau. Consider, for example, his praise of the invention of property as a form of "progress" and his general defense of the liberalizing ethical consequences that follow from a regime devoted to the promotion of commerce and the protection of private property (82, 142–43). For all of his apparent indebtedness to Rousseau, Ferguson is no less a student of Adam Smith.

20. Ibid., 138.

21. In fairness to Ford, it should be noted that he was evidently much loved and admired by the Navajo Indians of Monument Valley, many of whom he employed as actors and crew for several of his films, including *Fort Apache.* In 1948, when heavy

snowstorms threatened to cut off the area from much-needed food and fodder for live-stock, Ford used his military connections to organize an airborne relief effort, Opera-tion Haylift, that delivered supplies to the Navajo. Ford's own paternalistic relations with the Navajo thus mirror the sort he celebrates in *Fort Apache*. For more details on Ford's relations with the Navajo, see *Monument Valley: John Ford Country*, a 2006 documen-tary film produced by Turner Entertainment and Warner Brothers included among the extra features on the Warner Brothers DVD edition of *Fort Apache*.

22. Jean-Jacques Rousseau, *The Discourses and Other Early Political Writings*, trans. and ed. Victor Gourevitch (Cambridge: Cambridge University Press, 1997), 167.

23. Ibid.

24. It is in their roles as "dropouts" that Crabb and Morgan most closely resemble Rousseau's "solitary walker"; see Jean-Jacques Rousseau, *The Reveries of the Solitary Walker*, trans. Charles E. Butterworth (New York: Harper Colophon, 1982).

25. For examples of the most up-to-date research by economic historians on Native American systems of property rights and the economic basis of indigenous American societies, see Terry L. Anderson, Bruce L. Benson, and Thomas E. Flanagan, eds., *Self Determination: The Other Path for Native Americans* (Stanford, CA: Stanford University Press, 2006), especially the following chapters: Craig S. Galbraith, Carlos L. Rodriguez, and Curt H. Stiles, "False Myths and Indigenous Entrepreneurial Strategies"; Bruce L. Benson, "Property Rights and the Buffalo Economy of the Plains"; and Ann M. Carlos and Frank D. Lewis, "Native American Property Rights in the Hudson Bay Region: A Case Study of the Eighteenth-Century Cree," 4–93.

26. Of the twenty-six soldiers charged with criminal offenses, only Lieutenant Wil-liam Calley was convicted of war crimes; he served three years of a life sentence before being paroled.

27. For the coinage of the term "acid western," see Rosenbaum, *Dead Man*, 51.

28. Ibid., 18.

29. I can't help but wonder what Sherman Alexie—a Spokane/Coeur d'Alene writer and director—might do were he to bring to the screen *Fools Crow* (1986), a novel set in 1870 among the Blackfeet during the Indian wars, written by James Welch, a member of the Blackfeet and Gros Ventre tribes.

30. Jarmusch's comments appear as a running interview with Rosenbaum, which the latter reprints selectively in his book *Dead Man* (32).

31. The phrase appears in Louis L'Amour, *Hondo* (New York: Bantam, 1953), 59; Jane Tompkins borrows the phrase for the title of her fascinating book *West of Everything: The Inner Life of Westerns* (Oxford: Oxford University Press, 1992).

32. Jarmusch himself attests to the connection between government sponsorship of the massacre of the buffalo herds and the attempt to exterminate the Native American tribes of the Great Plains: "There was a period in the 1870s. I think in 1875 well over a million were shot and the government was very supportive of this being done, because, 'No buffalo, no Indians'" (Rosenbaum, *Dead Man*, 27).

33. While such a practice was all too common in sixteenth-century Europe, the display of an American Indian in a cage in 1870 would seem to be either an anachronism or an example of Nobody's penchant for the tall tale.

34. Jarmusch in an interview gives credence to the notion that the United States conducted a form of biological warfare against Native Americans (Rosenbaum, *Dead Man*, 48). While it is unquestionably the case that Indians in the New World were nearly annihilated by the spread of diseases against which whites had developed an immunity, the basis for the story of a deliberate policy of infecting Native Americans by the distribution of infected blankets seems to rest primarily on a letter by Jeffrey Amherst, military governor of Canada from 1760 to 1763, in which he proposed to his subordinate, Colonel Henry Bouquet, that he help quell Chief Pontiac's uprising of 1763 by providing the rebellious Indians with blankets infected by smallpox.

35. On Depp's Native American heritage, see Rosenbaum, *Dead Man*, 21.

36. The scenes in Machine are reminiscent of those one finds in films such as *The Cabinet of Dr. Caligari;* in general, the sequence in which Blake seeks employment only to be turned away is perhaps meant to evoke K's comparable attempts in Kafka's *The Castle*.

37. Jarmusch explicitly calls Blake's hallucinations a "vision quest," a "really important ceremony of most North American tribes" (Rosenbaum, *Dead Man*, 70).

38. Ibid., 68. Nobody's many quotations from Blake's poetry are drawn principally from the latter's *Proverbs from Hell, Auguries of Innocence,* and *The Everlasting Gospel.*

39. See ibid., 47.

REGENERATION THROUGH STORIES AND SONG

The View from the Other Side of the West in *Smoke Signals*

Richard Gilmore

What is it that makes a western a western? Is a western a western because of where it is situated? Is the West of a western a place or a plot or an attitude, or is it some still more vague concept that includes all of these but is reducible to none? By location, *Smoke Signals* (Chris Eyre, 1998) is certainly a western, but location seems an especially insufficient criterion for identifying what makes a western a western. Richard Slotkin, in his book *Regeneration through Violence: The Mythology of the American Frontier, 1600–1860*, argues that the myth of the West is the founding myth of the American identity. He speaks of the founding fathers in "the American mythogenesis" as those "who tore violently a nation from the implacable and opulent wilderness."[1] Included in this "implacable and opulent wilderness" were the indigenous people of the land, and so they were part of the violence, the subjects of the violence, that brought forth the new nation. Slotkin says, "Myth describes a process . . . by which knowledge is transformed into power; it provides a scenario or prescription for action, defining and limiting the possibilities for human response to the universe."[2] The same could be said of stories in general. If the traditional westerns, novels and films, are part of the founding myth of the American identity, what role does, or can, a story from the other side of the myth, a story about indigenous people told by and from the perspective of indigenous people, play? *Smoke Signals* is just such a story, the first feature film that was written, directed, and coproduced by Native Americans. The question is a philosophical one, and it will take some philosophy to answer it.

Bruce Wilshire, in his *The Primal Roots of American Philosophy: Prag-*

matism, Phenomenology, and Native American Thought, finds, as his title suggests, the roots of American pragmatism, the unique philosophical contribution to world philosophy by America, in Native American thought. As Wilshire says of pragmatism, "It is original because it is aboriginal."[3] Both Ralph Waldo Emerson (1803–82) and Henry David Thoreau (1817–62) had many encounters with Native Americans, and both were deeply impressed with Native American ways of regarding and thinking about nature. Insofar as Emerson and Thoreau are responsible for writing our founding intellectual texts, as such contemporary philosophers as Cornel West and Stanley Cavell have argued,[4] they are also responsible for constructing some important elements of our American identity. That American identity as it is articulated in Emerson and Thoreau's transcendentalism and then later in the pragmatism of Charles Sanders Peirce (1839–1914), William James (1842–1910), and John Dewey (1859–1952), is profoundly inclusive, strives always for ways to sustain a relationship with complexity, is nondogmatic, and always has as its aim the amelioration of pain and suffering. At the same time, it is also an expression of the American character that has treated its indigenous people with such terrible violence and cruelty. This tension in the American identity comes to the fore when we consider the movie *Smoke Signals* as a part of the genre of the western.

Smoke Signals is composed of several overlapping and interweaving stories, but the core story is of the journey made by Victor Joseph (Adam Beach) and Thomas Builds-the-Fire (Evan Adams) to recover the truck and cremated remains of Victor's father, Arnold Joseph (Gary Farmer). They are Coeur d'Alene Indians living on the Coeur d'Alene reservation in Idaho. Arnold's remains are outside Phoenix, Arizona, where Arnold moved when he abandoned his family. Neither Victor nor his mother, Arlene Joseph (Tantoo Cardinal), have enough money to pay for his trip down to Phoenix, and that is how Thomas gets to go along. Thomas has saved enough coins and bills to pay for the trip for both of them and offers it to Victor on the condition that he, Thomas, go along with him. Victor is resistant to that suggestion because there have been tensions between the two since early childhood, but he finally relents.

The movie begins and ends with fire. Fire is the primary trope for the violence that is both perpetrated and suffered by all the major characters in the movie. It is also the primary trope for the possibility of regeneration. Although Victor seems to be the protagonist of the film, it is Thomas Builds-the-Fire who is at the center of this trope of fire, since it was his parents who had the huge house party on the Fourth of July that ended in fire, and it is Thomas Builds-the-Fire himself who, through his stories, will construct a narrative of redemption and regeneration that will be transformative for all.

Smoke signals are signals of distress, a form of communication that is designed to cross great distances. In the movie, of course, there are great distances to be communicated across: between Thomas and Victor, between Victor and his father, Arnold, between the reservation and the white world through which Victor and Thomas must travel to get to Arnold's remains, and between the Native American world in general and the world of non-tribal America, to which *Smoke Signals* is also meant to appeal.

Alexie says the following of his choice of "smoke signals" for the title of his screenplay:

> *Smoke Signals* fits for a number of reasons, for me. On the surface, it's a stereotypical title, you think of Indians in blankets on the plains sending smoke signals, so it brings up a stereotypical image that's vaguely humorous. But people will also instantly recognize that, in a contemporary sense, smoke signals are about calls of distress, calls for help. That's really what this movie is about—Victor, Thomas, and everybody else calling for help. It's also about the theme of fire. The smoke that originates from the second fire brings about the beginning of resolution. So I just thought *Smoke Signals* worked very poetically.[5]

There is a scene early in the movie with the young Victor and the young Thomas warming themselves around a fire in a barrel. Thomas is talking to Victor, but Victor is not responding. Thomas is talking about the colors of things that are revealed in fire, and then mentions that he has heard that Victor's father is living in Phoenix. Cruelly, Victor says, "What color do you think your mom and dad were when they burned up?" In the screenplay, although not in the movie, Thomas continues on the theme of Victor's father, and finally asks, "What does Phoenix, Arizona, mean?"[6] The figure of the phoenix exactly captures this idea of fire as element of both destruction and regeneration. In the voice-over Thomas describes Victor and himself as children of fire and ash. It is a reference to the violence that both have suffered from and also to the regeneration that both will need and seek.

There is a scene on the bus that Victor and Thomas are taking down to Phoenix in which Victor becomes exasperated with Thomas's constant storytelling: "I mean, you just go on and on talking about nothing. Why can't you have a normal conversation? You're always trying to sound like some damn medicine man or something. I mean, how many times have you seen *Dances with Wolves?* A hundred, two hundred times?"[7] And part of the joke is that Thomas *has* seen the movie that many times. So, there is a tragicomedy right there, a young Native American man learning how to be Native American by means of a movie made by Kevin Costner. That tragicomedy is compounded when we understand Slavoj Žižek's pointed critique of *Dances with Wolves* (Kevin Costner, 1990). Žižek compares *Dances with Wolves* to another movie from 1990, *Awakenings* (Penny Marshall). What the two movies have in common, according to Žižek, is a surface, official content and a latent, unofficial (but the real) content, which Žižek explains in terms of a principle of symbolic exchange. The official content of the movies is, respectively, the relationship between a doctor and his coma-stricken patients (*Awakenings*) and the relationship between a Civil War lieutenant and a tribe of Lakota Sioux Indians (*Dances with Wolves*). The real content of these movies, according to Žižek, is the creation of the couple, so that the real significance of the coma patients and the Indians is only to make possible the sexual relationships of the healthy white men. As Žižek says, "In *Dances with Wolves,* the role of the group of patients is taken over by the Sioux tribe which is also allowed to disappear in an implicit symbolic exchange, so that the couple of Kevin Costner and the white woman who has lived among the Indians since childhood can be produced."[8]

On the one hand, it is a pretty sad state of affairs, if also funny, when a young Indian man chooses to learn about being an Indian from a Kevin Costner film. Whereas *Dances with Wolves* influenced Thomas, another Hollywood movie made by non-Indians that influenced Sherman Alexie and Chris Eyre is the movie *Little Big Man* (1970), based on a novel by Thomas Berger and directed by Arthur Penn. Alexie has acknowledged the influence of *Little Big Man* on his writing of *Smoke Signals,* and there are at least two explicit references to *Little Big Man* in the later movie. The first is the repeated reference, with variations, to the phrase first enunciated by Old Lodge Skins (Chief Dan George) in *Little Big Man,* "It's a good day to die." That phrase becomes, in *Smoke Signals,* "Sometimes it's a good day to die. Sometimes it's a good day to play basketball," and "Sometimes it's a good day to die, and sometimes it's a good day to eat at Denny's."

The other clear reference is to the "contrary," Younger Bear (Cal Bellini), in *Little Big Man*. The "contraries" among the Human Beings (what the Cheyenne called themselves in the movie) were ones who did everything backward, saying good-bye when they mean hello or hello when they mean good-bye, or washing with dirt and drying themselves off with water. The contraries in *Smoke Signals* are Velma and Lucy, who drive all over the reservation backward and at one point give Victor and Thomas a ride in exchange for a story. Their names, Velma (Michelle St. John) and Lucy (Elaine Miles), are themselves references to the movie *Thelma and Louise* (Ridley Scott, 1991), a movie about two women who also do some crazy driving. I think Alexie and Eyre want us to laugh at the influence of *Dancing with Wolves* on Thomas, and with something like Žižek's critique in mind, to see the positive influence of *Little Big Man* on *Smoke Signals*. This is a very pragmatic move. It is a form of cultural critique that is undogmatic and ameliorative. The point is that being influenced by non–Native American movies is not necessarily bad, or that all movies made by non-Indians are bad, but that some movies made by non-Indians may do a kind of unperceived violence, and that this violence may best be counteracted with humor. In general, *Smoke Signals* deals with violence through humor, a humor that is tinged with sadness, which seems to be very characteristic of Native American thinking in general.

The early Americans were influenced by Native American practices, according to Slotkin in *Regeneration through Violence*. "We know that the colonists adapted their ways of living, farming, hunting, and fighting in order to survive in the Indians' world."[9] Suggesting that the colonists learned their adaptations from the Indians, Slotkin goes on to ask, "Did they [the colonists] also (to some degree) acquire an Indian-like vision of the New World?" Slotkin's long, attenuated answer to this question seems to be, basically, no. Near the end of his book Slotkin provides this contrast between "the tribesman" and the "white hunter":

For the tribesman, wilderness life, notwithstanding its requirement of hunting, was one of community rather than solitude. For the Indian the wilderness was home, the locus of the tribe that was the center of his metaphysical universe as well as his social existence. Even in moments of physical solitude, on a long hunt or a vision quest, the world community about him remained intact, for the gods and the wild animals were his fellows and kin. The border of tribal solidarity extended out from the village center to the edges of creation. The white hunter was an alien, paradoxically achieving a sense of relation to the world through an ordeal of profound physical, moral, and psychological isolation from society. His destiny was personal rather than tribal; his moral obligation was to himself, his "gifts," and his racial character, rather than to his fellows and his environment.[10]

In this passage, Slotkin refers to the center of the white hunter's moral universe being "himself, his 'gifts.'" "Gifts," and how one thinks about gifts, structures one's view of the world, opening up a way of contrasting the two worldviews, that of the tribal Indians versus that of the white colonists (westerner and easterner alike). I want to argue that the westerner, in *some* ways, has more in common with the easterner than with the tribal Indians, and that he is, in fact, just a more "savage" form of the easterner.

One of the things that distinguishes tribal culture from nontribal culture is their economies. In his book *The Gift*, Lewis Hyde contrasts gift economies with commodity or market economies. Tribal cultures tend to be oriented around gift economies, whereas nontribal cultures tend to be oriented around commodity or market economies. Ethical value in gift economies is based largely on how much a person gives away, whereas ethical value in market economies tends to accrue to the person who is able to accumulate the most.[11] Hyde associates gift economies with the basic principle of eros, while commodity economies are associated with logos.[12] Eros is a principle of connection, relationship, attraction, whereas logos is a principle of autonomy, distance, distinction. Both of these economies are, according to Hyde, economies of exchange. Both of these two economies generate a surplus, a remainder. In the gift economy, the remainder is the creation and sustaining of relationships, while in the commodity economy, the surplus generated is capital.[13]

The advantage of the gift economy to the individual who lives within it is that one has a large, supportive network of relationships, which gives meaning to one's life. The downside of the gift economy is that living within a large network of relationships entails the attendant responsibilities and moral constraints that such relationships demand. The advantages of living within a commodity economy are several: one is able, through capitalistic exchange, to secure a surplus of nonperishable capital that can provide security for the future. In addition, within the exchange relationship one's autonomy is maintained. Thus, no burdensome attendant moral or relational responsibilities are entailed other than the very basic ones that will guarantee sufficiently good relations to continue the exchange relationship in the future. The downside of the commodity economy of capitalist exchange is that deep relationships are not formed, there is a consequent lack of connection with other people, and one must live with a pervasive sense of alienation from other people.

The moral consequences of these two ways of living will be that the tribal Indians will tend to value relationships above all else, whereas the nontribal whites will tend to value autonomy and the accumulation of capital over all else. This is part of the significance of Thomas saying to Victor near the end of the movie, "Who needs money on the rez anyways."[14] Within commodity or market economies, there can be smaller gift economies—social groups, such as family or church—and in tribal communities, people will frequently have more of a commodity economy relationship with people outside their tribe.

Hyde contrasts gift property with commodity property in terms of movement and stasis: "The only essential is this: *the gift must always move.* There are other forms of property that stand still, that mark a boundary or resist momentum, but the gift keeps going."[15] That is, the gift economy depends on a constant circulation of gifts. Hyde refers to gifts as "anarchist property" because their possession is defined in terms of their being given up, recirculated, passed on to someone else. If one simply retains a gift without recirculating it, it loses its status as a gift and becomes a mere commodity. It is this despiritualization of gifts, of property, that, according to Hyde, the Indian wars were about. The war "that the American Indians had to fight with the Europeans" was "a war against the marketing of formerly inalienable properties. Whereas before a man could fish in any stream and hunt in any forest, now he found there were individuals who claimed to be the owners of these commons."[16]

As Hyde points out, tribal people will not only have a gift economy among themselves or with other tribes, they can also have a gift economy with nature itself, where there are exchanges of gifts between, as it were, the tribe or certain tribal members and nature. The classic example of this that Hyde refers to is the hunt. The deer that is killed is considered a gift from nature, and the hunter individually or the tribe communally will return some portion of that gift back to nature to maintain the health of the gift cycle.[17]

The originating gift in *Smoke Signals* is the potlatch-like supper party thrown by the parents of Thomas Builds-the-Fire. It is, not insignificantly,

I think, a Fourth of July celebration. Tribal wisdom about technology and change is, as Gregory Cajete explains, essentially conservative. "Because social value is gained by honoring mutual reciprocal relationships, spin-offs of Native science in technology are carefully applied. Adoption of technology is conservative and based on intrinsic need, and care is taken to ensure that technologies adopted and applied do not disrupt a particular ecology."[18] A wisdom that seeks relationship, harmony, and balance will be leery of the destabilizing effects of the intrusion of the new. It is hard to imagine more destabilizing intrusions of the new than those new things that the Fourth of July commemorates: the new government of the white Europeans (creating reservations for the Indians), gunpowder (fireworks), and alcohol. The delicate balance that the potlatch is designed to uphold and celebrate is horribly destroyed by these intrusive "technologies" introduced by the white Europeans.

There is a kind of alternate metaphysics that is associated with a gift economy that is well described by the American Indian Vine Deloria. In his essay "American Indian Metaphysics," Deloria says, "The best description of Indian metaphysics was the realization that the world, and all its possible experiences, constituted a social reality, a fabric of life in which everything had the possibility of intimate knowing relationships because, ultimately, everything was related. This world was a unified world, a far cry from the disjointed sterile and emotionless world painted by Western science."[19]

This metaphysics of universal relationship is very similar to the pragmatic vision of the universe in the philosophy of Charles Sanders Peirce. In his essay "The Law of Mind," Peirce describes the law of relationships in terms of the law of mind, which is "that ideas tend to spread continuously and to affect certain others which stand to them in a peculiar relation of affectability."[20] The law of relationships, the law of mind, is the law of the spread of influence through relationships. The spread of influence occurs in nature and in natural systems as well as in human social systems, and so for Peirce, mind operates in nature as well as in human beings. To be aware of the directions of this spread is to understand what Peirce calls the "personality" of a particular system, and so the world as a whole can be said, insofar as it manifests this spread throughout, to have a personality.[21]

There is a continuum of relationships. Signs of this continuum are made manifest by the spread of influence, just as the continuous surface of water may manifest itself in the action of waves. Another sign of the continuum is the nature of time, the way there is a continuity in time between past, present, and future. Peirce represents this continuity in terms of the "insistence," across time, of an idea. A past idea increases in its level of "insistence" as it more closely approaches the present. Similarly, the insistence of a future idea is most powerful the closer it is to the present, waning in power as it fades into the more and more distant future. Furthermore, there is continuity between past and future ideas; as Peirce says, "The future is suggested by, or rather is influenced by the suggestions of, the past."[22]

This idea of the real continuity of time is beautifully represented in *Smoke Signals*. Real, but latent or background, continuities between past, present, and future are powerfully made manifest and foregrounded via montage, the linking of one scene with the next. The general pattern is that a temporal portal is portrayed via a traditional spatial portal, a door or a window. The young Victor will walk into a doorway, and the adult Victor will walk out of a doorway, or the adult Victor will look out a window and the young Victor will appear outside that window. In this manner, the movie suggests that there are deep lines of connection between the past and the future. The present is the moment in which some kind of reconciliation, some kind of balance can be achieved between the events of the past and the potentialities of the future. The relationships that must be balanced are not just interpersonal, but intertemporal as well.

The primary mode of conveying important understanding about the universe for American Indians is through stories. In Western science knowledge tends to be propositional, whereas native wisdom tends to be narrative in structure. The Western scientist will kill a bird and cut it open to see how it works.[23] What the Western scientist is looking for are the general mechanisms that explain how the bird functions. The American Indian will live with the bird, attentive especially to an individual bird's anomalous behaviors, in order to understand the personality of a particular bird, as well as to learn some generalities about this bird species. This Indian way requires being responsive to anomalies, the particulars of things, special circumstances, and unusual events.[24] Understanding is constituted narratively, which is to say, through descriptions of relationships, interactions, developments, and conclusions. Since these narratives are essentially about relationships, they inevitably carry a certain ethical weight. That is, the acknowledgment of the reality of these relationships demands a certain respect for them.

The awareness of an underlying relational element is especially reinforced in Native American thinking because of their social system of clans. A person is born not just into a family, but also into a clan. A person's clan connections are often quite far reaching, both in distance and in terms of the variety of people with whom a person is connected. From the very beginning of one's life, one is raised within a large system of underlying connections and relationships that one is taught to observe and respect. One's very identity is relationally determined through one's clan. Furthermore, there is always a story about the origins of a clan, and a clan's origins will connect it to a specific animal—hence, there is a direct link between one's identity and the natural nonhuman (that is, from the Western, scientific perspective) world and the relationships that exist there.

One of the distinctive features of gift economies is that they are structured and maintained by stories. The fundamentally relational quality of these economies must be systematized and communicated among the economies' members, and this is done via stories. So stories, in tribal gift economy societies, serve an absolutely necessary and essential function. They are not mere entertainment; they also contain all the most important information and knowledge that sustain the community. The most important knowledge in tribal societies is not propositional knowledge such as that produced by Western science, but accounts of networks of relations that situate and give meaning to each individual entity within that network. The "bad" is when the system of relations is disrupted or breaks down. The "good" is when the system of relations is maintained or restored. Stories are the primary means of repair.

Smoke Signals begins with, and is permeated by, stories. And, of course, it is itself a story. The stories are about underlying relationships. They are about submerged narrative lines that are making their way to the surface. It is about latent stories becoming manifest stories, but for such stories to become manifest, someone has to listen. Part of the narrative of this story is how valuable stories are and how difficult it is to get people to listen.

When Victor Joseph is confused about what to do because he has just learned that his father has died far away in Phoenix, and he has no money to go there, and Thomas Builds-the-Fire offers him some money to go, but only on the condition that they go together, Victor does not like that idea. He goes to his mother, Arlene Joseph, for advice and she tells him a story: "You know, people always tell me I make the best fry bread in the world. Maybe it's true. But I don't make it by myself, you know? I got the recipe from your grandmother, who got it from her grandmother. And I listen to people when they eat my bread, too. Sometimes, they might say, 'Arlene, there's too much flour,' or 'Arlene, you should knead the dough a little more.' I listen to them.

And I watch that Julia Child all the time."²⁵ This story captures a lot of what I have been describing as core elements of American Indian philosophy. It is wisdom presented in a narrative form, as a story. It strongly emphasizes the ideas of connection, relationship, and respect. It has a definite ethical dimension. And, interestingly, amusingly, it points to an underlying holism with respect to the Julia Child reference. Wisdom and understanding can come from various sources. Wisdom is not an Indian thing or a white thing; it is a thing of the world and one must be responsive to it in all its forms, in all the ways it may come to one. This story is also very Peircean. For Peirce, truth does not belong to an individual, but emerges out of a community of inquirers. The essential components of that community are that the members of the community are interdependent, and they must experiment, and they must communicate with each other. Arlene does not tell Victor what to do. She gives him a story.

Presenting the advice she has to give in the form of a story is both an effective way of conveying all of the complex information that she has to give (a whole worldview of information) and a gesture of respect toward Victor. It signals not just her respect for his intelligence—her assumption that he will understand the point of the story—it also respects his right to form his own judgment on the matter. A story is not coercive in the same way that "advice" usually is. Victor, in turn, will hold up his end of this relationship by understanding what the story is about and letting its wisdom guide him in making his decision.

A final, but essential, component of this story Arlene tells her son is its humor. It is a very positive, inclusive humor that promotes intimacy and harmony in the relationship while it also warns and provides information about more effective (depending on others for help) and less effective (signing papers with white people) ways of going forward in the world. Humor is not just an interpersonal phenomenon, but a spiritual phenomenon as well. As Maureen E. Smith says in her essay "Crippling the Spirit, Wounding the Soul: Native American Spiritual and Religious Suppression," "Many tribes saw the need for humor in all of their most sacred ceremonies. It was often an integral part of religious ceremonies."²⁶

Another aspect of Native American philosophy is an emphasis on being in harmony with one's environment. This is not a different aspect so much as a different point of emphasis, since stories and song are ways of achieving that harmony. The idea of harmony here is not a notion of stasis, but is defined in terms of "completing relationships." As Vine Deloria says, "The

spiritual aspect of knowledge about the world taught the people that relationships must not be left incomplete. There are many stories about how
the world came to be, and the common themes running through them are
the completion of relationships and the determination of how this world
should function."[27]

Deloria gives the equation: power + place = personality. This is essentially
the same equation that Peirce gives for "personality." Deloria goes on to say,
"This equation simply means that the universe is alive, but it also contains
within it the very important suggestion that the universe is personal and,
therefore, must be approached in a personal manner."[28] Peirce comes to the
same conclusion, and, in fact, insists that anyone who really lets his or her
mind go, who lets the mind "muse," will come to the same conclusion.[29] This
is not mysticism. It is the acknowledgment that power and place inevitably
yield a kind of directional flow, yield a certain trajectory to a situation, and
to know the direction of that flow, the general trajectory of that situation,
is to understand the personality of that place. In this way, scientific method
will continue to prove inferior to the methods of American Indian philosophy as long as the methods of science refuse to acknowledge this personality aspect to the world.

Deloria goes on to say about the importance of completing relationships, "Completing the relationship focuses the individual's attention on the
results of his or her actions. Thus, the Indian people were concerned about
the products of what they did, and they sought to anticipate and consider
all possible effects of their actions."[30] To be in a position to be so present to
the moment, so alert to "all possible effects" of one's actions requires that
one be present to oneself. In addition to the power of stories to situate a
person within a context and to make manifest the relationships that obtain,
American Indians also make use of chants and song.

Smoke Signals is all about relationships that have been abandoned before
they were completed. Victor's dad runs out on his family, but his drinking
had been an impediment to complete relationship with his family for years
before he finally left. The young Victor most painfully feels the relationship
with his father is incomplete and expresses his despair at this first by responding to his dad's question, "Who is your favorite Indian?" with "Nobody!"
and later by breaking all of the remaining beer bottles against his father's
truck. Arlene, witnessing Victor's despair, and in frustration and anger at
her incomplete relationship with Arnold, all but drives him out. Victor, as
a consequence, lives with the uncompleted relationship with his father, and

will not allow the completion of relationship with Thomas or anyone else. Arnold *is* a kind of "Nobody," a man lost to himself as well as to those he loves, a man committed to making himself "disappear."

In *Smoke Signals* gifts function within a worldview of interdependency. Thomas's gifts are his stories, as Arlene's gift to Victor is her story about making fry bread. Arnold, bereft of himself, is bereft of gifts, and can only leave and, in the end, leave the gift of his own longing for home. Velma and Lucy, well versed in the ways of the gift economy, will give the gift of a ride for the gift of a story, which Thomas promptly provides. Victor has learned only the version of being bereft of gifts from his dad's leaving, but with Thomas's help, and with what Suzy Song (Irene Bedard) steers him to see in what his dad has left for him, he learns the way of gifts as affirmations of relationships. He gives gifts of life. He saves the woman in the car accident by going for help. He shares Arnold's remains with Thomas. And finally, when Thomas asks him if he ever found out why his dad left, he tells Thomas, "He didn't mean to." That is both the truth, which is a gift, and a withholding of a part of the truth: the information that Arnold had killed Thomas's parents by starting the fire that consumed their home. As Sherman Alexie says, "That is, by far, the greatest gift Victor could give Thomas."[31]

The scene on the bus when Thomas and Victor have been evicted from their seats—or rather, their seats have been co-opted by a couple of white men—recapitulates in miniature much of the history of white-Indian relations in America. They relocate to the back of the bus. That is what they are forced to do; what they choose to do is begin a chant. The chant is about John Wayne's teeth and how you never really see them, and what they may really be like. The chant functions to realign certain forces for the two characters. They have been thrown into a situation in which they are in conflict with their environment by the meanness of the two white men. They achieve a kind of reattunement with their environment through song. It is an alternative to a direct confrontation, and yet reveals a remarkably sensitive insight into the dynamics of white-Indian confrontations. That is, their chant affirms their connection with an aesthetic, harmonic relationship with the world, while simultaneously observing the lack of a sense of the aesthetic in the unsmiling white men, with John Wayne as the paradigmatic example. The chant works for Victor and Thomas not unlike the way the process of musement works in Peirce's philosophy, that is, as a way of making oneself receptive to an understanding of the deeper lines of relationship and personality in a given context.

A final scene from the movie that I would like to consider is the final poemlike monologue recited in a voice-over by Thomas as he pours the ashes of Arnold Joseph into the Spokane Falls. The theme of the poem is how we can forgive our fathers.

How do we forgive our fathers . . . ? Maybe in a dream?

Do we forgive our fathers for leaving us too often or forever
When we were little?
Maybe for scaring us with unexpected rage
Or making us nervous because there never seemed to be any rage
   there at all?

Do we forgive our fathers for marrying or not marrying our mothers?
For divorcing or not divorcing our mothers?

And shall we forgive them for their excesses of warmth or coldness?
Shall we forgive them for pushing or leaning? For shutting doors?
For speaking through walls or never speaking, or never being silent?

Do we forgive our fathers in our age or in theirs?
Or in their deaths saying it to them or not saying it?

If we forgive our fathers, what is left?

As we hear these words we see the turbulent waters of the river as they flow beneath the bridge. I take this scene to be quite complicated, the river representing various different fluidities, manifesting various different currents and eddies of flow that correlate with various themes that occur within the movie as a whole. Time in the movie is certainly fluid and full of eddies, with portions that turn back on themselves according to certain subliminal forces, according to certain latent narratives. There is fluidity in the alignment of relationships, relationships that come into existence and seem to flow out of existence only to emerge once again later, perhaps looking completely different. All the relationships between the characters seem to take this form. Thomas and Victor seem inescapably bound to one another, but their acceptance of that connectedness ebbs and flows. The same could be said of the relationship between Victor and his father. The same could be said of the emerging relationship between Victor and Suzy Song.

Those who are wisest are least susceptible to this ebb and flow, and so have the most stable relationships. This seems to be true of Arlene's relationship with her son Victor and of the relationship between Thomas and his grandmother. It also seems true of the relationship between the now-sober Arnold Joseph and Suzy Song. There is a sort of stability, but not stasis. The strength of those relationships depends on the mutual acceptance of growth and change in those relationships, the ability "to anticipate and consider all possible effects of their actions" on the relationships.

The theme of fathers encapsulates all of these different threads. Deloria says,

> Education in the traditional setting occurs by example and not as a process of indoctrination. That is to say, elders are the best living examples of what the end product of education and life experiences shall be. We sometimes forget that life is exceedingly hard and that no one accomplishes everything they could possibly do or even many of the things they intend to do. The elder exemplifies both the good and the bad experiences of life and witnessing their failures as much as their successes we are cushioned in our despair of disappointment and bolstered in our exuberance of success. . . . For some obscure reason, non-tribal peoples tend to judge their heroes much more harshly than do tribal people. They expect a life of perfection.[32]

The wisdom of American Indian philosophy and of the philosophy of Peirce seem to converge on this ethical point, that life is an ongoing experiment in which failure is as necessary a part as any success that may be achieved. The proper attitude is not the expectation of perfection, or the expectation that failure can be avoided, but to see as well as one can the interrelations that tie all things together, to try to be responsive oneself to the flow of those relations, and to learn from the successes and failures of those that have gone before us.

This is the central teaching of pragmatism as well. We Americans are schizophrenic in the way we are torn between the demands of our market economy for autonomy and the constant acquisition of more commodities and the possibilities of relationship and amelioration that our own intellectual history of pragmatism promises. We, too, are versions of "Nobody" until we can find some way of resolving these tensions within us. The questions raised in the final voice-over of *Smoke Signals* are unanswerable, but the tensions they point out, the secret lines of narrative they suggest are not ones we can't bear. They are about dichotomies that, in their asking, point to greater achievable unities and resolutions. It is precisely through stories and song that these tensions can be transformed into wisdom, and what better place to get a little perspective on the flow of the world, to mix narrative and song than in a movie like *Smoke Signals*.

Notes

1. Richard Slotkin, *Regeneration through Violence: The Mythology of the American Frontier, 1600–1860* (Norman: University of Oklahoma Press, 1973), 4.

2. Ibid., 7.

3. Bruce Wilshire, *The Primal Roots of American Philosophy: Pragmatism, Phenomenology, and Native American Thought* (University Park: Pennsylvania State University Press, 2000), ix.

4. Cornel West, *The American Evasion of Philosophy: A Genealogy of Pragmatism* (Madison: University of Wisconsin Press, 1989); Stanley Cavell, *The Senses of Walden* (San Francisco: North Point, 1981).

5. Dennis West and Joan M. West, "Sending Cinematic Smoke Signals: An Interview with Sherman Alexie," *Cineaste* 23 (Fall 1998): 28.

6. Sherman Alexie, *Smoke Signals: A Screenplay* (New York: Hyperion, 1998), 9.

7. Ibid., 61.

8. Slavoj Žižek, "Alfred Hitchcock; or, The Form and Its Historical Mediation," in *Everything You Wanted to Know about Lacan (but Were Afraid to Ask Hitchcock)*, ed. Slavoj Žižek (New York: Verso, 2000), 11n3.

9. Slotkin, *Regeneration*, 6.

10. Ibid., 560.

11. Lewis Hyde, *The Gift: Imagination and the Erotic Life of Property* (New York: Vintage, 2007), xix.

12. Ibid., xxi–xxii.

13. Ibid., 201.

14. Alexie, *Smoke Signals*, 137.

15. Hyde, *The Gift*, 4.

16. Ibid., 157.

17. Ibid., 22–24.

18. Gregory Cajete, "Philosophy of Native Science," in *American Indian Thought*, ed. Anne Waters (Malden, MA: Blackwell, 2004), 53.

19. Vine Deloria Jr., "American Indian Metaphysics," in Vine Deloria Jr. and Daniel R. Wildcat, *Power and Place: Indian Education in America* (Golden, CO: Fulcrum Resources, 2001), 2.

20. Charles Sanders Peirce, *Collected Papers of Charles Sanders Peirce,* ed. Charles Hartshorne and Paul Weiss (Bristol, UK: Thoemmes, 1998), vol. 6, para. 104.

21. Ibid., vol. 6, paras. 155–57.

22. Ibid., vol. 6, para. 142.

23. Deloria, "American Indian Metaphysics," 11.

24. Ibid., 22.

25. Alexie, *Smoke Signals,* 29.

26. Maureen E. Smith, "Crippling the Spirit, Wounding the Soul: Native American Spiritual and Religious Suppression," in Waters, *American Indian Thought,* 117.

27. Deloria," American Indian Metaphysics," 23.

28. Ibid.

29. Peirce, *Collected Papers,* vol. 6, paras. 452–66. The essay is called "A Neglected Argument for the Reality of God," the first section of which is entitled "Musement."

30. Deloria, "American Indian Metaphysics," 23.

31. Alexie, *Smoke Signals,* 167.

32. Deloria, "American Indian Metaphysics," 45.

GO WEST, YOUNG WOMAN!

Hegel's Dialectic and Women's Identities in Western Films

Gary Heba and Robin Murphy

The myth of the Old West is rooted in a kind of nostalgia for the lure of the frontier and the freedom and challenges it presented, resulting in a quest focused on bringing order—western order—to an untamed world. More so than any other epoch in U.S. history, the American Old West has been mythologized in the collective unconscious of the country through the many iconic representations of this historical period in film. The popularity of the western genre in U.S film and television from the 1930s to the 1960s has left an indelible set of images on the popular imagination—stark, rugged landscapes populated by rough-hewn men with horses and guns. Homesteads were spare and devoid of any urban comforts. The heroes wore white hats, while the outlaws wore black. Native peoples were characterized as a cultural other who posed a threat that needed to be addressed, violently in most cases. The social contrasts represented in these films were, by and large, clearly drawn and unambiguous and have been criticized for being simplistic morality plays. Noticeably missing, however, from the catalogue of immediately recognizable western images above are images of women.

Women certainly appeared in western movies, often in starring roles; but compared to their male counterparts, their representations have not had the same iconic immediacy and value. As a result, women's identities in western movies remain to be constructed, not only through the narrative of the film, but through the minds of the viewers as well. In this study, we argue that although women's identities in westerns do not have immediately recognizable iconic status, their roles in these movies still provide markers of identity that characterize a certain cultural point of view, so that women's roles in westerns function not only dramatically, but rhetorically as well. Because of this, in the western, women characters are often perceived to possess emerging identities—identities that are formed through contrast with other identities—that is, their identities are constructed by means of dialectic.

The specific dialectic applied to this analysis is Hegelian in origin. Although the terms *thesis, antithesis,* and *synthesis* are often associated with Georg Wilhelm Friedrich Hegel's (1770–1831) dialectic, they are originally derived from Immanuel Kant (1724–1804), and Beiser notes that Hegel never, in fact, used this schema and opposed the use of any kind of schemata.[1] Though it was not a specific heuristic for him, Hegel was fond of thinking in threes, and his dialectic does, like the concept of thesis/antithesis/synthesis, have a tripartite structure and it functions in a similar way.[2]

Overall, the mission of Hegel's dialectic is to provide a process whereby ideas, and ultimately truth, can emerge. According to Fox, Hegel referred to the result of the dialectic process as *aufheben,* a term that has three distinct meanings important to this study: to preserve or maintain; to destroy or negate; and to elevate or transform. The complexity of meaning afforded by the term *aufheben* is a centerpiece of Hegelian thought, says Fox, because "the word itself is dialectical, in that it contains opposing yet coexistent and interdependent elements of meaning." The three meanings of the term also provide some insight into the stages and functions of each part of Hegel's dialectic: (1) the first understanding—to preserve or maintain; (2) the dialectical moment—to destroy or negate; and (3) the speculative moment—to elevate or transform. While Hegel's dialectic provides these three distinct "stages" for identity construction, it does not provide a clear vocabulary for discussing the identities established within these stages. In order to discuss differences in identity as they are represented in film, we have grafted concepts and terminology from Mikhail Bakhtin's (1885–1975) theory of the social functions of language onto Hegel's dialectic, as is explained below.[3]

The function of the first understanding is to posit something absolute and unconditioned, conceived in itself and by itself as if it were an independent entity, or a thing in itself.[4] At this stage, the identity of something is formed in contrast to things it is *not*. It is a kind of mechanical stage in which one separates items according to types, like an inventory. Described another way, the first understanding is analogous to Bakhtin's idea of a monoglossic discourse. According to Bakhtin, monoglossic utterances contain "the forces that serve to unify and centralize the verbal-ideological world."[5] Simply put, monoglossic discourse is the language of power that asserts its ideology uncritically, and its function is to reinscribe cultural myths of power and their representations. Semiotically, monoglossic discourse is a stage of unmarked terms. As described by Jakobson, every "linguistic system is built on an opposition of two logical contradictories: the presence of an attribute ('markedness') in contraposition to its absence ('unmarkedness')."[6] When the difference between marked and unmarked terms is morphological in nature, it is called formal marking, according to Chandler.[7] For example, "uncivilized" is a marked term because its attribute is the prefix "un." Any word or image constructed by a process of adding something to an existing, unmarked term, in this case, "civilized," becomes marked in this way. Although there are inherent cultural values attached to the terms civilized/uncivilized, in the first understanding value and evaluation are suspended for the time being. The function of the first understanding is descriptive rather than evaluative and is "the moment of understanding whose specific virtue is to make hard and fast distinctions between things, each of which it regards as self-sufficient and independent."[8] The main point to be made here is that the first understanding posits a kind of naive, tacit construction of knowledge and cultural identities. In terms of *aufheben*, it is the sense of the term that means to preserve or maintain.

During the second stage of Hegel's dialectic, the dialectical moment, what was posited to be absolute, unconditional, and self-sufficient in the first understanding is now questioned in those same terms, resulting in a logical contradiction. If the thesis is unconditional and self-sufficient, then the antithesis is that it is conditional and dependent. The dialectic is a result of addressing the necessary contradiction in this stage—that the object of analysis is both unconditional and conditioned and self-sufficient and dependent; it is not merely one or the other. The sense of *aufheben* invoked here is that of negation and destruction of the original thesis, much in the same way that Bakhtin's concept of heteroglossic discourse exists to challenge the inherent dominant ideology of monoglossic tradition. According to Bakhtin, heteroglossia "permits a multiplicity of social voices."[9] Unlike monoglossic discourse, heteroglossic alternatives consist entirely of marked signifiers; they are always situated linguistically as not part of the monoglossic territory.

The focus of the third stage of Hegel's dialectic, the speculative moment, is to resolve the logical contradictions established in the first two stages. Hegel attempts to resolve the contradiction by appealing to the argument of the whole, in which "speculative comprehension grasps and is the unity of all essential opposites."[10] By viewing the original proposition and its negation as parts in a larger whole, "we avoid the contradiction if we ascend to a higher level, to the standpoint of the whole," and the sense of *aufheben* invoked here is that of the elevation or transformation of what appears originally to be a contradiction. Unfortunately, Bakhtin has no corresponding term for this stage of dialectic; he discusses polyglossia, a hybrid merging of two genres, like "dramedy," but what occurs during the speculative moment goes beyond a simple combination of parts from two distinctly different binary entities— rather, it posits an identity that transcends and lies beyond the binary; that is, it creates something new, an identity that challenges traditional models of either/or identity construction.[11] For the purposes of this study, we use the term *x-glossic* to describe the phenomenon by which new identities are constructed dialectically.

To review, the analysis we undertake in this study is layered, combining Hegel's stages of dialectic, their parallels to Bakhtinian concepts of social language functions in creating identity and ideology, feminist perspectives on film, and analysis of audio/visual signs that stand as markers for codes of identity. The table below illustrates the interrelationships among the terms.

First Understanding	Dialectical Moment	Speculative Moment
Aufheben—maintain	*Aufheben*—negate	*Aufheben*—transform
monoglossic	heteroglossic	x-glossic
settler women	town women	transformational women
language	material	revisional codes
infantilized	sexualized	mythologized

The First Understanding: Monoglossia, Language, and Settler Women

In terms of women's roles and identities in mainstream western movies, the Hegelian dialectic can be easily merged with feminist film theory, and it can be argued that Hegel's philosophy correlates with what Ravenn calls "insights that are particularly important to feminists: (1) a descriptive analysis of the family as a social system whose inherent oppressiveness needs to be transcended; and (2) a model of intrapsychic and social liberation and harmony as precisely the true path of emergence from and rational transformation of the family."[12] First of all, in correlation to Hegel's first stage of "preserving or maintaining the unconditional," film or cinematic codes for the use of a female in a western dictate that the female character, especially the settler woman, first and foremost should be utilized as a narrative vehicle. When examining the relationship between the settler woman and the plot of the movie, it is obvious in most westerns that whatever her predicament, that situation, her dilemma and identity, is the central vehicle for the male character's actions. This is not exclusive to settler women in westerns, but is used consistently in the roles of settler women. In *West of Everything: The Inner Life of Westerns*, Jane Tompkins identifies the major roles women play in the western genre as victim; extension of man; motive for a man's actions; essential; and controllers of the power of language.[13] All of these roles can be said to be monoglossic in that they represent the most traditional roles available to women and act as tacit, or given, identities. Ultimately, they also all relate to a woman's conventional roles in the most foundational unit of society—the family. As a monoglossic construction, a woman's identity is most valued in terms of her ability to procreate. In addition to being the bearer of children, the monoglossic woman's identity also carries with it expectations that she will be a reservoir of the most traditional cultural values regarding family, community, and faith. In this sense the settler or pioneer woman can be seen to most represent this stage of Hegel's dialectic—essentialized and unqualified—as they are represented in western movies. These essentialized social representations can be considered positive, for as Simone de Beauvoir says, "The role of pity and tenderness is one of the most important roles of all those which have been assigned to women. Even when fully integrated into society, woman subtly extends its frontiers because she has the insidious generosity of life."[14] Though these representations can arguably be considered positive, in regard to the cinematic codes of language, the tendency of the woman's speaking part or dialogue is to be minimal, to be ignored by her male counterparts, and to be portrayed as cinematically superfluous. In addition, she often needs a translator to understand narrative situations and in cases where she does speak, her linguistic purpose is often limited to asking for help, which in turn simply furthers the male character's significance. Laura Mulvey, in "Visual Pleasure and Narrative Cinema," refers to this situation: "Woman then stands in patriarchal culture as signifier for the male other, bound by a symbolic order in which man can live out his phantasies and obsessions through linguistic command by imposing them on the silent image of woman still tied to her place as bearer of meaning, not maker of meaning."[15] In this, the essentialized linguistic value of the female western character "doing not talking" is maintained.[16]

Evidence of the cinematic language code for women being preserved in westerns can be found in a range of decades from the 1940s to the present. In *The Ox-Bow Incident* (William A. Wellman, 1943), set in 1885, the use of town women with speaking parts is limited to the character of Ma (Jane Darwell), who rides with the posse like a man to find the murdering cattle rustlers, and the character of Rose (Mary Beth Hughes), who is on the trail through Ox Bow, riding in a stagecoach with her new husband, much to the chagrin of the lead male. These two females have small but *significant* speaking parts in terms of the *male* narrative. Ma, for instance, jokes with the men like a man; her other linguistic impact is primarily to laugh garishly through most of the film, especially in the sequence of scenes leading up to the hanging. More significantly, she ends up being one of the "men" with enough *verbal* courage to volunteer to whip a horse from under one of the hanging victims, thus not only advancing the male agenda, but also participating in it like a man. Rose's dialogue is limited to announcing her marriage and return from California to visit and expressing her concern over the injured male who was shot. In this, she initiates the jealousy between the left-behind male lead and her newfound rich husband; however, in the long run, this speaking part makes no significant plot difference, though it does emphasize the cultural idea that "a woman is defined by her relation to man."[17]

This idea is also evident in *Appaloosa* (Ed Harris, 2008), set in 1882. The first time the film shows a woman is at about seven minutes, and she is a servant who meekly interrupts a group of men with a one-line warning of coming danger, thus furthering the *male* characters' purpose. Not until fifteen minutes into the film does the lead female, Mrs. French (Renée Zellweger), make her entrance. She gets off a train in town only to immediately ask the male lead for assistance with finding room and board and work as a musician. The male lead's sidekick does have a confidante in the main whore character, whose lines are used to explain Mrs. French's actions but not to notably *progress* the motives of the characters. This narrative insignificance of the female character is described by Mulvey:

> The presence of woman is an indispensable element of spectacle in normal narrative film, yet her visual presence tends to work against the development of a story line, to freeze the flow of action in mo-

ments of erotic contemplation. This alien presence then has to be integrated into cohesion with the narrative. As Budd Boetticher has put it: "What counts is what the heroine provokes, or rather what she represents. She is the one, or rather the love or fear she inspires in the hero, or else the concern he feels for her, who makes him act the way he does. In herself the woman has not the slightest importance."[18]

Likewise, neither of these two films uses female character *dialogue* to significantly advance the narrative.

Specifically in terms of the linguistic importance and role of the settler woman, in *The Searchers* (John Ford, 1956), set in 1868, the settler women are linguistically portrayed similarly to town women. The woman settler character dialogue is superfluous or is used to move the male narrative along. Though the settler woman seems to initially have more speaking roles, starting early in the film, the mother speaks to her husband only to let him know someone is arriving or to scold or direct the children, and the female children speak only to each other or to the family dog, further debasing the female child. Therefore, a linguistic hierarchy is established within the first scene and the monoglossic identity is maintained. Later in the film, when the motive for the male lead has been established, a female character, a mother of one of the boys who is joining the male's search group, asks the male lead not to go and implores him to be logical about his motives. He simply responds with something like "Get to the point, woman." Here, the language hierarchy is reinforced. Tompkins claims this "male silence suggests the inadequacy of female verbalization . . . it establishes male superiority and silences the one who would engage in conversation."[19] Though the woman is concerned about her son dying in the venture for revenge and wants to talk about the danger, the male lead dismisses her motive. Throughout the film, the male lead seems to hear what the female characters say, but fails to respond with anything more than a nod, if he responds to them at all.

At about forty-four minutes into *The Searchers*, the audience meets Laurie (Vera Miles), the love interest of a male character—the lead's sidekick Martin (Jeffrey Hunter). When Martin first speaks in the presence of Laurie, he speaks to her mother about Laurie, in third person. Laurie speaks directly to him, but primarily about their relationship. This kind of womanly or monoglossic talk, for Laurie, represents the bulk of her lines. She even talks directly to Martin about her role as a settler woman: to wash and mend. However, she also jokes with Martin about being bashful and warns him to watch out for her father's response to their courtship. Though her lines are plentiful, their content is limited to maintaining and preserving the cultural role of the settler woman as helpless and insignificant. For instance, a major plot-moving technique is that of a letter Martin sends to Laurie. Though Laurie insists the letter is personal and private, her father and mother override her privacy and insist she read it out loud. However, though this adds to her total number of lines and therefore increases her perceived linguistic importance to the male and audience, she is reading a man's words. Even further preserving the monoglossic dialectic, though the letter is addressed to Laurie, its content speaks more for Martin's narrative and motive and indicates no true regard or love for Laurie, even closing with Martin signing his entire name. So, despite her linguistic *capacity* in this plot-moving device and sequence, her character's linguistic *significance* is actually reduced to the equivalent of town crier or male narrative vehicle.

Tompkins claims this characterization is typical of the western: "There's nothing to [the women in westerns]. They may seem strong and resilient, fiery and resourceful at first, but when push comes to shove, as it always does, they crumble."[20] For instance, at the end of the film, the ultimate male motive—Debbie (Natalie Wood), the girl who was kidnapped by the Comanche—speaks from the identity of a native woman, not as a settler woman. She is depicted as a trickster through her ability to speak both the native's language and "American." This is interesting binary in relation to the men in the film who can speak and understand Comanche or Spanish; they are portrayed as knowledgeable and competent while their male monolingual counterparts are considered dim-witted. Debbie speaks both languages, but it appears to be trickery, not competence, to the male lead, who ultimately questions her loyalty to her white family. Her linguistic capacity threatens the male lead's power and dominance, so when the advantage moves to Debbie in this case, it challenges the control of the male lead, which results in the audience questioning her motives. Though her lines are minimal, instead of continuing the role of the settler woman/girl from the beginning, the end of the film indicates the lack of character conviction in her language ability and reinforces her *female* position as merely an uncomplicated plot vehicle.

In *Shane* (George Stevens, 1953), a strong depiction of the traditional roles of women is evident in the language content of the role of Marian (Jean Arthur), the main female character and a settler woman. She is linguistically introduced through her singing as she works inside. Then, without speaking to Shane (Alan Ladd), she suggests, not demands, that her husband invite him to dinner. Throughout the film, her lines are limited to scolding her son, her husband, and later Shane. She also consistently reminds her husband and son to be polite. Later in the film, her language significance is raised to the level of imploring as she begs her husband and Shane not to go to town to fight with "Isn't there anything I can say to change your mind?" In one stroke of vehemence, she adamantly tells Shane: "We all would be better off if there wasn't a gun in this valley." Of course, all of these elevated lines are disregarded by the men. The men cancel out her talk through action, which Tompkins says "always delivers the same message: language is false or at best ineffectual; only actions are real."[21] Therefore, the female character's opinion on these matters, and thereby her influence on the narrative, is moot, but the monoglossic identity is preserved.

The Dialectical Moment: Heteroglossia, Material, and Town Women

The second stage of Hegel's dialectic, "to destroy or negate," is easily evident in the way women are materially identified as the male spectacle in western films. In this, they are portrayed through their dress as sexualized objects; their mythos is accentuated through material visual codes. The women settlers of western films dress in practical clothes that allow them to do their womanly tasks in a harsh environment. In stark difference to the settler women—a practical, working, traditional role—the town woman—a wife/widow, a whore, or a servant—dresses differently in style and in fabric, serving to negate the monoglossic identity codes for women that inscribe them only in family-centric terms. The purpose of the heteroglossic function of language, like Hegel's dialectical moment, is to provide an alternative to the essentialist, tacit identity construction that characterizes monoglossic discourse. One way the female characters in westerns indicate their dialectic identity is through the visual code of costume. Where settler women dress practically, for work, town women often dress to attract men or attention in general. Necklines, material, and accessories act as symbols that complete the visual code. In this way, the identities of town women are materially constructed as heteroglossic, a contrastive identity to the one of the settler woman. The contrast between settler and town identities is the basis of the dialectical moment when the family-oriented values of the settler are seen in opposition to the more urban, cosmopolitan values of the town woman.

That is not to say that the two are mutually exclusive, but that through dialectic, identities emerge when the two are placed in contrast.[22]

In *The Searchers*, the women dress practically for frontier work; however, Laurie's character often changes from a dress to pants and back again, not only for the sake of the work she's doing, but also for the sake of her need to attract the attention of Martin. For instance, in the scene where the audience first sees them together, Laurie has her hair up and is dressed monoglossically in a practical cotton dress with an apron. Later, when she's brought her best horse for Martin to ride to follow after the male lead, she's let her hair down and is dressed like a man in a button-down shirt, pants, and boots, as if she's finished with her attempts to attract Martin, a seemingly heteroglossic move for the character. In this she moves to attain male power by subverting and reducing female dress to the means of objectifying the male gaze. However, in the wedding sequence, her hair is up, and she is, of course, dressed in a white, silky material and white shoes. Therefore, except for a special circumstance such as a trip to town, a funeral, or a wedding, settler women dress, monoglossically, to work. This use of practical dress shows the woman as a male spectacle in that she is valued by the male as an integral part of their frontier survival, for without her hard work in traditional roles, the family unit would likely dissolve.

The town woman, however, isn't as likely to have to work as the settler woman, and her dress, materials, and accessories drastically indicate this difference and help construct a heteroglossic identity. In *Appaloosa*, Mrs. French departs from the train dressed to the hilt in a striped, tight-fitting, neck-high dress of a silky fabric, a hat, and gloves—as opposed to *Shane's* Marian, who is seen going to town in a worn, loose cotton shirt and skirt, a jacket, and a ribbon in her hair. Add a parasol to Mrs. French's outfit and the picture is complete for an afternoon picnic with her beau. She is dressed heteroglossically as the unattainable, the proper woman, the high-society woman, for the admiration of man and to antagonize the other, lesser women. Correspondingly, even the whore in *Appaloosa* dresses in finer fabrics than the settler woman, and her role as sexualized male spectacle follows suit. She is dressed exotically in layers, with a low neckline and chest and waist emphasis to uphold the myth of the woman as sexual object. Both Mrs. French and the whore are also seen in their undergarments (heteroglossic) at different times in the film. In Mrs. French's case, it is depicted as ridicule for her behavior, but in the whore's case, it is sexualized as an intimate moment.

In *My Darling Clementine* (John Ford, 1946), set in 1882, the two main town woman characters are, again, a highbrow woman and a whore/entertainer. Both women dressed as heteroglossic, which accommodates the pleasures of men. The town woman Clementine (Cathy Downs) arrives on a stagecoach dressed in expensive fabric, a hat, gloves, a shoulder throw, and carrying a small handbag. Chihuahua (Linda Darnell), the whore, wears her hair half up and half down and dresses in Spanish-style dresses of fine fabric, elaborate ruffles, and low necklines. In *The Ox-Bow Incident,* the character of Ma, though a town woman, dresses like a man to be a part of the hanging posse. She obviously represents an antithesis to the myth of the woman as a sexual object, but the character of Rose follows the sexualized material code right down to the petticoat. It is clear that the myth of the town woman as a sexualized spectacle is reinforced in these heteroglossic material visual codes of the cinema.

An excellent example of the contrast in materiality between monoglossic and heteroglossic identities is found in *How the West Was Won* (John Ford, Henry Hathaway, and George Marshall, 1962), a sprawling epic that chronicles three generations of the Prescott family in its trek westward from Pennsylvania to California. The main narrative of the film focuses on the Prescott sisters, Eve (Carroll Baker) and Lily (Debbie Reynolds). Even their names suggest the kinds of ideological attitudes and values associated with each of them through the biblical resonances carried by their names. Eve, named after the first woman in the Bible, dresses plainly and practically for life on the trail, her long hair worn down and often unbrushed. She longs for marriage and family and actively pursues Linus Rawlings (James Stuart), a mountain man whom the family encounters early in its travels. As such, Eve is coded visually as a monoglossic version of woman, bound by the constraints of an identity that is grounded in a patriarchal version of family. In contrast, Lily's full name, Lilith, suggests the apocryphal Lilith, who in Hebrew folklore was Adam's first wife, and whose name is often associated with evil. Lily, though also dressed plainly, adds adornments like ribbons to her clothes and her hair, usually worn up. Lily longs for fine clothes and to go back east—she has no plans for family in her future. She is a singer who has already developed a reputation for her ability, and following that career will enable her to support herself without the necessity of being married. Like many men who came west in search of a kind of freedom and independence that was becoming increasingly less available as cities in the East grew larger, Lily is visually represented as a heteroglossic identity challenging ideas about a woman who is able to be financially and socially independent without a man.

The ideological differences between Eve and Lily manifest further in the divergent paths their lives take after their parents drown. Prior to the accident, there is a scene in which both daughters long for the East and fine clothes—they are on this journey only because it is what their father wanted, and as unmarried women they are obligated to follow their family. As such, both are divided about where their identities and their allegiances lie: with the settler values and family or with those of the town and independence, the dialectical choice being to maintain the values and lifestyle they have inherited or to negate it through an alternative. Before the accident, Eve is on the verge of choosing to negate her family heritage by going back east with her sister. After the accident, however, Eve has a sudden change of heart. Linus Rawlings, whom Eve has been pursuing as a husband, returns to ask for her hand in marriage and to urge her to go back east with him to St. Louis, but she sees the accident as a divine sign that they should settle on the spot where her parents died. Although she is presented with an alternative, more urban existence, Eve chooses the essential, monoglossic code of family, raises two sons with her husband, and lives the remainder of her days on that same spot. Therefore, though she is presented with a dialectical option, she is not *transformed* by it.

Eve's sister, Lily, is heteroglossically grounded and much more determined from the start to find a way to the city. After her parents' death, she sights a riverboat, and when we next see her, she is headlining a musical revue on board. In terms of the visual coding of identity, we see here a *complete* transformation of Lily: from a reluctant pioneer woman to a professional singer. Replacing the plainer clothing she wore in the first part of the movie, Lily now wears a brightly colored satin outfit, about the size of a contemporary one-piece bathing suit. Her hair is carefully styled, and she wears jewelry to accent her costume. Through revealing more of her body Lily's identity is much more highly sexualized; thus her ideological choice is represented visually as well as through her actions. Most important, the signification of her clothing indicates that she is independent, free from the confines of traditional family. In her highly sexualized identity, it is not surprising that Lily is ardently pursued by two men, who can also be seen to represent ideological and dialectical positions. One of the men, Roger Morgan (Robert Preston), is a successful rancher who offers Lily the monoglossic ideal of family and views her primarily as a breeding machine, reinforced by numerous references to her "fine body," and his comment that "For you, childbearing would come as easily as rolling off a log." Lily's comment to him is "A woman likes to hear something a little more inviting." Because Morgan's offer does not appeal to her ideologically, Lily's attention is caught by another man, Cleve Van Halen (Gregory Peck), a riverboat gambler. He is able to win Lily's affections where Morgan failed because Cleve is more ideologically attuned to her values. Neither Cleve nor Lily is interested in family, because both view life as an adventure that family would only restrict. Near the end of the movie, Cleve has passed away after he and Lily "won and lost a few fortunes," and Lily has a chance meeting with Zeb (Karl Malden), the older son of Eve. Zeb is starting his own family and invites Lily, somewhat ironically, to go west to California, an invitation that Lily accepts. Lily is older but still dressed in fine clothes, suggesting that even though she has agreed to become part of an extended family, her independent, heteroglossic identity remains.

In the movies we have examined, although heteroglossic identities for women exist as dialectical points of contrast, the heteroglossic woman's identity is overall shown to be transgressive because it goes against the grain of what is considered a traditional family and what the woman's role is in that family. As such, Lily's decision, like Debbie's in *The Searchers,* is a return to the fold of family that allows her a chance to redeem her original transgression.

The Speculative Moment: X-Glossia, Character, and the Transformational Woman

Hegel's dialectic third stage calls for elevation and transformation. Arguably, this transformation occurs more often in modern westerns—those produced after the 1970s. In these more modern westerns, the woman is most often elevated as x-glossic through place or landscape and is more often associated with being integral to nature or the natural way of things. The function of x-glossic discourse is to transform identities that are constructed outside of traditional binaries in which women are also transformed from male spectacle to audience spectacle. In other words, the male gaze–centered cinematic code is subverted in one way or another. From the feminist point of view, this is a necessary destruction of the implicit and mythologized social roles of women, and in this way the represented identities of these women are x-glossic—neither settler nor town woman nor combination of both, but a new subject position, a new identity that transcends the either/or, settler/town binaries and exists outside them. The codes of language and material that helped to establish the dialectical identities of monoglossic and heteroglossic ideologies have been revised or transformed, following Hegel's third stage of *aufheben,* to such an extent that they are no longer recognizable as either, and may not even have a name. Mulvey, too, emphasizes the importance of challenging the code: "Cinematic codes create a gaze, a world, and an object, thereby producing an illusion cut to the measure of desire. It is these cinematic codes and their relationship to formative external structures that must be broken down before mainstream film and the pleasure it provides can be challenged.[23] In essence, these codes are challenged in the x-glossic dialectic. For example, when Sharon Stone makes her first appearance in *The Quick and the Dead* (Sam Raimi, 1995), only her hair and facial features mark her as a woman—she is dressed like a man, she walks like a man, she talks like a man, she fights like a man, and she says almost nothing—for all intents and purposes, she is coded as being a woman, but she is behaving like a man. The revision of the code causes a rupture in both the traditional settler/town binary and, more important, the male/female binary that forces the need for a new codification for identity, the x-glossic.

  Two Mules for Sister Sara (Donald Siegel, 1970), set in 1867, and *The Quick and the Dead,* set in 1878, both portray women in transformative material/costume in relation to the cinematic code of dressing women as the male spectacle. Sara (Shirley MacLaine) spends most of the film hidden in a nun's habit, which allows her to maintain her trickster character. At the end of the film, Sara dresses like any well-to-do town woman, though a little more flashy and over the top, probably because of her whoring history and love for the dramatic. Ellen (Sharon Stone) spends most of the film with her hair down, dressed in dark leather pants with chaps, a white, loosely buttoned-down shirt, a long, dark riding coat, a large black cowboy hat, and boots. In one sequence, Ellen wears a fitting dress of fine fabric and hosiery for her dinner with the male lead. However, she remains true to her male-like garb in the end. These town women's identities are identified as x-glossic because they are not visually and materially coded as extensions of the male characters, nor are they the spectacle of the male gaze—they are something new. These women use their identities, built upon language and dress, as narrative vehicles for their *own* purposes, not because they are the identities they actually inhabit. If settler women are monoglossically coded, and town women are heteroglossically coded, then Sara and Ellen are neither.

Instead, we can see their identities as transformative and situated *outside* the monoglossic/heteroglossic binary—they are something new.

For example, the first distinct transformational characteristic of the x-glossic female character is linguistically situated. In the opening of *Two Mules for Sister Sara*, the film shows a monoglossic language predicament, with Sara crying for help, but quickly subverts and transforms this cinematic code to an x-glossic identity by giving Sara an equal footing in dialogue and banter with the male lead in terms of purposeful lines and the number of lines. Sara also speaks three different languages (English, Spanish, and French), and rather than that complicated linguistic practice being seen as the trait of a trickster, as it was for Debbie in *The Searchers*, Sara often progresses the main narrative by translating for the male lead. At the same time, the male character's motive is driven by Sara's request for help when he saves her from sure rape in the opening scene, which is partial to the patriarchal motives of the cinematic code; however, Sara's character utilizes the male motive to further her own intentions as the narrative progresses.

Analogous to the x-glossic dialectic of *Two Mules for Sister Sara, The Quick and the Dead* also subverts the language code for the female character of the western. Though the lead (Ellen) isn't given a name beyond "Lady" until well into the movie, most of Ellen's lines, like Sara's, are significant to the plot of the film, not just to the narrative of the male characters, and they are equal in number to those of the men. In fact, the men often offer her unsolicited advice that furthers her motives, but her conversations are rarely about *asking* for help or direction. For instance, in an integral scene about halfway through the film, a male character tells her to listen for the click before the clock chimes the hour, so she'll draw her gun more quickly. She doesn't reply but uses the information to her advantage. She also rarely responds to men in the film with the answers they expect. In one of the opening sequences, a blind boy asks her if she's interested in a variety of lotions and the like, and she replies, "Just shine my boots." In that same sequence, a recently released murderer approaches her aggressively and says, "I need a woman." She responds, unconcerned, "You need a bath." Admittedly, though Ellen's lead role is linguistically integral to the plot, as it should be, the other women in the film uphold the cinematic code: the girl servant/rape victim whose lines further the male narrative as well as the female lead's motive and narrative; one whore who speaks to show concern for a fallen gunslinger but whose lines are insignificant to the plot except to emphasize her role as a male spectator or admirer; and the extras: whores, town women, and native women who only "speak" in murmurs or cheers at the gunfights. Most of the women, except the lead and the girl victim, are linguistically ignored by their male counterparts as well as the audience. Even though many of the female extras in both films are monoglossic or heteroglossic in their language significance, both Ellen and Sara are viable lead female characters who have subverted the cinematic linguistic code established for female roles.

Another example that subverts the cinematic code for women in westerns on multiple levels is the recent *Bandidas* (Joachim Ronning and Espen Sandberg, 2006). This movie takes the female character as gunslinger portrayed in *The Quick and the Dead* and transforms her into a bank robber. The main characters, Sara (Salma Hayek) and Maria (Penelope Cruz), are paired ideologically. The setting is Mexico, and Maria is a farm girl living with her father. She dresses very plainly in what amounts to a peasant's clothes. In contrast, Sara is the daughter of the governor of Mexico back home on a break from her education in Europe, and we first see her dressed in expensive satin gowns. Here the material distinction between the two in terms of settler and town women identities is true to what we have seen in other films, but with an added layer of social class. Both are wronged when a New York banker devises a scam to essentially steal Mexican land so a railroad can run through the small town. Maria's father is shot when he refuses to sell his property for a peso, and Sara's father is poisoned when he learns of the plan the banker has to steal land. Both women are displaced from their typical lives and meet, by coincidence, when they both decide, separately, to rob the same bank at the same time. They team up and become infamous bank robbers through the course of the film, ultimately seeking revenge on the banker from New York. In the speculative moment presented to them, they choose to transform their identities radically, though for different reasons. Maria wants to rob banks to get money for the poor, like Robin Hood. Sara's goal is more self-interested; she wants to raise enough money to return to Europe. During the movie, however, Sara comes to see Maria's position, and they both enjoy the celebrity they have gained in the country, earning them the status of folk heroes.

Because the movie is set in Mexico, both women are initially "othered" because they are not Caucasian. Like Ellen in *The Quick and the Dead*, they are also transformed into a traditionally male role of bank robber. Unlike Ellen, though, the actresses who play Sara and Maria, Salma Hayek and Penelope Cruz, are acutely sexualized and spend a good portion of the movie arguing about who is a better kisser. Essentially, *Bandidas* is a woman's version of *Butch Cassidy and the Sundance Kid* (George Roy Hill, 1969) and other "buddy" movies that traditionally feature male leads. As female bank robbers, their characters represent both audience spectacle *and* male spectacle, further disrupting the cinematic codes for women in westerns by producing new, transformative identities for them to inhabit.

It is also important to examine the motivation of transformative female characters. It is not necessary for a female character to have a narrative motivated by distinctly female issues. The motivation for both Sara and Ellen and Maria and Sara is revenge, just like that of the typical western male lead; however, in all cases, the women have feminist agendas within the plot of revenge. In Sara's case in *Two Mules for Sister Sara*, she is motivated to return to her home and exact her revenge on the French invaders, but she also wants to protect her friends' livelihoods at the whorehouse. In the end, she not only saves Mexico and her friends, but also gets the man. Sara's character transforms the natural role of the nun into a cunning disguise to save a business that is the direct social-value opposite—a brothel. Similarly, Ellen's obvious narrative vehicle is personal revenge on the man who made her responsible for her father's death. Ellen also avenges a young girl who was raped and left unprotected by her own father and saves a man from his own past. Therefore, all of the characters in the westerns in this section revise the mythologized female spectacle, embrace the traditional code of the male, and challenge that code by disrupting the dialectic, which results in a new dialectic identity, the x-glossic.

Transforming Identity Construction

In conclusion, we have argued that the identities constructed for women in westerns have a variety of ideological and dialectical positions, and that identities emerge as a result of the confrontations between dialectical points of view. Using Hegel's dialectic as a means for examining identities in film allows us to clearly see how characters' roles are ideologically positioned in contrast to characters who negate or transform that ideology. Just as Hegel wanted his dialectic to be representative of an ongoing process, so, too, do audiences continually engage in constructing the identities presented to them in western films. While the earlier westerns we examined have an ideological tendency toward representing women's identities in ways that reinforce traditional social roles in the cultural master narrative, movies from the 1970s on demonstrate an increasing number of heteroglossic and x-glossic representations of women's identities in this genre that challenge those traditional identities. As such, the expanding roles for women in westerns during this period are mirrors of the larger social changes occurring in the United States, and also of Hegel's teleological view of dialectic: that it shapes not only individuals, but also societies through time.

Though the western genre is nowhere near as robust now as it was in the 1940s through the 1960s, the fact that westerns are still being made, and are being used as vehicles to represent women in alternative identities, is a sign of the genre's continued power and hold over the collective cultural imagination and of the role it plays in shaping audiences' ideological values regarding gender. It is our hope that the method of analysis employed here will be of use to others studying the structural and ideological dimension of identities in film. With the western film genre extending itself into space, "the final frontier," movies like Joss Whedon's *Serenity* (2005) will also help to shape the future trails left to blaze for establishing new, transformational codes of what it means to be a woman on the frontiers of identity.

Notes

1. Frederick Beiser, *Hegel* (New York: Routledge, 2005), 161.

2. Michael Allen Fox, *The Accessible Hegel* (New York: Humanities, 2005), 10.

3. Ibid., 46.

4. Beiser, *Hegel*, 167.

5. Mikhail M. Bakhtin, *The Dialogic Imagination: Four Essays*, trans. Caryl Emerson and Michael Holquist, ed. Michael Holquist (Austin: University of Texas Press, 1988), 270.

6. Roman Jakobson, "Verbal Communication," in *Communication* (a *Scientific American* book), ed. Dennis Flanagan et al. (New York: Freeman, 1972), 42.

7. Daniel Chandler, *Semiotics: The Basics*, 2nd ed. (New York: Routledge, 2007), 94.

8. Beiser, *Hegel*, 167.

9. Bakhtin, *Dialogic Imagination*, 263.

10. George W. F. Hegel, *The Encyclopedia of Philosophy*, trans. Gustav Emil Mueller (New York: Philosophical Press, 1959), 83.

11. Bakhtin, *Dialogic Imagination*, 305.

12. Heidi M. Ravenn, "Has Hegel Anything to Say to Feminists?" in *Feminist Interpretations of G. W. F. Hegel*, ed. Patricia Jagentowicz Mills (University Park: Pennsylvania University Press, 1996), 225.

13. Jane Tompkins, *West of Everything: The Inner Life of Westerns* (New York: Oxford University Press, 1992), 17, 40, 41, 44, 50.

14. Simone de Beauvoir, "The Second Sex," in *Feminist Literary Theory and Criticism,* ed. Sandra M. Gilbert and Susan Gubar (New York: Norton, 2007), 311.

15. Laura Mulvey, "Visual Pleasure and Narrative Cinema," in *Film Theory and Criticism,* 6th ed., ed. Leo Braudy and Marshall Cohen (New York: Oxford University Press 2004), 838.

16. Tompkins, *West of Everything,* 50.

17. de Beauvoir, "Second Sex," 302.

18. Mulvey, "Visual Pleasure and Narrative Cinema," 841.

19. Tompkins, *West of Everything,* 59.

20. Ibid., 61.

21. Ibid., 51.

22. This description corresponds nicely to Klaus Theweleit's women: the absent woman, the white nurse/chaste woman, and the red/enemy woman. It also supports the idea that males tend to view woman in the binary terms of virgin/whore. *Male Fantasies* (Minneapolis: University of Minnesota Press, 1987).

23. Mulvey, "Visual Pleasure and Narrative Cinema," 847.

BEATING A LIVE HORSE

The Elevation and Degradation of Horses in Westerns

Jennifer L. McMahon

> The souls of horses mirror the souls of men more closely than men suppose.
>
> —Cormac McCarthy, *All the Pretty Horses*

When one thinks of western films, certain stock characters come to mind. Cowboys, Indians, gunslingers, and homesteaders are some of the obvious examples. However, there is a character that is as—perhaps even more—elemental to the western: the horse. Horses are everywhere in westerns. Our heroes ride in—and out—on them. And yet, who thinks about them? In recent decades, increased scholarly attention has been paid to marginalized figures in literature and mainstream media. Studies on otherness have served to bring recognition to individuals and groups whose voices and value have been suppressed or distorted because of their misrepresentation, or lack of representation, in media of various sorts. However, little attention has been given to the role horses play in westerns.[1] As Jane Tompkins notes, despite their exhaustive analysis of other elements of the genre, as far as most "critics [of the western] are concerned [horses] might as well not exist."[2] She agrees with Harold Hintz that horses are an "important ingredient of Western movies," arguing that horses are in fact "indispensable" to the western to the extent that they are on-screen constantly and "affect our reactions subliminally."[3] This chapter will further examine the representation of the horse in westerns, particularly how most westerns both exemplify and perpetuate the conflicted relationship that Americans have with horses. While few animals possess the aesthetic allure for Americans that horses do, few are depicted as subordinate beings as frequently as horses. Whereas dogs are trained, horses are broken. As often as horses lope gracefully across the screen, they are roped, tied, hobbled, yoked, curbed, whipped, or ridden until they drop. Existential philosophy offers an explanation for the ambivalence that humans display toward horses, namely, their simultaneous desire to elevate and subjugate these animals.

Prominent existentialists such as Jean-Paul Sartre (1905–80), Martin Heidegger (1889–1976), and Friedrich Nietzsche (1844–1900) pay little attention to animals in their philosophic works; nonetheless, their existential theories can help explain the polarized relationship that humans have with horses. From an existential perspective, the ambivalence that humans display toward horses lies largely in the similarities that horses have to humans, the ontological insecurities that humans have, and the coping strategies that humans employ to assuage these insecurities. To the extent that humans see traits in horses that they themselves possess but dislike, horses become convenient objects upon which to transfer our own self-loathing and exact a psychologically satisfying dynamic of control. To the extent that horses manifest traits that humans seek to possess, they inspire both envy and admiration. Not only do we see these aspects of our relationship to horses in westerns, most westerns serve to reinforce our ambivalence.

Kindred Spirits: The Parallels between Horses and Humans

Before turning our attention to specific westerns, it is first necessary to discuss the similarities that exist between humans and horses. This will establish the philosophic basis for the ambivalent treatment of horses that westerns exemplify and encourage. Obviously, humans are very different from horses; however, they share some important attributes. One is anxiety. Horses are known for being skittish. Equine anxiety has obvious instinctual and evolutionary roots.[4] Horses are herbivores. As such, they are potential prey for other animals, not predators themselves. In the wild, horses are vulnerable to various environmental threats, including large carnivores, dangerous weather or terrain, and insufficient forage or water. The primary defenses that horses have developed to facilitate their survival are hypersensitivity to stimuli, a powerful flight instinct, physical agility, and speed. Horses are, by nature, highly alert and easily startled, and these characteristics serve to preserve both individual animals and the species as a whole.

Though humans are not as fleet of foot as horses, we, too, are hypersensitive beings who are predisposed to flight. Sartre and Heidegger agree on this.

According to Heidegger, human being is characterized by existential anxiety, or "angst."[5] He argues that anxiety is our primary emotion, our "fundamental mode of being-in-the-world." Sartre concurs. While we normally associate our anxiety with specific stressors, Sartre and Heidegger agree that anxiety is fundamentally about being. Heidegger indicates that humans are characterized by their "care" for being, and argues that "the being about which [human being] is concerned . . . is always its own."[6] Existential psychologist R. D. Laing refers to this self-oriented anxiety as "ontological insecurity."[7] Rather than being grounded in any specific external threat, ontological insecurity, or existential anxiety, is anchored in the awareness of personal vulnerability, our fragility. Arguably, to the extent that they are mortal, all living creatures are fragile; however, some are more so than others. Horses are hardy, but they lack the defensive arsenal of their predatory counterparts. The absence of large canines and sharp claws makes horses more susceptible than other animal species. Though their fleetness affords them a means to escape predators, the lightness of bone that gives them speed also renders them fragile. As any number of westerns show, horses break legs fairly easily, and one misstep can mean death. Though we don't shoot them if they break a leg, humans, too, are fragile. Though we are predators and occupy the topmost position on the food chain, our being is still tenuous. Our power lies in our wits, not in other natural defenses. Our existential anxiety is grounded in, and reminds us of, our vulnerability: our perennial susceptibility to physical injury and death. Our anxiety is primarily visceral, not reflexive. In short, it is something we know intuitively, but do not tend to think about formally.

While Heidegger distinguishes humans from other animals on the basis of their concern for being, his own theory of anxiety can be used to argue that humans are on a continuum that includes other animal species. According to Heidegger, all fear is grounded in anxiety. Fear is a second-order emotion predicated on angst.[8] Only beings who are aware that they are vulnerable to injury or annihilation display fear. By this logic, any being that displays fear must possess an awareness of its own vulnerability. Horses clearly display fear. They spook at shadows, bolt at thunder, and communicate their fear to others. Though horses don't possess higher brain function sufficient to allow them to "know" that they are anxious or analyze their anxiety the way that we do, anxiety is nonetheless a trait that humans and horses share. Indeed, our large brain affords us the potential for such hyperanxiety that we give horses a run for their money.

Just as humans share the trait of anxiety with horses, we also share the tendency to try to alleviate anxiety through escape. Though our flights tend to be more conceptual than actual, humans and horses are both predisposed to run. Whereas horses are literal escape artists, humans are figurative ones. The existentialists have even coined terms to describe our evasive tendencies. Whether they refer to them as "bad faith,"[9] "inauthenticity,"[10] or "philosophical suicide,"[11] they agree that when humans encounter something that elicits anxiety, our "immediate behavior with respect to [anxiety] is flight."[12] Because many of the things that terrify humans are mental, we flee through psychological diversion and denial. Just as we avoid physical confrontation, we run from unwanted truths into comforting fields of lies. Rather than accept responsibility for behavior, individuals often attempt to escape responsibility by shifting the blame to someone or something other than the self. For example, if caught surfing the Internet at work, a person might readily justify her action on the grounds that "everyone else is doing it," rather than admit acting irresponsibly.

This example alludes to a third similarity between humans and horses. They are both herd-bound. Like horses, humans are social animals. Both species exist in communities and exhibit social dependence.[13] Like horses, humans like to stand with each other and feed at the trough together. Humans and horses need others beyond their infancy; they retain that dependence throughout their adult life. Sartre and Heidegger both describe humans as fundamentally social. Heidegger asserts that we are social beings before we have a self and that we derive comfort from our "being-with-others."[14] While Sartre is alert to the potential that our relationships have to arouse discomfort, he too asserts that "being-for-others" is an essential aspect of human being, an aspect that is not only essential for physical survival, but also for proper psychological development and normal human function.[15]

In addition to wanting to be with others, we also want to be like them. Heidegger discusses how individuals try to be part of the "they," and agonize when they "diffe[r] from" from other members of their social group.[16] Arguably, this tendency to conform is what led earlier existentialist Friedrich Nietzsche to describe humans as "herd animal[s]."[17] He saw that despite the rhetoric of individualism, humans, like horses, are more comfortable in groups. Both horses and humans are ontologically tied to others, and as a consequence, they fear estrangement from their peers. That fear inclines both species to acquiesce to authority and stick with the herd.

Spurred by Desire: The Origins of Our Impulse to Dominate Horses

Of course, the fact that humans and horses share certain traits does not explain why humans have such an ambivalent relationship with equines, an ambivalence illustrated and reinforced by both classic and contemporary westerns. For that explanation we need to delve more deeply into the human psyche, our insecurities, and the way we manage anxiety. As mentioned previously, humans, like horses, are naturally anxious; however, unlike horses, humans actively reflect on their anxiety and the causes of it. To the extent that many of the causes of anxiety are intractable aspects of the human condition, reflection merely compounds our anxiety rather than alleviates it. To the extent our anxiety is really about our being, it is irremediable, a terminal condition. This leads Sartre to describe human being as a "troubled longing" that has "no possibility of surpassing its unhappy state."[18] Though humans have no ready solutions for their existential troubles, they do have various means of consolation. Though we often feel disempowered by existence, we have developed psychologically satisfying ways to assert ourselves, assuage anxiety, and thereby increase our sense of agency and power.

Nietzsche is well known for his Will to Power. In his view, all beings are expressions of the Will to Power and the Will to Power is nothing other than life.[19] By his account, all living things embody the Will to Power and desire to express that will. In addition, individuals experience frustration when their will is thwarted either by circumstance or conflict with another will. The conflict that arises between individual wills explains the animosity evident between animals, even social animals, like horses and humans, that are mutually dependent. Georg Wilhelm Friedrich Hegel (1770–1831) discusses this dynamic, as evident in humans, in the famous "Lord and Bondsman" section of his *Phenomenology of Spirit*. To the extent that Nietzsche's and Sartre's later accounts of social relations rely heavily on Hegel's work, these three figures can help us understand our desire to dominate others, horses in particular.

According to Hegel (and Sartre), human consciousness is not initially reflexive. Rather, it is thoroughly absorbed in experience. What prompts reflection, and ultimately self-awareness, is the encounter with another consciousness. Unfortunately, this initial encounter (and the others that follow) is not entirely pleasant. Encounters with others are problematic because the confrontation with another consciousness discloses to the individual the existence of another will, an "independent existence" whose wishes might be contrary to his, and that might threaten or even kill him.[20] As Hegel, Nietzsche, and Sartre agree, because of the intrinsic threat that others represent, social relationships are fraught with tension and conflict. As much as we depend upon others, others can endanger us. Our relationship to others is further complicated by the fact that we seek to define ourselves in opposition to them. Specifically, as much as we like to align ourselves with others, we also seek to prove ourselves independent of, superior to, them in order to placate the anxiety that they, and existence generally, generate. Hegel, Nietzsche, and Sartre agree that the desire to dominate is a natural impulse that arises out of our ontological insecurity.[21] Sartre even suggests that individuals are naturally "sadis[tic]" because the domination of others fosters a sense of physical and psychological security;[22] however, as Nietzsche discusses at some length, in a situation of conflict, not everyone can dominate. Rather, some individuals will be subordinates. The dynamic of domination causes the emergence of not only social hierarchies but also of resentment and "hostility" in the suppressed groups.[23] Individuals who are subject to the control of others seek to find ways to vent their frustration, express their power, and recoup their sense of ontological security. Though the philosophers mentioned discuss how this plays out only in human communities, clearly, if individuals are unable to dominate members of their own species, they may attempt to dominate members of another. This is where horses come in. Whether a human or another animal, subjecting another being to the force of one's will produces a sense of power and control. And size matters. The bigger the being is, the more substantial the return. Beating up someone smaller than you isn't as satisfying as taking on someone your own size or bigger. Likewise, leading a puppy on a leash is not the same as leading a 1,200-pound stallion.

From an existential perspective, the psychological satisfaction humans get from hunting wild animals and owning domestic pets stems largely from the fact that both activities affirm the power of the individual by rendering—in the former case literally—an animal subject to human will. This also explains our fascination with animal training and obedience. We demand—and delight in—animal obedience because their compliance feeds our hunger for control. The bigger the animal one masters, the more satisfying is its subjection.[24] To the extent that most horses are five to ten times a person's weight, compelling their compliance is deeply satisfying. Importantly, horses command human interest not only because they are large, but also because they are "volcanic force[s]," "dynamic material presence[s]" that impress us with their "sheer energy."[25] We desire to dominate horses not simply because of their size, but also because in subjecting them to our authority we "appropriat[e]" their power and thereby prove our own.[26] As Tompkins asserts, horses are "colonized subjects." They "don't start out as [our] pals; they have to be forced into it." Westerns illustrate and emphasize this. In Hegelian fashion, westerns depict "a kingdom of force and conflict where humans and animals vie for dominance and define themselves by competing with each other." More often than not, they show "horse[s] becom[ing] [our] servants." The subjugation of horses is psychologically satisfying because "a man astride a horse illustrates the [satisfying] possibility of mastery of self, of others, of land, [and] of circumstance."[27] What Tompkins does not fully explain is why horses, more than any other animal, are the focal point of domination in westerns. Cattle are driven, but horses are broken. Horse-breaking scenes are stock elements in westerns and bronc-riding remains one of the National Professional Rodeo Association's most popular events. This special interest in breaking horses begs explanation.

Hippomania: Our Unique Fascination with Equines

Clearly, the simple desire to prove one's power by breaking the will of another being explains why humans enjoy engaging in or observing acts of domination. The fact that individuals are not generally given social license to dominate other humans, or feel incapable of it, makes animals easy targets. Likewise, watching such acts on-screen provides vicarious satisfaction when real experience is unavailable or undesirable. The question is: Why are horses particularly appealing? Obviously, horses can do things for humans that other animals cannot. They can work cattle and pull wagons. They are faster and generally more tractable than oxen. A rider on horseback can cover more ground than a person on foot and is elevated from some of the dangers, such as snakes, to which the latter is exposed. Because of their various uses (and the fact that they submit to being put to those uses), horses were essential to the settling of the American West. The settling of the West literally rode on the back of the horse. Horses also served an important function historically for many Native American tribes. While commitment to realism explains the ubiquitous presence of horses in westerns, it doesn't explain the special focus on their domination that is evident in them. This special interest issues from the fact that horses embody traits we both loathe and love.

Ironically, the traits we loathe in horses are the traits that we share with them. To the extent that we would like to purge ourselves of these traits, we seek to discipline them out of horses. As discussed previously, humans and horses are anxious, herd-bound beings who are predisposed to flight. Though horses cannot, humans can reflect on their being, and unfortunately, when we do, we do not always like what we see. Sartre argues that we usually don't. In particular, we do not like the fact that we are anxious, dependent, and inclined to run. It's not hard to see why we don't like anxiety. Anxiety is uncomfortable. Worry and fear are not fun. Neither is dependence. Dependence links one's being to something that is beyond one's will and control. This is anxiety provoking and therefore unpleasant. The tendency to run is distasteful because it smacks of weakness. The one who runs is the one whose will is weaker. Whether it is for natural or cultural reasons, we read a predisposition toward flight as an indication of cowardice.

The positive traits that horses possess also make them targets. As Tompkins states, horses embody "all that is desirable and precious about living things . . . [including] the blamelessness and vulnerability of the body and its inborn desire for pleasure."[28] Horses symbolize even more than that. We love horses for many reasons. As Tompkins rightly notes, we love them for their innocence and purity and for the fact that they do not seem to suffer the way that we do. We also love them for their sheer beauty and remarkable athleticism. Horses are striking animals. Their fluid elegance, elasticity of movement, and natural grace are captivating. Moreover, in a country where the national symbol could as easily be a horse as an eagle, horses embody other powerful ideals including freedom, grace, and community. To the extent that we aspire to these qualities, we admire horses for having them.

Unfortunately, as much as we admire and celebrate horses for their possession of traits such as beauty, freedom, and grace, we also envy their possession of these qualities. Part of our desire to subjugate them derives from our wish to "posse[ss]" what they have.[29] As Sartre discusses, in seeking to dominate others, individuals strive to appropriate power and prove their own authority. Maintenance and validation of the individual subject is achieved through the objectification or suppression of the Other. This is illustrated clearly in the treatment of horses in westerns. Horses are frequently shot to create a protective barrier to gunfire and are traded for goods and services. They are broken in order to confirm the power of the individual on their back. Their feelings are not usually considered relevant. Their welfare tends to be considered only to the extent that it relates to their exchange value.

Though horses are commonly objectified, it is interesting to note that the horses that command the greatest interest and respect from us, and from characters in westerns, are those that retain their spirit and resist being reduced to objects. The rogues, not the nags, have enduring appeal. These are the horses that serve as characters rather than as background in our beloved westerns. Existential theory also sheds light on why we love these horses. According to Sartre, what human consciousness really wants is not to reduce others to objects but to possess another consciousness as subject. While reducing someone to an object is empowering, we prefer to dominate others as subjects, not objects. We want to dominate "a freedom as freedom," while simultaneously (and paradoxically) "demand[ing] that this freedom as freedom should no longer be free."[30] It is for this reason that Hegel asserts that the goal of the conflict between individuals is domination, not death. Though death more effectively removes the threat posed by another, it denies the individual the psychological satisfaction that comes when another freedom willingly accepts and acknowledges the power of the self. To the extent that horses are powerful symbols of freedom, when we harness them or ride them and they accept that situation, we get exactly what we want—we control a freedom as freedom.

Westerns and Horses

As other essays in this collection examine, westerns have an enduring appeal in part because they serve the purpose of wish fulfillment. They satisfy our nostalgia for a less alienating, preindustrialized time, a time when we were closer to nature, when our labor produced tangible and worthwhile results, and when things were clearer—morally speaking. Of course, it's not clear that this time ever actually existed, but we want it nonetheless. We idealize western heroes like Marshal Will Kane (*High Noon*, 1952) because they embody traits we seek to have. They are loners who are unruffled by danger and refuse to run regardless of the risk.[31] While we aspire to be like the archetypal heroes of the classic western, the horses in westerns (and horses generally) exhibit qualities we are more likely to share. As mentioned previously, to the extent that they exhibit characteristics that we possess but also despise, horses are convenient objects upon which to transfer our own self-loathing and enact a disciplinary regime designed to punish and transform.[32] As traditionally practiced and depicted in westerns, and often illustrated by the hero himself, the act of breaking penalizes horses for exhibiting their natural traits, and forces them into manifesting the traits we seek not only in them but also in ourselves. Training transforms nature by reconditioning natural response. Natural equine responses, like running and bucking, are denied their efficacy and associated with a negative consequence. Unnatural reactions like internalizing aggression, and facing and approaching danger, are rewarded. Interestingly, this process is analogous to that discussed by philosopher Michel Foucault in *Discipline and Punish.* Just as he asserts that human bodies are subject to control and reconditioning in and through the process of socialization, the bodies of horses are subjected to disciplinary techniques that force a compliance that is contrary to instinct. With both humans and horses, the ultimate goal of training is to produce "docile bodies."[33] In subjecting horses to our control, we reenact the processes to which we ourselves were subject. In Hegelian terms, slave becomes master.

The horse-breaking scenes in *All the Pretty Horses* (2000) and *The Horse Whisperer* (1998) illustrate this "disciplinary model" clearly.[34] In the former, the horses are herded into a corral. One by one they are separated from the comfort of the herd, caught, and bound tightly with ropes. To encourage quicker submission, their noses are hobbled to their hind legs so that their efforts at resistance will actually use the horse's own strength to command compliance. When they kick or run they yank their own nose. The harder they resist, the more punishing it is on their tender noses. In the novel that serves as the basis for the film, McCarthy describes how the process demeans and terrifies the colts. He says the colts look like "circus" animals "trussed up by children" and that the main character, John Grady Cole, "remorseless[ly] . . . rende[rs] . . . [the] fluid collective selves [of the horses] into [a] condition of separate and helpless paralysis." Denied any means of escape and "trailing their hackamore ropes . . . [so as] not to tread upon them and snatch their sore noses," the horses "stood waiting for they knew not what with the voice of the breaker still running in their brains like the voice of some god come to inhabit them." After the breaker finishes with the horses, their being is irrevocably altered: "The mustangs that had circled the potrero like marbles in a jar could hardly be said to exist . . . the animals whinnied . . . as if someone among their number were missing, or some thing."[35] Despite the fact that his methods demean the horses, Cole (Matt Damon) is described as the best horseman in the land.

A similar elevation of coercive methods is seen in the film *The Horse Whisperer.* After traditional round-pen techniques that bear an interesting similarity to Jeremy Bentham's (1748–1832) panopticon[36] fail to compel compliance, the main character, Tom Booker (Robert Redford), uses a different but equally forceful technique to break Pilgrim. He ultimately "lays" Pilgrim down, a euphemism used to describe when a person ropes the legs of a horse in such a way as to force it to the ground. To keep the horse prostrate, a person using this technique will either hog-tie the horse's legs or sit on the animal's neck to prevent it from getting back to its feet. Booker uses ropes to bring Pilgrim to the ground and sits on his neck to keep him there. Because it robs them of their one real defense, flight, laying a horse down is one of the most frightening things one can do to it. While Booker indicates that he is merely asking Pilgrim to choose whether he'll let someone ride him, being forced to the ground and having someone sit on your head would certainly be coercive if were we talking about doing it to a human. After all, though both the original novel and the film version intentionally align the traumatized protagonist, Grace MacLean (Scarlett Johansson), with her traumatized horse, despite Grace's initial resistance, Booker doesn't take her to the mat to inspire her compliance. Again, though he employs coercive methods, Booker is championed as an exemplary horseman.[37]

To be fair, both *All The Pretty Horses* and *The Horse Whisperer* articulate the love we have for horses as much as they illustrate our tendency to try to dominate them. They trade as much on their audience's fascination with horses as the satisfaction associated with watching them get broke. Poignant scenes in which the protagonists speak to the horses and stroke them softly counterbalance the coercive training sequences. Similarly, multiple scenes focus exclusively on the beauty of the horse and the quiet communion possible between horse and rider. Films such as *Hidalgo* (2004), *The Electric Horseman* (1979), and the classic *Lonely Are the Brave* (1962), also glorify horses and celebrate our relationship with them.[38] To the extent that the aforementioned films foreground our interest in and affection for horses, they, more than most other westerns, demonstrate that our relations with horses are not based simply on the impulse to dominate. Instead, they allude to the possibility of a more productive bond. These films illustrate an important fact: we have a profoundly positive connection to horses.

Though the traits we share with horses can compel a negative reaction, they can also serve as the basis for a positive empathic bond. Humans sense a powerful kinship with horses because of our common characteristics: our mutual sensitivity and similar subjection to social restraint. Like horses, we feel ourselves "saddled" with obligations, and often reduced to the status of an object. Our bosses "ride" us, and while normally fearful of consequence, we occasionally find ourselves "bucking authority"—"tossing our heads," as it were. Similarly, while we like to think of ourselves as individuals, we often find ourselves anxiously looking to others for validation and, more often than not, following the herd's lead. Western films both illustrate and capitalize on the kinship with horses that humans experience. They utilize it by having horses serve as symbolic surrogates for their human counterparts, illustrating on-screen what humans feel they have lost, or hope to possess. This is nowhere more evident than in the classic *Lonely Are the Brave*. Though the film is normally looked at as a requiem for the Old West, a film focused on the death of cowboy culture, it also illustrates the poignant relationship that a person can have with a horse. Arguably, the protagonist in the film, Jack Burns (Kirk Douglas), has no better friend than his horse, Whiskey. The film "identifi[es]" the plight of the protagonist with that of his horse as they struggle to find a place for themselves in a brave new world of high-speed commerce.[39] In the closing scene in which Jack and Whiskey are killed trying to cross a highway in the rain, horse and rider serve as a poignant symbol of the price of modernity.

In addition to illustrating the kinship humans have with horses, western films also illustrate the delight that people can derive from their relationships with horses. They depict the loyalty and camaraderie that can exist between humans and horses, a joy that comes not merely from tactile bonding and the pleasure of nonverbal communication but also from the mutual trust and friendship that can develop between an individual and a horse. These traits are exemplified in *Hidalgo*, a film based on the life of legendary horseman Frank T. Hopkins (1865–1951) and his horse, Hidalgo. In the film, while Hopkins (Viggo Mortensen) rides Hidalgo and races him for prize money, rather than regard his horse as a subordinate, he sees Hidalgo as an equal, a partner. He talks to Hidalgo, expresses genuine concern over the horse's welfare, and horse and rider display mutual respect and affection. Importantly, Hopkins also repeatedly refers to his horse as "brother." The use of this familial term shows that Hopkins sees his horse not only as an equal, but also as intimately connected to himself, as a member of his immediate family. As the film suggests, Hidalgo is Hopkins's closest friend. And when Hopkins repeatedly tells his friend, "Let 'er buck," he expresses his willingness to let his horse be a horse. This phrase also foreshadows the end of the film, in which Hopkins releases Hidalgo back into the wild to run with a herd of mustangs he purchased and spared from extermination at the hands of the U.S. Army.

Though its plot is predicated on less amiable relations to horses, *The Electric Horseman* concludes in a similar fashion to *Hidalgo*. In this film, former rodeo champion Sonny Steele (Robert Redford) rescues the racehorse Rising Star from an exploitive situation in which the horse is being drugged so that he will be placid enough to parade on-stage alongside showgirls who are promoting breakfast cereal at Caesar's Palace in Las Vegas. Like Hopkins, Steele empathizes with the horse and detests his exploitation. To save the horse, Steele elects to release him into the wild. The closing scene in which the stallion lopes freely toward a group of mares contrasts sharply with the scene for which the film is known: Steele atop the horse, both figures draped in lights, man and horse reduced to an advertising gimmick. The endings of *Hidalgo* and *The Electric Horseman* command a powerful response in audiences. Like many other western films, they allude to the duality of nature and culture and display a clear preference for the former. Audiences delight as bridles and saddles are removed and the horses are liberated. We thrill as the horses gallop into an open landscape, celebrating not merely their liberation, but also the way that release satisfies our latent desire for freedom from constraint.

As thrilling as the endings of *Hidalgo* and *The Electric Horseman* may be, the open future they depict for these horses, or horses generally, is not realistic. The endings serve the purpose of human wish fulfillment, not fact. While the liberation of horses on-screen serves as an apt symbol of our own desire for autonomy, there are now very few places in this country where horses can run wild, and even in those places, horses usually remain at the mercy of humans. In order to ensure sufficient grazing for cattle and adequate acreage for new home building, thousands of horses are rounded up every year off public land by the Bureau of Land Management and put out for adoption or auction, with some animals going for slaughter.[40] The situation for horses is very much as the ending of *Hidalgo* suggests. In the world today, horses exist at the will and whim of humans. They are bought and sold, run and bred. They live and die at our discretion. Horses don't have any choice in this matter, but humans do. We can choose to relate to horses in a responsible manner or an exploitive one; however, we cannot just set them free. Our world is not one of fiction, where ample space exists for all. Horses are beings that exist alongside us in the world, and humans, for the time being, control that world. Our actions exert tremendous influence on the species that surround us, horses included. Though we can use our knowledge of horses against them in order to dominate them and satisfy our own desire for control, we do not have to do so. Our empathic connection can inspire us to display greater sensitivity to horses.

We can return to Hegel and the existentialists for guidance. Just as Hegel describes the instinct to dominate that influences our relation to horses, he also denies that individuals can achieve their full potential in the context of unequal relations. This is what inspires Hegel to argue for the need to transcend one-sided relationships of domination to achieve relations of reciprocity. According to Hegel, though others arouse discomfort, humans need others, and full human potentiality can be achieved only through mutuality. His dialectic encourages humans to go beyond their tendency to dominate one another and progress toward more egalitarian relationships. Though Hegel was not thinking of animal-human relations, arguably his ideas can be applied to them. Clearly, our humanity is measured not only by our treatment of other humans, but also by our treatment of other species and the environment. Likewise, our humanity evolves not only in conjunction with our human interactions, but also through our nonhuman ones. For the benefit of other beings and our own, we should resist our inclination to dominate horses and seek greater mutuality with them, mutuality like that illustrated in *Hidalgo*.

Learning from Horses: Letting Go, Turning In, Hooking On

One might ask at this point what larger purpose seeking out and celebrating mutuality with horses serves. After all, only a relatively small percentage of the U.S. population has concrete relations with horses. This is true; however, the conflicted relationship with horses that westerns tend to exemplify and promote is significant because of what it says about humans generally, not merely those who work with horses. Rather than promote the acceptance of our nature, most westerns reflect and reinforce our dissatisfaction with it, and they do so in part through their portrayal of horses. As Tompkins states, "The desire to curb the horse and make it submit to human requirements is as important to Westerns as [any] desire for merger or mutuality."[41] Most westerns serve up lone heroes who embody our desire for absolute autonomy and fortify the ambivalent relationship we have with horses by celebrating their violent subjugation. However, because they foreground the deep affection we have for horses, westerns such as *Hidalgo, All The Pretty Horses, The Electric Horseman,* and *The Horse Whisperer* have the potential to inspire critical reflection both on the ideals of horsemanship that most westerns endorse and on our general attraction to these punitive techniques. As much as we have nostalgia for the world of the western, the treatment of horses that is characteristic of the genre reduces humans as much as it does horses. As this essay shows, the psychodynamics that influence our relationship to horses exert an influence on other relationships as well.

Whether one rides horses for recreational or professional purposes, that activity presumes relations of power. This essay is not suggesting that people give up riding and hand over the reins to the horses, or that we deny ourselves the pleasure of observing or owning horses. Instead, it simply suggests that we consider the psychological basis for the ambivalent relationship Americans have to these animals, a relationship that is depicted in and reinforced by most westerns. When it is subject to scrutiny, we can see that the nature of our relationship to horses often has more to do with our relationship to ourselves than it has to do with equines. Our relationships with horses are often dictated more by our own desires than by any recognition of theirs. Often we ride horses in order to prove something to ourselves. Even those who have never swung a leg over a horse delight in watching them be broken because not only does that act satisfy the desire to dominate, it also glorifies the subjugation of instincts we regard as weak.

While the analysis offered here holds particular significance for those who work with horses, it is equally relevant to those who don't. Obviously, for those who work with horses, the insights provided here might help individuals: (1) limit the transference of negative emotion in the course of training; (2) discourage the immature demand for control that often results in the inappropriate or disproportionate application of punitive techniques; and (3) encourage more empathic, productive, and nonviolent relations to horses. For those who don't work with horses, the remarks provided here might influence greater critical reflection upon our cultural attitude toward horses and more informed popular dialogue regarding public policy related to equine industries such as horse racing. However, there is another, even more compelling benefit.

Ultimately, understanding the nature of our relationship to horses increases our understanding of ourselves.[42] This yields an increased ability to determine both our own being and our being with others. As existentialists like Sartre emphasize, humans have the freedom to determine their nature because we stand in a unique position with respect to our natural inclinations. While humans are nothing other than highly evolved animals who are subject to various sorts of impulses, unlike other animals, our consciousness gives us the ability to decide whether we are going to act on those impulses or not. As Sartre indicates, consciousness affects a "break in being," and that capacity to dissociate from experience is the foundation for freedom.[43] It is what keeps human action from being completely determined by inclination. With this freedom in mind, we can look at the impulses and emotions discussed earlier in this essay, namely, the impulse to dominate, an impulse that is aggravated by our own self-loathing. Rather than act on this impulse, an impulse that influences numerous important relations, not merely those with horses, we can resist it and elect to act on other motives, motives perhaps grounded less in our own anxiety about what we are and more about what we hope to be.

While we are shaped by our evolutionary heritage, our hardwired responses, our primal fears and desires, we can choose how we react to that history. Though we cannot change the fact that we are anxious and social, we can choose not to let our anxieties compromise our relationships with other beings. Of course, this isn't easy; however, it is easier if we learn to accept ourselves. Self-acceptance is critical because, as suggested here with horses, much of the ambivalence we display toward other beings is anchored in our own insecurity. Though existentialists like Sartre recognize that aspects of our being are troubling, at the same time he sees existence as "a perfect free gift."[44] In advocating authenticity, he encourages individuals to admit and accept the human condition. Though we don't like everything about existence or everything about ourselves, we are "indebted" to our environment, and human by virtue of the traits we possess.[45] Our anxious nature is what anchors our capacity for deep concern. Our fragility grounds our potential for profound existential appreciation. Our social nature serves as the foundation for genuine empathy, community, and solidarity. We need to embrace the traits we possess and that horses mirror to us, rather than act on our visceral desire to expunge them. We can take our lead from horses.

In order to be ridden, horses have to get past their initial impulse to duck (more accurately, buck!) and run. What is amazing is that most of them "let go" of their primal fear, "turn in" to us, and let us ride them without us having to use excessive force.[46] We are in a similar situation to that of horses. We exist in a situation of constraint and we have to find a way to deal with it productively. To function at an optimum level, we also have to get past some of our initial impulses. Ironically, it may be easier to ride an unbroken horse than it is to get most people past their ontological predilections. Perhaps we could learn from the colts in *All the Pretty Horses*. There, despite the severity of the methods used and their transformative effects, the horses somehow retain their grace. They adapt to their condition, "hook on" to their new situation, and, as McCarthy puts it, move "with great elegance and seemliness." Like the colts, the thoroughbred stallion that Cole trains retains his power and grace and even delights in being ridden. When Cole returns from prison, the stallion is "glad to see him," and when they head out for a ride, the horse is so exuberant he "[can] find no gait within his repertoire to suit the day."[47] We could take a lesson from these horses, and horses generally. They adapt to their situation without surrendering their grace. When given the opportunity, they take delight in life. They do not seem to exhibit the self-loathing or social anxiety that we do. If we would do more of the same, we would be better off. Though often cynical, Sartre alludes to this possibility. He uses the term *grace* to refer both to the state of the individual and to interpersonal relations that are characterized by "reciproc[ity]" rather than dominance.[48] Though he asserts that grace is rare, it is an ideal that the authentic individual exemplifies. It is an ideal that bears similarity to that described by Heidegger. Though Heidegger asserts that a "will to mastery" dominates most people, he says this will operates to the detriment of all living things.[49] As a result, he urges individuals to lay down their desire to dominate, and instead to hasten to the "call . . . [of] conscience," a call that reminds us of our connection to other beings and the environment.[50] He urges us to "spare and husband" other beings, rather than subjugate them, and "to stay with [them]" in such a way as to "free [them to] their own presencing."[51]

Though it depicts our tendency to dominate horses, *All the Pretty Horses* also illustrates an ideal of human-horse relations, an ideal of grace and mutuality to which we might aspire not merely with horses, but with other humans. At the end of the novel and at great personal risk, Cole rescues his horse Redbo. Though horse and rider have been separated for some time, Redbo recognizes Cole's voice and whinnies to him from the darkness of the barn. Cole takes Redbo, along with Rawlins's and Blevins's horses, and heads back to the States.[52] While riding Redbo, Cole realizes the depth of his connection to his horse. He "found he was breathing in rhythm with the horse as if some part of the horse were within him breathing and then he descended into some deeper collusion for which he had not even a name." Cole finds profound solace in this collusion, and the intimate link between horse and rider is reinforced in the final scene as Cole and Redbo move off into the darkening landscape, a world where Cole seems to feel at home only with his horse, and where the shadow of horse and rider is like that "of a single being."[53] Unfortunately, rather than allow themselves this degree of connection with either another human or an animal, people often flee it. All too often, like horses on their first experience in the round pen, we run the perimeter, our noses tipped to the outside, searching for a way out. From the existentialist perspective, life is a pen with no outside; there is no place to escape. While we can spend our lives running, we have another option. As a seasoned horseman might say, we can choose to let go, turn in, and hook on. If we would, more than our relations to horses would benefit.

Notes

This essay is dedicated to all my pretty horses. You have tolerated my imperfection with immeasurable grace and good humor and have undoubtedly helped make me a better person. One couldn't ask for better friends. I am also grateful to B. Steve Csaki, Ken Hada, Mark Walling, and Steve Pedersen for their thoughtful comments and helpful suggestions on an earlier draft of this essay.

The epigraph is taken from Cormac McCarthy, *All the Pretty Horses* (New York: Vintage International, 1992).

1. In *West of Everything: The Inner Life of Westerns* (New York: Oxford University Press, 1992), Jane Tompkins dedicates a chapter to the significance of horses in the western, one of the few scholarly efforts to analyze the subject. This essay draws from her subtle and penetrating analysis and attempts to supplement her work on the subject by offering an existential explanation for what she argues is the "contradiction horses in westerns embody" (104). Other works that warrant recognition are Jenni Calder, *There Must Be a Lone Ranger: The American West in Film and in Reality* (New York: Taplinger, 1974); Harold Hintz, *Horses in the Movies* (New York: A. S. Barnes, 1979); and Lillian Turner, "The Golden Horse on the Silver Screen," *Montana: The Magazine of Western History* 45, no. 4 (1995): 2–19. Calder, Hintz, and Turner all agree that horses are essential to the enduring appeal of the western; however, they do not go to great length to explain why.

2. Tompkins, *West of Everything,* 90.

3. Hintz, *Horses in the Movies,* 11; Tompkins, *West of Everything,* 90, 92.

4. See Jeanna Fiske Godfrey, *How Horses Learn: Equine Psychology Applied to Training* (Lincoln, NE: Authors' Guild, 2005). The author describes horses as "flight rather than fight animals . . . [who] under most conditions . . . would rather run from enemies than stand and fight to protect [themselves]" (12).

5. Martin Heidegger, *Being and Time,* trans. Joan Stambaugh (Albany: State University of New York Press, 1996), 166.

6. Ibid., 176, 171, 40.

7. R. D. Laing, *The Divided Self* (New York: Random House, 1969), 40.

8. Heidegger, *Being and Time*, 177.

9. Jean-Paul Sartre, *Being and Nothingness*, trans. Hazel Barnes (New York: Washington Square, 1956), 110.

10. Heidegger, *Being and Time*, 40.

11. Albert Camus, "An Absurd Reasoning" in *The Myth of Sisyphus and Other Essays*, trans. Justin O'Brien (New York: Vintage, 1991), 41.

12. Sartre, *Being and Nothingness*, 78.

13. In *How Horses Learn*, veterinarian Godfrey describes horses as fundamentally "contactual," social beings that "see[k] warmth and protection from members of [their] own species" (4).

14. Heidegger, *Being and Time*, 113. To demonstrate that humans are essentially social, Heidegger looks to the phenomenon of loneliness. Loneliness, he argues, is predicated on sociality. Only a being that needs others of its kind experiences a sense of lack at their absence. For further discussion, see *Being and Time*, 113.

15. Sartre, *Being and Nothingness*, 301.

16. Heidegger, *Being and Time*, 118.

17. Friedrich Nietzsche, *Beyond Good and Evil*, trans. Walter Kaufmann (New York: Random House, 1966), 118.

18. Sartre, *Being and Nothingness*, 503, 140.

19. Nietzsche, *Beyond Good and Evil*, 48.

20. Georg Wilhelm Friedrich Hegel, *The Phenomenology of Spirit*, trans. A. V. Miller (Oxford: Oxford University Press, 1977), 112.

21. In *How Horses Learn*, Godfrey discusses "dominance hierarchies" in equine communities, hierarchies she asserts are "also evident in many animal species including *Homo sapiens*." These hierarchies produce "a social ranking of the individuals within a group according to their relative dominant and/or submissive tendencies" (12).

22. Sartre, *Being and Nothingness*, 494. It is important to note that Sartre does not use the term *sadism* to refer specifically, or even primarily, to sexual relationships. Though the predisposition to sadistic behavior can be expressed in a sexual fashion, Sartre uses it to refer simply to the tendency humans have to objectify others. He also asserts that individuals try to escape their freedom (bad faith) by treating themselves, or allowing themselves to be treated, as objects. He uses the term *masochism* to refer to this type of bad faith.

23. Friedrich Nietzsche, *Twilight of the Idols*, trans. R. J. Hollingsdale (New York: Penguin, 1968), 49.

24. In his article "The Causes of Animal Abuse: A Social-Psychological Analysis," Robert Agnew lends support to the position taken in this essay. There he asserts that individuals often experience a "desire to dominate" (187) animals and often "compensate for feelings of weakness or vulnerability by exerting power and control over animals" (192). Because mastering animals is psychologically satisfying, their domination provides

individuals with a "convenient mechanism for coping with strain . . . and to manage . . . negative emotions" (197). Agnew's article can be found in *Theoretical Criminology* (1998): 177–209, http://www.sagepublications.com (accessed May 21, 2009).

25. Tompkins, *West of Everything*, 95, 94, 89.

26. Sartre, *Being and Nothingness*, 478.

27. Tompkins, *West of Everything*, 101, 97, 100, 99, 101.

28. Ibid., 103.

29. Sartre, *Being and Nothingness*, 475.

30. Ibid., 478, 479.

31. Though it is beyond the scope of this essay to examine, it could be argued that our fascination with western heroes has also an existential foundation. Just as our captivation with horses has existential roots, one could argue that the archetypal western hero commands an enduring interest by virtue of the fact that he embodies traits we desire to have. Specifically, among other things, he fulfills our desire to escape the existential traits we share with his horse: namely, anxiety, social dependence, and a predisposition for flight.

32. Again, Agnew's "The Causes of Animal Abuse" supports this claim. There he argues that certain animals are more frequent targets of abuse by virtue of the fact that they "possess traits we do not like" (187). In the case of horses, the traits we do not like are the ones we share with them.

33. Michel Foucault, *Discipline and Punish*, trans. Alan Sheridan (New York: Vintage, 1977), 135.

34. Tompkins, *West of Everything*, 126.

35. McCarthy, *All the Pretty Horses*, 105, 107, 111.

36. The term *panopticon* refers to a design for a prison advocated by philosopher Jeremy Bentham. For further information, see Jeremy Bentham, *The Panopticon Writings*, ed. M. Bozovic (London: Verso, 1995), 29–95. The circular design of the panopticon allows for a small number of prison personnel to oversee a substantial number of inmates from a central position. Moreover, the fact that the guards are invisible to the inmates heightens the sense of surveillance while in theory allowing the guardhouse to be empty without any reduction in punitive effect. Michel Foucault comments exhaustively on the panopticon in *Discipline and Punish*. He argues that the design uses "visibility [as] a trap" (200), and compels obedience by "induc[ing] . . . a state of conscious, permanent visibility" (201). Foucault notes that the power of the gaze is used in cultural contexts to command obedience like that described by Bentham. The round-pen technique that is used to break horses employs the power of optics and a circular design in a way similar to the panopticon. The trainer stands in the middle of the pen, "a laboratory of power" (204), looking at the horse. To facilitate training, she applies visual and physical pressure on the animal. Like other herd animals, horses have predictable flight zones, areas that compel the flight response if one enters them. Thus, physical pressure refers not primarily to physical contact with the animal, but to physical proximity suf-

ficient to compel flight. When a horse behaves in a fashion desired by the trainer, pressure is let up. The trainer averts her gaze and turns away from the horse. This removes the trainer from the animal's flight zone and allows the horse to experience the reward of relaxation. The technique intentionally manipulates anxiety in order to recondition natural response. For additional discussion of the power of optics, namely, how sight relates to dominance, see Maxine Sheets-Johnstone, *The Roots of Power: Animate Forms and Gendered Bodies* (New York: Open Court, 2003).

37. It should be noted that the breaking scene in the film version differs dramatically from the original novel. In the novel, Booker does not hobble the horse or lay it down. Nicolas Evans, the author of *The Horse Whisperer* (New York: Random House, 1996), the novel upon which the film is based, has stated that the natural horsemen Tom Dorrance, Ray Hunt, and Buck Brannaman were the inspiration for his novel (http://nicholasevans.com/faq/faq/asp). These people employ nonviolent training practices grounded in equine psychology and are outspokenly critical of coercive and punitive methods traditionally used to break horses. For further information on their techniques, see Tom Dorrance, *True Unity* (Sanger, CA: Word Dancer, 1994); Ray Hunt, *Think Harmony with Horses* (Streetsboro, OH: Ag Access, 1991); and Buck Brannaman, *Believe: A Horseman's Journey* (Guilford, CT: Lyons, 2006).

38. At the same time, all these films suggest that our relationship with horses is often dysfunctional. To the extent that most of them not only illustrate but also elevate the use of coercive methods, the ideals of horsemanship displayed in the films are ones we should question.

39. Tompkins, *West of Everything*, 102.

40. For official statistics on wild horse and burro removal and adoption, see the U.S. Department of the Interior, Bureau of Land Management Web site, http://www.blm.gov (accessed January 9, 2010).

41. Tompkins, *West of Everything*, 97.

42. In *West of Everything*, Tompkins concurs, stating, "The way people treat the world around them—animals, the land, other human beings—reveals something about themselves" (119).

43. Sartre, *Being and Nothingness*, 126.

44. Jean-Paul Sartre, *Nausea*, trans. Lloyd Alexander (New York: New Directions, 1964), 131.

45. Martin Heidegger, "The Question concerning Technology," in *The Question concerning Technology and Other Essays*, trans. William Lovitt (New York: Harper & Row, 1977), 7.

46. These terms are used in conjunction with round-pen training and refer to the stages of equine response. When placed in a round pen, a horse that is unacquainted with or fearful of humans will tend to run the perimeter of the pen, its nose tilted to the outside, looking for a way out. The energy displayed by the horse reflects the animal's degree of anxiety or concern. Eventually, when the horse realizes that it cannot flee, it

will "let go" of the idea of getting out of the pen. Its focus will shift to what is going on inside the pen. It will start to "turn in." This shift is initially visual, as the horse starts eyeing the trainer, but it becomes a physical shift when the horse elects to approach the trainer in the pen. When the horse not only predictably looks to the trainer but also turns to him and follows him around the pen, it has officially "hooked on." This behavior indicates that the horse's attention is on the trainer, that it is listening and willing to engage. It is what well-known natural horseman Monty Roberts refers to as "joining up." For further information on his techniques, see his *The Man Who Talks to Horses* (New York: Random House, 1997).

47. McCarthy, *All the Pretty Horses,* 107, 225.

48. Sartre, *Being and Nothingness,* 521, 475.

49. Heidegger, "The Question concerning Technology," 5.

50. Heidegger, *Being and Time,* 253.

51. Martin Heidegger, "The Turning," in *The Question concerning Technology,* 42; Martin Heidegger, "Building Dwelling Thinking," in *Poetry, Language, and Thought,* trans. Albert Hofstader (New York: Harper & Row, 1971), 151, 150.

52. Importantly, Cole also releases the grullo mustang into the wild before returning to the United States. This act parallels the release of the horses in *Hidalgo* and *The Electric Horseman,* and demonstrates Cole's recognition that he has no legitimate claim on the horse. Though he bears affection for the horse and would benefit from having an additional horse in his remuda, he nonetheless returns him to his original "free" state.

53. McCarthy, *All the Pretty Horses,* 266, 302.

SELECTED BIBLIOGRAPHY

Adams, Les. *Shoot-Em Ups.* New Rochelle, NY: Arlington House, 1978.

Aquila, Richard, ed. *Wanted Dead or Alive: The American West in Popular Culture.* Urbana: University of Illinois Press, 1996.

Armitrage, Susan, and Elizabeth Jameson, eds. *Writing the Range: Race, Class, and Culture in the Women's West.* Norman: University of Oklahoma Press, 1997.

Bataille, Gretchen, and Charles Silet, eds. *The Pretend Indians: Images of Native Americans in the Movies.* Ames: Iowa State University Press, 1980.

Bazin, André. "The Western, or the American Film Par Excellence" and "The Evolution of the Western." In *What Is Cinema?* translated by Hugh Gray, 2:140–57. Berkeley: University of California Press, 1971.

Berman, Russell A. *Fiction Sets You Free: Literature, Liberty, and Western Culture.* Ames: University of Iowa Press, 2007.

Blew, Mary Clearman. *Bone Deep in Landscape: Writing, Reading, and Place.* Norman: University of Oklahoma Press, 2000.

Brownlow, Kevin. *The War, the West, and the Wilderness.* New York: Knopf, 1979.

Buscombe, Edward, ed. *The BFI Companion to the Western.* New York: Atheneum, 1988.

Buscombe, Edward, and Roberta E. Pearson, eds. *Back in the Saddle Again: New Essays on the Western.* London: British Film Institute, 1998.

Calder, Jenni. *There Must Be a Lone Ranger: The American West in Film and in Reality.* New York: Taplinger, 1974.

Cameron, Ian, and Douglas Pye, eds. *The Book of Westerns.* New York: Continuum, 1996.

Carmichael, Deborah A., ed. *The Landscape of Hollywood Westerns: Ecocriticism in an American Film Genre.* Salt Lake City: University of Utah Press, 2006.

Cawelti, John G. *The Six-Gun Mystique.* Bowling Green, OH: Bowling Green Popular Press, 1971.

———. *The Six-Gun Mystique Sequel.* Bowling Green, OH: Bowling Green Popular Press, 1999.

Clapham, Walter. *Western Movies: The Story of the West on Screen.* London: Octopus, 1974.

Cohan, Steven. *Masked Men: Masculinity and the Movies in the Fifties.* Bloomington and Indianapolis: Indiana University Press, 1997.

Corkin, Stanley. *Cowboys as Cold Warriors: The Western and U.S. History.* Philadelphia: Temple University Press, 1997.

Coyne, Michael. *The Crowded Prairie: American National Identity in the Hollywood Western.* New York and London: I. B. Tauris, 1997.

Davis, Robert Murray. *Playing Cowboys: Low Culture and High Art in the Western.* Norman: University of Oklahoma Press, 1992.

Davis, Ronald L. *John Ford: Hollywood's Old Master.* Norman: University of Oklahoma Press, 1997.

Davis, William C. *The American Frontier: Pioneers, Settlers, and Cowboys, 1800–1899.* Norman: University of Oklahoma Press, 1999.

Deloria, Philip. *Playing Indian.* New Haven, CT: Yale University Press, 1998.

Deverell, William. *A Companion to the American West.* Malden, MA: Blackwell, 2004.

Everson, William K. *A Pictorial History of the Western Film.* Secaucus, NJ: Citadel, 1969.

Fenin, George. *The Western: From Silents to the Seventies.* New York: Penguin, 1973.

Folsom, James K., ed. *The Western: A Collection of Critical Essays.* Englewood Cliffs, NJ: Prentice-Hall, 1979.

French, Peter A. *Cowboy Metaphysics: Ethics and Death in Westerns.* Lanham, MD: Rowman & Littlefield, 1997.

French, Philip. *Westerns: Aspects of a Movie Genre.* New York: Oxford University Press, 1977.

Horwitz, James. *They Went Thataway.* New York: Dutton, 1976.

Kasson, Joy S. *Buffalo Bill's Wild West: Celebrity, Memory, and Popular History.* New York: Macmillan, 2001.

Kitses, Jim. *Horizons West: Directing the Western from John Ford to Clint Eastwood.* New ed. London: British Film Institute, 2004.

Kitses, Jim, and Gregg Rickman, eds. *The Western Reader.* New York: Lunebright, 1998.

Kolodny, Annette. *The Lay of the Land: Metaphor as Experience and History in American Life and Letters.* Chapel Hill: University of North Carolina Press, 1975.

Lachman, Ron. *Women of the Western Frontier in Fact, Fiction and Film.* Jefferson, NC: McFarland, 2001.

Lenihan, John. *Showdown: Confronting Modern America in Western Film.* Urbana: University of Illinois Press, 1985.

Limerick, Patricia Nelson. *Legacy of Conquest: The Unbroken Past of the American West.* New York and London: Norton, 2000.

———. *Something in the Soil: Legacies and Reckonings in the New West.* New York and London: Norton, 1987.

Loy, R. Philip. *Westerns and American Culture, 1930–1955.* Jefferson, NC: McFarland, 2001.

Marubbio, M. Elise, ed. *Killing the Indian Maiden: Images of Native American Women in Film.* Lexington: University Press of Kentucky, 2006.

Milner, Clyde. *A New Significance: Re-envisioning the History of the American West.* Oxford: Oxford University Press, 1996.

Milton, John. *The Novel of the American West.* Lincoln: University of Nebraska Press, 1980.

Mitchell, Lee Clark. *Westerns: Making the Man in Fiction and Film.* Chicago: University of Chicago Press, 1996.

Nachbar, John G. *Focus on the Western.* Englewood Cliffs, NJ: Prentice-Hall, 1974.

Pettit, Arthur C. *Images of the Mexican American in Fiction and Film.* College Station: Texas A&M University Press, 1980.

Place, Janey Ann. *The Western Films of John Ford.* Secaucus, NJ: Citadel, 1973.

Prats, Armando José. *Invisible Natives: Myth and Identity in the American Western.* Ithaca, NY: Cornell University Press, 2002.

Rainey, Buck. *Western Gunslingers in Fact and on Film: Hollywood's Famous Lawmen and Outlaws.* Jefferson, NC: McFarland, 1998.

Rollins, Peter C., and John E. O'Connor, eds. *Hollywood's Indian: The Portrayal of the Native American in Film.* Lexington: University Press of Kentucky, 1998.

———. *Hollywood's West: The American Frontier in Film, Television, and History.* Lexington: University Press of Kentucky, 2005.

Russell, Don. *The Lives and Legends of Buffalo Bill.* Norman: University of Oklahoma Press, 1960.

Saunders, John. *The Western Genre: From Lordsburg to Big Whiskey.* London: Wallflower, 2001.

Simmon, Scott. *The Invention of the Western Film: A Cultural History of the Genre's First Half-Century.* Cambridge: Cambridge University Press, 2003.

Slotkin, Richard. *Gunfighter Nation: The Myth of the Frontier in Twentieth-Century America.* New York: Atheneum, 1992.

Smith, Henry Nash. *Virgin Land: The American West as Symbol and Myth.* Cambridge, MA: Harvard University Press, 1950.

Stanfield, Peter. *Hollywood, Westerns, and the 1930s: The Lost Trail.* Exeter, UK: University of Exeter Press, 2001.

Studlar, Gaylyn, and Matthew Bernstein, eds. *John Ford Made Westerns: Filming a Legend in the Sound Era.* Bloomington: Indiana University Press, 2001.

Tompkins, Jane. *West of Everything: The Inner Life of Westerns.* New York: Oxford University Press, 1992.

Tuska, Jon. *The American West in Films: Critical Approaches to the Western.* Westport, CT: Greenwood, 1985.

Walker, Janet, ed. *Westerns: Films through History.* New York: Routledge, 2001.

Warshow, Robert. "Movie Chronicle: The Westerner." In *The Immediate Experience.* Cambridge, MA: Harvard University Press, 2001.

Wright, Will. *Sixguns and Society: A Structural Study of the Western.* Berkeley: University of California Press, 1975.

———. *The Wild West: The Mythical Cowboy and Social Theory.* London: Sage, 2001.

CONTRIBUTORS

SHAI BIDERMAN is a doctoral candidate in philosophy at Boston University and an instructor in the Bet-Berl College and the College of Management, Israel. His research interests include the philosophy of film and literature, the philosophy of culture, aesthetics, ethics, existentialism, and Nietzsche. His publications include articles on personal identity, language, determinism, and aesthetics. He has also written about the TV shows *Seinfeld, South Park, Lost, Family Guy,* and *Star Trek* and the films *Minority Report, Kill Bill, Down by Law, Intolerable Cruelty,* and *Rope.*

PAUL A. CANTOR is Clifton Waller Barrett Professor of English at the University of Virginia. He has taught at Harvard in both the English and government departments, and served on the National Council on the Humanities. He has published widely on popular culture, on topics from science fiction to pro wrestling. He has essays in volumes in the University Press of Kentucky's Philosophy of Popular Culture Series, Blackwell's Philosophy and Popular Culture Series, and Open Court's Popular Culture and Philosophy Series. His *Gilligan Unbound: Pop Culture in the Age of Globalization* was named one of the top nonfiction books of 2001 by the *Los Angeles Times.*

LINDSEY COLLINS is a doctoral candidate in the History of Consciousness program at the University of California, Santa Cruz. Her doctoral dissertation, "Trial by Mountain: The Politics of Suffering and Healing in Difficult Landscapes," explores how the recent phenomenon of women's recovery climbs creates cultural landscapes of health, risk, and survivorship. Her research interests include feminist theory, identity theory, and gender theory. She has a special interest in the relationship between identity and spatial place, particularly in how place is experienced differently due to varying gender socialization.

B. STEVE CSAKI holds a doctorate in philosophy from the State University of New York, Buffalo. He specializes in comparative philosophy, and is particularly interested in exploring the parallels that exist between Zen Buddhism and classical American pragmatism. He has published essays in volumes including *The Lord of the Rings and Philosophy* and *Finding the Ox: Buddhism and American Culture.* From 1998 to 2006, he was visiting professor at Centre College in Danville, Kentucky, where he taught courses in philosophy, humanities, and Japanese, and served as the coordinator for the Japanese program. Csaki has now relocated to central Oklahoma, where he is an independent scholar and cattle rancher. He owns and operates Watershed Ranch with Dr. Jennifer L. McMahon.

DOUGLAS J. DEN UYL is vice president of educational programs at the Liberty Fund. He holds a master's degree in political science from the University of Chicago and a PhD in philosophy from Marquette University. Den Uyl has taught at Tulane University and Bellarmine University, where he was chairman of the philosophy department. His research interests include political philosophy and ethics. Most recently, he published *God, Man, and Well-Being: Spinoza's Modern Humanism*.

WILLIAM J. DEVLIN is assistant professor of philosophy at Bridgewater State College. His fields of interest are the philosophy of science, theories of truth, Nietzsche, and existentialism. His publications include articles on Nietzsche, ethics, and aesthetics, and on films including *Twelve Monkeys* and *The Terminator*.

DAW-NAY EVANS teaches philosophy at both DePaul University and the School of the Art Institute of Chicago. He is the inaugural recipient of DePaul University's Michael Mezey Excellence in Graduate Teaching Award. His interests include moral and political philosophy, moral psychology, ancient Greek philosophy, modern German philosophy, African American philosophy, the philosophy of film, the philosophy of religion, and Nietzsche. Evans is the author of review essays in the *Journal of the History of Philosophy, Journal of Nietzsche Studies, Classical Review,* and *Philosophers' Magazine*. He is also a member of the review board for *Philosopher's Digest*. Currently, Evans is finishing his dissertation, "Nietzsche and Classical Greek Philosophy: Essays on Socrates, Plato, and Aristotle," at DePaul University.

RICHARD GAUGHRAN is assistant professor at James Madison University, where he teaches American and world literature in the English department. He is a former Fulbright Scholar for American Studies in Skopje, Macedonia, and has worked on literary translations from Macedonian to English. Recent scholarly articles include one on Larry Brown's *Rabbit Factory* (in *Larry Brown and the Blue-Collar South*) and a contribution to *The Philosophy of the Coen Brothers* as part of the University Press of Kentucky's Philosophy of Popular Culture Series.

RICHARD GILMORE is associate professor of philosophy at Concordia College. He received his master's and doctoral degrees from the University of Chicago. His areas of specialization include pragmatism, Wittgenstein, aesthetics, and film and philosophy. He has multiple publications, including the book *Doing Philosophy at the Movies* and essays in *The Philosophy of the Coen Brothers, The Philosophy of Neo-Noir, The Philosophy of Martin Scorsese,* and the *Journal of Speculative Philosophy*.

KEN HADA is associate professor in the Department of English and Languages at East Central University in Ada, Oklahoma, where he teaches American and ethnic literature and humanities courses. Some of his recent critical writing appears in *American Indian Culture and Research Journal, College Literature, Southwestern American Literature, Ethnic Studies Review,* and *Papers on Language and Literature.* His current research interests include eco-criticism and issues of place in fiction and poetry. He serves as area chair for Literature: Eco-Criticism and the Environment for the annual Southwest/Texas Popular Culture Association meeting held in Albuquerque, New Mexico. Ken has also authored two collections of poetry: *The Way of the Wind* and *Spare Parts.*

GARY HEBA is associate professor in the scientific and technical communication program at Bowling Green State University. He has published in the areas of film, visual rhetoric, multimedia development, and Web design.

DEBORAH KNIGHT is associate professor of philosophy, Queen's University at Kingston, where her research focuses on the philosophy of art, in particular the visual and narrative arts. She has published on Scorsese's *The Age of Innocence* as well as *The Matrix,* Hitchcock and suspense, *CSI, Blade Runner,* and *Dark City,* and on topics in the narrative arts including tragedy, comedy, sentimentality, and empathy.

GEORGE MCKNIGHT recently retired from Carleton University's School for Studies in Art and Culture, where he taught in the film studies program. Besides his research interests in British cinema and the film industry, he has published (with Deborah Knight) papers on Hitchcock, suspense, *CSI,* the philosophy of horror, and *Memento.*

JENNIFER L. MCMAHON is associate professor of philosophy and English and chair of the Department of English and Languages at East Central University. McMahon has expertise in existentialism, aesthetics, and comparative philosophy. She has published articles in journals such as *Asian Philosophy,* as well as numerous essays on philosophy and popular culture. Among others, she has chapters in *Seinfeld and Philosophy, The Matrix and Philosophy, The Lord of the Rings and Philosophy, The Philosophy of Martin Scorsese, The Philosophy of TV Noir, The Philosophy of Science Fiction Film,* and *House M.D. and Philosophy.* McMahon owns and operates with Dr. B. Steve Csaki Watershed Ranch in central Oklahoma, where they live with their two children, six horses, four dogs, an increasing number of barn cats, and about one hundred cows.

DAVID L. MCNARON is associate professor of philosophy at Nova Southeastern University in Fort Lauderdale, Florida. His areas of teaching and research include philosophy of science, philosophy of mind, and ethics. He grew up watching westerns on TV. His favorites were *Have Gun, Will Travel, Rawhide,* and *Maverick.*

STEPHEN J. MEXAL is assistant professor of American literature at California State University, Fullerton. His research concerns the relationship between literary narratives and political identification. Recent articles have appeared in *MELUS, English Language Notes, Studies in the Novel,* and the critical anthology *Eco-Man: New Perspectives on Masculinity and Nature.* He is currently at work on a manuscript on liberalism and the Western literary sphere.

MICHAEL VALDEZ MOSES is associate professor of English at Duke University. He was educated at Harvard, New College, Oxford, and the University of Virginia. He is the author of *The Novel and the Globalization of Culture,* editor of a collection of critical essays, *The Writings of J. M. Coetzee,* and coeditor of *Modernism and Colonialism: British and Irish Literature, 1900–1939.* His articles and reviews have appeared in *Kenyon Review, Modernism/Modernity, Latin American Literary Review, South Atlantic Quarterly, Modern Fiction Studies,* and *Literary Imagination* as well as in essay collections from Harvard, Duke, and Cambridge University presses. He has written on *The X-Files* and *Millennium* for the University Press of Kentucky's collection *The Philosophy of TV Noir.* His main interests are in nineteenth- and twentieth-century Irish, British, postcolonial, and third world literature and theory. Professor Moses is currently at work on a book project, "Nation of the Dead: The Politics of Irish Literature, 1890–1990."

ROBIN MURPHY is assistant professor in East Central University's Department of English and Languages. Her main research interests are in civic and visual literacy and their correlation to trauma rhetoric, culture studies, and feminist theory.

AEON J. SKOBLE is professor of philosophy and chair of the philosophy department at Bridgewater State College. He is the coeditor of *Political Philosophy: Essential Selections,* editor of *Reading Rasmussen and Den Uyl: Critical Essays on Norms of Liberty,* and author of *Deleting the State: An Argument about Government,* as well as author of many articles on moral and political philosophy. This is his fourteenth contribution to a volume on philosophy and popular culture, and he coedited *The Simpsons and Philosophy, Woody Allen and Philosophy,* and *The Philosophy of TV Noir.*

INDEX

Bushido, 146–47
Butch Cassidy and the Sundance Kid,
    288n9, 325

Cabinet of Dr. Caligari, The, 290
Cajete, Gregory, 298
Calley, William, 289n26
Camus, Albert, 203, 215–18, 218n1
capitalism, 4, 71, 84, 124, 134, 280
Castle, The, 290n36
categorical imperative, 158, 173, 174,
    176, 180–82, 189–99, 224
Cavell, Stanley, 292
Chandler, Daniel, 311
Chaney, Lon, Jr., 175
Cherokee, 159, 283
Cheyenne, 267, 273–77, 295
Child, Julia, 301
Christianity, 153, 168n24, 206–7, 282
Christie, Julie, 242
cinematic codes, 313–14, 321–25
civic liberalism, 71, 77, 80
civilization, 4, 31–32, 41–47, 51n38,
    51–52n40, 52n41, 52n42, 52n44,
    75, 109n27, 126–35, 149–51, 268,
    281–82
civil society, 41, 44, 77, 80–86, 114,
    131, 140, 144, 267, 272, 288n12
Civil War (U.S.), 22, 83, 89, 101, 107n2,
    139, 141, 149
clans, 139, 299–300
Cleef, Lee Van, 22, 151,179, 237
Clinton, Bill, 171, 182
Cochise, 265–70
code of the West, 6–7, 65
Coen brothers, 190, 222, 238, 242
Coeur d'Alene Indians, 289n29, 292
Cohen, Leonard, 13, 27, 243, 250, 252,
    256, 257n3
cold war, 4, 71–85, 86n3, 109n24
Columbus, Christopher, 261–62

commerce, 93, 122–28, 136, 288n19,
    340
communism, 71, 78
community, 4–5, 28n2, 32, 39, 84, 115–
    22, 124–30, 139–46, 149–66, 193–
    96, 228, 241–45, 248–50, 252–55,
    276, 295, 300–301, 313, 336, 344
compassion, 130
*Conquest of America, The: The
    Question of the Other,* 261–63
Conrad, Joseph, 278
consequentialism/consequentialist,
    173, 176–77, 181
Constant, Benjamin, 178
Cooper, Gary, 14, 31, 171, 182, 192,
    221, 245
Cooper, James Fenimore, 286
Costner, Kevin, 7, 264, 278, 280, 294
costume, 317, 320, 322
Cowboys, The, 4, 55, 59, 63, 64
Cree, 286, 289n25
Crowe, Russell, 70, 72, 84, 100, 102
Culp, Robert, 215, 218, 220
Custer, General George Armstrong,
    266, 276–77

Damon, Matt, 338
Dances with Wolves, 7, 264, 278–80,
    294–95
Dante, 284
Darnell, Linda, 242, 319
Darwin, Charles, 205
Day, Laraine, 98
Dead Man, 7, 264, 280–87, 287n1,
    288n8, 289n27, 289n30, 289n32,
    290n34, 290n35, 290n37
Deadwood, 5, 9n3, 113–36, 136n5,
    137n5, 137n6, 137n7, 137n8,
    138n28, 138n38, 167
Deadwood: Stories of the Black Hills,
    113, 136

CPSIA information can be obtained at www.ICGtesting.com
Printed in the USA
BVOW04*0756210714

359539BV00007B/5/P

9 780813 125916